People Disrupted

People Disrupted

Doing Mission Responsibly among Refugees and Migrants

EDITORS

Jinbong Kim
Dwight P. Baker
Jonathan J. Bonk
J. Nelson Jennings
Jae Hoon Lee

WILLIAM CAREY
LIBRARY

www.missionbooks.org

Published by William Carey Library
10 W. Dry Creek Cir.
Littleton, CO 80120 | www.missionbooks.org

William Carey Library is a ministry of
Frontier Ventures
Pasadena, CA 91104 | www.frontierventures.org

Dwight P. Baker, Lois I. Baker, Craig A. Noll, copyeditors
Dwight P. Baker, interior design
Jay Matenga, cover design
Craig A. Noll, indexer

Printed in the Republic of Korea
22 21 20 19 18   5 4 3 2 1 BP

Contents

Foreword

Icontinue to have high appreciation for the vision of the Korean Global Mission Leadership Forum and for its role in calling for accountability in the conduct of the Christian world mission.

This volume is the outcome of the multinational case studies and responses presented at KGMLF's 2017 consultation held in Sokcho, Korea, on the subject "Migration, Human Dislocation, and Accountability in Missions." The studies presented deal with significant issues in Christian mission and address the case of North Korean migrants, the sufferings of Iraqis fleeing from war, African refugees, Syrian refugees in Lebanon, overseas Filipino workers, the situation of refugees in Europe, and other refugee cases.

Two points of special note: As Timothy K. Park mentions in his concluding summary, churches in the world should be concerned both with mission *for* scattered people and with mission *by* scattered people.

Also as Jonathan Bonk observes, "It is difficult for human societies to expand the category of 'we'—but it is absolutely essential that Christians within those societies do so, so that 'we' encompasses not only family, tribe, and nation, but also stranger, alien, and even enemy. . . . It seems easier for us to serve refugees outside of our countries than to make room for them inside our countries."

With my sincere wish for the continuing efforts of the Korean Global Mission Leadership Forum, I value this book and recommend it to Christian workers to read and to study these reports and discussions of real life in Christian mission.

David J. Cho
East-West Center for Missions Research and Development
Seoul, Korea

Foreword

What is the church's experience and responsibility with regard to refugees, immigrants, migrant workers, and other people on the move? How does direct interaction with the lived realities of displaced individuals and groups shape the faith practice of Christ-followers, even as these relationships form new communities? How do the situations of diasporas, mass migration, and widespread voluntary and involuntary relocation worldwide call for new attention to the identity and needs of one's neighbors, and how do they invite new opportunities in church leadership and mission?

These are some of the starting questions addressed by participants in the Fourth Korean Global Mission Leadership Forum (2017) as they considered the theme of migration, refugees, and human dislocation in Christian world mission. Population movement is, of course, integral to biblical and church history; the authors in this volume remind us to approach and to interpret human migration with a missional lens, alert to the ways in which God's purposes are often effected through migrants. The very people often classified by a region's current residents as unwelcome aliens and suspect foreigners are the very ones that God's people are charged to love as themselves: protecting from oppression, extending justice, and treating as citizens out of honor for God.

The need to give special recognition and care to those who are aliens and strangers stems from the unique risks and vulnerabilities that migrants face. Those with uncertain political identities, people of minority ethnic or religious groups, and all who are removed from their familiar contexts and are thrust into a new setting suffer some degree of loss in their transitions. As this volume powerfully reminds us, modern human migration flows are not comprised of nameless or faceless beings. Rather, dislocated people such as Suri,

Suleiman, Lorie, and Oscar bear the image of God. It is through patient accompaniment with them though the daily level practical processes of finding housing and confronting discrimination—and by learning to know their children—that countercultural witness to love of neighbor occurs.

Throughout biblical history and today, God uses migrant communities to influence the places which receive them, and dislocations are woven into the missional present and future of the church. Diasporas become vibrant missionary sending hubs. Immigrants revitalize waning congregations. Migrant laborers and asylum-seekers, exercising their spiritual gifts within the new communities to which they relocate, bear witness to the Gospel of Jesus in which the so-called margins are the center, demonstrating how healing and hope happen in the kingdom of God.

Each author has shared profound truths from texts and from direct experience in vital lived relationships. For these we are grateful. May their insights enrich your experience and serve to inspire the wider church toward accountability in welcoming, embracing, and following the newcomers and strangers in our midst.

Laura S. Meitzner Yoder
John Stott Chair and Director
Program in Human Needs and Global Resources
Professor of Environmental Studies
Wheaton College
Wheaton, Illinois, USA

Foreword

Throughout history, migration has been a major source of change and a central feature in human development. But the sheer magnitude and relentlessness of migrant movements in recent decades defy easy analysis. There are more persons on the move globally at the start of the twenty-first century than at any other time in human history. Hundreds of millions of people are living outside their country of birth, and unprecedented numbers (reportedly half of them children) have fled their homes because of conflict, persecution, and violence. This global migrant crisis has generated major geopolitical challenges in some regions and overwhelmed some of the world's poorest countries. Global migration is also contributing to unprecedented levels of sustained interaction between diverse cultures and peoples once separated by great physical distance. Almost everywhere, but most notably in wealthier Western societies where cultural anxieties have contributed to the rise of nationalist movements, rising foreign-born populations increasingly evoke resentment and hostility.

For the global church, these developments raise complex issues, especially in relation to the missionary task. To start with, Christians constitute nearly half of international migrants. This statistic correlates with the recent demographic and southwards shift within world Christianity; for international migrants are predominantly non-white or born in the "Global South" (and more originate from Asia than from any other region). But, while the Christian element points to the vast missionary potential of migration, it also confirms that large numbers within the family of faith are affected by high levels of instability, violence, and suffering. In any case, the multidirectional global migrant movements and the dynamic transnational networks they generate have radically transformed the context or environment in which many churches around the world do mission. How churches and mission organizations respond is often complicated by intense debates around immigration, deep cultural bias among Christians themselves, and fraught questions about Christian witness in relation to issues of social justice.

DILEMMAS AND INNOVATION

In the meantime, the swelling tide of migrants and displaced persons has also triggered a multitude of ministries and missional initiatives. The issues are not the same everywhere. But, given the global dimensions of this new reality, the need to share and examine the lessons and limitations of diverse approaches around the world is great and pressing.

Therein lies the intrinsic value of this compendium. It delivers fourteen case studies that depict and appraise (through respondents) specific missionary endeavors—carried out by churches, mission agencies, and other organizations—among migrants and displaced communities in different contexts around the world. These accounts put a human face on cold statistical data and convey the critical and complex considerations that missionary outreach among (and by) migrant populations entail—in part because both involve boundary-crossing. A number of themes stand out: in many parts of the world, social prejudice, ethnic pride, and ethnocentrism among Christians place powerful barriers in the way of outreach to immigrants or collaboration with immigrant Christians for effective mission; everywhere, indigenous believers, whether embedded in transnational networks or part of diaspora populations, represent the most effective missionaries to their own communities or societies; for vast populations of Christian migrants in various regions of the world, Christian witness often carries great risk and requires uncommon courage (overseas Filipino workers in the Middle East and elsewhere being a major example); effective ministry among the world's displaced multitudes places the church at the very heart of the struggle, pain, and maltreatment that refugees, asylees, and other immigrants experience on a daily basis from oppressive human systems.

In the final analysis, faithful witness involving immigrants often radicalizes Christian mission because it raises complex questions with no easy solutions. In almost every situation, effective witness requires innovative strategies, collaborative (or multi-cultural) measures, prophetic voice or vision, and deep reservoirs of Christlike compassion. All of which call for thoughtful missiological reflection.

CROSSING BOUNDARIES

In addition to showcasing the dilemmas and innovative strategies that migration and mission elicit, this volume incorporates crucial historical and biblical perspectives. Human migration not only permeates the biblical record but has also been, as Andrew Walls explains, "a significant, and often a determining, factor in many different ways throughout Christian history" (43). Moreover, the movement of Christian migrants (so prominent in the present time) has historically played a major role in cross-cultural expansion of the faith. A series of stimulating biblical reflections by Christopher Wright provides additional missiological insights. He notes that Yahweh's "saving intention for *all nations*" (27) is reflected in his impartiality and love for the foreigner, an understanding that carries profound implications for the global church at a time when xenophobic rejection of vulnerable immigrant populations is rife. It is also noteworthy that, in the divine economy, the suffering and disgrace of violent displacement can serve missionary purpose, as migrants develop a new sense of responsibility for those among whom they live. Most important, the Gospel message of redemption through Christ and the promise of a new creation remains powerfully relevant in the face of the large-scale suffering and global systems of exploitation that contribute to the rise of displaced populations.

In the arena of Christian missions, theory naturally lags behind practice. So, the combination of lived (real life) experiences and critical reflection presented in this volume makes it a great resource for twenty-first-century missiological study. The new age of migration signals the tragedies of a fallen world. This, in and of itself, requires a Christian response. But, from a Christian perspective, unprecedented migrant flows have also transformed the global missionary landscape, subverting old paradigms and calling forth new understandings. Due to a multitude of migrant-missionaries, Christian mission in the early twenty-first century is a global, multidirectional, decentered undertaking in which rich and diverse expressions of the faith are readily manifest. We are reminded that throughout the ages the church has been most effective in fulfilling the missionary task when the people of God have been willing (or compelled) to cross boundaries.

Jehu J. Hanciles
Associate Professor, Brooks Chair of World Christianity
Candler School of Theology
Emory University
Atlanta, Georgia, USA

Preface

As followers of Christ, how should we respond to the daily reports of suffering and toil that refugees undergo? Perhaps Jesus—who called us to "love your neighbor as yourself" (Matt. 22:39 NIV)—was himself a refugee on this sinful earth from his home in heaven. And perhaps that is why the Bible describes him as someone who "empathize[s] with our weaknesses" (Heb. 4:15 NIV).

In my role as a missionary, I have been an immigrant for over twenty-five years, but I know little about the experience of refugees. My only exposure to refugees came when I was on the staff of a mission organization in the United States. My family and I lived in the organization's apartment building that also hosted asylum seekers from countries including Iraq, Syria, and Tanzania. During the short time we had together, my heart broke as I witnessed the hardships they were experiencing, but of course I could not fully understand their pain.

But when, after ten years of service with my family with that mission organization, I was laid off overnight, I felt like a refugee: I was in a foreign country and suddenly without a job or a place to live. To make matters worse, the layoff meant that my family and I would no longer have medical insurance; it was very difficult to secure funds for treatment for my younger son, who had severely injured his leg. I was devastated.

It would be wrong to suggest that the pain and disappointment I felt at the time were comparable to the suffering experienced by refugees forced to leave their beloved homes through no fault of their own. But I had a glimpse of that agony in June 2016 as I left the mission organization that had become my American "home."

All my plans for my life seemed to have collapsed. What was going to happen to the vision the Lord had given me in 2008 to start the Korean Global Mission Leadership Forum (KGMLF) and to publish the discussions in English and Korean? Exhausted both mentally and physically, I could not see any light at the end of the tunnel. Yet there was one thing I could still do: I could cry out to the Lord in prayer at the dawn of each morning (Ps. 5:1–3).

As I prayed, God revealed through his people that he willed for KGMLF to continue. Jonathan Bonk, a spiritual leader and distinguished mission scholar, has been my mentor for the past twelve years. His spiritual judgment, discipline, and leadership made possible the first KGMLF in 2011 and KGMLF's growth thereafter. Thankfully, he agreed to serve as president of the board of trustees of a new organization, Global Mission Leadership Forum (GMLF), that would carry KGMLF forward. Dwight Baker, who had been in charge of the English publication of KGMLF volumes from the beginning, gladly became the first secretary of GMLF. These brothers in Christ stood by me during the most difficult times of my life. Attorney James Whitney helped throughout the process of registering GMLF as an NGO.

Jae Hoon Lee, senior pastor of Onnuri Community Church, has unconditionally supported KGMLF since 2013. He has continued to be an encouragement to KGMLF, including by inviting J. Nelson Jennings, vice president of GMLF, to serve Onnuri Community Church as a mission pastor, consultant, and international liaison. Jennings has since been of service not only to Onnuri Community Church, but also to the broader church and Christian ministry in Korea and other countries around the world. In the process of planning for KGMLF 2017, I benefited greatly from Nelson Jennings's wisdom and advice.

God helped to clarify my path when Hyung Joong Yoon, senior pastor of Hong Kong Korean Exodus Mission Church and one who has been a spiritual comrade for over twenty years, called me from Hong Kong to share the conviction he received while praying that God desired for me not to leave the New Haven area but to build a new organization to sustain KGMLF. In addition, many mission leaders in Korea, including Steve Sang-Cheol Moon, executive director of the Korean Research Institute for Mission who has been a colleague since 2011, extended sincere encouragement in the new endeavor.

And thus, a new organization called Global Mission Leadership Forum was born. The 2017 KGMLF meeting, the first hosted under the new GMLF organization, took place at Kensington Stars Hotel in Sokcho, Korea, near beautiful Seorak Mountain. It met November 7–10, 2017. KGMLF's success was largely due to the wholehearted financial and personnel support provided by Young Hoon Lee, senior pastor of Yoido Full Gospel Church, and Jae Hoon Lee, senior pastor of Onnuri Community Church, both in Seoul. I am also grateful for the generous gift from Jongbu Hwa, senior pastor of Namseoul Church; support by Jae Chul Chung, director of Asian Mission (who also supported KGMLF 2015), and Hong Sung Chil, chair of the Missions Department of the New Haven Korean Church, Hamden, Connecticut (Do Hoon Kim, senior pastor).

I must thank Jae-Han Jung, mission pastor of Yoido Full Gospel Church, and YFGC staff—including managing secretary Sang Ha Lee—who provided lodging and transportation for forum participants. And I bless Mrs. Jung Hee Hong and her team, EZER, who again exemplified true servanthood by showing everyone at the forum what life-giving serving and welcoming look like.

The dedication and sacrifice of more than thirty Onnuri Community Church staff members enabled the forum to run smoothly. With gentle leadership Hong Joo Kim, head mission pastor, and mission pastor Jung Hoon Son directed all of the logistics of 2017 KGMLF. Words cannot express my deep gratitude for each staff member who served the forum with joy and humility.

Finally, I would also like to thank Abe Kugyong Koh, pastor of Korean Grace Presbyterian Church, Fort Lee, New Jersey, USA, for his great effort in translating the English edition for simultaneous publication in Korean. I especially wish to express my thanks to Duranno Press and William Carey Library staff for their dedication and cooperation. I am so thankful for my wife, Soon Young Jung, and my two sons, who have helped and encouraged me in many ways behind the scenes.

This book gathers the richness of KGMLF 2017, albeit incompletely. As the book goes to press, I have two wishes. First, I pray that refugees, immigrants, and North Korean defectors will no longer be treated as sojourners or strangers, but as members of our families and as neighbors. Second, I hope that the book will inspire Christ's followers and churches around the world to "love your neighbor as yourself" in more concrete and proactive ways. Maranatha!

Jinbong Kim
Managing Director of GMLF
Coordinator of KGMLF

Preface

I begin my preface with some personal memories.

Fourteen key Korean mission executives and mission pastors took part in the first planning meeting for the Korean Global Mission Leadership Forum, held at the Seoul Club on March 1, 2010. The meeting was hosted and paid for by Mr. Young Hyun Jung and Mrs. Sook Hee Kim, staunch supporters of missions and the parents of Soon Young Jung, wife of my colleague, Dr. Jinbong Kim. Among those who took part were Dr. Keung-Chul (Matthew) Jeong, Dr. Hyun Mo (Tim) Lee, Rev. Dr. Shin Chul Lee, Rev. Dr. Wonjae Lee, Dr. Sang-Cheol (Steve) Moon, Rev. Dr. Nam Yong Sung, Rev. Dr. Yong Joong Cho, Rev. Shinjong (Daniel) Baeq, Dr. Kwang Soon Lee, and Rev. Dr. Seung Sam Kang. They agreed that a forum on accountability should be convened at the Overseas Ministries Study Center (OMSC), and they assured us of their willingness to cooperate. The theme around which the resulting inaugural forum was to be organized was "Missionary, Mission, and Church Accountability: Implications for Strategy, Integrity, "and Continuity.

In my June 10, 2010, report to the OMSC Board of Trustees in New Haven, Connecticut, I gave an enthusiastic account of this planning meeting, little realizing that the envisaged forum would become much more than a one-time event, but would establish the pattern for several more forums to follow.

With the able assistance of my colleague Rev. Jinbong Kim, serious planning for the first forum got under way. It succeeded far beyond our modest hopes! A group of forty-eight men and women gathered at OMSC, February 10–14, 2011, where—by means of presentation and group discussion of case studies and responses—they bravely tackled complicated issues relating to financial, administrative, strategic, and pastoral accountability practices and lapses.

The forum was a great blessing to those of us who took part, and through the publication of Korean and English versions of the ensuing book—*Accountability in Missions: Korean and Western Case Studies* (Wipf & Stock, 2011)—its blessings were spread wider still. The practicality, the honesty, the professional and intellectual vigor, and the spirituality of both the intent and the outcomes of the forum made it clear that something *significant*—not huge, not mighty, not numerically impressive, but *seminal*—had been launched. It was our "cloud as small as a man's hand rising from the sea" (1 Kgs 18:44 NABRE), signaling God's blessings to come. A model of vigorous cross-cultural interaction and constructive cross-cultural collaboration—and of sharing both widely through multilingual publications—had been born. It was a model that could be employed to address other complex but overlooked issues bedeviling missions regardless of the sending or receiving country, mission society, or denomination involved.

Three more biennial forums followed: in 2013 in New Haven, in 2015 in Sokcho, and in 2017—the one whose content is featured in this book—again in Sokcho. Each successive forum seemed better than the previous one, as planners, participants, and hosting institutions learned from experience. At each gathering, key mission leaders from Korea and from around the world explored a range of complex, mission-related accountability challenges, resulting in several more publications in Korean and in English, including *Family Accountability in Missions: Korean and Western Case Studies* (OMSC Publications, 2013); *Megachurch Accountability in Missions: Critical Assessment through Global Case Studies* (William Carey Library, 2016); and now this volume, *People Disrupted: Doing Mission Responsibly among Refugees and Migrants* (William Carey Library, 2018).

This is how it came to be that on November 7, 2017—after careful planning for presenters, respondents, facilitators, travel, accommodations, hosting, and all of the other details crucial to a successful forum, and with the generous support of the sponsoring congregations and mission organizations—more than eighty mission and church leaders from around the world were welcomed to Sokcho by Dr. Jinbong Kim, now the managing director of the Global Mission Leadership Forum and the principal vital energy behind the event.

With Dr. Jinbong Kim, we prayed and prepared for this occasion for two years, and the presence of these scores of leaders was evidence that God had answered our prayers. In the spirit of Colossians 3:23, some gave generously, even sacrificially, of their financial resources; others joyfully devoted their time and intellectual energies; many shared their gifts of wisdom and knowledge in the presentations and responses that constituted the presentations of this forum and the chapters of this book; others—such as Dwight Baker, Lois Baker, and Craig Noll—toiled diligently behind the scenes, editing the manuscripts, correcting errors, clarifying meanings, and making sure that each offering was the best that it could be; still others cheerfully undertook the daunting task of making sure that all the manuscripts were available in both Korean and English, so that the book would be available in both languages.

Special acknowledgment must be made of the indispensable role played by Dr. Jinbong Kim, whose inspiring vision, personal sacrifice, organizational gifts, and unstinting effort have been the essential catalyst whereby all the other contributions have been combined into this well-formed and useful forum; to the sponsoring churches and their pastors; to Yoido Full Gospel Church for graciously providing accommodations in Seoul and then transporting international and many Seoul-based forum participants to and from Sokcho; to Onnuri Community Church and their staff for providing unparalleled hosting of every person and every aspect of the forum in Sokcho; and to Ezer Community Fellowship for lovingly preparing exquisite refreshments beyond what anyone present could have asked or thought!

As we look back, it is with thanksgiving that all of us who have been in any way associated with the forum and with the book that you hold in your hands acknowledge a verity that has been attested throughout the history of our Lord's merciful dealing with those who seek to follow him faithfully: God's power is made perfect in our weakness, and little is much when God is in it (2 Cor. 12:9; Mark 6:37–43).

Jonathan J. Bonk
President
Global Mission Leadership Forum

1

North Korean Migrants in South Korea: How Can the Korean Church Best Serve Them?

Ben Torrey

In this chapter I provide a brief look at the experience of North Korean migrants who have come to South Korea with the expectation of settling there. It is based on my experience, study, and research from 2003 to the present. During this time I have worked with these migrants as presenters, consultants, and participants in a number of educational, religious, and social settings, including personal interactions and interviews. I have also continuously tracked the situation of North Korean migrants in South Korea through the news media, journal articles, and other means.

In April 2007 I made a ten-day trip to North Korea with Christian Friends of Korea (www.cfk.org), an NGO, and from the beginning of September to mid-December 2008 I worked in North Korea as a food distribution monitor for a US food aid program. During this time, as a member of a team covering seventeen counties in North Pyongan Province, I worked with North Korean officials and visited numerous homes and institutions in various cities, towns, villages, and collective farms. This responsibility provided many opportunities for conversations and discussions with local officials and residents. During that period, I also made trips to Chagang Province and to the capital, Pyongyang. These experiences in North Korea were extremely valuable for deepening my understanding of the differences between the worldviews, culture, expectations, and society of North and South Korea. They all gave me a greater sense of the context that North Korean migrants find themselves in, in the South, especially as they compare their experiences before and after migration.

Rather than being an academic research work based on rigorous interviewing standards that focuses on a specific concern, this chapter presents what I have learned from the above exposure to North Korea, augmented by direct interviews with seven emigrants of various backgrounds and ages (ranging from fifteen to forty-seven years old) who have settled in South Korea. The fundamental question I seek to answer is, What is the church's responsibility toward these migrants, and how might it better carry out that responsibility?

Throughout this chapter, except where the official political terms are appropriate, I refer to the familiar "North Korea" and "South Korea," not the official political designations (respectively, Democratic People's Republic of Korea, DPRK, and Republic of Korea, ROK). Also, I refer mainly to "migrant," not "refugee" or "defector" (*talbuk ja* or *talbuk min*), though in a few cases "refugee" is appropriate for individuals who have fled from North Korea and have not yet made a decision whether to migrate elsewhere.

BASIC FACTS AND STATISTICS

A review of some key statistics will provide a general picture of the severe difficulties facing North Koreans who are successful in emigrating to South Korea.

Number of migrants. ROK Ministry of Unification figures released on November 13, 2016, showed that a total of 30,005 North Koreans had arrived in South Korea since the end of the Korean War.[1] Large numbers of North Koreans began arriving in South Korea during the late 1990s because of famine in the North. Of these, 71 percent were women, a figure that was expected to rise to 80 percent by the end of 2016.

Statistics concerning the total number of migrants leaving

---

1. Yi Whan-woo, "Seoul Bolsters Efforts to Embrace Defectors," *Korea Times*, November 22, 2016, 5.

North Korea over the past twenty years vary significantly, running anywhere from 100,000 to 300,000, with some sources, such as official Chinese estimates, as low as 10,000 (in 2010), which is clearly unrealistic, considering that, by the end of 2009, close to 18,000 North Koreans had arrived in South Korea alone.[2] Many of those who left North Korea returned, many continue to live in China, for the most part illegally, and a much smaller number have migrated to Russia, Europe, or the United States, either directly from North Korea or from China or (in a few cases) South Korea.

Employment. Many sources and personal accounts indicate that North Koreans in South Korea frequently move from job to job, not staying very long in any one position, whether as an employee or as the owner of a small business. It is believed that nearly 40 percent of North Korean migrants are currently unemployed. A significant number of those who have left jobs or are currently not seeking employment give health issues as the primary reason.[3] In 2012, according to the Database Center for North Korean Human Rights, 47.3 percent of North Koreans ages 20–29 living in South Korea were not economically active, compared with 39.4 percent of South Koreans in the same age group.[4]

Education. North Koreans of all levels of education have a difficult time either transferring their North Korean education to the South Korean context or catching up to South Korean grade levels

2. Courtland Robinson, "North Korea: Migration Patterns and Prospects," NAPSNet Special Report, November 4, 2010, nautilus.org/napsnet-speical-reports/north-korea-migration-patterns-and-prospects.
"North Korean Defectors," *Wikipedia*, https://en.wikipedia.org/wiki/North_Korean_defectors; cited as "Bukhanitaljumin Huynhwang" [Status of North Korean defectors], Ministry of Unification. Resettlement Support Division.

3. Elizabeth Shim, "North Korea Defectors' Health Issues Obstacles to Employment, Seoul Says," UPI, September 22, 2016, www.upi.com/Top_News/World-News/2016/09/22/North-Korea-defectors-health-issues-obstacle-to-employment-Seoul-says/4871474567942.

4. Go Myong-Hyun, "Resettling in South Korea: Challenges for Young North Korean Refugees," Asan Institute for Policy Studies, Issue Briefs, August, 2014, 9, http://en.asaninst.org/contents/resettling-in-south-korea-challenges-for-young-north-korean-refugees/.

or standards. Professionals in the fields of medicine and engineering have found that skills and certifications acquired in the North are either obsolete or do not measure up to South Korean standards. They need to gain further education and new certifications. Primary and secondary students face additional problems in that their education in the North in recent years has been substandard because of the virtual collapse of the North Korean societal infrastructure. They have also suffered because of the migration process itself, spending time, often in hiding, in China and traveling to South Korea. North Korean migrant students in South Korea have a school dropout rate of as much as six times the national average.[5] Middle and high school students, often in their twenties, attend some of the numerous alternative schools focused on migrants. I know of four such alternative schools.

Health. Because of the near starvation across North Korea in the late 1990s and chronic poor nutrition or malnutrition in the years since, the average body weight and height of North Koreans are considerably less than those of their South Korean peers: for boys, 11.1 kg lighter in weight and 10.1 cm shorter in height; for girls, 3.8 kg less in weight and 7.2 cm in height.[6] Both tuberculosis and hepatitis are serious health problems in North Korea, and many migrants leave the country already infected with one or both of these diseases. In addition, female migrants often experience human trafficking and sexual slavery or assault in China, resulting in not only trauma, but also a high incidence of sexually transmitted disease.[7]

The incidence of post-traumatic stress disorder (PTSD) is very high among North Koreans because of their having endured famine, witnessing family members die from starvation, witnessing public executions and violence, experiencing violence and torture, human trafficking, and a host of other traumas. Practitioners report that 30 percent of migrants suffer from PTSD.[8]

5. Ibid., 7.

6. Ibid., 3.

7. These comments are based on numerous conversations with health care givers and educators working with North Koreans in South Korea, knowledge of individual migrants, and comments by NGO staff involved in humanitarian assistance both to North Korea and to migrants in China and South Korea.

8. Go Myong-Hyun, "Resettling in South Korea," 5–6; Jin-Heon Jung,

Suicide. According to the World Health Organization, South Korea has the second highest rate of suicide in the world and the highest rate among OECD countries.[9] In September 2015 a South Korean news report stated that the suicide rate among North Korean migrants was 15.2 percent, which was "about three times the national average."[10] Many reasons are given for this sad figure—despair at separation from loved ones and longing for home that is so near yet impossible to reach, chronic inability to gain meaningful employment, with accompanying economic distress, loss of children during the passage through China, stresses of trying to adapt to a culture that is more different than expected, along with ill health and psychological trauma. There are other reasons as well, each one an individual tragedy.[11]

THE CHURCH AND MIGRANTS ON THE MOVE—CHINA

One frequently hears that some 80 percent of refugees escaping to China from North Korea become Christians; that is, they choose to associate with missionaries and churches and are likely to profess conversion and seek baptism.[12] For those who settle in South Korea, however, only 10–20 percent actually attend church on a regular basis. Many reasons are given for this disparity. Perhaps the most frequently observed is that conversion is viewed simply as part of the process of getting from North Korea to South Korea rather than as a truly life-changing event.

Migration and Religion in East Asia: North Korean Migrants' Evangelical Encounters (New York: Palgrave Macmillan, 2015).

9. "Suicide in South Korea," *Wikipedia*, https://en.wikipedia.org/wiki/Suicide_in_South_Korea.

10. Elizabeth Shim, "More North Korean Defectors Report Dissatisfaction with Life in South," UPI, September 9, 2015, www.upi.com/Top_News/World-News/2015/09/09/More-North-Korean-defectors-report-dissatisfaction-with-life-in-South/4301441810531.

11. I have heard of several incidents of mothers being separated from children, going back to China to find them, without success, and subsequently taking their own lives. At the same time, I know several people who were successfully united after years of separation.

12. My comments in this section are based on years of interaction with North Korean migrants in South Korea, numerous news reports and papers, and conversations with teachers, pastors, and others ministering to or caring for migrants.

Over the years since the famine of the late 1990s, networks and systems of brokers, helpers, safe houses, and an underground railroad have developed. Many North Koreans enter China to earn money as laborers or traders with the intention of returning home. Some of these persons have traveled back and forth numerous times either legally or illegally. In China, many have had contact with Chinese-Korean (*chosun-jok*) Christians and churches. Often local Christians provide assistance. Churches and missions have been involved with networks providing safe houses and assistance in migrating through the underground railroad. The system of paid brokers came into being to help North Koreans escape the North and travel through China. Because of these networks and the extensive movement back and forth, those entering China, especially illegally, are often aware that places showing crosses—Christian churches and ministries—are places to turn to for help.

Migrants in the system of safe houses and the underground railroad have a variety of experiences, both good and bad. In some cases, individuals spend months locked into apartments or other hideouts, with little or no exposure to people other than the ones providing the housing. They are expected to take part in daily early morning prayer, to participate in extensive Bible study, and to accept evangelistic teaching. Those who "convert" may be given priority for assistance in moving on toward the dreamland of South Korea. Some migrants have indicated that this process has been traumatic and harbor anger because of it. Others, perhaps the majority, accept it as a natural part of the process of moving from North Korea to South Korea. The process is familiar because of the routines of daily and weekly self-criticism, study, and public "worship" of the leader required in North Korea. And, it should be noted, some individuals indicate that they have joyfully and freely embraced Christianity without experiencing any pressure or duress whatsoever.[13]

---

13. Two sources offering good discussion of various aspects of this experience are Shin Ji Kang, "Postcolonial Reflection on the Christian Mission: The Case of North Korean Refugees in China and South Korea," *Social Sciences* 5 (2016): art. 67, www.mdpi.com/2076-0760/5/4/67, doi: 10.3390/socsci5040067; and Jung, *Migration and Religion in East Asia*, chap. 3, "North Korean Crossing and Christian Encounters."

THE CHURCH AND MIGRANTS SETTLING DOWN —SOUTH KOREA

Upon arrival in South Korea, North Korean migrants automatically receive ROK citizenship, for the ROK Constitution states that all of the Korean peninsula is ROK territory, and therefore all people born anywhere in this territory are citizens. Migrants are sent immediately to a secure facility where they undergo a period of interrogation by the National Intelligence Service and the National Police Agency to determine whether they might be spies sent by the North Korean government.[14] This period may last from a few days to weeks or possibly months, depending on the situation.

Following this interrogation period, migrants are sent for a period of three months to Hanawon, an orientation center operated by the Korean Hana Foundation under the auspices of the Ministry of Unification. During this time, they learn about life in South Korea; they are introduced to South Korean democracy, capitalism, and the economy, and they have classes in civics, history, and other subjects. Religious study and worship are offered by evangelical Protestant, Roman Catholic, and Buddhist groups, with the Protestants being by far the largest contingent. These groups hold Bible studies, prayer meetings, and worship services inside the secure Hanawon precinct. Material assistance is often provided by churches as well. The whole effort is one of active proselytizing.

The government has a strong interest in influencing the new migrants to be model South Korean citizens with a strong anti-Communist, anti-DPRK perspective. The time at Hanawon begins a process of suppressing the migrants' sense of being North Koreans, which continues on beyond the three-month orientation period. This process is generally aided by Protestant churches, schools, and ministries that work with the migrants, for these programs consider assimilation and anti-Communism as important elements of being good Christian citizens.

Much of the training program in Hanawon is focused on employability. Jin-Heon Jung makes a salient point in *Migration and Religion in East Asia*:

14. "North Korean Defectors," *Wikipedia*.

With reductionist rather than cultural relativist points of view, the state settlement system as a social force tends to keep "Otherizing" the migrants, while depoliticizing them. In other words, [the] South Korean state regime that has pursued the normalization of inter-Korean relations based on ethnic nationalism is likely to incur an identity crisis by marginalizing the migrants, and thus they find themselves expected to become nothing other than productive laborers.[15]

After their time at Hanawon, migrants are provided with housing in various parts of the country, and they receive basic economic assistance for a limited time.[16] Those who have not completed elementary or secondary school, especially if they are orphans or are unaccompanied by parents, may voluntarily enter one of the various private alternative boarding schools (most of them run by Protestants) that have been established for them.

Once migrants have been set up with housing and a modest subsidy, they are largely left to their own devices. While they may be encouraged to participate in church and may be contacted by any of the small number of small- to medium-sized churches established by or for migrants or by targeted ministries of megachurches, many migrants simply cease attending church. Migrants may have understood church participation as being part of the requirements for entering the country, but after passage of an initial period of time in the South, they often show little interest in ongoing church participation. Other reasons include difficulty in finding churches that are friendly toward them. Churches in the vicinity of their lodgings are quite likely to be unfamiliar with, and may be resistant to, North Korean migrants. Some migrants have spoken of their disenchantment with South Korean churches, whose sermon styles remind them of North Korean propaganda. A persistent emphasis on tithing and service to the church is alienating to them—in some cases also reminding them of the constant requirements in North Korea for "voluntary" contributions and labor for State projects.

15. Jung, *Migration and Religion in East Asia*, 90.

16. The amount and duration of assistance have been reduced over time. Intended to help migrants become economically self-sufficient, the amount is generally considered to be insufficient. Assistance may also include preferential enrollment in college and tuition assistance.

DIFFICULTIES OF LIFE IN THE SOUTH

Many difficulties that migrants face in South Korea have already been mentioned, but there are many others. Unfamiliarity with South Korean work and study ethics, along with language and cultural barriers, makes it very difficult for migrants to stay in one job or occupation, or to remain in school through graduation. The migrants must deal with a chronic sense of displacement and questioning of identity. Many suffer extreme loneliness and grief over separation from family and friends in the North. One study conducted a number of years ago recorded that men, unemployed or retired, would spend large portions of the day sitting together drinking *soju* (Korean rice wine/whisky) and expressing their longing to return to the North.[17] Furthermore, a very small but increasing number of migrants either have returned or are actively seeking to return to North Korea. In 2015 some 700 North Korean migrants to South Korea were unaccounted for. Many of these people are suspected to be in China seeking a way to return to the North; others have left illegally for Europe or North America.[18]

Migrants report discrimination and bullying because of their accent or when their place of origin is revealed. Many try very hard to hide their North Korean origin and work hard to change their accent. Communication in the South is often quite difficult because of extensive but subtle and poorly understood differences in culture and language. North Koreans are very direct in their speech, unlike South Koreans, who prefer to be indirect. North Koreans will readily say No, something that is very difficult for South Koreans to do. (South Koreans normally resort to stock phrases such as "it would be difficult" or "I'll let you know later.") When no follow-up is forthcoming, South Koreans simply understand that the speaker has no intention of

17. The author of this study withdrew it from publication and, for security reasons, requested that the author's name not be used and that the study not be cited.

18. "Almost 700 N. Korean Defectors' Whereabouts Unknown," Yonhap News Agency, September 27, 2015, http://english.yonhapnews.co.kr/search1/2603000000.html?cid=AEN20150927000500320; Choe Sang-Hun, "A North Korean Defector's Regret," *New York Times*, August 15, 2015, www.nytimes.com/2015/08/16/world/asia/kim-ryen-hi-north-korean-defector-regret.html?_r=0; Shim, "More North Korean Defectors Report Dissatisfaction with Life in South."

following through; North Koreans, however, are offended by a lack of response. North Koreans commonly complain that South Koreans are liars, while South Koreans consider North Koreans to be extremely rude. Neither side realizes that they are seeking to communicate across a cultural and linguistic divide. Migrants report that it may take as many as three years before they are comfortable communicating with South Koreans. Feelings of alienation and confusion are exacerbated when both parties to a conversation assume they are speaking the same mother tongue.

Another source of difficulty is the need to hide the effects of trauma. I have a good friend, a migrant seeking to help other migrants, who operates a coffee shop to employ migrants and help them work their way into management positions. He told me that he has discovered that such customer-focused service business is not appropriate for North Korean migrants, because they must continually smile and be welcoming to the customers, even though "inside they are weeping."

For migrants there is also the issue of, on the one hand, finding no sympathy but, on the other hand, of being "used." South Koreans generally are not interested in hearing the experiences of migrants. Church and mission organizations, on their part, often showcase such stories, which may cause the migrants to feel used.

POSITIVE CHURCH EXPERIENCES

While the above comments indicate that the interaction of churches with migrants is complicated, to say the least, and may be fraught with a number of issues, there is also a bright side to the picture. All of the migrants whom I interviewed for this chapter were very positive about their current situations and able to talk about their hopes, dreams, and aspirations.

One was a man in his late twenties about to graduate from agricultural college. He has the dream of developing organic farms and encouraging people to eat healthily. While he is now happy with his life in the South, it was not always so. Having arrived in South Korea in 2008 after about two years in China and Thailand, he sought to fulfill himself with material acquisitions and alcohol. One day, two evangelists from a church near where he lived knocked on his door. He welcomed them in, offered them tea, and after conversation, agreed to accompany them to church. He went a few times. This was his first real contact with Christians. Then in

2010 he was in a serious automobile accident because of driving after heavy drinking. While he was in the hospital, the two evangelists and the pastor of the church came to visit him. It was because of the accident and the concern expressed by this group that he concluded he needed to turn his life around and that he could do that only through the help of Jesus Christ. He made a thorough confession of his sins and a commitment of his life to the Lord. He now says that if he had not met Christ at that time, he would not be alive now.

Another man came to faith through reading the Bible while in a detention center in Thailand. He has continued to grow in his faith through the years since and is reaching out to other migrants to lead them into better lives and to a deep faith in Christ. He currently leads a monthly prayer meeting that includes migrants, South Koreans, and foreigners. He has also stated that without his relation to the Lord, his life would have been a disaster. His experiences included an extensive period in China in virtual slave-labor conditions.

A woman in her twenties is currently enrolled in college working toward a social service degree while also working as a manager in a coffee shop. She has a strong relationship with the Lord but states that she needs to grow in a spirit of obedience. Prior to her conversion she had no concern for anyone and no purpose to her life. Now she is deeply concerned for others and wants to help other migrants with their struggles in the South. After reunification, she wants to go back to North Korea, open a coffee shop, and start a church.

These are a few examples of how coming to faith in Jesus Christ has changed the lives of migrants who had experienced great trauma and suffering, who had little purpose in their lives, and who were filled with despair. One of the things that has been important for these and others whom I have known or interviewed, in addition to their conversion, is their sense of renewed identity as North Koreans. Some have gone back to referring to themselves as *Chosun* (the word used in the North for Korea), as opposed to *Hanguk* (the word used in the South). They have been free to do so because the intimate church communities of which they have been a part recognize the diversity of culture and value it, unlike the majority of South Korean churches, which seek to transform the migrants into "good South Koreans."

CONCLUSIONS

As I have reflected on the situation of North Korean migrants in South Korea and the church's role in helping them, I see that perhaps the greatest thing that the church can do is to accept the idea that North Korean migrants do not need to become South Koreans. Much of their culture and background have indeed been shaped by Communism and other North Korean ideology and by the idolization of the leaders. At the same time, much of South Korean church culture has been shaped by anti-Communism and nationalism within a strongly Confucian cultural context. I believe that each can learn from the other; both sides can enrich each other's faith and life if there is open acceptance of and respect for the differences. It would be good for church programs that are often aligned (frequently without conscious thought) with South Korean political priorities and that have developed under South Korean assumptions to be reshaped so as to appreciate the differences in culture between the North and the South. Ideally, churches could work toward greater mutual understanding rather than demanding that migrants conform to South Korean culture.

A favorite Scripture passage of mine is Revelation 21:24, 26 (KJV): "And the nations of them which are saved shall walk in the light of [the city]: and the kings of the earth do bring their glory and honour into it. . . . And they shall bring the glory and honour of the nations into it." Every nation will have its glory to bring into the New Jerusalem. I see this passage as referring to the best in the diverse cultures of the nations, including the different cultures of North and South Korea.

We must keep in mind the need for a strong, loving community that can provide healing and acceptance, and we must not forget the work of the Holy Spirit in bringing about true conversion and transformation in a person. All of my interviewees indicated that their conversion and coming into an intimate relationship with Jesus Christ was the single most important thing in bringing them from despair and emptiness to a life full of joy, even in the midst of their grief and struggle. Outreach programs for North Korean migrants should not be focused simply on church attendance or on giving personal testimonies; rather, they should be built around inclusion in organic communities of faith and worship where there is strong long-term commitment to one another, where there is no "other," no outsider. In such communities, empowered by the Holy Spirit, migrants become settlers and better citizens without having to become South Korean, without having to deny their origins, their own culture, or their background.

QUESTIONS FOR REFLECTION

1. One of the conclusions of this chapter is that it would be good for the South Korean church to accept North Korean migrants as North Koreans who do not need to become South Koreans. How might the church be able to give North Koreans a sense of welcome without calling for them to become something other than what they are? How can the church, at the same time, minister to the real needs of North Koreans with compassion and wisdom?

2. What are some of the ways that the South Korean church might be able to help North Korean migrants adjust to South Korean society without surrendering the migrants' personal identity or yielding to the competitive pressures of that society?

3. After reflecting on Revelation 21:24, 26, ask, What might be considered to be aspects of the glory and honor of North Korean life and culture?

4. How might the South Korean church provide North Korean migrants with a strong, loving community that provides healing and acceptance?

5. How can the South Korean church meet the challenge of sharing the Good News of Jesus Christ as an expression of genuine love and lead North Korean migrants to true conversion without either real or perceived coercion?

Response
to
"North Korean Migrants in South Korea"

Peter Lee

Ben Torrey has both traveled in North Korea and worked with North Korean migrants in South Korea. The reflections he offers in "North Korean Migrants in South Korea: How Can the Korean Church Best Serve Them?" are founded on a depth of knowledge and firsthand experience. In short compass he offers much insight into the situation North Korean migrants face at various stages of life in South Korea.

In my comments here I wish to enrich the perspective Torrey provides by bringing a Korean American perspective to the discussion and by highlighting several missiological considerations. Tensions currently facing the Korean peninsula, especially considering the instability, even unsustainability, of the government of North Korea, mean that attention should also be given to the potential for a massive influx of migrants into South Korea.

NORTH KOREANS WANT
TO BE TREATED AS HUMAN BEINGS

As a Korean American, I have been involved in mission to North Korea for over thirty years. I have noticed that North Koreans want to be treated as human beings rather than as "North Koreans." North Koreans who have managed to reach South Korea, as soon as they have learned South Korean intonation, hide their North Korean identity in school, in the workplace, and even in church. Only when they socialize with North Koreans does their accent reflect who they are. They do not show pride in being North Korean, nor do they desire to be identified as North Korean migrants. The reason is not that they want to lose their identity as North Koreans, but that they wish to escape discrimination in South Korea. In many places, South Koreans label them "North Korean refugees," which carries an unfavorable connotation and causes them to be treated differently. For this reason they seek to hide their identity.

It is not by accident or even intentionally that South Koreans, including Christian South Koreans, do not easily allow North Koreans to enter their circle of friends. The people of Korea like to maintain that Koreans are pure blooded, or "Bae-Dal Min-Jok," in descent, even though, genetically speaking, it is not true that all Koreans have a "pure" Korean ancestry, The term "Bae-Dal Min-Jok" gained circulation during the Japanese colonial period (1909–45) as a means for sustaining national unity. Some believe that the word originated over 6,000 years ago. Consequently, Koreans tend to keep themselves distant from persons of other nationalities, races, and regions. Both South and North Koreans tend to associate only with people from the same town, same schools, and same blood relationships. Until recently, few Koreans traveled abroad or lived in other nations, which meant that most Koreans lacked extensive experience of different cultures. Therefore, when someone new shows up in their communities, it usually takes a long time for that person to gain a sense of belonging. Unless someone brings in outsiders and introduces or sponsors them, it is very difficult for them to become part of the mainstream of their new community. When Korean-Chinese have come to Korea, they have typically been treated as second-class citizens and have had a difficult time becoming members of the mainstream. The situation of North Korean migrants is worse, for they are treated as third-class citizens.

I thus totally support Torrey's statement that "the greatest thing that the church can do is to accept the idea that North Korean migrants do not need to be become South Koreans" (12).

CHRISTIAN CONVERSION WHILE IN CHINA

North Korean migrants frequently spend a shorter or longer period of time in China before coming to South Korea. Torrey states that "those who 'convert' may be given priority for assistance in moving on toward the dreamland of South Korea" (6); more specifically, he states that "in some cases, individuals spend months locked into apartments or other hideouts, with little or no exposure to people other than the ones providing the housing" (6). I find this generalized statement a bit disturbing; it needs to be balanced by considering the many genuine ministries and missionaries who are giving their lives to bring the Gospel to North Korea and who are helping North Koreans to accept Jesus Christ as their Lord. I am certain that some North Korean migrants have had negative experiences in China, yet many have come to the Lord with the help of missionaries. Many of those who discontinue attending church after arriving in Hanawon (the "orientation center operated by the Korean Hana Foundation under the auspices of the Ministry of Unification," as Torrey states; see p. 7) do not do so because of ill treatment received from missionaries, but because they no longer think that they need help from God.

MISSIONAL PERSPECTIVE
ON NORTH KOREAN MIGRANTS

When North Koreans arrive in South Korea, they face cultural shock in all areas of life: language, economy, people, food, and much more. The two nations have been separated for three-quarters of a century, living under totally different political and economic situations. The people of North Korea live under Communism, socialism, and Kim Il-Sungism. Their communal life is so different from that of South Koreans that most people in the South would find it inconceivable.

North Koreans must bow to Kim Il-Sung's statue, hang pictures of Kim in their homes, protect the pictures of Kim instead of saving their own drowning child, and worship Kim Il-Sung as a living god by keeping a badge on their left chest. The children of Christian martyrs are not given education beyond elementary school. Someone who complains about a bad harvest or tells friends about life in Japan is in danger of being sent to political prison. The country has two Protestant churches, one Roman Catholic church, and one Russian Orthodox church; all are located in Pyongyang. The government claims that there is freedom of religion, but having a Bible is treated as treason. Being a Christian carries a sentence of fifteen years in political prison, where the life expectancy is less than three years.[1]

To make matters worse, having grown up under Communism, North Koreans have been trained from childhood to watch for—and report on—the wrongdoings of others and to distrust others. In order to survive, they refuse to acknowledge any wrongdoing but strongly defend themselves at all costs. Weekly peer meetings for self-criticism ingrain an outlook of strident self-defense and of ignoring the viewpoint of others for the sake of simple self-protection.

When North Koreans arrive in South Korea, they go through a three-month orientation at Hanawon. They must then make many decisions: where to live, which school to attend, what to wear, what to buy—and the list goes on. Although they experience new freedom, they now face unaccustomed choices.[2] While in North Korea they did not have to make many decisions, for the government assigned rations for food and clothes and dictated their place of residence, their job, and other life necessities. The many choices found in South Korean supermarkets, for example, were not part of their experience. Although North Koreans appear to understand the South Korean dialect, they are confused and puzzled over many foreign words found in markets, on the streets, and in public, as well as on television.

In view of these cultural, language, and lifestyle differences, the South Korean church should view migrants from a missional perspective. The church can act as the agent of love and care in helping the migrants to settle. In doing so, the church can share the love of Jesus Christ, and the North Korean migrants may come to know the Lord. The church has the opportunity to be an agent of reconciliation between North and South Koreans.

NORTH KOREAN MIGRANTS ARE INNOVATORS

Through ministry to the 30,000 North Korean migrants in South Korea, the church can learn lessons in preparation for the opening of North Korea in the near future or whenever it occurs. A caution,

1. Soon-Ok Lee, *Eyes of the Tailless Animals: Prison Memoirs of a North Korean Woman* (Bartlesville, OK: Living Sacrifice, 1998).

2. Soon-Hyung Yi, Youn-Shil Choi, and Meejung Chin, *Buk-han-yi-tal-ju-min-eu jong-kyo-kyung-hum* [Religious experience of North Korean refugees] (Seoul: Seoul National Univ. Press, 2015), 126.

however, is in order. Current migrants must be distinguished from the North Korean populace in general. Current migrants do not represent the norm or majority among North Koreans; instead, early migrants would fit into Everett Rogers's category "innovators."[3]

As innovators, these were people open to seeking something new, to living outside of their norm, and to leaving North Korea in seeking a different life. If they had not been innovators and outsiders in relation to the North Korean mainstream, they would have stayed with the rest of the population. Being innovators, they moved to find a better place to live. These people will therefore be the best evangelists to North Korea when the nation opens, providing freedom to share the Gospel and to worship God without restrictions.

ANTICIPATING MASSIVE MIGRATION

Since 1990 many scholars and experts have predicted the collapse of North Korea. When North Korea does collapse and opens up, we can expect up to one-sixth of the population to be displaced. Forecasts predict that between 220,000 and 4 million people will migrate to South Korea, China, Japan, or Russia.[4] Although North Korea's collapse has not happened and we do not know when it will happen, we need to be prepared for a massive migration. The church needs to prepare Gospel tracts in the North Korean dialect, to develop methodologies of evangelism adapted to people who are accustomed to communal life as opposed to using individualistic approaches to evangelism, and to figure out other ways of reaching North Koreans for Christ.

When North Korea opens, some theological questions will

3. See Everett M. Rogers, *Diffusion of Innovations*, 5th ed. (New York: Simon & Schuster, 2003; orig. pub., 1962). Rogers divides populations into five categories: innovators (2.5 percent), early adopters (13.5 percent), early majority (34.0 percent), late majority (34.0 percent), and laggards (16.0 percent). Innovators are the first to act on new opportunities.

4. See Youn-Young Kim, "Dae-Ryang-tal-buk-nan-nin yu-yip dae-bi kyung-chal-eu dae-ung-ban-an" [A study on counter measures by Korean police against massive influx of North Korean defectors], *Chee-an-jung-chak-yun-ku* [Journal of police policy] 29, no. 2 (September 2015): 116; and Kwang-joo Son, *Buk-han-teuk-jing-eu Gup-byun-sa-tae-wha dae-ryang tal-buk-nan-min yeu-bang tong-jae dae-check* [Prevention and control policy against an unanticipated North Korean crisis and large-scale North Korean defections], National Defense Institute Policy Seminar (2013), 36.

arise. How should the church deal with those who have left the church by denying Christ? How should the church receive those who claimed that they were Christians yet also wore Kim Il-Sung's badge? The church needs to be prepared to offer open and full fellowship to underground believers. But without theological preparation for reuniting them to the church, their differences will lead to splits instead of to church unification.

Current migrants may be able to be a blessing by serving as intermediaries. Having learned South Korean culture and acknowledging the Gospel message, can they be prepared to receive and assist the coming mass of North Korean migrants?

CONCLUSION

Currently, fifty to sixty churches composed of North Korean migrants exist in South Korea.[5] Most of these churches are small in membership, and they are not financially stable. More than one hundred North Korean migrants are students in theological training.[6] The South Korean church needs to embrace these North Korean migrant churches and theological students. Many issues and problems can be resolved if they work together. God may have sent North Korean migrants to South Korea so that from them South Koreans could learn about North Koreans, all for the sake of bringing the Gospel to North Korea.

5. Kyung-Nam Lee, "The Issues of Mission to North Korea," *Han-Kook Gi-dok Kong-bo*, no. 3093 (June 2, 2017).

6. "Conference on North Korean Refugees," *Yon-Hap Gi-dok News* (February 28, 2014).

2

"And you are to love those who are foreigners . . ." (Deut. 10:12–19)

Christopher J. H. Wright

Deuteronomy is a good book to begin with in considering a biblical response to the challenges of migrations, refugees, displaced peoples, and diaspora populations, for it presents itself as the preaching of Moses to people in exactly that situation: the Israelites in the generation after the exodus. It is, in many senses, a book "on the boundary": the boundary between wilderness and promised land; boundary between past promise and future fulfillment; boundary between the culture of Egypt, then the liminal phase of the wilderness, and the culture of Canaan ahead.

How should such people relate to their God, to one another, and to those in their midst who do not "belong"? Deuteronomy as a whole has immensely challenging theological insights, as well as practical instructions for such circumstances. And it is all based on the saving grace of God. Remember that although the book is regarded as law, it is all founded on the historical act of redemption, on the exodus.

Deuteronomy 10:12–19 is unquestionably one of the richest texts in the Hebrew Bible, exalted and poetic in its language, comprehensive and challenging in its message. It purposely tries to "boil down" the whole content of the book into memorable phrases, packed and pregnant, rich and resonant with all the surrounding preaching. It is like a mini-symphony of biblical faith and life. It begins with a five-note opening chord and then moves on to a two-movement surprise symphony.

And now, Israel, what does the LORD your God ask of you but to fear the LORD your God, to walk in obedience to him, to love him, to serve the LORD your God with all your heart and with all your soul, and to observe the LORD's commands and decrees that I am giving you today for your own good?

To the LORD your God belong the heavens, even the highest heavens, the earth and everything in it. Yet the LORD set his affection on your ancestors and loved them, and he chose you, their descendants, above all the nations—as it is today. Circumcise your hearts, therefore, and do not be stiff-necked any longer. For the LORD your God is God of gods and Lord of lords, the great God, mighty and awesome, who shows no partiality and accepts no bribes. He defends the cause of the fatherless and the widow, and loves the foreigner residing among you, giving them food and clothing. And you are to love those who are foreigners, for you yourselves were foreigners in Egypt.[1]

A SINGLE MUSICAL CHORD WITH FIVE DISTINCT NOTES IN HARMONY (10:12–13)

And now, O Israel (NRSV). Rather like Paul's "therefore," after all the teaching, warning, and admonition of chapters 1–9, the words "and now, Israel" indicate a transition to a strong conclusion.

What does the LORD your God ask of you but . . . ? The intention is to get down to basics and show that the claim of God upon the covenant people is not complicated, but fundamentally simple. It is not "simple" as in "easy"—if obedience were *easy*, there would be little need for these chapters full of encouragement, warning, and promise. But it is simple, meaning that there is only one God to be obeyed, and he has made his will very clear (see Deut. 30:11–13). So although there are many individual commands and instructions, a single thread runs through them all.

This sentence (vv. 12–13) is like a five-note musical chord. Each note has its own distinct tone, but taken all together they sound forth in a harmony that expresses the whole content of Deuteronomy and the Torah—*to fear . . . to walk . . . to love . . . to serve . . . to observe.* With a similar purpose, but with different words, Micah 6:8 asks the question "What does the LORD require of you?"

---

1. Unless noted otherwise, Scripture citations in this chapter are from the New International Version.

and answers it with a triplet of phrases that summarize the prophetic preaching, in the same way that these phrases summarize the Torah: "to act justly and to love mercy and to walk humbly with your God." Micah gets the five words of Moses down to three. Jesus later got them down to two: "Love the Lord your God. . . . Love your neighbor as yourself" (Matt. 22:37, 39).

Let's hear each note.

To fear the LORD your God is to have a basic respect and reverence for the covenant Lord, which permeate all other attitudes (see Deut. 5:29; 6:13; 10:20). It means to take God seriously, to put God first. And for Proverbs, it is the beginning of wisdom.

To walk in all his ways (ESV) is to imitate God (see Deut. 5:33; 8:6; 11:22). It means to see what God is like, to observe what God does, and then to seek to reflect God's character and ways in your own life. In Genesis 18:19 God says that this intention was the purpose of calling Abraham—so that his people would be taught to walk in the ways of Yahweh God, not in the ways of Sodom and Gomorrah.

To love him is to have and to express covenant loyalty and obedience flowing out of gratitude (see Deut. 6:5; 11:1, 13, 22). According to Jesus, it is the first and greatest commandment, and here it stands as the central note of the whole chord. For Deuteronomy, and for Jesus, love must be shown in obedience. "If you love me, keep my commands" (John 14:15; see also 14:23 and 1 John 4:19–21).

To serve the LORD your God with all your heart and with all your soul is virtually identical to "loving" God, but with the added metaphor of bonded service to the one who has bought and therefore owns the people. Israel had been slaves of Pharaoh. Now they were freed from that bondage, but freed *into* the service of Yahweh their God (see Deut. 6:13; 10:20; 11:13).

To observe the LORD's commands is to give careful, conscientious, and constant attention to the terms and stipulations of the covenant relationship (see Deut. 7:11; 11:1, 8, 13, 22). Once we have gotten our orientation right and understand that all our obedience flows from gratitude and grace, then we can get down to the detailed study of God's Word and all that God requires of us. Our obedience needs to be based on love and grace, in order to avoid legalism. But there is a right place for careful attention to all of God's Word.

For your own good. Just two words in Hebrew (*ləṭôb lak*, "for good for you"), this phrase condenses all the blessings that Moses elsewhere expansively describes. Through obedience, Israel could enter into secure possession of the land, enjoy long life, receive all of God's plentiful gifts, and prosper (see Deut. 5:29, 33; 6:24; 30:15–20). It also condenses the important ethical point that the law itself was a gift of God's grace for the benefit of human beings, not something God just imposed for his own pleasure. As Moses has already pointed out (Deut. 4:6–8), observing the law is wisdom—it not only pleases the giver of the law, but it also benefits the keeper of the law. "Obedience is good for you."

We need to correct the idea that, for Old Testament Israel, the law was in itself some kind of burden or merely an external legalistic requirement. It did become distorted in that way by the time of the New Testament, and so we can see how Jesus and Paul had to deal with people who had turned it into such a burden. But in the Old Testament, the law is a blessing and a gift, for people's own good—as the psalmists recognized: read Psalms 1, 19, and 119. Obeying the law was never intended as a means of deserving God's salvation or blessing, but rather as the way of responding to his salvation and continuing to enjoy salvation's blessings.

A SURPRISE SYMPHONY (10:14–19)

The six verses of Deuteronomy 10:14–19 are carefully structured as a pair of matching triplets: verses 14, 15, 16 and verses 17, 18, 19. Each set has an opening, hymn-like exaltation of Yahweh with resounding superlatives (14 and 17). The middle verses describe something surprising about God's action or character (15 and 18). The concluding verses are commands for Israel to respond appropriately (16 and 19). This stereophonic effect enriches the impact of the whole symphony.

14 Hymn	17 Hymn
⇓	⇓
15 Surprise	18 Surprise
⇓	⇓
16 Response	19 Response

FIRST MOVEMENT

The first movement, consisting of verses 14–16, contains three parts.

The hymn: God owns the universe! Verse 14, with wonderful rhythmic cadence, affirms the universal exaltation and cosmic ownership of Yahweh (see 1 Kings 8:27; Pss. 24:1; 33:6–8; 47:7–9; 68:34; 95:4–7; 115:16; 148:4–13; Jer. 10:10–13). There is absolutely nothing in creation "up there" or "down here" that does not belong to him. And if absolutely everything belongs to Yahweh (and the text could hardly have found more emphatic words to say so), what was left to be franchised out to other deities?

Yahweh's absolute ownership of the whole of the universe has at least two implications. The first is *ecological*: since the earth is the Lord's (and not ours), then he is the landlord, and we are the tenants. We are accountable to him for how we use it and care for it. And these are not merely "environmental" issues, for climate change is affecting most severely the poorest of the world, and many of them are migrants or displaced persons. Indeed, in some parts of the world, the impact of climate change is what is driving so many people to leave their homelands.

The second implication is *missiological*: Jesus Christ made the same claim—"all authority in heaven and on earth has been given to me" (Matt. 28:18). The whole earth belongs to Christ by right of creation, redemption, and inheritance. So wherever we go in his name (whether as migrants or as those who minister to them), we are walking on his property. There is not an inch of this planet that does not belong to him. So there is therefore no need for fear and no place for dualism; whatever power and influence Satan has is *usurped and illegitimate*. The earth is the Lord's.

The surprise: Yet God loves you! The Hebrew word *raq*, translated "yet," emphatically introduces a contrasting or surprising point. The wonder is that a God of such cosmic, universal ownership should have focused his affection on the insignificant ancestors of insignificant Israel. This verse echoes Deuteronomy 7:6–8 in expressing the wonder of Israel's election. There the surprise was that God should have chosen Israel though it was so small. Here the surprise is because God is so great. In both cases, the message is that Israel's election was based on nothing in itself that had evoked God's favoritism, but solely in the character and action of this amazing God.

It is important to read each of these two verses (14 and 15) in the light of the other. On the one hand, the God of universal ownership exercised his sovereignty in the particular choice of Israel. On the other hand, the God who loved and chose Israel is the God who owns the whole world. Thus the universality of God must not be separated from the particularity of God's electing love. Neither, however, must the particularity of God's action in Israel be severed from the universality of God's cosmic ownership of the world (the same dual truth is expressed in Exod. 19:4–6).

Missiologically, it is vital to keep these two great biblical truths integrally related to each other. Otherwise we can end up in one of two dangers. The first danger is to conclude that, if everything and everybody belongs to God, then all distinctions are dissolved between those who are the people of God and those who are not yet. The second danger is the temptation to infer from God's love for God's own people that God hates, or at least has no interest in, the other nations. The balance found in these verses protects us from the unbiblical extremes of a monistic universalism that destroys all distinctions, on the one hand, and a narrow exclusivism that denies or restricts the universality of God's love, on the other hand. In the immediate context of our topic, we need constant reminding that God loves the foreigner, migrant, and refugee, just as much as he loves us.

The response: Therefore, repent! We might have expected words of praise and encouragement to follow verses 14 and 15. But instead, Israel finds a double-barreled call to repentance aimed at their hearts and necks (v. 16). For Israel, being the elect people of God was not so much a privilege as an awesome responsibility that could prove highly dangerous. The way this summary call for repentance follows an exalted statement of election that is rhetorically and theologically very similar to Amos 3:2, where the uniqueness of Israel's relationship with Yahweh is stunningly followed by the words "therefore I will punish you."

In Deuteronomy 10:16 the Israelites are admonished: "Circumcise your hearts." Literal circumcision was the sign of covenant membership, but it could also be used metaphorically with the ears (Jer. 6:10 Heb.) or the heart to speak of willingness to hear and obey the Word of God (e.g., Lev. 26:41; Deut. 30:6; Jer. 4:4; 9:26; Ezek. 44:7–9). This phrase describes an inner commitment to obey God and so to live out the meaning of the physical sign in the flesh. Paul says the same thing in Romans 2:28–29.

SECOND MOVEMENT

The second movement, verses 17–19, also contains three steps or parts.

The hymn: God rules the universe! The second triplet begins in verse 17 with another burst of hymnody, similar in form to verse 14, but with its emphasis not so much on God in relation to the created order (heavens and earth) as on God in relation to all other spiritual realities. The expression "God of gods and Lord of lords" (also "heavens of heavens," the Heb. of v. 14) expresses a superlative. It means Yahweh is the highest God and the supreme Lord. Whatever other spiritual realities may exist, they are all subject to Yahweh. He rules and governs all forces of every kind within his created universe. This truth is emphasized again and again in the Old Testament (e.g., Pss. 24:8; 95:3; 136:2–3; Neh. 9:32; Isa. 42:13).

The text does not say merely that Yahweh is the only God for Israel (while allowing for the legitimate jurisdiction of other national deities) but affirms that Yahweh is the supreme God over all. Yahweh's sovereignty is not just covenantal, but cosmic. The conviction expressed poetically here seems very similar to the conviction expressed politically (and with scant regard for diplomatic niceties) at the international conference of Middle Eastern states in Jerusalem circa 594 BCE by Jeremiah (see 27:5–11). The same truth was acknowledged with surprise by the object of that word, Nebuchadnezzar himself (Dan. 2:47; 4:25, 34–35). Yahweh, the God who owns the world (v. 14), is also the God who runs the world (v. 17).

The affirmation of Yahweh's universal ownership and universal lordship in verses 14 and especially 17 is a claim that conflicted with the cultures around them. Israel lived in an ancient Near Eastern macro-culture as religiously plural as that in any era in which God's people have had to live. Yet Israel's claims regarding the universality of Yahweh stood out against the surrounding polytheism.

Similarly—and with greater missiological relevance for Christian claims within the modern controversy over religious pluralism—the fact that early Christian worship could apply such language to Jesus (Rev. 17:14; 19:16; see also 1:18 and elsewhere) shows both the determination of New Testament Christians to affirm the universal lordship of Christ in ways that clashed with all the religious plurality of their context and also their determination to do so within a consistent framework of scriptural monotheism. They saw no incompatibility, in other words, in including Jesus in the affirmation of Deuteronomy 10:14, 17 (see 1 Cor. 8:4–6).

Unlike human lords and so many of the members of ancient Near Eastern pantheons, Yahweh had no favorites and no price (v. 17b). The expression "shows no partiality" is literally "he does not lift up faces"; that is, he does not base decisions on selective favoritism. This understanding might seem to be in considerable tension with verse 15 until we remember that Deuteronomy has already explicitly excluded the idea that God's election of Israel was some kind of favoritism (7:7; 9:4–6). Unfortunately, the very notion of divine election is still frequently caricatured and dismissed by Christians as divine favoritism. We need to take note that the statement of God's love for *Israel* in verse 15 is bounded by (and so to be understood in relation to) affirmations of God's ownership of *the whole earth* (v. 14), on the one side, and of God's *impartiality* (v. 17), on the other. It should not be pulled out of that context and defined in a way that denies either of those enveloping truths. It was precisely because of God's love and saving intention for *all nations* that God called and chose Abraham and his descendants to be the vehicle of his redemptive action in the world for the sake of the world. *The particular and the universal must be held together.* And our doctrine of election must be seen within the missiological frame of God's cosmic purpose as revealed in the whole biblical narrative.

The surprise: Yet God loves the foreigner! In verse 18 we once again have a surprise. If God is the supreme ruler, who should benefit when he exercises his "God-ship" in practice? In some ancient Near Eastern royal texts the exaltation of national gods is commonly followed by the exaltation of the royal household. It was human kings who basked in the reflected glory of the ruling gods. The gods ruled, and kings benefited. But who, in this wonderful doxological definition, are the beneficiaries of Yahweh's supreme lordship? *The fatherless and the widow and . . . the foreigner!*

Nothing could be more characteristic of Israel's countercultural faith. The majestic monotheistic superlatives of verses 14 and 17 are harnessed, not to the glory and power of the wealthy and strong, but to the needs of the poor, the weak, and the vulnerable (the same pattern is seen in Isa. 40:28–31). The rest of the law will demonstrate that this social concern was no facade. Rather, the fundamental character of Yahweh expressed so succinctly here, and enjoined on Israel in verse 19, pervades the legal sections of Deuteronomy and explicitly shapes much of the practical social legislation. Our text is saying, "Here is the God you worship, Israel! This is who your God loves and cares for. Now, then, how should you therefore live?"

God *"loves the foreigner . . . giving them food and clothing."* This declaration reinforces the previous point about God's impartiality. God's love for Israel should never be seen as sheer favoritism, for that is not God's way. The impartiality of Yahweh is seen in that he not only loved Israel's forebears but he also loves the foreigner. Exactly the same word is used. And then, the additional phrase that Yahweh feeds and clothes the foreigner undoubtedly echoes the way God had fed and clothed Israel in the wilderness (Deut. 8:3–4). What Yahweh had done for Israel was, quite simply, typical of him. Yahweh is the God who loves foreigners and feeds and clothes them. When the Israelites were the foreigners in Egypt and then in the wilderness (v. 19b), God provided for them. For that is what God is like and what God does.

Once again we find this remarkable balance between the particularism of Yahweh's action for Israel in redemption and covenant, and the universality of his character for all people, on which that behavior is based. His action for Israel was paradigmatic *for them,* but it was also paradigmatic *of God.* Jesus drew the same lessons about the generosity and breadth of God's love from nature and applied them with a similarly radical ethical thrust to the love of foreigners (Matt. 6:25–34; 5:43–48).

The response: Therefore, you are to love the foreigner! In verse 19 we have Deuteronomy's equivalent of Jesus' "second greatest commandment," similar to Leviticus 19:18 and 34.

This commandment is remarkable first of all because it is totally rooted in the character and action of God. What does it mean to "walk in all his [God's] ways" (v. 12 KJV)? Verse 19 gives the answer. The ways of Yahweh in verses 14–19 begin with condescending love for the ancestors of Israel and climax in practical love for the strangers in Israel, the foreigners. In between these two all-embracing dimensions of Yahweh's love are sandwiched impartiality, integrity, and commitment to justice. God is love, so to walk in God's ways will entail the exercise of practical love; that is what it means (in the Old Testament and in the New Testament) to live in imitation of God (see 1 John 3:17; 4:20–21).

Second, the commandment is remarkable in specifying the object of such love. Moses skips over, as it were, the two other love commands that might have naturally followed—to love God and to love fellow Israelites as neighbors. He jumps to the most radical and demanding of the list—to love the foreigner.

Why does Moses do this? Was it perhaps because he assumed that if Israel could demonstrate practical love to *foreigners*, they would be likely to sustain other aspects of the social laws that God was giving them? Or was it perhaps the insight that love for foreigners will always be the first feature of any society to evaporate in times of social pressure and conflict? Xenophobia, exploitation, and precisely the kind of scapegoat politics that Israel suffered in Egypt are much more typical in our world today, as the response to migrants all over the world has shown. Whatever the reason, singling out that particular love commandment in such a lofty context is astonishing.

It is worth noting that the Hebrew verb form *wə'āhabtā* (and you [sg.] shall love) occurs only four times in the Old Testament: Deuteronomy 6:5 and 11:1 (the LORD your God) and Leviticus 19:18 (your neighbor) and 19:34 (the alien). Deuteronomy 10:19 supplies the only occurrence of the plural form *wa'ăhabtem* (and you [pl.] shall love), and it reinforces Leviticus 19:34 exactly.

The instruction in Deuteronomy 10:19 is only one of many places in Israel's law where God's heart for the homeless, landless, and family-less is expressed. The foreigner is placed alongside widows and orphans as being particularly vulnerable and in need of protection. If this position applied to those who were foreigners within the land and community of Israel itself, how much more does it apply to those who are driven from their own lands and have no place to call their own—as is true of so many millions in today's world. Here are just a few other examples of what God expected from Israelites in their treatment of foreigners.

Protection from abuse	Exod. 22:21; Lev. 19:33
Justice in the courts	Deut. 24:17–18; 27:19
Fair employment	Deut. 24:14–15
Access to food	Deut. 24:19–22
Equality before the law	Lev. 19:33–34
Generous provision	Deut. 10:17–19

Finally, we may note that in these six rich verses Israel is required to respond to God's universal reign and gracious action in only two ways, expressed in the two imperatives: "Repent!" and "Love the foreigner!" (vv. 16, 19). It is challenging to sense the way Jesus drank deeply from the wells of Deuteronomy's spirituality and ethic when teaching about the kingdom of heaven—"Repent, for the kingdom of heaven is at hand" (Matt. 4:17 NKJV)—and in giving his radical command "Love your enemies" (Matt. 5:44, see 43–48).

3

Migration in Christian History

Andrew F. Walls

Migration has been a recurrent feature of human life throughout history. It is also a theme that runs through the Bible. The book of Genesis introduces us to two main categories of migration. One is the Adamic, represented in the expulsion of Adam and Eve from paradise, where the migration is punitive, indicating deprivation and loss. The second category, the Abrahamic, is represented in the divine call to Abraham to leave his settled homeland (in the highest of contemporary civilizations) to assume the life of a nomadic herdsman, with the promise of receiving a better land for his children—though he had no children at that time. Adamic migration recurs many times in the story of Israel, as the inevitable outcome of the nation's faithlessness to God, culminating in the lament of Jesus over the fate of Jerusalem, which killed the prophets and eventually rejected its own Messiah. Abrahamic migration is reflected in the exodus from Egypt and the eventual settlement of Israel in the Promised Land; and when, in accordance with the Deuteronomic law, the Israelite farmer brought the firstfruits of his land as an offering to God, he recalled that his ancestor was a wandering Aramean, a perennial migrant with no land of his own. In the New Testament, Abraham, the migrant seeking a better land, is taken as the prototype of the Christian both by the apostle Paul and by the writer to the Hebrews; the Christians addressed in 1 Peter are called refugees; and the Letter of James describes its readers in terms usually applied to the dispersion of Jews from Palestine across the world.[1]

It is no surprise, therefore, to find that many developments in Christian history have been connected with migration, as a number of recent studies have highlighted. In this chapter, we will take a brief look at several of these developments.

THE JEWISH DISPERSION

Let us begin by reflecting on a migration that began in the antenatal period of Christianity: the Jewish Dispersion, or, to use the Greek word, diaspora—the scattering of the Jews over the Greco-Roman world and the Middle East and beyond both, which took place over several centuries after the return from exile in Babylon.

Jews settled all over the Hellenistic Greek-speaking world, bringing with them their Scriptures, their worship of God, and their complete rejection of all other divinities. As is common among migrants, the generations born abroad increasingly adopted the language of the people among whom they now lived, and this factor led to a development that was to be important for early Christianity. In Alexandria, the Hebrew Scriptures were translated into Greek, and that Greek translation was to become the first Bible of the early church. Because these writings were so old—many of them much older than such great writings as Plato's *Dialogues*—they could not be easily dismissed as worthless by the Hellenistic world, which distinguished itself so sharply from the "barbarians," who had no literature. Nor was the Greek Septuagint the only gift of the Dispersion to early Christianity. Similar processes in the Middle East, where Syriac was widely spoken, led to Syriac translations of the Hebrew Scriptures and provided another part of the early church there with its first Bible. The history of Bible translation begins with migration.

In the New Testament, the importance of the Jewish Diaspora to the establishment of the early church is clear. The crowd that heard the apostolic preaching at Pentecost included Dispersion Jews from all over the Mediterranean, the Middle East, and North Africa. In his Pentecost speech in Acts 2, Peter makes it

---

1. The theme of migration in the Bible is discussed in Andrew F. Walls, "Toward a Theology of Migration," in *Crossing Cultural Frontiers: Studies in the History of World Christianity* (Maryknoll, NY: Orbis Books, 2017), 49–61.

clear that the promised Messiah is for them: the promise is "for those afar off" (that is, for Israelites of the Dispersion), as well as for those "that are near" (that is, for those living in Jerusalem and Judea). When persecution broke out following Stephen's death and most believers in Jesus fled from Jerusalem, it was to the Dispersion in Phoenicia, Cyprus, and Antioch that they went— often, no doubt, to relatives or friends. Some of those in Antioch took the epoch-making step of sharing the news about Jesus with Greek-speaking pagans and thereby produced the model of the bicultural church, which was soon to be replicated elsewhere, opening the faith to Gentiles.

Antioch became the base for the mission of Paul and Barnabas, and the accounts in Acts represent them as regularly beginning their mission in the synagogues of the Jewish Dispersion, but often finding the readiest response among the Gentiles, the proselytes and Godfearers on the edge of these communities. It was only after complete rejection on the part of Diaspora Jewish communities that the missionaries, as in Acts 13, deliberately turned to the Gentiles. Paul's mission to the Gentiles (himself a Dispersion Jew eloquent in Greek and knowledgeable about Greek culture) was thus rooted in the Jewish Dispersion, even though it often resulted in disruption in the synagogues and opposition from those Jews who rejected the preaching of the Messiah.

What we know from the Acts of the Apostles about Paul's missions in the Roman Empire is almost certainly also true of other places where we know little or nothing of how the church began. Alexandria, for instance, had a huge Jewish population, and it would be surprising if Jewish followers of Jesus were not its first missionaries. Even in India, if, as there are good grounds for believing, the apostle Thomas was its first evangelist, it is reasonable to suppose that what first took him there was the knowledge that a Jewish community was settled there.

The initial spread of the Christian faith in the earliest centuries thus owed much to the huge, complex migration of Jewish people out of Palestine.

ARAB MIGRATIONS AND THE CHRISTIAN FAITH

We readily recognize the significance for Christianity of the Arab movement out of the Arabian Peninsula following the death of the Prophet Muhammad, when Arabs invaded and asserted their rule over Egypt, Syria, and Iraq, all of them at that time Christian territories. We readily recognize also that the Hijra, the migration of Muhammad and his companions from Mecca to Medina in 622, was crucial in the rise and development of Islam. But there was another Arab migration, of Syriac-speaking Arab Christians, that was to spread Christian living and teaching across much of Asia. This migration was partly a product of economic developments, in particular the silk trade from China. Syriac-speaking merchants moved and settled across Central Asia, bringing with them their families and their Christian faith, and churches sprang up in regions as far distant from each other as Siberia and Sri Lanka. But the migration also had a missionary dimension. Syriac Christianity had a radical youth movement, the Children of the Covenant, which seems to have been the seedbed of a missionary movement based on devoted people schooled to endure harsh living conditions. Through them various Central Asian people groups converted to Christian faith. The missionaries reached peoples surrounding the Chinese Empire and translated the Scriptures into the Mongol and Manchu languages, creating new scripts for the purpose. In the year 635, as the famous Nestorian Inscription records, the missionaries reached the court of the emperor of China and began to translate parts of Scripture and other Christian books into Chinese. This early dawn of Chinese Christianity may have faded in later centuries, but it remains an important development. The Gospel reached China in the same period that it was being received in northern England.

Syriac Christian migration also brought strength to the church in India, when persecution of Christians in the Middle East led numbers of them to move to South India. We must conclude that migration—sometimes voluntary, sometimes forced—was a significant factor in the early Christian history of Asia. Missionaries are themselves migrants for the sake of the Gospel.

MIGRATIONS AND SOUTHEAST ASIA

Migration has also been important for Christianity in Asia in more recent times. Let us consider the long history of Chinese migration into Southeast Asia and the Pacific Rim. In the early nineteenth century, when China was closed to missions and to all outside influences except strictly regulated trade, the area we now call Malaysia became the base for a China mission-in-waiting. Gospel preaching in Chinese to Chinese audiences went on steadily in Melaka; there the Anglo-Chinese College pursued the study and teaching of Chinese language and culture, and there James Legge began his monumental research on the Chinese classics. Such activities could not at that time be readily carried out in China. In Melaka, Bibles and other Christian literature in Chinese were printed and, in the regular trade with China, passed into the Chinese Empire. In Melaka new migrants from China—such as Liang A Fa, who was to become the first ordained Chinese Protestant minister and a hugely influential writer—heard the Gospel and turned to Christ.

The opening of China to missions did not end the Christian significance of the southeast Pacific Rim and its migrant population. The area has continued to have an important function in mission. Its Chinese community, periodically refreshed from China, has continued to be important in Christian terms. The Chinese and Indian communities, in each case the outcome of complex movements of migration, now provide the Christian base in Malaysia and Singapore, and the Christian components of these communities have had influence far outside their own boundaries. Nor should we forget that after 1950 the area resumed for a time its former position as China mission-in-waiting and as the source of Christian literature in Chinese.

Continuing connection with China has been a feature of this area. One example is in the remarkable work of the Chinese evangelist John Sung, at first noted for his evangelistic campaigns in China but afterward for the dramatic response to his preaching in Singapore and elsewhere.

MIGRATION AND KOREA AS A BASE
FOR WORLD MISSION

In the reports of the World Missionary Conference in Edinburgh in 1910 and of the meeting of the International Missionary Council held in Tambaram, India, in 1938, Korea occupies a sort of niche. It was recognized to be part of East Asia, and in general the patterns of mission activity there had been developed in China and Japan. Yet Korea was different from its neighbors. Though it was a relatively new field for Protestant missions, solid progress was visible. Such words as "miracle" could be used of Korea's self-supporting church, and "Pentecost" of its early twentieth century revival movement. The main energies of Western missions were directed to China, Japan, and India, where immense cultural and political movements were taking place.

But God was perhaps quietly preparing the church in Korea for a special place in world mission.

Some aspects of that preparation are described in the Tambaram report, where we catch glimpses of the building of a Bible-reading, financially self-supporting church able to look beyond itself and its own interests, as well as of a body of committed, disciplined, and well-taught Christian workers being assembled. Meanwhile, in the political field, the movement for national independence (with which Christians were closely associated) carried the preparation further, and Korea emerged from colonial status before many other parts of the world.

Then came fiery trials. First, a devastating war, bringing about a huge displacement of population, in which areas where the church had taken deepest root suffered most disturbance, bringing disruption and exile for many. Later came the division of the nation. Perhaps the deep sense of longing that has issued from the division of the nation—and the retreat of a large part of the nation into an isolation as difficult to penetrate as that of the old Hermit Kingdom—has been part of the divine preparation of Korea for its world mission. The line dividing the nation is Korea's equivalent of the Wailing Wall in Jerusalem—a visible token of suffering and of hope deferred.

But there were other dimensions of the divine preparation of Korea for a world missionary vocation. Rapid economic growth and technological development—backed by well-educated leadership (already noted in the Tambaram report as an aspect of Korean church life)—were combined with awareness of the world outside and a global consciousness, which is always a prerequisite for mission activity. And these things were especially characteristic of a category of the Korean population that the war and displacement greatly enlarged: the Korean diaspora.

Diaspora has a long history for Koreans. Reports from both the Edinburgh and the Tambaram conferences devote attention to the Korean communities in China, in the islands of the China Sea, and in Russian Asia, and the extent to which they were sharing in the Korean movement to the Christian faith, so visible in Korea itself. Koreans overseas were not only the focus of evangelization, but also the evangelists themselves. Later events enlarged the diaspora, and one part of it, the diaspora population in North America, became of special importance and significance, both in its numbers and in its effect.

Many factors made North America a magnet for Koreans wishing to emigrate—or forced to do so—and a network of churches across the continent was one result. These churches were important for the way in which they helped new arrivals through the sometimes traumatic business of settlement, lending their assistance both to Christians and to non-Christian families. It is clear that this work played a part in leading many to faith in Christ.

The ancient language of Korea—preserved over the centuries, despite all the cultural and political influences from Korea's larger neighbors, and fostered as part of missionary policy—was a treasured part of national identity, and the Korean churches in diaspora naturally retained it. A postmigration generation emerged, however, that fully shared that identity and revered its heritage, but that had also developed familiarity with the English language and by this means entered into the wider discourse of world missions conducted in the English language. Their position recalls the experience of the Jewish Dispersion in Alexandria that led to the Septuagint.

Churches of the Korean diaspora have become a notable feature of North American Christianity, becoming perhaps the most prominent nationally of the churches of the recent migrations to North America. They are part of a wider presence of Asian Christian influence in America, in which younger generations, aware of their Asian heritage but at the same time at home in American culture and the English language, begin to contribute beyond their ethnic bounds, in particular as they enter the ministry of indigenous American churches.

The Korean diaspora in the West linked Korean Christians with the Western bases of world mission at a crucial time, when those bases were struggling to maintain their activities, with diminishing human and financial resources as a result of the recession from Christianity in the West, especially in Europe. Here, Korea proved a valuable source of missionary recruits. The Korean diaspora in the West also ensured that, to a large extent, the new missionaries, who usually came from the postmigration generations, could operate effectively in English, avoiding disruption of traditional lines of communication in the missions that they now joined. English was also in many cases the official language of the countries to which they went as missionaries. By these means, Korea became a useful component within what was left of the older missionary movement from the West.

In Britain, where the rate of Christine decline was markedly faster than in North America, this process was particularly noticeable. Perhaps I may be allowed a personal reminiscence. Over a period in the 1970s and early 1980s, I taught an annual study course for the missionary candidates of a well-known British non-denominational evangelical mission agency. In the early years the missionary candidates were almost all British; in the later years, Korea and Brazil were supplying an increasing proportion of the candidates.[2]

The Korean presence within Western mission organizations was only one of the routes within this period by which Korea became significantly involved in world mission; the churches of South Korea, and often large individual congregations, were by this time organizing for missionary activities across the world. In several different ways, therefore, the postwar Korean diaspora in the West has had a significant part in the emergence of the Korean world missionary movement.

The World Missionary Conference held at Edinburgh in 1910 marked the high point of the missionary movement from the West. One volume of that conference's multivolume report was entitled "Home Base of Missions." At that time, the home base clearly lay in Europe and North America, with some help from Australia and New Zealand, and the authors of the report saw little likelihood for that situation to change soon.

The situation today is totally different. The West is no longer the home base of mission; rather, it is increasingly becoming a major mission field itself, requiring the reevangelization of an increasingly complex and multilayered non-Christian culture. The home base of mission is now spread across the world; mission ini-

2. As a general assessment, this seems to me a fair statement. Some notable research, however, indicates that overseas mission has not been given high priority among younger Korean Americans. See S. Steve Kang and Megan A. Hackman, "Toward a Broader Role in Mission: How Korean Americans' Struggle for Identity Can Lead to a Renewed Vision for Mission," *International Bulletin of Missionary Research* 36, no. 2 (April 2012): 72–77.

tiatives may develop almost anywhere in the world and be directed almost anywhere else in the world. Sub-Saharan Africa and Latin America are potentially major home bases of world mission. Other home bases are emerging in Asia. Various factors point particularly to Korea, and soon to China as well, as major home bases of world mission. And in each of these cases, the diaspora is likely to be a vital aspect of that base.

A MIGRATION THAT SHAPED
THE MODERN WORLD ORDER

The Jewish Dispersion gave direction to the whole future history of the Christian faith. The other migrations that we have considered had particular relevance to Christian history in Asia. Had we time, we could explore many other movements of migration and diaspora that have been crucial to the Christian story in Europe, in Africa, and in the Americas. But before we conclude, let us consider two other migrations: one that ended in the twentieth century, because it has influenced the geopolitical setting of our own time, and one that began in the twentieth century, because it highlights needs, resources, and opportunities in world mission today.

I call the first movement the Great European Migration. Some aspects of this migration are often obscured by concentration on certain particular aspects of it, such as colonialism and imperialism. Colonialism and imperialism are in fact special modes or processes in a wider phenomenon that took place between the beginning of the sixteenth century and the middle of the twentieth. During those four and a half centuries, huge numbers of people left Europe for lands beyond Europe. There was no single motive: some went as soldiers and conquerors, some as traders, some as administrators, some as missionaries. The commonest motive, however, was to find for themselves or their children a better life or a fairer society than they could find in Europe at the time.

This movement of people out of Europe was one of the formative influences on what we may call the modern world order, the order of the world in which we grew up. The migration brought new nations into being, as peoples of European descent settled in lands overseas, sometimes merging with the original population, sometimes far outnumbering it. In this way all the nations of the Americas—North, Central, and South—came into being, as did

Australia, New Zealand, and other countries. Europeans established control of the seas, enabling them to set up their rule over much of the world—most of Africa, large parts of Asia, and all of the Pacific region—as various European states created empires. Their control of the seas and their empires gave them dominance in world trade and the capacity to institute other migrations. In the largest of these forced migrations, a huge piece of Africa was broken off and put down in North, Central, and South America, as millions of Africans were transported into slavery across the Atlantic. Smaller migrations followed in the interests of trade, as Chinese and Indian workers were brought to the Caribbean or Indians to Fiji. One European power, Russia, expanded overland rather than by sea, right across Asia to the Pacific.

One of the new nations created by the Great European Migration, the United States of America, eventually reached such a size of population and such a degree of economic power as to outstrip the powers of Europe itself, with the partial exception of Russia.

The world order established by the Great European Migration was subject to strains arising from rivalries between the European powers. The eruption of these tensions in the First World War foreshadowed the coming implosion of that world order; the Second World War took that process further. Following that war the empires of the European powers were steadily dismantled; a host of new nations emerged in Asia and Africa. And the Great European Migration itself came to an end; its last phase consisted perhaps of the founding of the State of Israel in 1948 with the migration of many European Jews to Palestine. Otherwise, though migrations within Europe increased, migrations out of Europe dwindled to a trickle.

Let us consider the religious effects of the Great European Migration. When the migration began around 1500, Christianity was the religion of Europe, so much so that Europe was thought of as Christendom, the Christian part of the world. In Christendom, everyone was baptized in infancy; all were regarded as Christians living under Christian law and ruled by Christian princes. The lands closest to Europe on the south and east were under Muslim rule, but Europeans knew little about people living beyond the Muslim world before the great voyages at the end of the fifteenth and in the sixteenth centuries. As those new worlds were revealed to them by these voyages, it was natural for them to desire that these peoples should be Christian and thus part of Christendom. In one part of the world, what we now call Latin America, this desire was effected by conquest: Mexico, for instance, was named New Spain, and an attempt was made to impose the laws, customs, and faith of Old Spain. In a few places, as happened at the mouth of the Congo River, existing states voluntarily adopted Christianity on the European model. But in most of Africa and in Asia voluntary conversion did not take place (save for a time in Japan), and conquest was beyond European capacities. The powers of Europe, generally speaking, abandoned projects to impose Christianity and concentrated on their economic and political interests. Under British rule in India, Hinduism acquired new vitality and adjusted to the scientific and technological influences introduced from the West. In Sri Lanka Buddhism revived under British rule. In Africa and Southeast Asia, Islam expanded under colonial rule beyond anything achieved by jihads. And in the twentieth century, perhaps the fastest recession in Christian history began. The center of that recession lay in Europe, which had once thought of itself as Christendom. Before long, the same processes of de-Christianization were appearing in North America also. By the end of the twentieth century over half of the world's professing Christians were Africans, Asians, or Latin Americans, for the twentieth century had also seen an intensification of Christian faith in Latin America and a huge accession to it in some parts of Asia and, above all, in sub-Saharan Africa.

How had this shift come about? One development cannot be ignored: the growth of the missionary movement from the West. It did not emerge from state initiatives; indeed, European states sometimes tried to control, divert, or block missionary activity. The movement arose from the radical Christians within Christendom, those who, like the Children of the Covenant in earlier Syriac Christianity, wanted to be Christians to the roots. Missionaries, unlike conquerors, had to persuade and demonstrate, but not compel. They had to learn languages and to find a place in other societies.

The movement developed first in Catholic southern Europe, employing the renewed monastic orders and religious societies of dedicated men and women for the supply of its personnel. Later, in Protestant northern Europe, when the Pietist and Evangelical movements had prepared the spiritual ground, voluntary societies became the basis of missionary organization.

We have seen that the Great European Migration effectively came to an end in the middle of the twentieth century following World War II, amid the dismantling of European empires and the emergence of new nations. We have noted also that the world order that the Great European Migration had created began to give way to another. In this new geopolitical order it seems certain that Asian powers will play an increasingly large part.

A MIGRATION OF OUR TIMES

The migration not only ended, it went into reverse. Over the decades since World War II, millions of people from Asia, Africa, and Latin America have moved into Europe and into the lands where people of European descent have settled and been made into nations, as in North America and Australia. This migration has brought African and Asian and Latin American religious and social patterns into the West in ways unknown while the Great European Migration was still in progress. This Great Reverse Migration (as I like to call it) has not only made Islam and Hinduism and Sikhism religions of the West, it has also brought large numbers of African and Asian and Hispanic Christians into the West at the very time when Christianity has been in rapid recession in Europe and in a slower but still marked and continuing decline in North America. The West, once the Christian part of the world, is increasingly a post-Christian society, and its post-Christian character is most marked in the cultural and intellectual spheres. The West is in need, not so much of revival, but of reevangelization: cross-cultural evangelization of an increasingly non-Christian culture. In this situation, the post-Western Christianity of Christians from Asia, Africa, and Latin America may be an important resource. It is well to consider the significance for world mission and for Asian mission of the Great Reverse Migration.

The Great Reverse Migration seems set to continue, though amid controversy and pain. The Western nations do not, for the most part, want migrants, but they need them: migrants are essential to their economies. Nor can we forget that the Great Reverse Migration is being augmented by the flow of refugees from the most distressed parts of the world.

CONCLUSION

Migration, then, has been a significant, and often a determining, factor in many different ways throughout Christian history. It is well to remember the apostle Paul's characterization of Abraham, called out of the comfort of settled city life to the wandering life of a nomadic herdsman, with the hope of future reward for his children in a better land. Paul sets forth Abraham the migrant as the pattern of Christian life, and the author of the Epistle to the Hebrews calls Christians strangers and exiles in search of a city whose builder and maker is God. This identity is as true now, in an age of post-Western Christianity and a post-Christian West, as ever it was in times past.

QUESTIONS FOR REFLECTION

1. This chapter identifies "Adamic" and "Abrahamic" forms of migration in Scripture. Are these categories mutually exclusive in Scripture, or do elements of the Abrahamic sometimes flow into "Adamic" situations?

2. Consider how far the postexilic Dispersion of the Jews offers a model of the experience of modern migrants over several generations.

3. Much of the chapter is concerned with movements of migration within Asia or of Asian migrants. Consider some examples of how migration has influenced Christian history in Africa, the Americas, Europe, or the Pacific region.

4. What place should the development that this chapter calls "the Great Reverse Migration" have in thought, prayer, and action related to Christian mission?

Response
to
"Migration
in Christian History"

Jongboo Hwa

Our thanks and appreciation to Andrew Walls for presenting a very broad picture of migration indeed—from Adam and Abraham to the Jews and the Arabs, then to China, Japan, and Korea. Next came the five centuries of migration out of Europe, and then the great flow of peoples back into the West, with every indication that this most recent movement will continue to radically reshape our world—including our world of mission.

In light of Walls's presentation, I offer three comments on migration and world mission in our times.

WE MUST APPROACH AND INTERPRET MIGRATION IN AN ACTIVE AND MISSIONAL WAY

Today, migrants such as the Syrian refugees in Europe or the Rohingya fleeing from Myanmar to Bangladesh or the many Africans crossing into Europe have become an increasingly critical international issue. With this crisis as backdrop, Walls offers a truly fresh and challenging reinterpretation of both biblical history and church history from the broad perspective of migration. On the one hand, migration can be seen as punishment, starting with Adam's expulsion from paradise and evident throughout the sinful history of Israel. On the other hand, migration can also be redemptive, as seen in the call of Abraham. The view of migration as redemptive, rather than punishment, is enriched by the promises and blessings of God. Viewed in this light, New Testament saints, as well as missionaries of today, stand as voluntary and blessed migrants.

Through international migration, God is fulfilling his plan and will for the world. Not only the Bible, but the entirety of Christian history can be interpreted in terms of migration. Walls perceptively argues that this modern flow of refugees and their great difficulties are not just a misfortune that requires a humanitarian response—which they are and do. We need also to respond in a missional and prayerful way, recognizing that God's redemptive plan is at work. Because of the unfortunate circumstances today's migrants face, one can easily dwell on the need to grieve and mourn with them. But even while working to meet their needs, we need to change our approach and attitude to proactively take this mission opportunity to save the lost and glorify Christ as part of God's greater economy.

THE ROLE OF THE KOREAN CHURCH IN WORLD MISSION

At the height of the mission conferences sparked by the 1910 World Missionary Conference in Edinburgh, particularly the 1938 gathering in Tambaram, India, Korea received sparse attention, being only briefly referred to during reports on China, India, and Japan. This Korean church—at that time largely neglected—is now working incessantly to mobilize people and resources for world mission today. In many ways this reversal in status illustrates the difference between human thoughts and what God sees. Though it is natural to elevate the importance of a nation's or region's strategic value when approaching world mission, perhaps we should reconsider. Rather than focusing on the visible and worthwhile, should we not also regard the weak and lesser valued? It is time to set aside prejudice and instead serve every nation with our utmost for the sake of God's kingdom (Isa. 55:8–9; 1 Cor. 12:21–25). This biblical outlook needs to be applied to our fields of ministry as well.

As a country that has experienced colonization and a devastating civil war, Korea offers an important message and perspective on world mission. With Western missionaries facing increasing racial and religious tension throughout the world, the call for the Korean church to send more missionaries becomes increasingly urgent. Furthermore, if the Korean church is faithful to this call to mission, the result will be a great testament to the world of how God can make use of a weak and divided people.

The Korean church abroad also offers a great mission resource; the Korean diaspora is present all around the world but particularly in North America. Korean Americans hold strongly to their Korean heritage but have received a high quality education and have faithfully grown in their immigrant churches. In particular, they are fluent in English, and they can grasp and embrace the mandate for world mission. They have the potential to be a resource especially prepared by God, able to offer a contribution to world mission beyond the scope of Korean nationals. But greater effort needs to be made to synergize and integrate the mission work underway inside Korea and that undertaken among the Korean diaspora. It may be appropriate to create organizations to unify and harmonize this mission effort. The wider national and diasporic Korean church needs to make a greater effort to work in close cooperation so as to maximize our contribution to world mission.

THE FLOW OF MIGRATION AND MISSION THROUGHOUT WORLD HISTORY

The perspective on world history from the sixteenth to the mid-twentieth century offered by Andrew Walls views imperialism and colonization through the lens of migration. What he calls the Great European Migration—massive migration out from European nations—led to the founding of the United States and Canada, the countries of Central and South America, Australia, and New Zealand. It created the world order that we live in today. Unfortunately, over time these migrations led to a diminishment of faith and moral character. Traditional pagan religions have resurfaced in the nations colonized by the West. As a result, Western colonial expansion did not lead to the spread of the Gospel or the expansion of Christianity in the way many had hoped. Instead, its fruit has included the revival of traditional religions, not the revival of Christian faith. This result should lead us to pay more attention to purely missionary efforts and the preaching of the Gospel. The life of our Savior, and Christian history itself, show us that the Gospel is not received through imperialism or nationalism. It is received joyfully through service and sacrifice.

Today, what Walls calls the Great Reverse Migration is occurring in counterflow to the Great European Migration. In the period since World War II, millions of people from Africa, Asia, and South America have migrated to Europe and the long-established nations of the West. The religious results have been mixed. On the one hand, foreign religions have infiltrated and weakened the European church. On the other hand, Christian immigrants have helped strengthen the Western church. By its very nature, the church needs to be more international, less limited or defined by race, region, culture, or nationality. The Gospel bars any discrimination: "There is neither Jew nor Gentile, neither slave nor free, nor is there male and female, for you are all one in Christ Jesus" (Gal. 3:28 NIV). This unity and removal of barriers describe the character and beauty of the church. Sadly, the church has often not lived up to its calling on this point. Reverse migration in particular has brought with it such negative features as terrorism, religious conflict, and great resistance to social movements. Even so, we must not forget that God is the Mover of history and that the church constantly needs to pursue deeper Christlikeness as we respond to the current global migration with hopes and prayers for a new era of world mission, one that will fully engage the body of Christ, East and West, South and North.

4

Migration and Human Dislocation: Accountability in Christian Missions from an African Perspective

Jesse N. K. Mugambi

The topics of migration, human dislocation, and accountability in Christian missions are significant in reflecting broadly on the history of migration out of and within Africa, from the perspectives of both outsiders and insiders. The *International Migration Report 2015* summarizes the statistics of international migrants by major areas of origin, classified by area of destination. Consider the following facts:

- The number of international migrants worldwide has continued to grow rapidly between 2000 and 2015, reaching 244 million in 2015, up from 222 million in 2010 and 173 million in 2000.
- Nearly two-thirds of all international migrants live in Europe (76 million) or Asia (75 million). Northern America hosted the third largest number of international migrants (54 million), followed by Africa (21 million), Latin America and the Caribbean (9 million), and Oceania (8 million).
- Women compose slightly less than half of all international migrants. The share of female migrants fell from 49 percent in 2000 to 48 percent in 2015. Female migrants outnumber male migrants in Europe and Northern America,

while the reverse is true in Africa and Asia, particularly western Asia.

- In 2015, of the 244 million international migrants worldwide, 104 million (43 percent), were born in Asia. Europe was the birthplace of the second largest number (62 million, or 25 percent), followed by Latin America and the Caribbean (37 million, or 15 percent) and Africa (34 million, or 14 percent).
- The 2030 Agenda for Sustainable Development not only includes several migration-related targets but also encourages countries to disaggregate targets by, inter alia, migratory status.[1]

According to statistical highlights, 34 million Africans crossed their national borders as migrants in 2015, out of a total continental population of 1,186,178,282 (2.86 percent). The UN report *Trends in International Migrant Stock: The 2015 Revision* indicates that the number of international migrants has grown faster than the world's population. In 2015 most international migrants living in Africa, or 87 percent of the total, originated from another country of the same region. For Asia, the figure was 82 percent; for Latin America and the Caribbean, 66 percent; and for Europe, 53 percent. In contrast, a substantial majority of international migrants living in Northern America (98 percent) and Oceania (87 percent) were born in a major region other than the one where they currently reside.[2]

As of March 2016 the refugee and asylum seeker population in Kenya was 597,683, with about 70 percent from Somalia (UNHCR).[3] The United Nation's *International Migration Report 2015: Highlights* placed the aggregate number of international migrants in Kenya in 2015 at slightly over 1 million persons.[4]

1. United Nations, Department of Economic and Social Affairs, *International Migration Report 2015: Highlights* (2016).

2. UN Dataset, *Trends in International Migrant Stock: The 2015 Revision*, www.un.org/sustainabledevelopment/blog/2016/01/244-million-international-migrants-living-abroad-worldwide-new-un-statistics-reveal.

3. See https://reliefweb.int/report/kenya/kenya-country-profile-updated-april-2016.

4. United Nations, *International Migration Report 2015: Highlights* (2016), 28.

SIGNIFICANCE OF AFRICA

Most of the published narratives about Africa have non-African authors, reporting their own perceptions, as observers, about Africa and Africans. Rarely have the perspectives of Africans about themselves been accessible abroad. In this chapter, I seek to present an African perspective, though not a comprehensive one, based on a combination of academic research and personal experience.[5] Africa features prominently in the Bible (esp. in the Old Testament), particularly on themes related to migration and human dislocation. The Roman Province of Africa (Africa Proconsularis) was a very important part of the Greco-Roman civilization.

According to articles in the *National Geographic*, there is consensus among leading archaeologists, geneticists, and population geographers that human migration out of Africa began about 130,000 years ago. From the equatorial zone, Africans traveled northward along the Nile Valley and eventually crossed into Asia and Europe. They reached Europe about 40,000 years ago. They arrived earlier in the West Pacific, about 67,000 years ago, in North America about 20,000 years ago, and in the furthest point in South America, about 13,000 years ago.[6] Genetic evidence indicates that all humans are related to each other, irrespective of present-day racial identity. Africa is the cradle of humankind. In Kenya several well-preserved archaeological sites present evidence of the earliest human way of life.

Little is known about the religiosity of our earliest ancestors, but there are indications that they preferred living with, rather than against, a sense of the sacred. The ecological crisis in the world today is partly attributable to human interventions that disrupt nature's processes through depletion, pollution, and outright destruction of natural resources.

The history of early Christianity is inseparable from that of North Africa, from which the whole continent of Africa got its name.[7] Three Roman Catholic popes were African: the

---

5. For earlier initiatives toward an Afrocentric approach to African Christianity, see for example Lamin Sanneh, *Translating the Message* (Maryknoll, NY: Orbis Books, 1986); and Ogbu Kalu, ed., *African Christianity: An African Story* (Trenton, NJ: Africa World Press, 2007).

6. See https://genographic.nationalgeographic.com/human-journey.

7. See Thomas Oden, *How Africa Shaped the Christian Mind* (Downers Grove, IL: IVP Academic, 2006); and Kwame Bediako, *Theology and Iden-*

fourteenth, Victor I (188–99); the thirty-second, Miltiades (311–14); and the forty-ninth, Gelasius I (492–96).[8] Several important councils and synods of the early church were convened at Carthage, where Tertullian taught, and at Hippo, where Augustine was bishop. Alexandria was an important center of Christianity, alongside others in Europe and western Asia.[9] The Coptic Church traces its history from the first century, and the Ethiopian Orthodox Church goes back to the fourth century. No European church has early beginnings comparable to those of early African Christianity.[10]

---

tity: The Impact of Culture upon Christian Thought in the Second Century and in Modern Africa (Oxford: Regnum Books International, 1992).

8. For the African popes, see www.stbensparishmilwaukee.org /about-us/history/black-history-profiles/african-popes.

9. H. R. Drobner and S. S. Schatzmann, *The Fathers of the Church: A Comprehensive Introduction* (Peabody, MA: Hendrickson, 2007).

10. The Council of Nicaea, which effectively inaugurated European Christianity, was convened under the authority of Emperor Constantine in 325. By that time North Africa had established church traditions for longer than two centuries. Pope Victor I was the first Christian author to write theological works in Latin. Before Victor's time, Rome celebrated the Mass in Greek, and he may have been the first Roman bishop to use a Latin liturgy. Latin masses, however, did not become widespread until the latter half of the fourth century. Pope Miltiades is very important in the history of Roman Catholicism. He was pope when Emperor Constantine issued the Edict of Milan in 313, officially extending religious toleration to Christianity within the Roman Empire. It was the Edict of Milan that made the Council of Nicaea possible; it also paved the way for the Edict of Thessalonica (380) by which Emperor Theodosius I established Christianity as the Empire's sole authorized religion. Pope Gelasius I, the third pope of African origin, strongly affirmed the primacy of Rome and promulgated the doctrine of the Two Powers, insisting that the emperor bow to the will of the pope in spiritual matters. He had worked closely with his predecessor, Felix III, especially in drafting papal documents. He continued Felix's policy of affirming the decrees of the Council of Chalcedon and refusing to compromise with the emperor and the patriarch of Constantinople regarding the Monophysite controversy, thus perpetuating the East-West split known as the Acacian Schism. He also worked effectively to suppress the celebration of the pagan festival of Lupercalia, which was replaced with the Christian holiday of Candlemas.

For authoritative and concise summary of the only three African Catholic popes, see *New World Encyclopedia*, www.newworldencyclopedia.org /entry/Pope_Victor_I; www.newworldencyclopedia.org/entry/Pope_M iltiades; and www.newworldencyclopedia.org/entry/Gelasius_I.

For millennia Africa has been the home for Africans, a refuge for people from other continents, and home for the ancestors of humankind. The biblical profile of Africa and Africans is mainly positive and constructive: Africa is a place of refuge, abundance, wealth, peace, and generosity, with exceptions under particular rulers. Likewise, the earliest narratives of travelers to tropical Africa portray a profile of dignified and cultured communities, hospitable and generous. Such are the accounts of the earliest European visitors to Angola, Ghana, Mali, Uganda, Zimbabwe, and Zululand. The narratives change to negative profiles when colonization replaces exploration.[11]

The trade in Africans as commodities for sale and purchase across the Atlantic Ocean, for three centuries between 1560 and 1860, was perhaps the most inhuman treatment any person could inflict on another.[12] Incongruously, there were Christian chaplains on the slave ships, and some churches participated in the trade. According to the Trans-Atlantic Slave Trade Database, 12.5 million Africans in all were shipped to the New World, with only 10.7 million surviving the dreaded Middle Passage, disembarking in South America, the Caribbean, and North America.[13]

COLONIZATION, CONQUEST, COMMERCE, CHRISTIANITY, AND CIVILIZATION

The modern Western missionary enterprise in Africa, entangled with European imperial expansion, emphasized more the discontinuity and superiority of European culture than it did the holiness, magnificence, eternity, and omnipotence of God as understood and appreciated in African religions. The Coptic and Ethiopian Orthodox Churches have maintained a very strong link with the

11. See, for example, Leo Frobenius, https://archive.org/stream/voiceo fafricabei01frobuoft/voiceofafricabei01frobuoft_djvu.txt.

12. See http://thomaslegion.net/historyofslaveryintheunitedstateso famerica.html. Henry Louis Gates Jr., professor at Harvard University, has written lucidly about the complexity of the lucrative trans-Atlantic slave trade, particularly with reference to the issues of demand and supply for the 352 years between 1514 and 1866. See his article "Ending the Slavery Blame-Game," *New York Times*, April 22, 2010, www .nytimes.com/2010/04/23/opinion/23gates.html.

13. Trans-Atlantic Slave Trade Database, http://hutchinscenter.fas.har vard.edu/research-projects/projects/trans-atlantic-slave-trade-database.

biblical narrative, while retaining their distinctive worldview and cultural heritage. In the rest of Africa tens of thousands of African Instituted Churches have arisen, including newer Pentecostal and charismatic churches. Underlying this highly pluralistic expression of African Christianity is the affirmation that God the Creator is the source of all power and authority, exceeding that of any human person or institution. In *Concepts of God in Africa*, John Mbiti has documented this focus and strong conviction from his research on 550 African communities from across the continent.[14]

Ontological *discontinuity* between Christianity and the African religious heritage became the core of Western missionary indoctrination in Africa. At that time, however, ontological *continuity* would have helped to bridge the gap between the rulers and the ruled. Missionary indoctrination denied the relevance of African history, asserting that African history began only with the advent of European colonization. As late as the 1960s and 1970s, African scholars were debating with their European professors about the existence or nonexistence of African history.[15] This ontological dislocation has been much more oppressive than physical dislocation under imperial rule and settler colonialism. Africans were dispossessed and also dislocated from their ancestral homelands; even more significantly, they were dispossessed of their cultural and religious identity in the name of Christian mission.

Theologically, African converts knew that the colonizers had no divine authority to colonize Africa. Politically and physically, however, they did not have the power to resist successfully. Under these circumstances—in the context of oppression, dislocation, and exploitation—their Christian faith became stronger, rather than weaker. African Christianity today is thus the outcome of four elements: (1) the African cultural and religious heritage, (2) the history of Christian missions in Africa, (3) the African presence in biblical narratives, and (4) the African presence in the early history of Christianity. These four elements inform African Christian theological reflection today.

14. John S. Mbiti, *Concepts of God in Africa*, 2nd ed. (Nairobi: Acton, 2012).

15. See, for example, https://davidderrick.wordpress.com/2010/06/09/there-is-no-african-history.

CATEGORIES OF MIGRATION AND DISLOCATION
WITHIN AFRICA AND ABROAD

Broadly, there are at least twenty categories of migration and dislo-cation of Africans abroad and within Africa, which can be grouped in three clusters: permanent/irreversible, short-term/reversible, and uncertain. The following list summarizes this categorization:

Permanent/irreversible
1. Migration (prehistoric)—Africa as the cradle of humanity
2. Slavery (Americas and Asia)—16th to 19th centuries
3. Emigration (documented)—relocation by choice
4. Marriage (foreign spouse)—voluntary

Short-term/reversible
5. Diplomatic corps—according to protocol
6. International NGOs—according to contracts
7. Business—according to visa
8. Migrant worker—according to contracts
9. Refugee—according to UNHCR
10. Exile—at the discretion of host nation
11. Visitor—according to visa
12. Student—according to visa
13. Sport—Olympics, soccer, etc.
14. Medical treatment—according to visa
15. Religion—according to visa
16. Tourist—according to visa

Uncertain
17. Ecological—flight from drought and floods
18. Political—flight from political unrest
19. Undocumented—discreet and illegal
20. Asylum seeker—at the discretion of host nation

The challenge of migration and dislocation within Africa is mainly in the "uncertain" category, arising particularly from eco-logical disasters and political instability. Most of the continent of Africa is arid or semiarid, except the zone along the equator and the small temperate zones on the northern and southern tips of the continent. People who live in the arid and semiarid zones are ecologically vulnerable, owing to prolonged periodic droughts and the scarcity of water for domestic use, agriculture, and livestock. Political instability arises from Africa's imperial history, specifically from the Berlin Conference (1884–85), in which European powers carved up the continent of Africa among themselves, without any regard for or consultation with Africans themselves.

Both the League of Nations after World War I (1914–18) and the United Nations and its various organizations after World War II (1939–45) consolidated rather than diminished the interests of the imperial powers in their African colonies. In response, African leaders mobilized and campaigned for liberation, which culminated in the establishment of sovereignty for most African nations by 1963, when the Organization of African Unity was founded. A few territories remained without sovereignty, the last of which were South Sudan and Western Sahara. During the struggles for sovereignty there was a great deal of dislocation, the consequences of which are still evident today. A return to peace and stability after decades of political strife is always a challenge. No African nation can claim to have fully stabilized politically.

Until African nations evolve political systems that resonate with the African cultural ethos, political instability will remain inevitable, with the attendant occasional dislocations. In 2013 the African Union published *Agenda 2063: The Africa We Want*, a document that provides guidelines for permanent political solutions.[16] The approach endorsed in Agenda 2063 represents a continent-wide strategy, rather than national and regional options. Likewise, dislocations resulting from ecological disasters will remain inevitable until African nations design coping strategies that provide for permanent settlement of communities.

CHRISTIAN MISSION AS AN ASPECT OF GLOBALIZATION

African converts to Christianity discern God's intervention in history, despite the discouragements they have experienced in missionary and colonial encounters. The translation of the Bible into African languages has been the most important factor in the promotion of Christianity in Africa. Not all African communities

---

16. For *Agenda 2063*, see www.un.org/en/africa/osaa/pdf/au/agen da2063.pdf.

have the Bible translated into their languages, however, and only one community has a version translated into its own language by one of its own scholars as the sole translator.[17] African Christianity thus has a long way to go before it becomes fully mature, which would mean being able to carry on theological debate in African languages.

While struggling against imperial domination and missionary tutelage, African Christians embraced the Gospel and appropriated it in struggles for liberation and reaffirmation of their dignity, which had been trodden underfoot by imperial subjugation. In his book *Joyfully Christian, Truly African,* John G. Gatu lucidly articulates this paradoxical position.[18]

Between 1910 and 2010 the percentage of Christians worldwide who lived in Europe dropped dramatically from 66.3 to 25.9 percent. Within this same century, the percentage of Christians worldwide in Africa and the Middle East made an even more dramatic change, rising from just 2.1 to 24.2 percent. Similarly, clear growth occurred in the Asia and Pacific region (from 4.5 to 13.1 percent of the worldwide total) and in the Americas (from 27.1 to 36.8 percent).[19]

The dramatic demographic growth of Christianity in Africa signifies the importance that Africans attach to the Christian faith, which has become an anchor for their quest for liberation and in the assertion of their dignity as human beings, despite the horrific dehumanization and oppression they have endured. The dramatic numerical growth of independent churches among African Americans corresponds with a similar phenomenon in tropical Africa, as documented in the research of David Barrett and Allan Anderson.[20] African Americans also have formed their own independent

17. The first sole-author translation, done by John S. Mbiti, of the New Testament from original Greek into an African language is *Utianiyo wa Mwiyai Yesu Kilisto* (Nairobi: Kenya Literature Bureau, 2014). This pioneer initiative should encourage other African scholars to devote themselves to study of the biblical languages.

18. John G. Gatu, *Joyfully Christian, Truly African* (Nairobi: Acton, 2005).

19. For Pew Research graphs, see, for example, http://assets.pewresearch.org/wp-content/uploads/sites/11/2012/07/christianity-graphic-01.png.

20. David B. Barrett, *Schism and Renewal in Africa* (Oxford: Oxford Univ. Press, 1968); and Allan H. Anderson, *African Reformation: African Initiated Christianity in the Twentieth Century* (Trenton, NJ: Africa World Press, 2001).

churches, breaking away from the dominant European-American denominations. This response correlates with that of African Independent Churches and confirms the challenge of ecclesiastical dislocation in both Africa and North America.[21]

On matters pertaining to human migration, dislocation, and Christian accountability, history has taught us to look hard at the realities on the ground, not simply at idealistic theories. For example, when "globalization" became a catchword in discourses about diplomacy, commerce, and religion, its proponents anticipated an era in which there would be free movement of people, services, goods, and capital. The world, it was hoped, could and would become a "global village."

It is widely recognized that this picture of globalization has not materialized. Travel across national borders has become more restrictive than ever; exports and imports are much more restricted and regulated, and flow of capital is monitored much more rigorously than at any earlier period in human history. International treaties and protocols do not seem sufficient for standardizing relationships between nations. Host countries welcome or reject migrants according to their respective immigration policies, not according to the needs of the applicants.

As of 2015 the United States was home to over two million people who were born in Africa. This number represents a considerable increase since 1980, due largely to a change in legislation to allow entry for people fleeing "conflict-ridden areas." Half of the more than two million migrants came from only five countries: Nigeria (327,000), Ethiopia (222,000), Egypt (192,000), Ghana (155,000), and Kenya (136).[22]

Immigrants move not only with their belongings but also with their identity, religion, and self-understanding. Physical dislocation requires readjustment both religiously and ideologically. This insight helps to explain the rise of churches for immigrant communities in Europe and North America. In his research on African-led churches in Europe, Kwabena Asamoah-Gyadu observes that the African Christian diaspora is contributing toward vibrant expres-

21. On this point, see, for example, Gayraud Wilmore, *Black Religion and Black Radicalism*, 2nd ed. (Maryknoll, NY: Orbis Books, 1998).

22. See www.pewresearch.org/fact-tank/2017/02/14/african-immigrant-population-in-u-s-steadily-climbs.

sions of Christianity in various European countries. Not only are there churches whose membership is entirely African, but others are fully integrated with members from the host nation, yet with African leadership.[23] Mission and evangelization, as biblical mandates, are no longer the monopoly of missionaries from Europe and North America to the rest of the world. In the twenty-first century, participation of the African diaspora in Christian mission and evangelization is vibrant, influential, and innovative, attracting attenders and converts from the host countries. The term "diaspora," which originally referred to Jews who were scattered outside Israel, has acquired much wider usage in the study of religion, especially with reference to migrant African Christians in Europe and North America.

The African diaspora has no expectation of returning to Africa, although Africa is cherished as the original home. A significant number of Africans are *academic* and *political* migrants, but in Europe the majority of Africans are *economic* migrants. For Africans forcefully uprooted from Africa as slaves, the Americas and the Caribbean became lands of bondage, and their masters were oppressors. In contrast, the masters regarded their new homelands as the Land of Promise. For these dialectically opposed communities, the Gospel message evoked different expectations, as detailed by such scholars as James H. Cone, Robert Hood, and Peter Paris.[24]

AFRICAN CHRISTIAN THEOLOGY OF REAFFIRMATION

Until the beginning of the twenty-first century, it was taken as normative for missionaries to come from Europe and North America to Africa to spread Christianity, even to countries and areas where Christianity was already established. Religion statistics indicate that, in many countries of Europe and North America, Christianity is no longer the dominant religion. Instead, secularism has become normative. In view of the decline of adherence to Christianity in

23. Kwabena Asamoah-Gyadu, "African-Led Christianity in Europe: Migration and Diaspora Evangelism," *Lausanne World Pulse Archives*, issue 7 (2008). See Andrew F. Walls, "Mission and Migration: The Diaspora Factor, " *Journal of African Christian Thought* 5, no. 2 (2005): 3-11.

24. James H. Cone, *The Spirituals and the Blues* (New York: Seabury Press, 1972; repr. Maryknoll, NY: Orbis Books, 1992); Robert Hood, *Must God Remain Greek?* (Minneapolis: Fortress Press, 1991); Peter Paris, *The Spirituality of African Peoples* (Minneapolis: Fortress Press, 1994).

countries that previously sent missionaries to Africa, it is logical that African Christians seek to re-evangelize Europe and North America. Such a proposition now can seem awkward because Africa is still generally perceived as a continent that receives rather than gives. Missionaries to Africa came, and continue to come, uninvited. Yet it is thought inconceivable for Africans to travel uninvited to Europe and North America as missionaries or evangelists, even if they could afford to do so. Such imbalance in relations has more to do with imperial history than with the Gospel.

This lack of reciprocity points to the question of power relations in the history of Christian missions. As a Roman citizen, the apostle Paul was able to travel freely around and across the Mediterranean Sea to preach the Gospel, a privilege that Jesus' original disciples did not enjoy. Such privileges have been important for the spread of Christianity, but they ought not to be taken for granted. Paul could appeal to Caesar when his rights were infringed, but none of the other apostles could do so. Negotiations in global organizations are characterized by endless tugs-of-war, particularly between the so-called developed and the so-called developing nations. Such disputes are common in such bodies as the WTO, UNCTAD, and IPCC.[25]

Throughout the twentieth century, struggle against imperial domination preoccupied progressive African leaders, many of whom participated in various capacities on the side of their respective colonizers during the two world wars. The modern Christian missionary enterprise is entangled in this paradoxical history. Participation of Africa in the global economy takes its cue from this historical background.[26]

In *Agenda 2063*, in anticipation of the first centenary since formation of the Organization of African Unity in 1963, Africans outlined seven aspirations for their continent. The fifth of these

25. Joseph Stieglitz, *Globalization and Its Discontents* (New York: Norton, 2002), 34.

26. On this point, see Bediako, *Theology and Identity*; Sanneh, *Translating the Message*; Oden, *How Africa Shaped the Christian Mind*; John S. Mbiti, *New Testament Eschatology in an African Background* (Oxford: Clarendon Press, 1971); J. N. K. Mugambi, *Christianity and African Culture* (Nairobi: Acton, 1992); David T. Adamo, *Africa and Africans in the New Testament* (Lanham, MD: Univ. Press of America, 2006); David T. Adamo, *Africa and Africans in the Old Testament* (Eugene, OR: Wipf & Stock, 1998).

focuses on culture: "An Africa with a strong cultural identity, common heritage, shared values and ethics." This aspiration can best be realized with strong emphasis on the cultural and religious heritage of Africa, with its firm foundation on African religiosity. African Christianity and African Islam will thus have African cultural identities, allowing them to distinguish African expressions of Christianity and of Islam from expressions of these religions in other cultures. Although all Christians necessarily affirm the core tenets of Christianity, the universal appeal of Christianity is vindicated by the distinctly local expressions of those core tenets. Similarly, the universal appeal of Islam is vindicated by the distinctly local expressions of Islamic faith. Such universal appeal helps to hold people of faith together, while local expressions help to reaffirm the identity of believers in their respective local contexts. Christian theology at its best helps to mediate in the dialectical tension between the universally valid affirmations of Christianity and the contextual relevance of those affirmations. Likewise, Islamic theology at its best helps to mediate in the dialectical tension between the universally valid affirmations of Islam and the contextual relevance of Islam across cultures.

Individuals and communities who are forced to endure dislocation and migration often hold on to faith as their last recourse. Religious texts are testimonies of individuals who, through faith, endured suffering and triumphed in the end. This principle holds true, irrespective of specific religion, culture, race, class, or gender. Despite abuses of particular religions, including Christianity and Islam, these religions maintain a core of affirmations that sustain those who hold on, under the challenges of dislocation and migration.

QUESTIONS FOR REFLECTION

1. Since the apostolic period, Christian missionary outreach has involved migration of missionaries and their influence on the peoples they encounter. With illustrations, discuss both the positive and the negative consequences of such cross-cultural encounters.

2. Throughout history there has been a close relationship between Christian missionary outreach, commercial enter-

prise, and imperial expansion. With illustrations, comment critically on this proposition.

3. The expansion of Christianity across cultures is inconceivable without human migration. Critically comment on this proposition, giving specific illustrations.

4. The global demography of Christianity corresponds with the global expansion of commerce and civilization. Comment critically on this proposition.

5. Human migration is one of the core themes of the canonical biblical narratives. Discuss this proposition.

6. The future demography of Christianity will be shaped by the patterns of human migration in the twenty-first century. Comment critically on this statement.

7. David Livingstone lobbied in Europe for expansion of Christianity, Commerce, and Civilization as the keys toward the "development" of Africa. Comment critically on this statement.

8. Discuss the presence of Africa and Africans in the canonical biblical narratives.

9. Discuss the role of Africa in the global future of Christian missionary outreach.

10. Human migration is one of the core themes of church history. Comment critically on this proposition.

Response
to
"Migration
and Human Dislocation"

Inho Choi

The history of Christianity in Africa reaches back to the very founding of the church, and when we consider the continent as a whole, the church has been present in and part of Africa ever since. As the information so masterfully marshaled by Jesse Mugambi shows, international migration and refugee flows of the past quarter to half century raise new questions for the church and issues that are vital for the shape of mission today. For one thing, under circumstances of oppression, dislocation, exploitation, and migration, the Christian faith in Africa has—counterintuitively—become stronger, rather than weaker. But instead of speaking about Africa as a whole, in this brief response I wish to focus on one country, Kenya, the country of Mugambi's birth and career as an educator and professor. It is also the country in Africa with which I am best acquainted, for I have served there as a missionary since 2003. Using two stories of wounding, I wish to weave together a reflection on the path of mission in our turbulent era. Can it be that those who have experienced wounding can more fully and directly be ministers of God's grace to others likewise wounded?

WOUND

According to Mugambi, the majority of transnational migrants in Africa originate from another country of the same region. Most migrants present in Kenya today have come from neighboring East African countries. One of the main reasons that migration and dislocation lie at the root of African political and ethnic conflict is that the Western imperial powers made boundaries for their colonies (which later became the boundaries of the newly independent African nations) according to their own benefit, not that of the African people. The effect was simultaneously to place many diverse ethnic groups together within a single nation and to divide numerous ethnic groups between two or more nations. The short period of time allotted to the new nations' formation has not allowed for melding of such cultural and ethnic diversity.[1] In many African countries ethnic solidarity, which has been around for thousands of years, is far stronger than people's sense of national solidarity, which has been a part of their life for only a few decades.

The Africa just described was ripe for conflict, and during my time in Kenya I have witnessed one such ethnic conflict.

THE MARSABIT MASSACRE

On July 12, 2005, during my time as a missionary in Marsabit County in northern Kenya, 500 armed bandits from the Boran tribe across the Ethiopian border raided the town of Turbi, killing members of the Gabra tribe. This attack included a primary school. Altogether at least fifty-three people were killed, including twenty-one primary school children. A day later the Gabra took revenge. A group of them went to the Gabra town of Bubisa, where they killed two Borana families, including an infant.

The killings in Bubisa were done right in front of an Italian Roman Catholic missionary who was using his vehicle to try to drive the two families to safety. Bubisa was known to be a strong Catholic town, and the missionary recognized some persons in the group of attackers who he knew were members of the Roman Catholic Church. When the missionary begged the Gabra for mercy, they refused, saying, "We are not Catholics anymore; we are just Gabra," and then went on with their killing. A Boran refugee from Galacha, a Gabra town, who married a Gabra husband and had lived more than ten years in that town, escaped to the mission compound where my family was living and stayed with my fam-

1. Mkwazu Changwa, "Causes of Conflicts in Africa," Rural Development, February 15, 2009, http://maendeleoyajamii.blogspot.co.ke/2009/02/social-change.html.

ily until the conflict calmed down. I will never forget the fear and anger on her face.

The town of Marsabit itself has a mix of several tribes and churches. Each ethnic group has its own tribal church in town.

AFRICANS AS WOUNDED HEALERS

Colonization and war have been part of Korean experience, just as they have been in African history. It may help Korean Christians to understand the hurt African Christians have undergone at the hands of Western missionaries if they consider the difference between the missionaries' status during the colonization of Korea and during that of Africa. For Koreans, the question to be asked could be, What if the missionaries who brought Christianity to Korea had been Japanese who were part of the Japanese colonizers? When Mugambi writes that "politically and physically" Africans "did not have the power to resist [their colonizers] successfully" (53), it was because they had no help in resisting. The Korean experience was much different. Christianity gave energy and motivation for independent movement and resistance against Japanese imperialism. But also, and very significantly, many missionaries from the West supported the Korean resistance movement and became deeply involved. Some missionaries were deported, and others were imprisoned and tortured.[2] The missionaries faced persecution by the Japanese government alongside the Korean Christians as members of the same body of Christ.[3] Besides preaching the Gospel, they suffered together with us.

We should be careful, however, in judging the work of Western missionaries in Africa. We must avoid devaluating the core of the Gospel, which, thank God, they did bring to Africa, even though they themselves were weak vessels and were sinners who mistreated Africans and African culture. If we fail to discriminate between the message and the messengers, we might lose sight of the power of evangelism, which our Lord made as a tool for spreading the Gospel all over the world (see 1 Cor. 1:21). To help the church in Africa overcome a barrier that still exists in the mod-

2. Bruce Hunt, *For a Testimony* (London: Banner of Truth Trust, 1966), 13.

3. Byoung Gil Lee, "Missionary Roy M. Byram's accusation of Japan" [in Korean], *Revival and Reform* [in Korean], August 30, 2015, www.ksco ramdeo.com/news/articleView.html?idxno=8836.

ern world in the form of political, social, and economic imbalances, we do well to remember the challenge posed in 1971 by the late John Gatu, when he called for a moratorium on the sending of missionaries and advocated a policy of self-reliance for the African church.[4] According to Emele Mba Uka, Gatu wanted to "restore the cultural integrity of the African so that the authentic African religious beliefs and worldviews could be respected."[5]

STORY OF THE RENDILLE

A personal experience from 2010 strongly reminded me of the importance of African values. I work with the Rendille people, a minor ethnic group of northern Kenya, many of whom are nomads. One day Susan, a local Christian woman, asked me to take her to her sister's village. She wished to go because, while her sister and her brother-in-law were away herding livestock, their house had burned down. She wanted to bring her nephew and nieces back to her home. Since her sister lives in a distant traditional village, I brought her with me in my car. When we arrived, I could not recognize her sister's house. It had totally burned down, and even all her pots had melted. On the way back, feeling pity for the children and the family, I asked Susan how much it would cost to build a house of the same type, that is, a small dome-like structure built with sticks and boxes and covered with a big cloth. I really wanted to help them.

Before long, however, I totally forgot about the burned house, and a few weeks later I remembered my promise. So I asked Susan about it, but she said that people in the village had already built a house for her sister. The townspeople had said, "When Susan's sister and her husband return home, if they find their house gone, how sad they would be! So let's build a house for them." I was deeply touched. Susan commented that this generous action was part of their tradition and culture. I realized that if I had helped them, I could have gotten in the way of their great tradition! And I learned values that I had not heard of before and had not found in Korea.

4. C. Peter Wagner, "Colour the Moratorium Grey," *International Review of Mission* 64, no. 254 (April 1975): 165–76.

5. Emele Mba Uka, *Missionaries Go Home? A Sociological Interpretation of an African Response to Christian Missions* (Frankfurt: Lang, 1989), 192.

CONCLUSION

Africans hold great values—deep faith in God, a general hospitality, and a great sense of community—which we should learn and respect. But traditional attitudes of African hospitality have increasingly given way to public discontent and strong xenophobia. Hostility and tension flare up when local populations see—through external assistance—generous food aid being given to refugees.[6] In conflict zones, national governments often view the influx of large numbers of refugees as a security threat.[7] It will be significant if African churches can recover the prominence of generous hospitality as a step of accountability in mission toward migrants. As Henri Nouwen writes, "Hospitality is a central attitude of ministers who want to make their own wounded condition available to others as a source of healing."[8]

Churches can start with forgiveness. Nelson Mandela emphasized this point, stating, "Forgiveness liberates the soul, it removes fear. That's why it's such a powerful weapon."[9] Mandela himself experienced many difficult times, including discrimination and being thrown into prison. Despite these trials he chose to forgive and not to take revenge by mistreating the opposition. May African churches likewise forgive their own opposition and become wounded healers.

Nouwen gives us great insight here: "A Christian community is therefore a healing community not because wounds are cured and pains are alleviated, but because wounds and pains become openings or occasions for new vision. Mutual confession then becomes a mutual deepening of hope, and sharing weakness becomes a reminder to one and all of the coming strength."[10]

African Christianity has suffered many deep wounds, but it

6. Jehu J. Hanciles, *Beyond Christendom: Globalization, African Migration, and the Transformation of the West* (Maryknoll, NY: Orbis Books, 2008), 215.

7. See, for example, Nancy Agutu, "Refugees Must Go, Kenya Says," *Star News*, May 6, 2016, www.the-star.co.ke/news/2016/05/06/refugees-must-go-kenya-says_c1345961.

8. Henri J. M. Nouwen, *The Wounded Healer: Ministry in Contemporary Society* (New York: Doubleday, 1979), 105.

9. Thomas Ashe, "Nelson Mandela," *Love and Forgiveness in Governance*, December 11, 2013, http://blogs.shu.edu/diplomacyresearch/20 13/12/11/an-exemplar-of-forgiving-prisoner-nelson-mandela.

10. Nouwen, *Wounded Healer*, 94.

also has strong faith, a tradition of tolerance and warm hospitality, and a community-centered mind-set, all of which are hard to find in developed countries. Africans are good at taking care of their traditional communities. But they must be encouraged to enlarge their understanding of community, not only to take care of their own clans or ethnic groups, but also to serve their nations as a whole with their strong faith—and eventually to go further and to encompass the world within the scope of their vision.

May our Lord richly use African Christians to awaken Western countries and even Korea as wounded healers!

5

Iraqi Christian Refugee Worship Communities of Jordanian Evangelical Churches

John H. N. Chung

For 1,500 years Iraq, along with Lebanon, Syria, Palestine, Jordan, and Egypt, has maintained its Christian heritage, dating from the early church, despite the opposition of Islam. In 1987 there were over 1.4 million Christians in Iraq, which represented 8 percent of the total population. In 2003 Iraqi Christians numbered 1.5 million, or about 6 percent of the country's population. But in 2016 the number of Christians in Iraq had fallen to an estimated 275,000; the rest have fled the country.[1] In Jordan, the council of evangelical churches consists of five denominations. In the order of the year in which they registered with the government, they are Christian and Missionary Alliance (1927), Nazarene Church (1951), Evangelical Free Church (1955), Assembly of God (1957), and Baptist Church (1957). Anglican and Lutheran churches are also registered but are distinct from those five evangelical churches.

At three points in recent history—after the Gulf War (1990–91), after the Iraq War (2003–11), and after the emergence of ISIL (June 2014)—I have served Iraqi Christian Refugee Worship Communities (ICRWCs) in Jordan, under the umbrella of various evan-

---

1. See Michael W. Chapman, "2003, Christians in Iraq 1,400,000 — 2016, Christians in Iraq 275,000," CNSNEWS.COM, www.cnsnews.com/news /article/michael-w-chapman/2003-christians-iraq-1-400000-2016-christi ans-iraq-275000.

gelical churches in Jordan.[2] Most of the refugees I served came from Assyrian (Nestorian), Chaldean Catholic, Syrian Orthodox, and Syrian and Armenian Catholic Churches, with only a few coming from Protestant backgrounds. Under the reign of Saddam Hussein only five Protestant churches existed in Iraq (two in Baghdad, one each in Basra, Mosul, and Kirkuk), all of them Presbyterian. That is, a considerable portion of the Orthodox and Catholic Christians from Iraq came to experience evangelical churches for the first time through the ICRWCs they encountered in Jordan.

AFTER THE GULF WAR

After the Gulf War (from August 2, 1990, to February 28, 1991), all the airports and borders of Iraq were closed; only the border with Jordan remained open. Iraqi refugees escaped their country and entered Jordan with the dream of emigrating to the West. They were granted refugee status by the UN refugee agency (UNHCR) until they could be resettled in Western countries. For their benefit, ICRWCs were organized inside existing churches in Jordan. The story of the ICRWC at Christian and Missionary Alliance (C&MA) church in Jabal Amman provides a good example.

JABAL AMMAN C&MA CHURCH

Jabal Amman is one of the seven hills that originally made up Amman, the capital city of Jordan. The pastor of the Christian and Missionary Alliance Church (CCJA) located there is Yousef Hashweh. His parents were from Gaza, Palestine, and he has a special affection for refugees. In 1991 CCJA initiated an ICRWC as a Tuesday evening meeting. With Romail, an Iraqi pastoral candidate and colleague, I started participating in this ICRWC in October 1994. During this period, I had been looking for a partner in my ministry. Every Tuesday evening the worship service had a different preacher: Yousef, his brother Victor, other local pastors, and visiting foreigners. But there was no Iraqi among the preachers, neither were there small-group meetings. I started to pray for the recruitment of small-group leaders and preachers among the Iraqis. When Romail and I met we believed that we had found the

2. Jiries Habash, "Evangelical Churches in Jordan," *MEATE* [Middle East Association for Theological Education] *Journal* 6, no. 1 (December 2011): 1–15.

answer to each other's prayers, so I brought him to my house to live with my family.

A small group soon was formed at my house that brought together a number of Romail's friends. He had become a committed believer after having personally accepted Jesus while he carried out his military service during the Gulf War. I could relate to his experience, for I personally had the chance to trust the Lord more deeply during my experience of the Gulf War while serving as a missionary in Bahrain, my first mission field.[3] He and I met when he came to Jordan on his way to study at a theological college in Egypt or Lebanon, as there was no theological college in Iraq.

The small group moved its meetings to CCJA in the first week of January 1995. Sargon, the lay leader and coordinator of this ICRWC, played an important role. Unlike the already existing Tuesday evening meetings, the small-group gatherings were held on Friday during the day, the Muslim holy day and the first day of the weekend in Jordan. We realized that the CCJA building was a much more appropriate space for these meetings than my home. First, the building was available for use because, while mosques are open on Fridays, local churches are usually closed; second, meeting in the church building allowed us to operate openly and without suspicion, under the protection of a legally established local church.

At that time, it was not common for Arab pastors to publish sermon transcripts or notes. But with Romail's help, every week I prepared sermon notes, added questions, and distributed them; the next week I gathered and checked the answer sheets and redistributed them. Quiz times, supplemented with little prizes, attracted the attention and participation of the church members. As many members from nonevangelical backgrounds were new to personal Bible study and were largely unfamiliar with Scripture, this step provided a unique opportunity to acquaint them with the Bible. At the time of this writing, my sermon manuscripts and their related questions are available on online; they are also being transmitted to my companions via an online social network.[4]

3. From September 1989 to February 1992, I was the senior pastor of the Korean-speaking congregation of the National Evangelical Church in Bahrain.

4. See www.elhaya.org, a website managed by the Society for World Internet Mission (SWIM), which belongs to Onnuri Community Church.

In the spring of 1995 Sargon emigrated to Australia. Right before he did, Younan, a friend of Romail's, came from Iraq to Jordan and became the lay leader of the ICRWC at CCJA. The more Iraqi refugees came to Jordan, the bigger the Tuesday and Friday meetings grew, at times exceeding 200 people in attendance. Before and after the Friday meetings, various additional ministries developed, such as a youth group, women's meetings, and a choir.

Around the same time, Korean church leaders visited Jordan and Iraq. One of them was a board member of Korea Food for the Hungry International (KFHI).[5] Following this visit, KFHI began to support our ministries. We helped to sponsor a health clinic for Iraqi refugees at CCJA. We also provided meals after the Friday meetings, hosted conferences for them at nearby campsites, and opened a brethren residence house (BRH), where Romail and Iraqi brothers lived together.

We saw fruit from our ministry as leaders began to arise from within the ICRWC. In October 1995 Jordan Evangelical Theological Seminary (JETS; www.jets.edu), the first evangelical theological institution in Jordan, opened with the purpose of training leaders in the Arab world, and I became a lecturer in its master's program. Six members from the ICRWC at CCJA, including Romail and Younan, were admitted. The number of Iraqi students increased every semester, and by 1997 there were over thirty.[6] Many of them had encountered an evangelical church for the first time after arriving in Jordan.

We also, however, saw certain limitations and boundaries arise from within the ICRWC itself. Beginning in 1996 the Muslim-background Iraqi brother I had met previously, whom I will call "F," stayed at the BRH. He assisted me in the preparation of sermons and my lectures at JETS in place of Romail, who had to

5. In summer 1995 the Iraqi government hosted the world peace conference in Baghdad and invited world church leaders. I was included in the delegation of Korean church leaders headed by Elder Sangdal Doo, a board member of KFHI. At the conference I delivered a lecture in English, with Mahir Abdul Ahad, the representative of Life Agape Iraq, providing Arabic translation. Later he introduced to me an Iraqi Muslim-background believer (MBB) he called "F," whom he had trained.

6. The Korean churches in the Middle East contributed to a scholarship fund for the Iraqi students at JETS. The contributions received were distributed to JETS and to individual recipients.

concentrate on his studies at JETS. "F" later went on to enroll at JETS himself, where Imad Shehadeh, the president of JETS, evaluated him as the best student of the year. Nevertheless, the Iraqi leaders of the ICRWC decided to bar him from the ICRWC's meetings, asking that he and I instead meet privately in my home. This decision stemmed from their distrust and discomfort at having a former Muslim in their community. "F" later found a warmer welcome in a Jordanian church.

The rejection "F" encountered contrasted with the experience of "M," another Muslim-background brother from Egypt. The ICRWC had no problem working with him. When he heard from another member that a Korean was preaching in Arabic at our church, he visited a Friday meeting. Afterward, Romail presented him the Gospel in person. Within two weeks, he had read all of my collected sermon notes and answered all the questions. At that time, I was also involved in a Bible study with Egyptian Coptic Christians, and I invited him to join. The others were initially uncomfortable around him, but he presented his testimony and was invited by a member named Muaiyad to return the following week. Muaiyad's name means "one who helps." In response to his invitation, we went to the meeting the following week, only to discover that because of an accident at work Muaiyad had passed away. We came to believe that "M" took the place of Muaiyad. Eventually, "M" also became a student at JETS. He did so with my recommendation, and he later started to lead the meeting himself.

The contrast between the experience of "F" and that of "M" demonstrates the importance of the historical ties that give various Arabic-speaking groups a unique sense of communion with each other. The same impulse that leads some persons to thrive in an ICRWC or in a Bible study group composed of Egyptian Coptic Christians when they are not interested in joining the regular service of a local Jordanian church—that is, the desire to fellowship with their compatriots, in a familiar dialect and with shared backgrounds—was also the impulse that led them to reject an Iraqi Muslim-background brother but not an Egyptian one. Furthermore, because of the critical role played by one member and the accident that befell him, "M" became a leader among the Coptic Christians.

During the summer of 1996, the Friday meetings of the ICRWC at CCJA underwent a huge change. At that time I transferred the regular preaching duties to Younan. One and a half years had elapsed since I began the Friday meeting, and Younan had been preaching occasionally for the Tuesday meetings of the ICRWC before that. (Many guest preachers from inside and outside the church shared in preaching for the Tuesday meetings.) But transferring the preaching privilege for the Friday meetings from me to Younan was a significant step; it marked the first time an ICRWC had full-scale preaching leadership by an Iraqi pastor.

The women's gathering and youth group also became more energized. Milad, the worship service accompanist and a student at JETS, began to lead the youth group. With some leaders of the ICRWC at CCJA, we began to pray for new ICRWCs to be planted among Jordanian churches. To that end we began to meet with local leaders, some of whom expressed resistance. For example, some of the leaders argued that Jordanians and Iraqis were both Arabs serving the same Lord and questioned why the refugees should have separate worship communities. But with the help of five local church regions, more ICRWCs were formed, one by one.

AFTER THE IRAQ WAR

Twelve years after the Gulf War, US president George W. Bush invaded Iraq with the purpose of removing Saddam Hussein and bringing democracy to Iraq. The Hussein regime collapsed in short order, on April 9, 2003. Three years before that war broke out, however, I had been called to do home missions, and in June 2000 I returned to South Korea.[7] I revisited Jordan during my next two winter vacations and made a tour of various ICRWCs. In the third year, I heard the news that the Iraqi regime had collapsed and immediately returned to Jordan and visited Iraq.[8]

The following summer I visited Iraq again. Then in January 2004 I left my family in Jordan and went to do ministry in Iraq,

7. My home missions assignments were to serve as a professor at Asia United Theological University/Asian Center for Theological Studies and Mission (ACTS) and as director at the headquarters of the Seoul-based Middle East Team (founded in 1984).

8. Baghdad Presbyterian Church asked Korean church leaders, who had led a medical service team from KFHI, to build a theological seminary. The board (David Sangbok Kim served as chairman) for the Iraq Evangelical Seminary (IES) was organized in Seoul, and in the summer of 2003 I visited Iraq to help launch IES.

having previously completed the home missions work to which I had been assigned in South Korea. But contrary to my expectations, the situation in Iraq only got worse, and I had to return to Jordan, where my family was waiting for me. Meanwhile, more Iraqi refugees emerged. While the former wave of Iraqi refugees fled only to Jordan because its border with Iraq was the only one open, this time the refugees also fled to Syria, Turkey, and Lebanon. While the post–Gulf War refugees were mostly Shiite Muslims, Kurds, and some Christians, the post–Iraq War refugees, because of the Shiite domination of power, were mostly Sunni Muslims and Christians.

The departure of the refugees from the Gulf War and the influx of new refugees from the Iraq War directly affected the ICRWCs. As members of the ICRWC at CCJA resettled in the West or returned to Iraq, the Tuesday meetings dropped in size, and the Friday gatherings eventually ceased altogether. ICRWCs at other churches also diminished in size or stopped meeting. But the ICRWC at the Evangelical Free Church of Ashrafiya (FECA) was still meeting, giving me the chance to serve this ICRWC.[9] Following the Iraq War, more and more Iraqi refugees crowded into Jordan, and the ICRWC at FECA was revitalized.

A crisis fell upon this community. After completing a new building in 2009 in Khalda, a newer and more expensive neighborhood, the church wanted to end its ministries in the Ashrafiya neighborhood. In fact, most of the Jordanian members had already moved to the Khalda area, and they were excited about beginning new ministries there. But a few Jordanian members who could not afford to move there, as well as the ICRWC, did not share their excitement. I was thankful for having been able to freely serve ICRWCs related to evangelical churches in Jordan, and I earnestly asked God for his guidance. By the grace of God, FECA survived, and I was able to serve the Jordanian church as well as the ICWRC.[10]

9. FECA was planted by Roy Whitman, the first Protestant missionary in Jordan, where he served more than sixty years. An old piano that his wife, Dora, brought from the United Kingdom is still at FECA.

10. Jerias Habash, moderator of the EFC, played a role in the survival of EFCA. The church in Ashrafiya owned 450 square meters of land and an old building with a market value of JOD60,000 (which in 2017 would be equal to a value of about US$85,000). In the arrangement brokered by Habash, one-third of the property was distributed to the Ashrafiya con-

Over a ten-year period, beginning in 2004, the majority of the Iraqis who participated in this ministry also eventually left Jordan, either emigrating to the West or returning to Iraq. By 2014 our work with the ICRWC had mostly wound down, and our ministry at FECA was mostly with the local Jordanian congregation. We did not anticipate that yet another wave of refugees was to come.

AFTER THE EMERGENCE OF ISIL

After the US invasion led to the destabilization of Iraq, many Christians from Baghdad, rather than leaving the country, moved to Christian villages in the vicinity of Mosul in northern Iraq. Unfortunately, that was the very region in which the rampaging Islamic State of Iraq and the Levant (ISIL) emerged in June 2014. This blow fell eleven years after the Iraq War had broken out and two and a half years following the official withdrawal of US forces. The Christians of Mosul scattered into Iraqi Kurdistan. Though some still remain there, others fled abroad without any promise of return. The ancient Christian church of Mosul, whose history spanned nearly two thousand years, was completely uprooted. Many local churches in Jordan welcomed the Iraqi Christians who arrived there.

ONGOING ROLE OF THE EVANGELICAL FREE CHURCH OF ASHRAFIYA

In September 2014 I began to minister in a new ICRWC at FECA for Iraqi refugees who had fled the most recent wave of violence. A few Syrian Christians who had escaped from the civil war in that country also participated in these ministries.[11] Botros, an Egyptian pastor, became my partner; unlike during the Gulf War or the Iraq War, few prepared leaders were among the Iraqi people who arrived. As with the previ-

---

gregation and two-thirds to the Khalda congregation. The former then gave the latter JOD40,000, in effect buying out its portion. The money that enabled the Ashrafiya congregation to make the purchase was donated by an elder of the Qatar Korean Church.

11. Many Jordanian churches provided aid for Syrians, but worship communities were not organized for the Syrian Christians. Since most Syrian Christians were pro-government, their residences were relatively safe. Therefore, unlike Muslims, they tended to stay in Syria or to move to Lebanon, rather than to Jordan.

ous waves, most of the church members among the refugees had been raised Catholic or Orthodox.[12]

Though the number of refugees increased, the FECA church building could contain only about 40 people. To meet the need, the ICRWC added a second floor with room for 120 people.[13] Then a children's club was opened that taught English, Arabic, and other subjects. The club was overseen by Fawzi Atta, an Egyptian-American missionary, and was staffed by his wife, Linda Atta; partner missionaries; and Iraqi Christian refugees with teaching experience. The role played by the club was immense, for many members could not afford to send their children to private Christian schools but did not want them to attend public schools, where they would have to study the Qur'an and Islam. Later, after financial assistance from Caritas, an NGO of the Roman Catholic Church, provided opportunity for the children to attend a Christian private school, the children's club was closed.

SHMEISANI BAPTIST CHURCH

Jiries Abugazala, whose grandfather fled to Jordan from Palestine, planted Shmeisani Baptist Church (SBC) in 1995. With SBC's Jordanian members, he is currently ministering with a special affection for the refugees. Iraqi refugees have occupied a special place in his heart ever since he was invited to preach at various ICRWCs when he first planted the church. When I was serving FECA's ICRWC, he and his church members became proactively engaged.

In early 2016 my wife, Grace, and I, along with Pastor Botros and his wife, Salwa, transferred the pastoral ministries of the ICRWC at FECA to the Jordanian leaders, and we began to serve the ICRWC at SBC. In early 2017 it consisted of about 80 Christian Iraqi refugee families. I led the participants in memorizing weekly Bible verses and doing presentations at the church. Attendance averaged 130 people. We also had a partnership with Emmaus Correspondence School, which distributed free Bible study materials.[14]

12. Mosul Presbyterian Church, the only Protestant church in Mosul, had few members, and it was closed after Elder Munthir Al-Saqa of the church was martyred in 2006.

13. The funding for this expansion was provided by the Korean board of Iraq Evangelical Seminary.

14. See, in Arabic, www.lifeismore.net; for English, go to https://emmauscourses.org.

In addition, we created the Baraka Center for the refugees (*baraka* is Arabic for "blessing"). The church members, who live in narrow houses, like to have fellowship in the center's building, which is spacious and commands an unimpeded view. Small-group Bible studies and mentoring are going well at the center. We have led retreats in the Ajloun mountain area. We also continue to provide financial and material assistance; unlike the previous refugee waves, the most recent group left relatively suddenly and therefore came to Jordan with very little. As a result, their needs are higher. Our Lord knows how desperately the current refugees need relief, unlike the post–Gulf War and post–Iraq War refugees, and provides for them.[15]

CONCLUSION

Quite a few people among the post–Gulf War and post–Iraq War refugees from Iraq received the love of Christ through ICRWCs formed under the umbrella of the local Jordanian churches. Once they began to be assured of their salvation, they became active in studying the Word of God and even began to become church leaders. In all three waves of displacement, the ICRWCs grew largely through word of mouth in the tight-knit Iraqi Christian communities. The ICRWCs' growth was also directly tied to the refugees' circumstances: they could not work legally, so they had much free time to gather as a community and to study the Bible at home. Also, they often came to the church looking for material assistance and afterward became involved.

Some were trained as church ministers, some were installed as leaders within evangelical churches, and some trained at JETS to become pastors of evangelical churches. Some who left for the United States and Canada, various countries in Europe, and Australia and New Zealand are now serving churches in those countries. Among the students at JETS in Jordan who trained to become pastors, some have become ministers to Arab churches abroad.[16]

15. The board of IES covers the rental cost of Baraka Center. The Board for Special Needs (BSN) in the Netherlands; Hanna Massad, pastor of the ICRWC of CCJA; and my other connections support many of the ministry expenses of the ICRWC at SBC.

16. Sahir, who ministered to the ICRWC at FECA, is now ministering to an Arab church in Toronto, Canada. Dawood, who ministered at the ICRWC of the Anglican church in Marka, served an Arab church in

And several graduates of JETS have gone back to Iraq and served various evangelical churches there.[17]

Some Christian refugees from Iraq who came to Jordan after the rise of ISIL have had the good fortune to be resettled elsewhere. I hope that they will be welcomed by churches in the West, but there are many more refugees who still remain in the land of Jordan. Still more refugees continue to arrive. I hope that Jordanian evangelical churches will have a zeal for ministry to them and that global churches will love and support them.

QUESTIONS FOR REFLECTION

1. Both Jordanians and Iraqis speak Arabic (the same literary language, though the colloquial dialects are different). Therefore, is a distinct worship community for Iraqi Christian refugees needed? If so, why? What principle can we draw from the contrasting experiences faced by MBBs "F" and "M"?

2. Some Iraqis have left their old church traditions and worship communities to join the evangelical church community; others have not. Mahir, the representative of Life

---

New Zealand for a long time and recently moved to Sydney, Australia, to minister there. Sami, who ministered at the ICRWC of FEC in Hashmi Shamali, is also pastoring an Arab church in Sydney. Hermezm, who was a leader of the ICRWC at CCJA, is ministering at an Arab church in St. Louis, Missouri. Milad, who ministered at the ICRWC of CCJA, lives in the United States but visits Iraq to minister there. Habil, who graduated from JETS and then served as a professor at JETS, now ministers at an Arab church in San Diego, California. Both "F" and "M," who came from Islam, now serve respectively where God has led them to serve.

17. Younan, pastor of the ICRWC of CCJA, returned to Iraq and became the pastor of Baghdad Assyrian Presbyterian Church. But he fled to the United States to escape a death threat, becoming first a tentmaking pastor in Chicago and then an itinerant pastor in many areas of the world, including Jordan. Romail also returned to Iraq and taught as a professor at JETS Baghdad and Erbil; now he is serving a church in Kitchener, Ontario, Canada. Estawri graduated from JETS and then returned home to become the pastor of Basra Presbyterian Church; he is now pastoring in Phoenix, Arizona. Sabri, who served the ICRWC of the C&MA church in Madaba, is now the senior pastor of Erbil Baptist Church. Michelle, who ministered in the ICRWC of the Nazarene church in Jarka, is still serving in Erbil. Haitham, who completed the master's program at JETS, has been the senior pastor of Kirkuk Presbyterian Church.

Agape Iraq, belongs to the latter group. He recognized the Gospel during his study in England and became a full-time minister, but he still belongs to the Catholic community. What principle can we draw from this example?

3. What is, should be, or can be the role of the Iraqi and Arab diaspora for the Iraqi and Arab churches? How can non-Iraqis and non-Arabs support and enhance that role?

Response
to
"Iraqi Christian Refugee Worship Communities"

Wissam P. Kammou

I appreciate John Chung's opening a window for us into the lives of Iraqi refugees in Jordan and beyond. He recounts the reception they received from Christian ministries in Jordan and details their ongoing ministry in countries all around the world. I write as a former refugee who was welcomed by the Iraqi Christian Refugee Worship Communities (ICRWC) of which Chung writes. I now serve as a minister in Iraq. In gratitude for the ministry of the ICRWC, I seek to add details that can enrich our understanding of difficulties that press upon Christians within Iraq and the Middle East generally, as well as mentioning ongoing fruit of the ministry carried out by the ICRWC.

BACKGROUND

Christianity has a long history in Iraq. According to some Eastern Church traditions, Christianity spread to Mesopotamia, the area of modern Iraq, late in the first century. The Gospel was taken there from Jerusalem by two disciples of the apostle Thomas. One of these disciples was Thaddeus of Edessa, who is thought to have been one of the seventy elders whom Jesus sent out (see Luke 10:1), and the other was his disciple Marris.

Many churches and monasteries were built in Iraq after Christianity became the common faith of most of the population. The seventh-century Islamic invasion and conquest became a sad turning point for the history of Christianity in Iraq. In accord with Islamic law, Christians were forced to embrace Islam or to pay heavy taxes or even face death. Since that time, Christians in Iraq have consistently faced persecution. The intensity of the persecution has varied, depending on the various Islamic groups that ruled over Iraq.

RECENT HISTORY OF IRAQI CHRISTIANS IN IRAQ

The modern country of Iraq came into being under British protection in 1921, with independence achieved in 1932. During the past century many different governments have ruled Iraq, with a varied mix of liberal and more strict Islamic conviction. Throughout the twentieth century, a relatively stable ratio of Christian, Jewish, and Yazidi minorities continued to live in Iraq, but eventually the number of Christians started to decline because of Iraq's unsuitable political climate. Official statistics are not available for the number of Christians in Iraq, but unofficial estimates indicate that approximately 1.4 million Christians were living in Iraq in the late 1980s and beginning of the 1990s. Unfortunately, those numbers were already decreasing and eventually declined sharply as unsuitable conditions pushed Christians to emigrate.

WAVES OF IMMIGRATIONS OF IRAQI CHRISTIANS

During the Iran-Iraq War (1980–88), Christians were still persevering in Iraq. But waves of emigration began after the start of the US-led Gulf War of 1990–91 and then steadily increased during the subsequent economic embargo (1990–2003). Many Christians, including my family, found a way to escape to the West through Jordan. With the collapse of Saddam Hussein's regime following the US-led invasion in 2003, the rate of emigration grew. In the following years, many Christians fled, especially to the city of Amman and to Jordan in general, where they found refuge. Fortunately, many of them also found a warm welcome provided by Christian ministries such as the ICRWC, which were attached to evangelical churches. The ICRWC welcomed Iraqi refugees whatever their religious background, affiliation, or denomination.

After the Islamic State (ISIS) invaded Iraq (2014–17) and captured a large proportion of its territory, large numbers of Christians either became displaced internally or emigrated to nearby countries such as Jordan, Turkey, and Lebanon. Many of these refugees came from Mosul, Qaraqosh, and the Nineveh Plains. Qaraqosh, part of the Nineveh Governorate, had been regarded as the largest Catholic community in the Middle East. All of its population was displaced, and many of its people emigrated. Fortunately, organizations such as the ICRWC were on hand to welcome those who emigrated to Jordan.

Through the successive waves of emigration and persecution, many refugees accepted the Lord as Savior and were discipled and trained. Numbers of them are now active church members, leaders, and pastors in their final destinations in the West. But also it is exciting to know that some of them have returned to Iraq, either to serve in already existing churches or to begin new churches and ministries.

NEW CHURCHES AND NEW MINISTRIES

The goal of the ICRWCs is to raise up a new generation of believers and leaders who have a passion to serve the Lord wherever their final destination may be. This outcome is the fruit that arises from providing a warm environment, thoughtful care, periodic pastoral visits, material provisions, relief work, medical care, hospitality, places to meet, and food given with an open hand. Such are the tools used in outreach to Iraqi refugees, reflecting a clear vision and strategy.

In the remainder of this response, I mention two examples of fruit from the ministry of the ICRWCs.

SABAH A. ANAEE, CHRISTIAN & MISSIONARY ALLIANCE CHURCH, MOSUL

Brother Sabah Anaee (1950–2016), who is well known in Jordan as Abu Karam, left Baghdad in 2000 with his wife and three boys. They moved to Jordan because of the difficult economic situation brought on by the economic embargo during the 1990s. He had in mind to migrate to Canada as a final destination, but the Lord had a completely different plan for him and his family.

Abu Karam, a simple believer, participated in ICRWC meetings and after a while was asked to become a member of the ICRWC board. From 2001 to 2006 he served as pastor of an ICRWC; in December 2006 he was called by God to return to Iraq, specifically to Mosul. At the time many radical Muslims were active in Mosul, and many Christians were being killed, including Munthir Alsaka, an evangelical elder who was serving the Lord in the national Presbyterian Church. Pastor Haytham received gunshot injuries in an attack and became paralyzed. Catholic archbishop Faraj Raho was killed. Many Catholic and Orthodox priests were killed or kidnapped, and many churches were bombed.

Yet, Abu Karam had assurance from God that he was to start a new ministry in Mosul. He and his wife, Faeza Anaee, launched meetings and worship services in their newly rented house in Mosul. Many people joined their meetings, and they began a small- group ministry similar to what they had practiced in Jordan.

After a period of several months with much fasting and prayer, Abu Karam and his wife took the courageous step of moving from being an underground group meeting in their home to becoming a public gathering as a Christian & Missionary Alliance church. Again, many people came forward to join the various ministries of the church, including the small groups, discipleship training, public services, and Sunday school. Abu Karam's oldest son, also named Karam, undertook theological studies in Lebanon in preparation for leading the church in Mosul.

After the crises caused by ISIS, Abu Karam and Faeza Anaee, along with their three sons and most of the dispersed congregation, were internally displaced and settled in Erbil, Iraq, where they found a warm welcome from the pastor and ministers of the Christian & Missionary Alliance Church. The two churches merged into one, and Abu Karam served God faithfully there until he passed away in June 2016. His widow, Um Karam, and three sons are still serving the Lord in Erbil. One son is now an assistant pastor serving in worship, preaching, and leading small groups. He is also manager of the church's relief program.

The family of Abu Karam and Faeza Anaee realize and testify that they are direct fruit of the ICRWC ministry in Jordan. They make it a point to encourage everyone who goes to Jordan to become part of the ICRWC meetings. As I was preparing this response, I met sister Faeza Anaee herself. She emphasized the importance of having such a ministry in Jordan and urged every church to support this ministry, for the ICRWC provides a significant opportunity for evangelism, discipleship, and the equipping of potential leaders.

SABRI H. PAULUS, ERBIL BAPTIST CHURCH, ERBIL

Brother Sabri (b. 1969) became a follower of Christ in 1993 while living in Baghdad. He had been a soldier during the US-led Gulf War, serving as a member of a Scud missile crew. His crew was to fire missiles into Israel, an extremely dangerous assignment. He eventually left his post, fleeing toward the Turkish border, but was caught and imprisoned. He was scheduled to be executed, but somehow he managed to escape. The results were not good personally, for he turned to behavior that was increasingly sinful. In 1993 an Iraqi Armenian talked to him about the Gospel and gave him a Bible. For the next thirty days Sabri read the Bible, which totally changed his life. As a new believer, he attended the few evangelical church meetings that were available in Baghdad.

In 1994 Sabri decided to emigrate to the West through Jordan. There in 1995 he began attending the newly formed ICRWC meetings. In 1997 he enrolled in the Jordan Evangelical Theological Seminary (JETS). Upon completion of the bachelor's program, he felt called in January 2003 to go back to Iraq, where the rest of his family lived. He visited both Baghdad and Kurdistan, Iraq's northern region. He finally decided to settle in Erbil, Kurdistan, where he joined some existing ministries.

The language of Kurdistan is Kurdish, which is unrelated to Arabic. Nevertheless, in November 2006 Sabri and his wife, Nahla, began holding meetings in Arabic in their house. Several people joined these meetings, especially those who had fled from the severe sectarian war being waged in Baghdad in 2006–8. The experience he had gained while attending the ICRWC meetings in Jordan and the biblical knowledge he acquired at JETS were very beneficial to him in this work as he sought to help, take care of, teach, and pastor the internally displaced people at that time. The same was true later when ISIS invaded (2014–16), which caused massive displacement of Iraqi Christians.

In 2015 Brother Sabri was ordained as senior pastor for Erbil Baptist Church, the church that he had planted in 2006.

CONCLUSION

These are two examples of ordinary believers who, through the ministry of the ICRWC and training at JETS, became leaders and pastors. God called some refugees who fled to Jordan to return to

Iraq to plant new ministries there. Other refugees, however, God called to start new ministries in other places around the world. John Chung is to be thanked for drawing attention to the vital ministry performed by the ICRWC and JETS.

6

The Importance of Migrant Missions in South Korea

David Chul Han Jun

According to the *Korean Herald*, one out of every seven people in the world is a migrant.[1] The United Nations Development Program, which monitors intercontinental migrant movements and conditions, states that migration contributes to human development and increases individuals' financial, health, and educational well-being.[2] Now considered the "new nomads," such people move from one location to another. This movement includes migrant workers everywhere, as well as multiple ethnic groups living side by side in most of the world's metropolitan areas. I believe this phenomenon represents a God-given opportunity for world mission. In this chapter I consider the unprecedented opportunities for evangelization that the Republic of Korea has been given, considering the large numbers of foreign workers, students, and members of multicultural families who have immigrated to our homeland.

The earliest use of the term "diaspora" referred to the scattering of Israelites outside their homeland at the time of the Babylonian exile. Most of the Jewish population were taken away as prisoners or fled to other countries. Even in exile, however, God

1. "New Nomadic Era," *Korea Herald*, October 5, 2009.

2. United Nations Development Programme, "Human Development Report2009,"http://hdr.undp.org/en/content/human-development-report-2009, 3.

reminded them of their true identity as people who were called to be a light to the nations.

After the resurrection of Jesus, the Holy Spirit descended upon the disciples on the day of Pentecost in Jerusalem. Luke records quite a list of peoples, a mixture of God-fearing Jews and converts to Judaism from many places, who, on this occasion, heard in their own language about "God's deeds of power." They included "Parthians, Medes and Elamites; residents of Mesopotamia, Judea and Cappadocia, Pontus and Asia, Phrygia and Pamphylia, Egypt and the parts of Libya near Cyrene; visitors from Rome (both Jews and converts to Judaism); Cretans and Arabs" (Acts 2:9–11 NIV). The apostle Peter addresses one of his letters to "God's elect, exiles scattered throughout the provinces of Pontus, Galatia, Cappadocia, Asia and Bithynia" (1 Peter 1:1 NIV). Similarly, the Letter of James addresses "the twelve tribes scattered among the nations" (1:1 NIV).

In Acts 8 we read about the great persecution in Jerusalem that scattered all but the apostles, causing the believers to go "throughout the countryside of Judah and Samaria" (v. 1), and ultimately to the ends of the world. This dispersion was certainly a painful event for them personally, yet God's sovereign will was being fulfilled in history, for they began to spread the Gospel of Jesus Christ everywhere.

God is now using the Korean diaspora as a missionary tool. During the Japanese occupation of Korea (1910–45), Japan forcefully sent many Koreans to Sakhalin Island (and the Soviet Union relocated many Koreans in the vicinity of Vladivostok to central Asia). As it has turned out, more than half a century later, some descendants of these Koreans have helped Christian missionaries in the former Soviet Union, especially with translation into the local languages. Some Koreans in the diaspora in mainland China have also been useful in supporting missionary work. In all, over seven million Koreans are now living outside of Korea.[3] I believe that this number represents an extremely important resource for mission in the twenty-first century. The recognition and use of the Korean diaspora may be one of the most important strategies for the future of Korean overseas mission.[4]

---

3. See "Korean Diaspora," Wikipedia, https://en.wikipedia.org/wiki/Korean_diaspora.

4. David Chul Han Jun, "World Christian Mission through Migrant

In the late 1980s, during a time of significant Korean modernization, a number of manufacturing factories emerged that depended heavily on employing migrant workers. Typically, such factories had poor working conditions and offered low wages, and local Koreans were not interested in employment there. The influx of such workers and other immigrants has continued to the point where today Korea is home to over two million foreigners, or about 4 percent of the total population of South Korea.[5]

The foreign workers who entered Korea to work in the factories, as well as other immigrants, have naturally enough brought their own culture with them. Many Koreans, however, have not been ready for an intercultural coexistence, and this attitude has led to a host of cultural conflicts, which have become a problem in our society. Simply put, we who live in Korea need to grow to understand each other's cultures; in particular, we who are Christian need to use this unique opportunity for God's kingdom.

THE PREDICAMENT OF MIGRANT WORKERS

My observation has been that overall the treatment of foreigner workers in Korea and their living and working conditions are improving. The minimum wage, compensation and benefits, dormitories, and provision of help centers against abuses of human rights have all been upgraded. Nevertheless, some factory owners still take advantage of migrant workers. For instance, foreign workers are required to have their current employer's permission before they can leave their present position to find a better job, and some factory owners are reluctant to grant such requests. Also, these workers often find it difficult, if not traumatic, to live in a new society. To some extent, every migrant experiences this trauma, which is more severe for some than for others. Loneliness and fear are common feelings among migrants, yet we native Koreans are often very slow to understand, and even slower to sympathize with, such burdens.

Workers in South Korea and through the Korean Diaspora" (presentation at Tokyo 2010 Global Mission Consultation and Celebration, Tokyo, May 2010).

5. See "Foreigners in Korea," Wikipedia, https://en.wikipedia.org/wiki/Foreigners_in_Korea.

The Korea Labor Institute and the Korea Women's Policy Institute conducted a study of how Koreans in factories with migrant workers viewed and interacted with these employees. One survey investigated how Koreans in these factories communicated with their foreign workers, asking whether the former used Korean or English or a translator from another language, or whether they simply relied on hand gestures to communicate with their foreign workers. The results showed that the Koreans relied most heavily on speaking Korean (62.3 percent) or on the use of hand gestures (about 30 percent). This ratio was consistent, regardless of how long the Koreans had been working along with migrant workers. As one can imagine, such communication cannot be very efficient or satisfying to either party.

Table 6.1. Means of Communication
with Foreign Workers in Korean Factories

Work experience with foreign workers	Speaking Korean %	Speaking English %	Through interpreter %	Using gestures %	Other %
< 1 yr.	59.7	5.2	0.0	33.8	1.3
1–2 yrs.	66.4	3.6	0.7	28.6	0.7
2–4 yrs.	57.5	7.5	1.4	30.8	2.7
> 4 yrs.	67.9	5.2	3.0	23.9	0.0
Average	62.3	5.4	1.3	29.3	1.2

Source: The data for this table are drawn from Gae Taek Oh, Jung Hwan Lee, and Kyu Yong Lee, "Koreans' Perception of Migrant Workers" [in Korean] (Seoul: Korean Labor Institute, 2007), 60.

Note: Due to rounding, totals may not equal 100.

For migrant workers who know little or no elementary Korean, it is obvious that such communication practices cannot result in effective sharing of directions or information. Although migrant workers receive language training both before and after their arrival in South Korea, the classes they take are relatively short and, in most cases, virtually useless for communicating in detail about their expected work responsibilities. These deficiencies in preparation explain the high level of stress migrant workers often feel, as well as the significant number of workplace accidents they are involved in.

Chon Eung Park, of the Ansan Immigration Center, has reported that significant percentages of the foreign workers in Ansan (the city with the highest concentration of foreign residents in Korea) have suffered human rights violations. In 2008 the grievances included discrimination (experienced by 27.7 percent), the withholding of identification credentials (26.7 percent), violence (15.5 percent), and forced labor (14.3 percent).[6] As long as such violations continue, migrant workers cannot enjoy working and living in South Korea, and the reputation of our country suffers accordingly.

Overall, prejudice is the biggest challenge that foreign workers face during their stay living and working in Korea. As Park's study points out, Korean workers are highly prejudiced against their foreign co-workers, with their differences in language, religion, and culture. This attitude reflects the Korean society's lack of experience in living harmoniously with foreigners. We should also note that many Koreans have no experience of life with foreigners simply because many areas of Korea have no resident non-Koreans at all.

In addition to fear of living in a new society, prejudice, and poor working conditions, migrant workers also have to deal with high levels of stress. Their lack of harmonious working relationships with fellow Korean workers increases their desire to give up staying in Korea. Manual labor is itself physically exhausting, but combined with experiences of physical or verbal abuse, wages delayed or paid only partially or not at all, withheld identification credentials, and constant prejudice, the stress often becomes unbearable, and the workers start to resent or hate Koreans. They might continue to work in the factories, but only for the sake of earning wages.

Churches and mission organizations have been coming forward to offer support and holistic care for immigrants as they try to cope with the difficulties of their life in South Korea. These ministries can be the means of meeting needs,

6. Chon Eung Park, "The Present Reality of Foreign Workers and Multicultural Policy Agenda" [in Korean] (paper presented at the Shinchon Forum 22, Seoul, May 2008), 36–37.

offering friendship, and opening hearts to be receptive to the Gospel message.

MISSION TO FOREIGN WORKERS:
FEATURES AND CHALLENGES

Since the 1990s, many churches and mission organizations have begun ministering to foreign workers in South Korea. At present, about 500 organizations are doing so. I would hope that many more Korean churches could take up such a ministry, but it seems that most churches lack knowledge of the needs of these foreign workers and of ways they could be involved in mission.

In some cases, mission work with migrants in Korea focuses mainly on trying to address human rights violations. One example is Haesung Kim, pastor of the House of Korean-Chinese, a missionary organization for Korean-Chinese that he started as a place for counseling migrant workers regarding their human rights. In contrast, evangelical churches and mission organizations focus their ministry to foreign workers on the Gospel, because their ultimate goal is see them become disciples of Christ. For example, Changsun Moon of the missionary organization WiThee International argues that some ministries to foreign workers are ineffective because they devote more energy to dealing with human rights than they do to teaching the Gospel.[7] He also points out that there is frequently a lack of expertise and cooperation between churches and mission organizations that work with migrant workers.

In some cases, however, mission organizations that work with foreign workers have realized the importance of pursuing a more holistic ministry, aiming to meet both physical needs of the workers (primarily regarding human rights) and the spiritual need of hearing and embracing the Gospel. Nasom Community (nasom. or.kr) and Onnuri Church's M-Center are two examples of centers engaging in such holistic ministry.

Mission to migrant workers in Korea can have an additional dimension, for it can become a bridge between local and worldwide missions that adds new dynamics to both. For example, churches and mission organizations can train committed foreign workers and can commission them, upon their return to their home coun-

----

7. See www.withee.org.

tries, to serve as missionaries to their own people. They would be ideal missionaries for they already speak the language and know the culture and, with the Lord's enabling, could effectively expand the kingdom of God. It would be wise to devote all the resources we can to preparing believing migrant workers to become missionaries to their own people.

FRIENDS OF ALL NATIONS

Friends of All Nations (FAN), in which I am heavily involved, is an organization that offers a variety of services to migrant workers, as well as opportunities for participation by other Christians.[8] It is led by a board of evangelical church leaders from various denominations and an executive committee that oversees the daily aspects of ministry. People serving as part of FAN have been committed to missions work for many years and have a variety of cross-cultural experience. Following Jesus' commandment to "love your neighbor as yourself," we seek to share the love of Christ with foreigners living in Korea. We view this ministry as our part in fulfilling the Great Commission to make disciples of all nations, as well as our opportunity to shepherd these believers. We work for their salvation and spiritual growth, as well as for their economic prosperity. We believe that migrants who truly believe and grow in the Gospel will thereby be equipped to share the Good News when they return to their home countries, including serving there as pastors and missionaries. The following list highlights several aspects of the work of FAN.

1. In reaching out to the 2 million migrant workers, foreign students, and multicultural families now in Korea, FAN works to fulfill the Great Commission by cooperating and networking with local churches and ministries throughout the country.

2. Through one-to-one discipleship, FAN shepherds and nurtures new believers in their faith. If they so desire, FAN makes available the support needed for them to attend seminary to receive formal Bible training.

3. FAN sponsors programs and volunteer opportunities that involve college students and young adults in its various

8. See http://fankorea.org.

ministries. In this way, volunteers can receive practical training in mission while developing their foreign-language and intercultural skills. Through these interactions with migrant workers, volunteers are exposed to various cross-cultural situations, as well as opportunities to learn about different religions, all of which helps prepare them for possible future work in missions.

4. FAN partners with overseas missionaries who have returned to Korea on furlough or permanently, bringing them in contact with migrant workers from the country of their previous service. In this way, these missionaries can continue an active ministry with people whose culture and language they know, as well as being a valuable bridge in linking FAN with different people groups.

5. FAN also connects foreign believers who are studying in Korea with foreign workers from the same country. These contacts facilitate the sharing of the Gospel with these migrant workers.

6. With the support of local churches, FAN seeks to provide a training ground for migrant workers who can then go as discipled, self-supporting missionaries with the goal of planting churches overseas.

By reaching out to the foreign workers already living in Korea, we are able to take advantage of a new type of harvest field. There is greater openness and responsiveness among these foreign workers, who are no longer bound by the cultural and religious pressures and restrictions that may exist in their home country. This is especially true among those of Muslim background, where evangelism is the greatest need. By drawing together the resources of the local churches, missionaries and laymen are able to make the most of this new context for evangelism.

FAN currently has ministries in thirty-five places throughout South Korea. As an example, the headquarters in Incheon sponsors worship services in five different languages: Filipino, Nepali, the Russian dialect spoken on Sakhalin, Cambodian, and English, usually with between 50 and 100 foreign workers in attendance. The Filipino community has a Wednesday night prayer meeting, a Friday all-night prayer meeting, a Saturday

Bible study, and a Sunday night discipleship training. A main goal of these services is to prepare those who take part to return to their countries as missionaries.

Mobilizing senior volunteers. In every outreach to migrant workers, there is a great need for volunteers and sponsors who can provide spiritual and financial support. Two likely sources for this help are returning and retired overseas missionaries. Former overseas missionaries have themselves been migrants and have experienced life in another country, making it relatively easy for them to understand the situation of migrant workers in Korea. Retired Christians who have not served as missionaries typically have particular skills and experiences that they can use in ministry with foreigners in Korea. They may also have a network of contacts who can be tapped to join them in becoming sponsors and volunteers in ministry. They usually do not have financial burdens, and their children are typically grown up and independent, so they can more easily and fruitfully devote themselves to this ministry in their golden years.

Chief characteristics of migrant mission: holistic ministry and discipleship. Effective mission to foreign workers must be holistic in nature. Their needs are many and deep, encompassing the physical (e.g., medical and legal) and the spiritual (e.g., counseling and growth with God in worship and obedience). The Bible is clear in commanding the people of God to treat well the strangers and visitors that come into our circles (e.g., Heb. 13:1–3). And we must remember that, according to Jesus' teaching, these needy ones are actually our neighbors (see Luke 10:25–37). Jesus was a friend of strangers, outcasts, and sinners—people who were despised and oppressed. We ought to treat our migrant brothers and sisters as Jesus did, loving them as ourselves (see Mark 12:31) and working to meet all their needs. Furthermore, we must obey our Lord's Great Commission, to "make disciples of all nations" (Matt. 28:19). When our migrant brothers and sisters open their hearts to us and to the Lord through our love, we must disciple them to obey and follow Christ, thus paving the way for Christ's second coming (see Matt. 24:14). Mark 12:31 and Matthew 28:19 are the key verses for FAN. And we sense a special urgency to equip migrant workers to become missionaries to their own countries.

According to Jesus' words in Luke 9:23, a true disciple is one who hears Christ's calling and then daily denies his or her own desires in order to follow Jesus. This invitation is wide open to anyone who hears Christ's voice and decides to follow him. Being a disciple and training others in discipleship is not just a program, but a commitment that is meant to lead to a complete transformation of one's life. This is the truth that we seek to share with our migrant brothers and sisters, praying that very many will make the commitment to follow wholeheartedly the Lord Jesus Christ.

MIGRANT MISSION NETWORK IN KOREA

At the end of 2008, several mission organizations cooperated in forming the Migrant Mission Network in Korea (MMNK), a ministry for coordinating and promoting missions to migrants in South Korea. This group's first major public event was the 2009 Korean Migrant Mission Expo, a mass meeting that consisted of missionaries to migrants and exhibitions of mission ministries to migrants. Through this meeting we were introduced to many migrant ministries and could share our collective knowledge and experience of these various ministries. It also clarified our vision for migrant ministry in South Korea. During the mornings at this expo, we presented various migrant mission ministries, and during the afternoons about 200 migrant mission organizations and around 7,000 foreign workers gathered together for mission festival meetings. These meetings gave us opportunities to communicate to Korean churches about the worldwide possibilities that migrant mission offers to world mission.

Prior to the formation of MMNK, it was very difficult to continuously build up the faith of foreign workers who are believers because of their frequent job changes and moving to new locations. Through MMNK we were able to better keep track of them and advise them more closely about ministry and training opportunities in their new locations. Though MMNK has officially ended, a loose network is maintained between the missionaries of cities and provinces. If necessary, we use the network to contact each other for help in serving the migrant population.

FAN AND CHURCH PLANTING

Several foreign brothers who have stayed and ministered in FAN have successfully developed ministries back in their home countries. These people were either foreign workers who had come to work in Korea or pastors who finished their studies while serving the diaspora population with FAN.

After finishing his studies in Korea, Pastor Arnel Gallaza returned to his homeland, the Philippines, where in 2011 he established a Bible school in Mindanao for training and equipping local pastors. This school is now a seminary that offers bachelor degrees in theology and master of divinity degrees. On occasion, I have led the discipleship training course "Train and Multiply" at this seminary.[9]

Huyen, Heung, and He are brothers from Vietnam who partnered with FAN while working and studying in Korea. Heung is currently ministering to house churches in Vietnam. These small groups have around ten members. Some are working closely with the international mission group Youth with a Mission, and others are actively involved in local churches and other ministries. Huyen and He are still in Korea finishing their seminary degrees. These men are good examples of migrants who are financially self-supporting while doing ministry.

Between 2001 and 2007 Mongolian migrants returning to their homeland started planting churches with the help of Korean church partners already in their hometowns. From 2008 to 2011 some of these churches gave birth to daughter churches that by now are fully self-sustaining, no longer needing the help of Korean church sponsors. As of 2014 there were 470 churches in Mongolia, 30 (6.4 percent) of which were planted by faithful Mongolian Christians who had returned from Korea, where they had been evangelized and nurtured. The fruits of their spiritual maturity produced seeds of faith in their home country.[10]

Pastor Hong Gwang Pyo is the head pastor of New Life Thai Church, which started in 2006. He is the chairman of the Thai Mission Network, a mission partnership of sixteen churches for

---

9. David Chul Han Jun, "Case Study of Church Planting through Diaspora Ministry in Korea" [in Korean], *Korea Missions Quarterly* 16, no. 2 (December 2016): 56–57.

10. Ibid., 53–54.

Thai workers in Korea. His church in Ansan also runs a shelter for foreigners where he trains them to be church planters through morning and evening Bible studies. He also trains these people to learn vocational skills such as coffee making, baking, and soap making—skills that may be of financial help to them when they go back to Thailand. Visitation and evangelism are vital in his ministry. Currently, his network has expanded to include fourteen cafes, two churches, and six small groups; since 2013, they have been part of the New Life Corporation.[11]

In Bucheon, Pastor Paul Sohn met Tit Bongsacha during Tit's recovery from a leg injury. One year of Bible reading and friendship prepared Tit for his calling. Now back home in Thailand, he and his wife completed Bible school and have planted house churches in five villages, with an average attendance of about twenty-five people each. These and other cases that are still being documented lead us to believe that discipling and training foreign migrants to return to their home countries as church planters is an effective way to more rapidly propagate the Gospel.[12]

CONCLUSION

If we want to make the greatest possible impact through our migrant workers' mission, we must train migrant Christian workers to become missionaries to their own people and must facilitate their working with other missionaries already serving in their home countries. We can network with them in their native countries by supporting their church planting efforts in every way possible. We need to focus particularly on training migrants who become missionaries to establish house churches.

It has been difficult to be consistent in nurturing the faith of migrant workers within South Korea because of their frequent job changes. MMNK helps to alleviate this situation by maintaining information about, and encouraging mutual support of, all the migrant ministries in South Korea. This network can also assist in providing ministries for missionaries returning or retiring from overseas. Recently, migrant ministries have expanded their focus from migrant workers from different countries to include ministries for foreign students, multicultural families, and young adults.

11. Ibid., 60–61.
12. Ibid., 61.

Such ministry groups can nurture their members' faith and can network with the other existing migrant mission groups. In addition, MMNK has a role to play in interacting with local churches in Korea, seeking to deepen and broaden their involvement in international mission efforts.[13]

May "the Lord of the harvest" (Matt. 9:38; Luke 10:2) find us faithful in preparing laborers—especially migrant laborers—for serving in his worldwide harvest fields!

QUESTIONS FOR REFLECTION

1. How can we motivate local churches to be involved in migrant mission?

2. What is the major problem deterring local churches from becoming involved in migrant mission?

3. How might local churches find workers for migrant mission so as to train them and to place them?

4. How can migrant mission programs of local churches network with other mission centers?

5. What should be the main focus of migrant mission? Should it be human rights? Should it be church planting?

13. This chapter is a condensed and updated revision of my chapter "A South Korean Case Study of Migrant Ministries," in *Korean Diaspora and Christian Mission*, ed. S. Hun Kim and Wonsuk Ma (Oxford: Regnum Books International, 2011), 207–22.

Response
to
"The Importance of Migrant Missions in South Korea"

Darrell Jackson

David Chul Han Jun's study of migrant missions is an updated and revised version of a chapter previously published in 2011 by Regnum Press.[1] After a brief biblical introduction to "diaspora," he refers to the 7 million Koreans who live in diaspora and who have been active in God's mission around the globe. Though important, these 7 million are not the focus of this helpful case study. Instead, Jun introduces the predicament of foreign migrant workers in Korea, currently estimated to number around 2 million.

Jun catalogs the range of difficulties foreign migrant workers have faced in Korea, including exploitation by employers (withholding of salary, unsafe workplace practices, abuse of rights), communication obstacles (language-learning), intercultural conflict, and prejudice (regarding language, religion, and culture). He expresses his concern and argues for the necessary involvement of Korean migrant missions among these workers. The grounds for his argument are not clearly stated, but we can say that they reflect a biblically informed ethic and missiology.

Developing his argument, Jun discusses the work of migrant ministries in Korea. From among five hundred examples, he high-

---

1. David Chul Han Jun, "A South Korean Case Study of Migrant Ministries," in *Korean Diaspora and Christian Mission*, ed. S. Hun Kim and Wonsuk Ma (Oxford: Regnum, 2011), 207–22.

lights ministries that address the spiritual and material needs of migrant workers in a more holistic way. In particular, he discusses the ministries of Friends of All Nations and the contribution of the Migrant Missions Network in Korea (MMNK). He concludes with a call to equip migrant workers for mission back in their countries of origin. More specifically, he anticipates that the MMNK will expand and grow as more areas of migrant mission are explored and developed.

INITIAL POINTS OF RESPONSE

First, I would like to express my appreciation to David Jun for the important and sympathetically critical research he has conducted. Second, may I be permitted to observe that the chapter reflects an unresolved tension? This tension exists, I would say, between the attention given to the missionary potential of the Korean diaspora abroad and the attention also given to the need for a more holistic approach to mission among migrant workers in Korea. I believe, however, that the tension can be resolved and that a more intentional missiology might do so. Or, a simpler way to resolve the tension would be to adopt a single focus on mission to migrant workers in Korea.

Third, may I suggest a point that I think deserves further theological and biblical reflection? Jun notes the observation made by other evangelical agencies that "some ministries to foreign workers are ineffective because they devote more energy to dealing with human rights than they do to teaching the Gospel" (91). Such claims, I would argue, require the presentation of a more robust and adequate biblical ethic for holistic mission.

Fourth, in developing a diaspora missiology, two theological and biblical sources are worth considering. The first of these would be for Korean migrant missions to explore together, from the Old Testament, the biblical injunctions concerning the mutual responsibilities between God's people and the aliens living in diaspora among them. Second, in the New Testament, the Great Commandment to "love your neighbor" sits at the heart of the Lausanne Movement's Cape Town Commitment and underlies any evangelical commitment to holistic mission.[2]

---

2. See www.lausanne.org/content/ctc/ctcommitment.

A MORE SUBSTANTIAL AND FOCUSED RESPONSE

I reflect here on six points of correspondence between what Jun presents and the Korean migrant community I know best—that of Sydney, Australia, the city that I now call home. This approach makes best use of my experience of mission leadership in three mission agencies (two Australian and one European).[3]

Seven million Koreans in diaspora. Of the 7 million Koreans in diaspora, the year 2016 found 123,000 residing in Australia; of this number 24,000 were Korean-Australians.[4] In 2006 the Korean diaspora in Australia was "the sixth largest Korean community outside of Republic of Korea."[5] Some 71 percent of Korean-born Australian residents self-identify as "Christian." In the same report, 40 percent of Koreans in Sydney reported attending church as their most frequent community activity.[6] Responses (out 312 Koreans residing in Sydney) to the question "What activities are you currently involved in [in] your local community?" can be seen in the accompanying table.

Activity	No. of people
Attend church	126
Sports and recreation	31
Cultural groups	27
Volunteer services	19
Youth services	6
Aged care services	1
Other	8
No community activities	117

3. My subheadings reflect observations presented in Jun's chapter.

4. Australian Bureau of Statistics, Annual Census, Canberra, 2016. For data on Koreans in Australia, see the file labeled "Cultural Diversity" archived at www.abs.gov.au/AUSSTATS/abs@.nsf/DetailsPage/2071.02 016?OpenDocument.

5. Sydney Korean Women's Association, *Needs Assessment Report of the Korean Community in the City of Sydney, 2011* (Sydney: SKWA, 2011), 7, citing Foreign Affairs Sub-Committee (2006); www.cityofsydney.nsw.gov.au /__data/assets/pdf_file/0011/109658/Report-Final-Needs-Assessme nt-Report-of-the-Korean-Community-in-the-City-of-Sydney-2011.pdf.

6. The table is adapted from SKWA, *Needs Assessment Report*, 30.

Gil-Soo Han and Joy J. Han note that the first Korean churches in Sydney were established in 1974. By 2010 the city had 151 Korean Protestant churches, with schism being a significant cause of the rapid multiplication.[7] An initial review I conducted in 2017 suggests that some consolidation has occurred, perhaps because of larger churches incorporating Koreans who were formerly attending smaller and less well-resourced churches.

Elementary communication by migrant workers. Several thousand Korean males traveled to Australia during and immediately after the Vietnam War. Many of the men overstayed their student or tourist visas and entered the "gray economy," working without proper documentation. Between 1974 and 1980 the Australian government extended a series of amnesties to individuals who had overstayed their visas, many of whom, lacking strong English-language skills, found employment in low-skilled, menial, and undesirable job sectors.

Koreans migrating to Australia during the 1980s and 1990s were generally highly skilled and educated, but they faced similar challenges in acquiring the necessary English-language skills to achieve the more desirable white-collar jobs. Migrants of this generation are notable for being the most likely to suffer from psychological and mental health disorders as a result of feeling unvalued and insignificant.[8]

Ministries that meet needs and offer friendship. Korean churches in Sydney have been an important point of social contact with other Koreans and have become key sites for affirming and nurturing cultural identity. Many who attended Sydney's Korean churches did so because the church formed a supportive and therapeutic community, particularly for the migrants of the 1980s and 1990s. For them, "the difficulties they face[d], whether psychological or physical, [were] relieved by the sermons they hear[d] in the Korean immigrant churches."[9] For

7. Joy J. Han and Gil-Soo Han, "The Koreans in Sydney," *Sydney Journal* 2, no. 2 (2010): 30.

8. Ibid., 27.

9. Gil-Soo Han, "Korean Christianity in Multicultural Australia: Is It

some church members, the social stigma attached to their low-status jobs, such as cleaning, could be relieved through serving as deacons or elders of their local Korean church. They worked as cleaners, but prayed as elders!

Many Koreans are not ready for intercultural coexistence. Kwang Chung Kim and Shin Kim, in writing of Korean American churches, note an "almost complete indifference to needs outside" their own Korean congregations.[10] These trends can also be observed in Sydney's Korean churches, despite the confident claim by Rev. Sang-taek Lee as long ago as 1989 that "we are here to influence and improve every part of the Australian society. . . . We should realize that God has sent us to Australia to carry out such missions."[11]

   Missiological analysis suggests that the insular location of Korean congregations within areas of high Korean population density is a further indication of Korean churches' reluctance to engage with ethnic difference, a conclusion implied as well, I think, by Jun's own case study.

Discrimination, forced labor, inadequate salary, physical and verbal abuse, delayed wages, withheld identification credentials. Korean migrants to Australia who arrived after the economic crash and International Monetary Fund intervention in Korea in 1997 came looking for a new start. They were unemployed or bankrupt, and they were traumatized. Koreans already living in Australia did not readily welcome them. New immigrants complained that they were being exploited by Korean employers and businesses. Gil-Soo Han discovered that "Korean migrants are not

---

Dialogical or Segregating Koreans?," *Studies in World Christianity* 10, no. 1 (2004): 123.

   10. Kwang Chung Kim and Shin Kim, "The Ethnic Roles of Korean Immigrant Churches in the United States," in *Korean Americans and Their Religions: Pilgrims and Missionaries from a Different Shore*, ed. Ho-Youn Kwon, Kwang Chung Kim, and R. Stephen Warner (University Park: Pennsylvania State Univ. Press, 2001), 93.

   11. Cited by Gil-Soo Han, "An Overview of the Life of Koreans in Sydney and Their Religious Activities," *Korea Journal of Population and Development* 35, no. 2 (1994): 74, www.ekoreajournal.net/issue/view_pop.htm?Idx=2848.

only the victims of racial discrimination, but are also exercising it, for example, Korean small business persons employing recent 'non-English speaking background' migrants at lower rates of pay than those earned by Korean workers."[12]

My students and colleagues share stories of newly qualified seminary students being encouraged to acquire a religious worker visa so as to enter Australia to begin working in a church. The church worker is then exploited, underpaid, and overworked. If such workers complain, they are warned that the church can withdraw their visa sponsorship. Those who become eligible for permanent residency after four years frequently leave that initial congregation and start their own. Some then sponsor other Koreans on religious worker visas and start the cycle of exploitation anew.

Use of the Korean diaspora for the future of Korean overseas mission. A Korean-Australian recently related to me the story of an elderly Korean missionary working in a deprived area of Sydney with a high aboriginal population. The missionary had limited proficiency in English but fed and loved the aboriginal community. My student had initially dismissed this man's missionary efforts, but later he attended the funeral of an aboriginal Christian and learned that the deceased had become a believer just a few months previously and was the fruit of that missionary's loving and faithful witness.

Han and Han suggest that Korean church growth in Sydney was due, in part, to "the presence of many theological graduates from Korea."[13] We can assume that some of them understood themselves to be cross-cultural "missionaries," for as Robert Buswell and Timothy Lee observe, "The Korean Protestant churches commissioned more missionaries than did any other national church except the United States."[14] For the great majority of Koreans in Sydney, however, the challenge of cross-cultural mission remains unrealized, for reasons already spelled out above.

12. Gil-Soo Han, "Korean Christianity in Multicultural Australia," 128.

13. Han and Han, "The Koreans in Sydney," 31.

14. Robert E. Buswell and Timothy S. Lee, *Christianity in Korea* (Honolulu: Univ. of Hawai'i Press, 2006), 2.

CONCLUSION

Even brief exposure to the Korean diaspora in Sydney highlights the need to develop intercultural practices of ministry that take their cue from the Messiah who came as a migrant to serve all. Understood in this way, for a Korean to work as a cleaner and pray as an elder can be interpreted as the hallmark of a truly missionary people in diaspora, liberated from the disabling effects of disempowerment, shame, and dishonor.

7

Multiethnic Ministry in Chicago: A Personal Testimony

Timothy Hong

I was an unbeliever until my freshman year in college, when a friend invited me to a Bible study group. After several months of participating in the group Bible study, I accepted Christ as my Savior. I found in him purpose and meaning for my life that I had earnestly sought but had never found anywhere. At that time I realized that a believer should live as a witness of Christ for all people in the world, as he commanded in Matthew 28:18–20, though I had no idea how I could obey this commandment in real life. I attended and finished seminary, but still I did not know how I could obey the commandment. After I immigrated to the United States in 1983 as a staff member of Evangelical Student Fellowship KOREA, however, the Lord opened a door for me to obey his commandment in a way I could never have planned or imagined. In this chapter, I would like to share how the Lord has enabled me to participate in the city of Chicago in his program of world evangelism.

A VISION FOR MULTIETHNIC MINISTRY

One day in the fall of 1987 several students studying at the University of Illinois at Chicago (UIC) asked me whether I could begin a ministry to students on campus. I prayed for God's guidance and was convinced that I should accept their request. So later that year I started doing ministry on campus. Most of the students who came to the ministry were Korean 1.5-generation immigrants; they were bilingual, speaking both Korean and English. When I was doing ministry for them, I spoke with them in Korean, and we had no problem communicating with each other.

One day after a couple of years in this ministry at UIC, the academic dean of the university invited me to a prayer breakfast in his office. On a wall I noticed many different charts of statistics for the university. One chart indicated that students from 100 different nations were currently enrolled at UIC. It struck me that I could reach out to the people of those 100 nations here on this one university campus. I remembered what the Lord said in the Book of Acts (1:8), "But you will receive power when the Holy Spirit has come upon you; and you will be my witnesses in Jerusalem, in all Judea and Samaria, and to the ends of the earth." I said to myself, "I don't have to go all over the world to reach out to the people of all nations. The ends of the earth are right here where I am standing. The Lord has given me a great opportunity to obey his Great Commission by reaching out to foreign students on this campus!"[1]

It was a new vision that I had never dreamed of, the excitement of which made my heart pound. That vision ignited my multiethnic ministry.[2] From that moment I was determined to obey the Lord's commandment to bring his Gospel to the ends of the earth by reaching out to all the foreign students on the campus. But at the same time I felt a heavy burden in my heart. In order to reach out to all the foreign students by preaching and teaching the Bible to them, I needed to speak English fluently. It seemed to me an impossible task, for I was already thirty-six years old and could barely speak English at all.

In my schooling back in Korea, most English classes were taught in such a way that students could read and write English grammatically, but spoken communication was not part of the curriculum. Although I had studied English many hours every week

1. David Boyd, *You Don't Have to Cross the Ocean to Reach the World* (Grand Rapids: Chosen, 2008), argues that "never before in the history of humankind have our populations been so mixed. All the major cities of the world are multicultural, and in this fact lies the potential to reach the whole world quickly and effectively" (148).

2. Hayward Armstrong emphasizes the importance for multicultural missionaries of a heartfelt conviction based on a vision granted by God; see his *M-Life Illustrated: Reflections on the Lives of Cross-Cultural Missionaries* (Lexington, KY: Rainer, 2016), 99–103.

for six years, I was unable to communicate in even the simplest sentences of English. The vision of multiethnic ministry, however, was too strong for me to erase from my heart. So I started preparing Bible studies, sermons, and prayers in English, which took three or four times longer than preparing the same things in Korean.

A few months after I started doing the English ministry, several Korean students who had faithfully participated in this work earnestly requested me to stop doing the ministry in English. They told me that the Korean students could not receive spiritual food through my English ministry as much as they did through my ministering in Korean. I was discouraged. I did not know for sure whether I should continue pursuing the vision.

CONVICTION FROM GOD'S WORD FOR MULTIETHNIC MINISTRY

For several months I struggled with my limited ability to teach and preach in English. One day I remembered the word in the Book of Exodus regarding God's calling of Moses in the desert. When Moses resisted God's call to him to go to Egypt to bring out the Israelites, he gave as a reason his lack of eloquence in speaking. And God answered him, "Who gives speech to mortals? . . . Is it not I, the LORD?" (Exod. 4:11). Encouraged with this word, Moses accepted God's call.

At that moment, the word touched my heart like a moving fire. I literally felt heat in my heart! The Word convinced me that it was God who had made my tongue and who would enable me to speak English fluently and thus be able to teach and preach the Gospel to all the foreign students. The conviction was so strong and vivid that I jumped up and down with joy several times.

From that moment, I kept holding on to that Word by putting Exodus 4:11 on the wall above my desk and on the dashboard of my car and meditating on it constantly. In reality, however, my English did not improve as I wished and expected. One by one, Korean students started leaving the ministry. Again I was discouraged. During that time, however, a couple of students from the United States and several other non-Korean students came to our ministry and were getting faithfully involved in it. I felt that the engagement of those students in the ministry was a sign of God's confirmation of his calling for my English-language ministry. I overcame discouragement and kept ministering to multiethnic students.

THE GIFT OF THE HOLY SPIRIT
FOR MULTIETHNIC MINISTRY

While I was ministering to students of different races and cultures, I noticed the existence of barriers that prevented students from being united in one spirit. Not only did differences of language cause barriers, but different views, attitudes, and traditions regarding specific issues and aspects of life also disrupted our unity. I started praying to seek God's wisdom and guidance to overcome these barriers.

One day while I was meditating on the words of Acts 2:1–11, I realized that the anointing of the Holy Spirit redeemed humanity from the curse of the language barrier. This curse attached to language was caused by human pride in building the Tower of Babel. It resulted in the scattering of humankind on the earth so that they were prevented from making a name for themselves by lifting up their accomplishments to the heavens (Gen. 11:1–9).[3]

On the day of Pentecost, the disciples of Christ, most of whom were uneducated and likely had not learned to speak foreign languages, were speaking more than a dozen foreign languages at once.[4] Speaking so many different tongues by the Holy Spirit "symbolized a new unity in the Spirit transcending racial, national, and linguistic barriers."[5] By the gift of tongues, the Holy Spirit enabled the disciples to overcome language barriers and to communicate the Gospel to people of different nationalities.

By this truth the Lord encouraged me to seek the gift of tongues of the Holy Spirit. Until that time I had tried to improve my English skill through my own efforts alone. I kept writing, reading, listening to, and speaking English for several hours every day. But I was unable to feel comfortable with teaching and preaching in English. I often felt awkward and embarrassed, self-conscious about my broken English.

In seeking the gift of speaking in tongues of the Holy Spirit, I learned a lesson, namely, that the language barrier that befell the

3. Gordon J. Wenham, *Genesis 1–15* (Waco, TX: Word, 1987), 246; Carl Friedrich Keil and Franz Delitzsch, *Biblical Commentary on the Old Testament*, vol. 1, *The Pentateuch* (Grand Rapids: Eerdmans, 1981), 175–76.

4. Scholars hold different opinions on what Luke meant by the "tongues" the disciples spoke. See John Stott, *The Spirit, the Church, and the World* (Downers Grove, IL: InterVarsity Press, 1990), 65–68.

5. Ibid., 68.

people who built the Tower of Babel signified more than simply the curse of being divided by speaking in different tongues. It also encompassed all kinds of problematic barriers that would "hobble man's attempts at cooperation once and for all."[6] Although people may speak the same language, communication barriers still exist which can lead to misunderstandings and disagreements. The cause of all barriers goes deeper than just language; at their root, these barriers are caused by humanity's sin of self-centeredness, pride, and rebellion against God.

By combining the meaning of the curse of the language barrier from the Tower of Babel with the redemptive gift of tongues of the Holy Spirit, the Lord convinced me that I could overcome the language barrier only if I completely repented of my pride, gave up all my selfish desires, and focused on seeking first his glory and his kingdom. I was determined to seek the gift of speaking in tongues from the Holy Spirit to preach the Gospel to all people in the world. From that time onward, I became free from any feeling of awkwardness or embarrassment caused by my broken English.

Ten years after I began this English-speaking ministry, I had an opportunity to visit Seattle. On the day of my return to Chicago, I stopped for breakfast at a fast-food restaurant near the Seattle airport. In the restaurant I met a young Caucasian man, a typical white person. We had breakfast at the same table, and he and I talked about the weather, our jobs, the reason for my visit to Seattle, and other topics. At the end of the conversation, he asked me where my hometown was. I answered, "My hometown is a small village in Korea." He seemed to be very surprised at my answer and said, "Really? I thought you were born somewhere in the United States." At the time I did not attribute any significance to his response. But on the flight back to Chicago, what he said came repeatedly to my mind. I felt that God had sent him to me at that moment to confirm that the Holy Spirit had anointed me with the gift of the tongue of English. I heard a very small voice in my heart: "Don't worry about English any longer. From now on, I will use you to do ministry for all people in the United States, including Caucasians."

6. Wenham, *Genesis 1–15*, 245.

THE FRUIT OF THE HOLY SPIRIT
FOR MULTIETHNIC MINISTRY

In 1999, about ten years after I started doing English-speaking ministry, our campus ministry turned into a local church.[7] I started facing challenges and problems that were different from those I had experienced in the ministry for students. Some of the adults were able to speak only a few words of English. Others were unable to speak English at all. Conflicts and uneasiness among different races in our ministry increased.

Sometime later, probably a year or two after our ministry turned into a local multiethnic church, I felt that our Spanish sisters were keeping a distance from me. I did not understand why they did so. One day I talked to a leader among them about my feeling of their changed attitude toward me and asked the reason. She answered, "Pastor, they don't feel any love from you."

I was surprised at her answer and responded, "Why? Don't they know how deeply I care for them and love them? God knows how much I love them!"

She replied, "They don't feel your love because you have never hugged them." This comment really shocked me. As a Korean man, I would never hug any woman in church to show my care and love—not even my wife. In our culture, a male pastor simply does not (and should not!) hug a woman in a public place, especially not in church. Through that incident the Lord taught me an important truth for a multiethnic and multicultural ministry.

The truth is that, first, I must be humble and flexible in identifying myself with people of different cultures and ethnicities, even if it makes me uncomfortable and seems radical when judged according to my own culture and traditions. As a Korean man, I grew up in a culture and tradition that were formed by Confucianism, which emphasizes strict separation between men and women in public places (e.g., it teaches that, beginning at age seven, boys and girls should never sit together). But the Lord gave me biblical grounds for adjusting or even sacrificing my comfortable traditions out of respect for people of other cultures and traditions. It is found in Paul's statement that he became "all

---

7. The church has kept the same name, Evangelical Student Fellowship, and the church and campus ministry are combined. See www.esfworld.us.

things to all people" for the sake of reaching out to the people of all nations (1 Cor. 9:19–23).

I learned, second, that I must connect Christ's love in me with people of other cultures in the same ways that they do. I must use the ways or means that they use, not what is comfortable for me. Even if I do everything I think shows my love, it may not be accepted as love if people of other cultures do not feel love from my attitude or behavior.

On one occasion I was concerned about the attitude of a brother who came from West Africa. During group Bible study meetings that I led, he always looked down and never lifted his head to look at me. After several meetings, I kindly encouraged him to make eye contact while I was talking. But he did not follow my advice and kept lowering his eyes during group meetings. I felt disrespected and ignored by him. Finally, I spoke with him personally about the issue: "Brother, didn't I encourage you to make eye contact with me while I am leading a group meeting? Is there any reason for you not to do so?"

He replied, "Pastor, in my culture, young people should not make eye contact with people who are older than they are, especially while they are instructing younger people."

This comment opened my eyes. The Lord taught me that I can connect in Christ's love with people of other cultures only when I "stop expecting everyone and everything to change to fit" me,[8] but instead "adjust to their culture in ways that they can relate to me and trust me."[9]

Oftentimes while I am doing multiethnic ministry for people of different cultures, I am frustrated by my misunderstanding of their behavior or attitude and by their misunderstanding of me in my behavior and attitude. The Lord always encourages me, however, with this word: "Love is patient; love is kind; love is not . . . rude" (1 Cor. 13:4–5).[10] You cannot manufacture this love by

8. Carissa Alma, *Thriving in Cross Cultural Ministry* (Lexington, KY: Pavilion, 2011), 73.

9. Armstrong, *M-Life Illustrated*, 132. Duane Elmer well explains how to develop skills and attitudes for building trust among people cross-culturally in his book *Cross-Cultural Connections: Stepping Out and Fitting In around the World* (Downers Grove, IL: InterVarsity Press, 2002), 108–10.

10. Some scholars interpret "rude" as "to behave [in an] unseemly way" or "to treat somebody in a wrong way"; see F. W. Grosheide, *Commentary*

your own effort; it is the gift of the Holy Spirit. I frequently affirm this verse, especially when I have trouble being patient with other people's behavior or attitudes: "Lord, I need patience by the fruit of the Holy Spirit; by this Spirit, enable me to be patient." I also frequently pray, "Lord, grant me the gift of cultural sensitivity to show your love to others in such a way that they will feel respected and loved."

GOD'S BLESSING

As of December 2016, the Lord had blessed our multiethnic ministry with people from thirty different countries spread across Europe, Africa, the Middle East, Asia, North America, Central and South America, and the Caribbean. As a witness to the way the Lord has blessed people in our multiethnic ministry, I share the following testimony of a brother, Samuel Lebbie, who came to Chicago as a refugee from Africa.

> I came to the United States as a refugee from Senegal, Africa, because of an Islamic terrorist threat against my life in 2015. A Japanese brother who was a member of the Evangelical Student Fellowship Church reached out to me. The church stood by me from day 1 in Chicago and took an extraordinary journey with me in terms of my needs. They hired an immigration lawyer to change my legal status from refugee to permanent resident.
>
> I received a work permit and Social Security number, which allowed me to stay and work in the United States. Eventually I got a job so that I could support not only myself but also my daughter in her first year at a medical college in Sierra Leone. The church also helped me practice driving and then obtain a driver's license. I have seen many immigrants who have been in the United States for years without having the opportunity to drive because they have neither a Social Security card nor a work permit. The church has also given me the opportunity to exercise my spiritual gifts by serving in the ministry.
>
> I have been blessed so much by God's love in the setting of the multiethnic ministry in ESF that I am praying every day that the

---

on the First Epistle to the Corinthians (Grand Rapids: Eerdmans, 1984), 307; and C. K. Barrett, *A Commentary on the First Epistle to the Corinthians* (Peabody, MA: Hendrickson, 1987), 303.

Lord may keep using me to bring his Good News to people from all over the world here in Chicago.[11]

Some of the leaders and pastors who have been trained in our multiethnic ministry have gone back to their home countries (the list includes Afghanistan, Benin, Cuba, Dominican Republic, India, Peru, and Philippines) and are serving in diverse ministries in our mission branches. Here is the testimony of a missionary, Suri Kumar:

I was born and raised in India. After finishing college in India, I came to the United States to study at a seminary in Chicago. After completion of my MDiv degree in Chicago, I joined the staff of ESF in October 2002. After joining ESF, I saw many wonderful things God did among people who were ethnically very diverse. They joyfully served the Lord in unity in diversity. And I acquired everybody's love and respect, although I was racially and ethnically different from them.

In May 2009 the Lord gave me a desire to go back to India to open a new ministry there. As soon as I returned to India, I started a mission branch of ESF in the city of Hyderabad. Although people in the city are not diverse in terms of ethnicity, they are very diverse in terms of religious affiliation, social class, and economic status. During the last seven years, the Lord has used me to reach out to young college students who are Muslims, the children of poor Hindu families, women and men who are underprivileged, and some people who are still regarded as higher class.

Jesus' love and the unity of the Spirit among diverse people, which I experienced in the multiethnic ministry in Chicago, have helped me to minister to diverse people in India joyfully every day.[12]

CONCLUSION

Although I have stumbled so many times with impatience toward people of different cultures, the Lord has been patient with me and has encouraged me to pursue the vision: "Today, the place you are living in is the ends of the earth. Keep witnessing my Gospel to the

11. Lebbie to Hong, email, January 2017. Lebbie is now a staff member of ESF in Chicago.

12. Kumar to Hong, email, January 2017. Kumar is an ESF missionary serving in India.

people from all over the world and send them back to their countries to bring their people to my salvation." I will keep pursuing this vision, agreeing wholeheartedly with Patty Lane's observation that "the multicultural nature of the United States is a tool that can speed the spread of the gospel throughout the world."[13]

QUESTIONS FOR REFLECTION

1. How do you define "a vision from God" for your ministry or mission? Have you ever received a vision from God as you define it? If so, how have you responded to the vision? What was the result?

2. Have you applied Paul's attitude of "becoming all things to all men" for effective evangelism (1 Cor. 9:19–23) to reach out to people who are different from you in terms of race, culture, or tradition? What have you learned while you have tried to apply Paul's attitude to your attitude?

3. What specific gift(s) of the Holy Spirit (Rom. 12:4–8) or fruit of the Spirit (Gal. 5:22–23) do you think you need most to reach out to people who are different from you in terms of race, ethnicity, culture, or tradition? How have you obeyed the Holy Spirit?

4. What is the racial or ethnic composition of the city or village where you live now? If your city has more than a single racial or ethnic group, have you done anything to reach across racial and ethnic lines? If you have, what was the result? If you have not, why not? If your city does not have ethnically diverse people, how will you obey the great commandment of the Lord in Matthew 28:18–20?

13. Patty Lane, *A Beginner's Guide to Crossing Cultures: Making Friends in a Multicultural World* (Downers Grove, IL: InterVarsity Press, 2002), 144.

Response to "Multiethnic Ministry in Chicago"

Sam George

Pastor Timothy Hong's chapter is very enlightening, particularly about his personal, cultural, and ministerial transformation. In this essay he shares honestly his vocational journey over three and a half decades as a missionary with its many triumphs and challenges, but at its very core Hong's chapter presents us with many lessons for all Christian workers everywhere. Living in Chicago and having personally known Hong's ministry, I consider it a great honor to present this response.

A SERIES OF CONVERSIONS

I would summarize Hong's missionary career in terms of four major shifts, or conversions. First, he begins with his *spiritual conversion* in his college years, noting that he was an unbeliever when he entered college and that a friend's invitation to a Bible study became life transforming. His acceptance of Christ as Savior and his call to ministry seem to have been closely interlinked. As he found meaning and renewed purpose in life in college years, I am not surprised that he first became involved with college-student ministries. As he wrestled with the idea of being a witness of Christ to all people, however, God surprisingly opened a door for him to relocate to the United States as a staff member of a Korean student ministry organization, and he came to Chicago in 1983 to begin a student chapter on a university campus.

The second major shift I read in his narrative is what I label a *calling conversion*, his call to multiethnic ministries. Hong was comfortable ministering to students in a Korean college context, but his geographic displacement to Chicago brought about a radical reorientation. Now he was seeking to reach people from many nations. In obedience to this expanded call, he faced many challenges, including rejection from Korean student leaders and the labor of acquiring cross-cultural ministry skills. These steps pose a major shift for people who have been captive to geographic and cultural bounds of faith. Displacement forces us to interact with people of diverse backgrounds and exposes our own cultural blind spots. We must understand that our call to ministry is not static, but evolves constantly over a lifetime of service. We are called to be faithful to the Master who calls, not necessarily to a particular ministry model, structure, or style. Such faithfulness produces greater humility and dependence on God, eventually proving good for the soul in our service to the Lord.

The third major shift Hong underwent was from student ministry to church ministry, what I will call *ministry conversion*. Though some may be called to a particular ministry for all of their lives, we must recognize that for others ministry might evolve over a period of time. Ministerial transitions should not be viewed as abandoning of the mission or as being disloyal. Some might move from missions to church ministry or vice versa. Others will move from church to academia, and yet others from a seminary to the mission field. The dynamic nature of Christian organizations in the twenty-first century—in which people may be available only for limited spans of time and in which there are constant turnovers—may be hard for mission agency leaders or heads of denominations to digest. But acknowledging this fluidity will help us gain a more comprehensive view of kingdom work and free us from a narrow and parochial view of ministry.

Finally, undergirding all of these conversions is what I will call *cultural conversion*. It is akin to the biblical account of Peter's vision in Acts 10 and the ensuing transformation of worldview to include Gentiles in the mission of God. It results in redefining boundaries of the mission of God far beyond our current geographic and cultural limitations. This conversion profoundly reorients our understanding of the Gospel and mission, and their ever-expanding nature to include all people everywhere. Cultural conversion exposes our biases and prejudices, while at the same time calling for a deeper soul-cleansing work in us in order to prepare us for greater missional impact in the world. In this process we gain a new, divine perspective and begin to see people differently, to develop a heart for different people and issues, to acquire new skills, and to experience new supernatural empowerment to carry out God's mission in the world both at a deeper level and across broader dimensions.

DIASPORA MISSIONS: STUDENT MINISTRIES AND MULTIETHNIC CHURCHES

Now I want to reflect on two major paradigms of mission that are present in Hong's narrative and to reframe them in the context of diaspora missions. The first is *ministry to international students.* We continue to see record numbers of students leave their families and home countries to go overseas for educational pursuits and research. Education abroad creates the most value by offering greater prospects and better knowledge creation and dissemination. Traditionally, countries that attracted international students were the United States, Canada, the United Kingdom, and Germany. In recent decades, however, many new countries—such as Australia, China, India, New Zealand, Qatar, and the United Arab Emirates—have become hubs of global education. Around the globe, international student ministries must remain a strategic focus of missionary work.[1]

God is moving, in ever-increasing numbers, students and scholars from all over world, even from countries closed to the Gospel, to go abroad for educational pursuits and research. They come in contact with Christians and are drawn to Jesus Christ through student ministries in host countries. This transitionary life stage holds enormous transformative potential as students probe personal beliefs and become open to explore alternative faith claims. University campuses are a strategic mission field that call for faithful witness and the caring presence of Christians. Many international students return home after completing their studies and become influential leaders of their nations. Effective ministry during the short window of students' college years in

---

1. Lausanne Committee for World Evangelization, *Diasporas and International Students: The New People Next Door*, Lausanne Occasional Paper 55 (2005), www.lausanne.org/content/lop/lop-55.

a foreign country can alter the future of nations and missions in other parts of the world.

The second major paradigm that appears in this chapter is *multiethnicity*. All of us are ethnocentric and are held captive within certain cultural boundaries. Missions is a boundary-breaking activity, and we see progressive boundary expansion that includes diverse people and cultures. Christianity has never been captive to any geography, culture, or people; it constantly moves with people on the move, resulting in the shifting of its center of gravity and the creation of new centers of Christianity. This diffusion across geographic and cultural lines creates new margins, each of which holds the potential to become a new future center of Christianity. Such an understanding of mission and of one's personal journey toward greater inclusiveness acts as an antidote to our self-centeredness, racial or cultural pride, and superiority complexes, while providing a new love for people unlike us and leading to our learning languages, cultures, and the traditions of people from other parts of the world.[2]

The Homogeneous Unit Principle has long been a major idea in missions and church growth conversations, but increased migration is creating unparalleled levels of heterogeneity in our societies and churches. I have therefore redefined the former acronym "HUP" as the "Heterogeneity Unity Paradigm." This new perspective holds immense potential for understanding the increased intercultural penetration we are seeing in the world as a result of unprecedented human mobility and diasporic interplays that are reshaping Christianity everywhere.[3] Loss and dislocation call out for a theology of otherness and diversity, which at the same time envisions a new basis of unity that lies beyond social or cultural commonalities. When the known and familiar world is left behind, it is replaced by diasporic settings that are unfamiliar and strange in which one lives as an "other." People in diaspora live in two worlds—one that they left behind yet to which they

2. See Global Diaspora Network, *Scattered to Gather: Embracing the Global Trend of Diaspora*, rev. ed. (Manila: Lausanne Committee for World Evangelization, 2017); Sadiri Joy Tira and Tetsunao Yamamori, eds., *Scattered and Gathered: A Global Compendium of Diaspora Missiology* (Oxford: Regnum Books International, 2016).

3. Sam George, *Diaspora Christianities: Global Scattering and Gathering of South Asian Christians* (Minneapolis: Fortress Press, 2018).

feel strangely connected, and one that they have adopted yet in which they feel estranged. Separation from home and hearth, coupled with sojourning in the land of another, never feeling settled or secure, produces the angst of disorientation, rejection, alienation, and discrimination. Assimilation into the dominant cultures of host nations and hybridized self-conceptions create much pain, confusion, anxiety, and a deep yearning for belonging. It is in this new, strange, and often oppressive context that the identity of an alienating otherness of diaspora is forged. At the same time, it can form the cusp of expansion for theological understanding of people, cultures, Gospel, church, and Christ.

With unprecedented means for mobility, communication, transportation, and interaction across all forms of cultural boundaries, human migration has become the defining feature of the twenty-first century. The word of caution that Andrew Walls offers may be pertinent as we realize the ever-growing need for unity amid the great diversity of twenty-first-century Christianity. He reminds us that "the Ephesian question at the Ephesian moment is whether or not the church in all its diversity will demonstrate its unity by the interactive participation of all its culture-specific segments, the interactive participation that is to be expected in a functioning body."[4] Christians worldwide can ill afford to express themselves in terms of disjointed Christianities. The basis of our unity is not doctrinal, nor is it structural or organizational. It is neither programmatic nor cultural, but rests on the lordship of Christ and the realization of the global body of Christ. The contemporary global scattering of people is not only advancing Christianity in unexpected ways, but is also stretching us to wrap our minds around a fuller vision of the body of Christ by bringing us face to face with Christians from all over the world, what the apostle Paul envisioned as the "fullness" of the body of Christ (see Eph. 1:23).

CONCLUSION

In conclusion, I would like to reframe this missionary life journey in four consecutive expanding ripples, continually realizing a grander vision of God and God's mission in the world. This

4. Andrew F. Walls, *The Cross-Cultural Process in Christian History: Studies in the Transmission and Appropriation of Faith* (Maryknoll, NY: Orbis Books, 2002), 81.

expanding vision is biblically anchored in the Great Commission (Matt. 28:19–20 and Acts 1:8). Our journey from Jerusalem to the ends of the earth involves a few stops or conversions along the way. The ever-expanding dimension of the mission of God calls for a series of conversions of our heart, eyes, hands, and feet such that we grow in our spiritual maturity, our calling, our intercultural skill, and a renewed commitment to God's mission. God weaves our geographic and cultural displacements in order to reorient us and to use us in new ways. All of our decenterings in life and missionary vocation make way for a fresh recentering of our focus on God and a new missional calling and impact. God scatters us in order to gather us in new ways, but then only to scatter us further. In these cyclical gatherings and scatterings, we find our identity in Christ, our meaning in life, and our mission in the world for the glory of God.

8

The Development of Mentoring Practices: Guidelines for Korean-Chinese in Yoido Full Gospel Church

Ildoo Kwon

As globalization draws the peoples of the world closer together, the church must understand the attitudes, skills, and abilities required of its leaders, who increasingly must realize the need for multicultural leadership. As James Plueddemann has stated, "World missions must be multicultural because the gospel is for everyone and the Great Commission is for all believers."[1]

Korea is the second largest missionary-sending country in the world.[2] World mission has been a passion for Korean churches from the early years of Korean church history. Korea also has the largest denominational churches in the world, including Baptist, Full Gospel, Methodist, and Presbyterian. Many Korean churches, however, are now facing challenges in missions because globalization is implicitly calling for changes in their leadership, which up till now has been almost exclusively monocultural.

Yoido Full Gospel Church (YFGC) has been one of the largest and most influential churches, not only in Korea but also in the world. YFGC has been a global church, commissioning 750 missionaries worldwide and leading major mission projects in various

1. James E. Plueddemann, *Leading across Cultures: Effective Ministry and Mission in the Global Church* (Downers Grove, IL: IVP Academic, 2009), 22.

2. Korea World Missions Association (KWMA), http://kwma.org /gnuboard4/bbs/board.php?bo_table=s_03&wr_id=44.

countries. This church, however, now faces new challenges and opportunities because of globalization, the advancement of technology, and new social movements as it seeks to gain a fresh perspective and find new ways to do mission. One of the biggest challenges facing the church is the need for it to adopt a more sensitive cross-cultural understanding of people who are currently part of the church but who come from different cultural backgrounds. Unfortunately, the church lacks cross-cultural pastors and for the most part has failed to recognize different cultures, all of which limits the church's ability to engage the new global challenges and opportunities present today.

Korean society has been monocultural for thousands of years. The language and culture remained largely unchanged until the country suffered a series of invasions by neighboring Japan, China, and, indirectly, Russia, which infiltrated lands with large expatriate Korean communities and allowed North Korea to invade South Korea in 1950. As a result millions of Koreans were forcibly displaced into these countries. For example, for almost three generations, an estimated two million displaced Koreans have been living in China, mostly concentrated in the northeastern region. They identify themselves as Chosunjok (Korean-Chinese). Over the last several decades, many Korean-Chinese have been returning to Korea because of the improved political relations between Korea and China and because of job opportunities created by the Korea's growing economy. Koreans, by and large, however, have not embraced returning Korean-Chinese as equal members of their society. Instead, they are treated as second-class citizens and are often discriminated against, even within the walls of Korean churches.[3] I have often witnessed conflicts and tensions between Koreans and Korean-Chinese arising from a failure to appreciate each other's cultural differences. Despite efforts by the Korean government to implement foreigner-friendly policies, discrimination is still blatant not only in Korean society at large, but also in the churches. Furthermore, the churches typically overlook the potential importance of the Korean-Chinese in missions. The Korean-Chinese understand the context of two cultures; this understanding is their strength and it gives them a significant advantage

---

3. Min Kee Ha, *Shattering the Korean Dream: Korean Chinese Experiences in Seoul, Korea* (Ann Arbor, MI: UMI, 2001), 206–8.

in doing mission. The diaspora Koreans have a vital contribution to make, I believe, in helping Korean churches address cultural challenges in the mission field.

For many years, YFGC's main mission strategy has been focused on sending native Korean missionaries to foreign countries to share the Gospel and provide relief for medical and social needs of the people. With globalization, however, which puts a premium on cross-cultural leadership, YFGC now faces new challenges in its world mission initiatives. Missions in China, in particular, have suffered serious setbacks, which have been attributed to government policies on religion that prohibit foreigners from influencing Chinese churches. It is time now to empower and mobilize Korean-Chinese Christians residing in Korea for missionary service in China, instead of continuing to send only Korean nationals. Such a shift may lead to engagement opportunities that will bring about a new level of effectiveness for mission work in China. Unfortunately, however, the Korean church has failed to recognize the potential role that Korean-Chinese Christians can play in world missions. Instead of Korean-Chinese Christians being envisioned as valuable mission agents in the mission field, they have often gone unnoticed and underappreciated in the church.

In light of the significant needs and opportunities just identified, I undertook doctoral study at Fuller Theological Seminary's School of Intercultural Studies to pursue these issues. In what follows I first explain the character of my research, its methodology, and my research findings. I then present proposed guidelines for multicultural mentoring at YFGC. I hope that they will help churches elsewhere that desire to develop the type of cross-cultural mentoring program discussed here. I conclude with some more general reflections on the place of multicultural mentoring at YFGC.

METHODOLOGY

The purpose of my research was to identify culturally appropriate mentoring practices and to develop guidelines for equipping Korean-Chinese Christians and empowering them to become future mission agents. I also wished to prepare guidelines for training multicultural pastors who can strengthen the multifaceted ministries of YFGC itself. To guide my study, I drew on Robert Clinton's mentoring theories and Geert Hofstede's theory of cultural dimensions, seeking to identify both the key factors present in mentoring practices and the significant role cultural differences play in a multicultural context.[4]

The research methodology I used consisted primarily of semi-structured interviews and surveys. The research pool was composed of Koreans, Korean-Chinese, and Chinese within YFGC, and through the interviews I sought to elicit information regarding YFGC's present mentoring culture. Using a written list of questions as a guideline for the interviews, I sought to determine the understanding of mentoring relationships held by the Korean-Chinese, their feelings related to mentoring relationships, and the expectations they held for such relationships. The questions for the semi-structured interviews were designed to identify key factors that would align with Clinton's mentoring theory, specifically, mentoring type, dynamics, and balance. The interview data were coded and analyzed, based on the frequency of key terms used by the interviewees.

Clinton's mentoring theory encompasses nine mentoring types, mentoring dynamics, and mentoring balance. He, along with the collaboration of Paul Stanley and Richard Clinton, provides guidelines that are useful for mentoring of Christian ministers.[5] Of the approaches available for examining the mentoring practices of YFGC's multicultural ministry, I found his to be the most helpful.

I also found the concept of cultural distance—which has been used to examine differences between national cultures in their ideas of what is good, right, and needed—to be useful as my

---

4. See J. Robert Clinton and Richard Clinton, *The Mentor Handbook: Detailed Guidelines and Helps for Christian Mentors and Mentorees* (Altadena, CA: Barnabas Publishing, 1991); J. Robert Clinton, *The Making of a Leader* (Colorado Springs, CO: NavPress, 1988); J. Robert Clinton, "Cross-Cultural Use of Leadership Concepts," in *The Word among Us: Contextualizing Theology for Mission Today*, ed. Dean S. Gilliland (Dallas: Word, 1989), 183–98. For Hofstede, see Geert Hofstede and Michael Harris Bond, "The Confucius Connection: From Cultural Roots to Economic Growth," *Organizational Dynamics* 16, no. 4 (1988): 5–21; and Geert Hofstede, *Culture's Consequences: Comparing Values, Behaviors, Institutions, and Organizations across Nations* (Thousand Oaks, CA: Sage, 2011).

5. See Paul D. Stanley and J. Robert Clinton, *Connecting: The Mentoring Relationships You Need to Succeed in Life* (Colorado Springs, CO: NavPress, 1992).

research progressed. For this aspect of my research, I used Hofstede's cultural dimension theory. He defines culture as "the collective programming of the mind which distinguishes the members of one group or category of people from another" and advocates using a multidisciplinary approach to analyze the relationship of cross-cultural values.

The foundation for Hofstede's theory of cultural distance dimensions rests on his study of almost 116,000 questionnaires in twenty different languages from seventy-two countries. He was able to identify the following five basic problems faced by every culture:

- human and social inequality; relationship with authority
- dealing with the unknown future and uncertainty
- dealing with relationships between the individual and the group
- emotional roles between men and women
- focus on the future or the past

Different cultures attempt to solve these problems differently, based on their cultural values. Within different cultures, leadership, organization, and motivation are shaped by a cultural scale that represents the different cultures' solutions for these five problems. For Hofstede, five main cultural dimensions—which correlate with the five basic problems that all cultures face—determine differences in cultural values related to work. For my research, it was important for me to identify differences in cultural values related to work held by Koreans, Korean-Chinese, and Chinese. For this purpose I conducted a survey using the questionnaire found in Hofstede's Value Survey Module 2008 (Korean and Chinese versions). This survey is widely utilized to compare culturally influenced values of two or more countries. It provided a measure of the cultural distance in values between Koreans, Korean-Chinese, and Chinese. It gave a basis for calculating a cultural distance index, which enabled evaluation of the cultural differences in values among these three groups of people in YFGC. The responses to the survey were tabulated by computer along five dimensions (power distance, uncertainty avoidance, individualism versus collectivism, masculinity versus femininity, and long-term versus short-term orientation) with an index being produced for each dimension.

In evaluating the relationship between mentors and mentees, culture is a critical factor. In my experience, an underlying cause of ineffective and irrelevant mentoring practices is lack of cultural understanding. With a focus on multicultural mentoring, Plueddemann states, "Today's generation of leaders in the global church must learn new skills and be willing to discard some of the styles that made them so effective in monocultural leadership." He explains that "church leaders must learn to cooperate with people who have radically different assumptions about leadership."[6] From its inception until becoming the global church that it is today, YFGC has thrived under monocultural leadership. But rapid globalization and the recent influx of immigrants show that the challenge of the future will be to develop programs that effectively take into account the country's and ultimately the church's growing diversity.

RESEARCH FINDINGS

As I pursued doctoral research, the results of my investigations (referred to as "findings") provided many practical ideas and suggestions for implementing a more successful mentoring model for the Korean-Chinese in YFGC. The findings show that, in terms of mentoring practices, significant differences in understanding exist between the Koreans and the Korean-Chinese who are part of YFGC.[7] The most important finding was that the Korean-Chinese in YFGC want to be treated as equal partners in church ministries and activities. The group felt the presence of discrimination and prejudice in the programs and on the part of the church leaders. On the one hand, in such settings, mentors need to be educated so that they can appreciate differences of culture and values. This awareness will work to remove stereotypes and prejudices they may have against the Korean-Chinese. On the other hand, development of the Korean-Chinese's leadership skills and abilities through effective mentoring can provide them with the opportunity to

6. Plueddemann, *Leading across Cultures*, 11.

7. My research findings are summarized in table 8.1 at the end of this chapter.

become church leaders within YFGC. Serving as leaders would ultimately demonstrate that the Korean-Chinese have successfully attained a status equal to that of YFGC's Korean leaders.

According to Stanley and Clinton, a spiritual guide is "a godly, mature follower of Christ who shares knowledge, skills, and basic philosophy on what it means to increasingly realize Christ-likeness in all areas of life."[8] My research showed that the factor that most attracted Korean-Chinese in YFGC to seek a mentoring relationship was the opportunity to receive pastoral advice from older and more experienced leaders. They hoped to receive spiritual care, guidance, and counseling from these leaders.

The mentoring relationships most commonly desired by the Korean-Chinese are "Upward Mentoring" (from older and more experienced leaders) and "Internal Peer Mentoring." The Korean-Chinese expect to expand their potential through relationships with older and more mature Christians. Through internal peer mentoring, they seek mutual growth and accountability. But for internal peer mentoring, the Korean-Chinese prefer to have a mentoring relationship with a Korean rather than a Korean-Chinese.

My research also showed that the Korean-Chinese have a difficult time working with other Korean-Chinese because of their background as a cultural minority in China. Wariness or even a hostile attitude toward groups from other hometowns in China impacts the bond and loyalty among them while they are living in Korea. Therefore, individual care and attention are needed. Korean-Chinese are very independent decision-makers and prefer to have care and attention on an individual basis, versus in a group. This preference stems from their background of belonging to a minority culture in China and from the prejudice and discrimination they have faced in Korea.

The Power Distance Index score from the Hofstede survey shows that the Korean-Chinese have a tendency to believe that the quality of learning depends on two-way communication. They want their voices to be heard in the process of learning. They also tend to believe that a decentralized decision structure is better and more efficient and that hierarchy in organizations means an inequality of roles. This tendency may be an important obstacle that

8. Stanley and Clinton, *Connecting: The Mentoring Relationships You Need*, 65.

the Korean-Chinese can overcome by learning more about YFGC's leadership practices. Understanding YFGC's decision-making process (and how it came into being) may make problems with it less acute, even though YFGC's hierarchical approach may not be the Korean-Chinese leaders' preferred style of decision-making.

The Individualism Index (IDV) and the Long Term Orientation Index (LTO) scores show that the Korean-Chinese have a strong shame culture, with saving face or preserving one's reputation as an important virtue. In a mentoring relationship, respecting the mentee's honor and dignity is therefore important for establishing trust in the relationship. In my research the Korean-Chinese received low IDV scores, which is consistent with their having a strong sense of loyalty based on their hometown in China. In mentoring relationships, then, the mentor needs to understand the place of one's hometown in the culture of the mentees in order to ease tensions and defuse potential hostility among the mentees.

The findings also show that the Korean-Chinese want their leaders to recognize their work and performance in the church. They want more recognition and encouragement from their mentors, along with the chance to exercise more freedom within their ministry.

The authoritative and charismatic leadership style in YFGC is another obstacle to establishing a healthy mentor-mentee relationship. The Korean leaders need to be willing to acquire a cross-cultural understanding and to be flexible in developing communication skills that take account of the cultural differences of their Korean-Chinese mentees. The Korean-Chinese need to understand the Yoido church system and policies. Mentors need, at the same time, to understand their mentees' culture and values, something that is necessary if stereotypes and prejudices against the Korean-Chinese are to be removed. Quite simply, we at YFGC need to recognize and embrace the Korean-Chinese as members of *our* church.

For Korean-Chinese, individual mentoring is more effective than group mentoring. According to the Power Distance Index (PDI) and interview results, the Korean-Chinese are very independent decision-makers and prefer care and attention as individuals, not as a group. It is important to note that the Korean-Chinese have a difficult time working with Korean-Chinese who come from different hometowns in China. The Korean-Chinese do want to maintain a close relationship with YFGC Koreans and the pastors, particularly in face-to-face pastoral care, yet all mentors should be aware of this factor in their cultural background.

EIGHT MENTORING GUIDELINES
FOR THE KOREAN-CHINESE IN YFGC

As an outcome of my research, I have identified eight main guidelines to help mentoring the Korean-Chinese in YFGC, which can assist in developing curricula and programs.

1. Equal treatment for Korean-Chinese in the church. Removing stereotypes and prejudices against the Korean-Chinese will improve the mentoring relationship. Also, church activities and ministry opportunities should be communicated in the native languages of all members in order to provide all with an equal opportunity to participate and serve.

2. Expansion of the leadership skills of YFGC pastors. To improve mentoring relationships, Korean leaders need to acquire cross-cultural understanding and develop flexible communication skills that will be sensitive to the cultural differences of Korean-Chinese mentees. Also, Korean leaders need to provide an orientation to the mentees regarding YFGC's culture and organizational structure.

3. Provision of pastoral care for Korean-Chinese church members. The church needs to invest time and resources in developing culturally appropriate programs to train pastors who can provide pastoral care and advice to Korean-Chinese members.

4. Understanding of group dynamics. It is important to understand the differences between the younger and the older generations of Korean-Chinese in order to communicate more effectively regarding the respective interests and needs of these two groups.

5. Mentor training. Mentors need to be educated to understand the differences in culture and values between Koreans and Korean-Chinese, for the purpose of removing stereotypes and prejudices against the Korean-Chinese.

6. Mentee training. To improve the mentoring relationship, Korean-Chinese need to receive training regarding the church's organization hierarchy, policies, and decision-making culture.

7. Modifying the Pastoral Credential Program for the Korean-Chinese. This program should be modified to allow parts of the exam to be conducted in Chinese, as needed by the mentees.

8. Exposure to ministry. More open and direct interaction is needed between Korean-Chinese and Koreans in YFGC. To improve the mentoring relationship, it is important for the church to open more ministry opportunities to the Korean-Chinese in the church.

FINAL COMMENTS

Approximately 100 Korean-Chinese are currently members of YFGC. This number may seem insignificant in a church of 480,000 members, yet we believe that God is interested in working with small and marginalized groups of people to use them to their full potential. God sees a mustard seed, not just as a small and insignificant seed, but also as a big and precious tree that one day will produce abundant life (see Mark 4:31–32). God is glorified when we reach out to people who are unnoticed and underappreciated and empower them to bring God's kingdom into our midst. Furthermore, I believe that God has chosen the Korean-Chinese to carry out the next wave of missions in China.

YFGC has been blessed with a group of talented multicultural people who are ready to engage in new global challenges and opportunities. The church needs to pay more attention to these individuals, thoughtfully establishing a program to recruit, train, and groom them to take a leading role in world missions.

Compared to other Korean churches, YFGC's leadership style is unique. Because of the history of YFGC and the influences of Korean society, it is also complicated when compared to that of other Korean churches. I believe that YFGC will not easily adjust its monocultural authoritative leadership style, which has been very effective and, until recently, has led to successful church growth. It is unfortunate that the mentoring practices of the current YFGC leadership have so far proven to be ineffective in grooming cross-cultural leaders and in forming disciples who can be catalysts in the mission fields, which would move world missions to the next level. Globalization and multicultural trends of the twenty-first century, however, clearly demand that church leaders adopt new attitudes and teach new skills to enhance the abilities of this church's leaders.

Betsy Glanville has said, "We are challenged to see the image of God in the 'other' who is very different from 'me.'"[9] Embracing Korean-Chinese Christians in the manner that I have proposed in this chapter will, I believe, enrich our own understanding of who we are, giving us a new appreciation of God's great love for us. As disciples of Jesus, we need to value differences and promote diversity within the body of Christ so that we can learn from one another. It is my prayer that this research will help to enable change and to enhance the way leadership at YFGC is practiced from day to day so it can more significantly strengthen the worldwide body of Christ.[10]

<><><><><><><><><><><><><><><><><><><><><><><>

Table 8.1. Summary of Research Findings in YFGC's
Korean-Chinese Mentoring Relationships

Mentoring dynamics

The Korean-Chinese were attracted to the YFGC leaders because of their desire for spiritual care, guidance, counseling, coaching, and ministry opportunities. In China, the leaders in the Chinese house churches lacked systematic and formal theological training. The Korean-Chinese want to find their identity and vision from their spiritual guide at YFGC.

Korean-Chinese wish to grow in faith and gain ministry insight through face-to-face pastoral care from older and more experienced

9. Elizabeth Loutrel Glanville, "Missiological Reflections on Difference: Foundations in the Gospel of Luke," *Mission Studies* 26, no. 1 (2009): 73, doi: 10.1163/157338309X442308.

10. This chapter is based on research done for my doctoral dissertation, "The Development of Mentoring Practices Guidelines for Korean-Chinese in Yoido Full Gospel Church" (DIS diss., Fuller Theological Seminary, School of Intercultural Studies, 2016).

mentors rather than to be assigned to younger leaders. They want to receive internal peer mentoring with Korean leaders, not with the Korean-Chinese.

Korean-Chinese want to be treated as equals to other Korean church members in YFGC. They do not want to be automatically assigned to a special Korean-Chinese service. They want the same opportunities to receive training in leadership as Korean members have.

Korean-Chinese want to follow mentors who are fair and unprejudiced in their mentoring process, who do not unconsciously and habitually stereotype foreigners.

Korean-Chinese want their mentors to recognize their progress and success. They also want to receive encouragement and spiritual guidance from the Korean leaders. They want to receive leadership and ministry training from the mentor and eventually become leaders of the church, like the Koreans.

Mentoring obstacles

The lack of cross-cultural mentors who can provide sensitive pastoral care, teaching, and guidance to Korean-Chinese becomes a great challenge in developing mentoring relationships with Korean-Chinese in YFGC.

Korean-Chinese in YFGC harbor feelings of disappointment and resentment toward Korean church members because of a lack of support and acknowledgment from the church. They face double isolation as a minority group in China and again in Korea.

Mentors need to be educated regarding the differences of cultural understanding and values between Koreans and Korean-Chinese; they need to remove stereotypes and prejudice against Korean-Chinese.

Korean-Chinese have a difficult time adapting to the Korean church culture. They are often confused and frustrated with Korean church leaders when they ask for quick results and frequently change policies and systems. Nor do they fully understand the authoritative and paternalistic leadership style of YFGC.

The authoritative and charismatic leadership style becomes an obstacle to establishing mentor and mentee relationships. Mentors fail to acknowledge the differences in culture between Koreans and Korean-Chinese, and they impose Korean culture and values on the mentees.

Power distance factors

Korean-Chinese believe that a leader does not necessarily have significantly more power or authority than the followers do.

Korean-Chinese tend to believe that a decentralized decision structure is better and more efficient. They want to have an equal two-way communication and to be consulted on matters and contribute their ideas as equal members of the church.

Individualism factors

Korean-Chinese have a strong bond and loyalty among others from their hometown in China. They may display hostility toward people from other hometowns.

Korean-Chinese have a strong shame culture that pays great attention to the expectations and attentions of others. They want mentors to offer advice in culturally sensitive ways that do not emphasize shame.

Uncertainty avoidance factors

Korean-Chinese have anxiety and a desire to avoid uncertainty.

Korean-Chinese are resistant to change.

Masculinity factors

In comparison with Koreans, Korean-Chinese are more aggressive and expect strong leadership from their leaders.

Korean-Chinese are attracted to large organizations.

Korean-Chinese want their leaders to recognize their work and performance. They long for mentors to show them undivided attention and to maintain a keen interest in their progress and achievements.

Long-term orientation factors

Both Koreans and Korean-Chinese have a shame culture and value persistence and perseverance.

Response
to
"The Development
of Mentoring Practices"

Samuel K. Law

Much appreciation should go to Ildoo Kwon for his research on the relationship between indigenous Koreans and diaspora Koreans, specifically Korean-Chinese. Indeed, because I have a certain level of familiarity with the Korean-American community in Seattle, Washington, with Korean students at Asbury Theological Seminary, and with Korean and Korean-Chinese students in Singapore and Korean Singaporeans, I know that the conclusions he has reached and the recommendations that he makes apply well beyond the Korean-Chinese in question. For example, the challenges Korean-Chinese face in Korean churches are the same challenges faced by second-generation Korean leaders in Korea, as well as other second-generation Koreans in the Korean diaspora.[1] Hence, because of the significant global footprint of Korean corporations and as the number of Koreans in diaspora grows, Kwon's study will become increasingly important as globalization transforms Korean society and Korean churches worldwide.

The focus of my response will be to further expand on Kwon's conclusions. First, as Kwon's research is descriptive, using Hof-

1. See Hyung Keun Choi, "Missional Conversion and Transformation in the Context of the Korean Protestant Church," *Mission Studies* 34, no 1 (2017): 53–77; and Sung Hyun Lee, "Marginality as Coerced Liminality," in *Realizing the America of Our Hearts: Theological Voices of Asian Americans*, ed. Fumitaka Matsuoka and Eleazar S. Fernandez (St. Louis: Chalice Press, 2003), 11–28.

stede's parameter for cultural differences, I wish to take the next step and propose a prescriptive response using the lens of Sherwood Lingenfelter's model of cultural adaptation. Second, since the experience of the Korean church with Korean diaspora believers is not unique, I seek to strengthen Kwon's prescriptive conclusions by expanding the context. Here I draw on lessons gained from the experience of the overseas Chinese church with Chinese diaspora believers. Third, I offer support for Kwon's conclusion that bicultural Koreans provide opportunities for Korean churches to engage in transformation to a new globalized Korean identity, that is, a "glocal" identity. As such, the intent of this response is to set Kwon's study in the larger global context and to bring the experiences of the global church into Korea's local context.

INTEGRATING MULTIPLE CULTURES

First, while Hofstede's work allows us to understand the differences and similarities across cultures, it is descriptive and, consequently, static; in reality, cultural interaction is dynamic and inevitably results in the transformation of all cultures involved.[2] All parties mutually enlarge their identities, becoming more than the sum of their parts when considered separately.

Sherwood Lingenfelter and Marvin Mayer use the incarnational model of Christ to describe this transformative process. They describe Christ's incarnation as a 200 percent entity, with Christ being 100 percent God and 100 percent human.[3] Neither nature is diminished by the other, and both natures are fully incorporated in the one person Jesus Christ. "Jesus" and "Christ" are integral to the Son of God.

Lingenfelter and Mayer argue that this model is also valid in cultural interactions, for the incarnational process is both descriptive and prescriptive. They acknowledge, however, that, because of human limitations, we can never be 100 percent in each culture; hence, they challenge us to strive to be at least 75 percent in each culture.[4] In other words, unlike the situation modeled by Jesus

2. Michael A. Rynkiewich, "The World in My Parish: Rethinking the Standard Missiological Model," *Missiology* 30, no. 3 (2002): 301.

3. Sherwood Lingenfelter and Marvin Mayer, *Ministering Cross-Culturally: An Incarnational Model for Personal Relationships* (Grand Rapids: Baker Academic, 2016), 4.

4. Ibid., 5.

Christ, the interaction will inevitably change us such that we are no longer 100 percent what we were originally; but equally true, we are augmented by the new culture. The result is that we become more—150 percent (i.e., 2 × 75 percent)—than we could ever have been if we had remained solely within our own culture. In the sacrifice of self-submission to the other, we are given the opportunity to expand the boundaries of our identity.

Furthermore, this process is not necessarily just two-sided; individuals can successfully integrate multiple cultures.[5] As each new culture becomes part of an individual, that individual becomes adept in transitioning and thriving in each.[6] Hence, it is possible for someone to become 225 percent (3 × 75 percent), 300 percent (4 × 75 percent), and more. Cultural adaptation should therefore not be seen as a weakness that is to be marginalized but as a strength that empowers one to move with near native proficiency in multiple cultures.

Consider, for example, Singapore's multicultural environment. Many Singaporeans are comfortable working in a multitude of Western and Asian contexts. Unlike monocultural ethnic groups that have a tendency to isolate themselves when in a foreign culture, Singaporeans can thrive in a variety of cultures. Limitations apply, naturally, for over time even Singaporeans inevitably develop a hunger for their beloved chicken rice and durian. Nevertheless, their multicultural identity enables them to move freely across cultures and excel in a multitude of contexts.[7]

People who are Korean-Chinese are therefore not to be viewed as being any less Korean, but in our globalized world, Korean-Chinese, as well as Korean-Americans, Chinese-Americans, Japanese-Brazilians, and so forth, are transnational. As 150-percent —or more—people, they are ambassadors who serve as bridges between their homelands and their adopted lands.

5. Fenggang Yang, *Chinese Christians in America: Conversion, Assimilation, and Adhesive Identities* (University Park: Pennsylvania State Univ. Press, 1999), 184.

6. Ted C. Lewellen, *The Anthropology of Globalization: Cultural Anthropology Enters the Twenty-First Century* (Westport, CT: Bergin & Garvey, 2002), 159.

7. Thiow Kong Ti and Edward S. K. Ti, *Singapore and Asia: Celebrating Globalisation and an Emerging Post-Modern Asian Civilisation* (Singapore: Partridge, 2014), 291.

LEARNING FROM CHINESE MULTICULTURAL CHURCHES

Second, just as Kwon's research contributes to the understanding of this widespread global experience—for the experience of the Korean-Chinese is shared by many other cultural groups—so the experience of other groups, including the Chinese overseas, may be enlightening for Koreans. Lessons of the Chinese church may be instructive for the Korean church as it wrestles with its relationship with Korean-Chinese.

It should be noted that Chinese are not necessarily monocultural in the way that Koreans are, for they have a multitude of coherent identities. A Chinese person may speak Cantonese, Hokkien, or Teochew, among other dialects or languages, and may differ from other Chinese in cultural aspects such as cuisine, social interaction, and even values. Nevertheless, the "Chinese" can be said to have a distinct cultural identity.

In the North American context, research has shown that multicultural Chinese churches, those that include multiple dialects, thrive better than do monocultural (single-dialect or singlelanguage) churches.[8] Furthermore, some cases in which monocultural Chinese churches have resisted including other cultural groups has led to both stagnation and conflict within the churches, often resulting in church splits.

Not only have multicultural, multilingual Chinese churches grown more and been more stable over time, but also bicultural leaders (i.e., leaders with backgrounds in multiple cultures) tend to be more effective as senior pastors and more able to mediate church conflicts, strengthen unity, and serve as catalysts to lead churches through change.[9]

For these reasons I would expand Kwon's recommendation for Koreans to mentor Korean-Chinese by making such relationships bidirectional. In other words, Korean churches should not only mentor Korean-Chinese, but they should also include the goal of having Korean-Chinese mentoring themselves, which can enable them to be more responsive to the impact of globalization. In interacting with Korean-Chinese, Korean churches will dis-

8. Samuel K. Law, *Revitalizing Missions on the Cusp of Change: Complex Systems Science Mazeways for Mission Theory amid Twenty-First-Century Realities* (Wilmore, KY: Emeth Press, 2016), 114.

9. Ibid., 106.

cover that the multicultural approach is but one small facet of a much broader trend. In reality, the issue is not merely one of mentorship, but more broadly of adaptation. In the case of Korean youth, the failure of Korean churches to embrace a multicultural identity has already resulted in significant losses in church attendance. Between 2004 and 2014, the percentage of Korean young adults in their twenties attending Korean churches dropped from 40 to 31 percent and from 45 to 37 percent for those in their thirties—together constituting the steepest declines in the overall percentage of Koreans attending Korean churches (from 54 to 50 percent).[10] Perhaps, in a way similar to the experience of the Chinese church, integration of bicultural leaders can enable Korean churches to adapt more readily to the inevitable cultural transformation being brought by globalization.

MOVING TOWARD A NEW "GLOCAL" KOREAN IDENTITY

Third, interactions with multicultural Koreans can serve to catalyze so far unrealized opportunities in which Korean churches can establish transformative processes and allow new identities to emerge. As Korean churches embrace the Korean-Chinese, for example, the expansion of relationships that will occur allows both groups to experience significant change, a process through which their identity is first deconstructed, then reconstructed.[11] As Kevin Vanhoozer argues, the best way to understand one's own culture is through the lens of a foreign culture.[12] As indigenous Koreans and Korean-Chinese mutually mentor each other, growing in expressing the Christlike attitudes of Philippians 2:1–11 in liminality, they experience the unique blessing of practicing the love of Christ in both cultures.[13]

Not only can such experiences help Korean churches to prepare for inevitable—and ongoing—transformation by globalization, but also—as Kwon argues—Korean-Chinese can help the large Korean missionary force to more fruitfully fulfill its calling to

10. Choi, "Missional Conversion and Transformation," 56.

11. Lee, "Marginality as Coerced Liminality," 11.

12. Kevin J. Vanhoozer, "One Rule to Rule Them All? Theological Method in an Era of World Christianity," in *Globalizing Theology: Belief and Practice in an Era of World Christianity*, ed. Craig Ott and Harold A. Netland (Grand Rapids: Baker Book House, 2006), 123.

13. Lingenfelter and Mayer, *Ministering Cross-Culturally*, xiii.

bridge cultures as ambassadors of the Gospel. The ability and skills embodied in newly bicultural Koreans can help equip Korean churches to better navigate the ever-rising tide of globalization.

CONCLUSION

In summary, Kwon's chapter has addressed a critical issue facing the Korean church. As with all societies in the twenty-first century, Korean society is increasingly becoming multicultural.[14] Hence, how the Korean church responds to the Korean-Chinese will indicate how it will respond to the inevitable changes brought by globalization. Rather than pursuing a unidirectional, hierarchical process of mentoring Korean-Chinese, Korean churches must be willing to expand the process reciprocally, allowing themselves to receive mentoring by Korean-Chinese and other Koreans with multiple compound identities, especially those found among its own young people. Together, such a transformative experience can be shared, thus bringing the cultural identities of Korean Christians to be 150 percent— or more. Such 150-percent missionaries can only enhance the impact of the Korean missionary force worldwide.

14 . Craig Ott, "Conclusion: Globalizing Theology," in Ott and Netland, *Globalizing Theology*, 309.

9

A Surprising Mission for Exiles
(Jeremiah 29:1–14)

Christopher J. H. Wright

How can we live as the people of God in the midst of a society and culture that dismiss or despise us at best, and may hate and persecute us at worst? We find ourselves asking this question in the contemporary world, but it is far from a modern query. Jews and Christians have faced it all through their history. For the people of Judah who found themselves in exile in Babylon it was agonizingly real. Indeed, "How can we live at all?" was what many of them wondered.[1]

But the biggest question that faced the exiles was, Where is the Lord? Where is Yahweh, the God of Israel, the God of the exodus, the God of the conquest, the God of David and all the promises made to him? Where is our God in the midst of such catastrophe? Does God have anything to say to his defeated, disgraced, dislocated, and despairing people?

To answer such questions, Jeremiah wrote the exiles a letter. Originally this letter was addressed to the first group of exiles, who left with Jehoiachin (in 597 BC), but its message became all the more relevant and hope-filled after the fall of Jerusalem (in 587 BC), as it was read and reflected upon by all the exiles who now faced their bleak future in Babylon. It was a letter that spoke into

1. This reflection on Jeremiah 29 is a slightly edited and adapted version of a chapter in my commentary *The Message of Jeremiah: Grace in the End* (Nottingham: InterVarsity Press, 2014), 289–97. The chapter in that book is itself based on many occasions when I have preached Jeremiah's letter.

the trauma and desperation of a people whose world had fallen apart. It is a letter that has profound meaning for those who find themselves in a similar situation today.

A SURPRISING NEW PERSPECTIVE:
FROM REFUGEES TO RESIDENTS (VV. 1–6)

Who was responsible for the Israelites being in exile in a foreign land? These verses give us two answers. On the one hand, the narrative introduction speaks about all "the other people *Nebuchadnezzar* had carried into exile from Jerusalem to Babylon" (v. 1).[2] But on the other hand, in the text of the letter we read God's own account: "all those *I* carried into exile from Jerusalem to Babylon" (v. 4). And this assertion is repeated in verses 7 and 14. So who did it? Nebuchadnezzar or God? The answer of course is both.

At the level of human history, what any observer would have seen was the army of Nebuchadnezzar carrying out his orders. There was terrible violence, suffering, cruelty, destruction, death, and loss—all the work of evil men doing evil deeds for which they themselves bore responsibility. Nebuchadnezzar did it.

But at another level, what the eye of the prophet saw (as he had seen and spoken of for years) was the hand of God behind the hammer of Nebuchadnezzar. It was God who had brought the Babylonians as agents of his judgment upon his recalcitrant people—as he had done in previous centuries through other imperial armies. God did it—or rather, to use Jeremiah's terms, Nebuchadnezzar did it, but functioning as Yahweh's servant.

This paradox was something many Israelites could not accept, no matter how long Jeremiah had prepared them for it. A more plausible explanation seemed to be that Yahweh had simply deserted them (asserted in Isa. 40:27), or that Yahweh had grown old and tired and had met his match at last—the gods of Babylon had defeated him. Perhaps they would be better off choosing other gods—as their wives had urged for years (see Jer. 44). But no, Jeremiah insists, *Israel* had been defeated and *Jerusalem* had been destroyed, but Yahweh, the sovereign Lord God of all creation (Jer. 27), was not defeated. On the contrary Yahweh was

2. Unless noted otherwise, biblical quotations in this chapter are from the New International Version.

as fully in control of events—even such shattering events—as he ever had been in their long history.

Ancient history is one thing. It would have been as easy for the Israelites as it is for us to look back to great events in centuries past and to affirm them as "the mighty acts of the LORD" (Ps. 106:2). Their psalms were full of that kind of celebration. But the present moment is something else. It is far harder to perceive and affirm the sovereignty of God in current events, when you are right up close to the puzzle and panic of them.

It is especially puzzling when God seems to be undoing all he has been doing up to this point. The repeated phrase "from Jerusalem to Babylon" (vv. 1, 4) has an ominous feeling that makes it more than mere geography. The whole history of the Old Testament had gone in the opposite direction: from the land of Babel (Gen. 11) to Jerusalem; from God's calling Abraham out of the land of Babylon to God's establishing his people in Jerusalem and Judea—and God's putting his name and his temple there. That was the flow of sacred history: to Jerusalem. But now it seems that the plot is unraveling. God has pressed the rewind button, and history is going backward.

I remember as a child the shock and horror adults expressed in talking about how the Chinese Communist Party had expelled all foreign missionaries in the early 1950s. It was hard to understand why God allowed it. Some thought it would be the end of the church and Christian mission in that country. Now, nearly seventy years later, there are more Christians in church every Sunday in China than in all of western Europe, including Britain. Sometimes we can see God's sovereignty only as we look back on history. The challenge, as it was for the exiles, was to discern God's sovereignty in the midst of the confusion of the present.

For the exiles, the question seemed to be, How could God reverse his plans? Did he no longer care about his promise to Abraham or his promise to bless all nations through the people of Abraham? How could that mission continue if God had hurled the people back to square one—back in fact to the very land Abraham had left behind?

Israel did indeed have a continuing Abrahamic mission, even in exile, as we shall see in a moment. But before the exiles could begin to contemplate that task, they needed to accept that it was by God's own sovereign will that they were now where they were.

And if that was a surprising perspective, they needed to get over the surprise and start getting used to Babylon. What had happened was under God's control, and it was not about to end soon. With this prophetic perspective, Jeremiah tells the exiles to settle down in Babylon for a stay that will last several generations (vv. 5–6). The language of these verses works in two ways.

First, such a perspective *turns refugees into residents*. The exiles were being told to accept where they were and to be there with God, who had put them there. They should not entertain hopes or belief in wild prophecies of an early return, which would keep them forever unsettled. They needed to settle into Babylon as their new home. Babylon would not be the nation's *permanent* home. But it was their *present* home, where the next few generations would reside. Prepare for it. Get on with the normality of building homes, farms, and families. Life goes on.

Second, the language of planting, eating, marrying, having children and grandchildren, and especially the instruction to "increase in number" (vv. 5–6), resonates strongly with Genesis. It is the language both of creation and of Abrahamic promise. For Israel in exile, there was the opportunity of a fresh creational start. And the God who blessed creation with fruitfulness and growth had promised the same to Abraham.[3] The language of increase also echoes Exodus 1:7, with the implication that, if the people continued to grow (after the decimation of 587 BC) even in a foreign land, God's redemption from this latter-day bondage lay ahead in a new exodus.

So the exiles must settle down, adapt and adjust to life in Babylon, and yet remain the people of Yahweh. One group who took this advice seriously was Daniel and his three friends. They were among the earliest of the exiles, taken probably when they were boys. There is no way of knowing whether they ever heard the letter of Jeremiah being read out, though it is perfectly possible that they did. At any rate, they behaved in a manner consistent with its advice. In Daniel 1 we see them accepting three aspects of Babylonian life and culture—Babylonian names, education, and jobs—before they draw a line and refuse to accept table dependence on the king (their refusal probably symbolizing total covenant loyalty). They accepted and adapted to where God

3. Genesis 1:26–28; 12:1–3; 17:3–6; 22:17.

had put them but remained faithful to God when an irreconcilable conflict of loyalties arose.

A SURPRISING NEW MISSION:
FROM MOURNERS TO MISSIONARIES (V. 7)

Spare a thought for the person who had to read out this letter publicly to the exiled community, especially when he reached verse 7, which is sensationally unexpected: "Also, seek the peace and prosperity of the city to which I have carried you into exile. Pray to the LORD for it, because if it prospers, you too will prosper." Imagine the angry response to such words among people in the early throes of being captives of war in a foreign, enemy land.

"Surely," they may have protested, "this letter has been intercepted by the Babylonian censor and altered. We know which city we should be praying for, and it most assuredly isn't Babylon. 'Pray for the peace of *Jerusalem*!' (Ps. 122:6). We know what we want for Babylon, and it certainly isn't peace."

> Daughter Babylon, doomed to destruction,
>   happy is the one who repays you
>   according to what you have done to us.
> Happy is the one who seizes your infants
>   and dashes them against the rocks
>   [—just as you did to ours!]. (Ps. 137:8–9)

Psalm 137 shows the wretched ugliness of the mood of the exiles on first arriving in Babylon, with their longings for home and their understandable desire for vengeance on their enemies. And here is this insufferable prophet from Jerusalem telling them to seek the welfare of Babylon and to pray for it! What an insult to their situation!

It was probably hard enough for the exiles to imagine that they could pray to Yahweh *in* Babylon, let alone that they should pray to him *for* Babylon. It must have seemed impossible—theologically, emotionally, and politically. But Jeremiah insists that this is the task before them. Once they could accept the perspective and the advice of verses 4–6 and had settled down as residents in Babylon, then they had an ongoing mission there. It was the Abrahamic mission of being the model and means of blessing to the nations. Such a responsibility turned mourners into missionaries. They should seek the *shalom* of their neighbors in Babylon, care for their welfare, and be agents of constructive peace and well-being in the communities in which they settled.

"But they are our enemies! They destroyed our city, slaughtered members of our families, and dragged us a thousand miles away to this pagan land."

"Pray for them," insists Jeremiah. "Seek their welfare." This word of Jeremiah to the exiles is possibly the closest we come in the Old Testament to the words of Jesus, spoken to people who felt like exiles in their own land under the heel of Roman occupation: "I tell you, love your enemies and pray for those who persecute you" (Matt. 5:44).

One might interpret Jeremiah's second phrase ("because if it prospers, you too will prosper") as self-interest. But it is no more so than one of the reasons Paul gives in 1 Timothy 2:1–2, where he instructs Christians to pray for pagan authorities. Jeremiah believed in the power of prayer (or rather in the power of the God who hears prayer). It is somewhat ironic that here the prophet who had been forbidden to pray for his own people in their own land instructs those same people to pray for their enemies in a foreign land.

Jeremiah's instruction makes several significant assumptions:

- that God could hear and answer prayer anywhere on earth;
- that God would hear prayer on behalf of those who were not his own people (see Solomon's prayer, 1 Kings 8:41–43, for a similar thought);
- that God could and would act for the blessing and welfare of the Babylonians if the Israelites would pray for them;
- that even in captivity, God's people could exercise a ministry that moves the muscles of God's providence in the world.

These are profoundly missional assumptions that should undergird our own sense of responsibility for the people around us, wherever we find ourselves, willingly or otherwise. Prayer is always a missional responsibility.

Once again, one wonders whether Daniel was among those who had heard this command and obeyed it throughout his life's work. We know he prayed three times a day (Dan. 6:10). Was Nebuchadnezzar at the top of his prayer list? If so, it would help explain Daniel's surprising reaction to Nebuchadnezzar's second dream, about the great tree that was chopped down and the man who would eat grass like an ox (Dan. 4). Suddenly Daniel realized that the dream was about Nebuchadnezzar himself. This man, who had destroyed Daniel's city and torn him from his home in childhood, was himself about to be chopped down! Should Daniel not have rejoiced that he had lived to see the day of his enemy's downfall? Surprisingly not. He was so upset he could not speak, and when eventually the king insisted on hearing the interpretation, Daniel offered him some advice about how to avoid the impending judgment. One gets the distinct impression that Daniel had come to have respect and even affection for his Babylonian monarch. Was that not the natural result of praying for him and seeking his welfare, as Jeremiah instructed? It is hard to go on hating someone when you pray for him or her every day.

Jeremiah's instructions here form part of a wider biblical tradition that God's people can serve God by serving wider society in various occupations. The stories of Joseph, Daniel, Nehemiah, and even Esther are Old Testament examples. Erastus, Corinth's director of public works (Rom. 16:23), is one such example in the New Testament. All forms of legitimate service can be ways to "seek the welfare of the city." Paul would have included them in what he generalized as "doing good" (Gal. 6:9)—a concept that did not merely mean being nice, but included concrete social benefaction, contributing to the public good of all citizens. It is a part of biblical teaching that is sadly neglected in many churches.[4]

Is there enough emphasis in Christian churches, especially in their preaching, on the Bible's teaching on good citizenship? Jeremiah told the exiles to "seek the welfare of the city" where they lived (v. 7 NRSV). Paul told Christian believers not only to pay their taxes but also to be "doing good"—a word that was commonly used for public benefactors, people who contributed to society. How can we give greater value and incentive to one another to be a blessing to the wider community in practical ways?

4. I have discussed more fully the Bible's teaching on what it means for God's people to exercise their mission in the public square of the "secular" world in *The Mission of God's People: A Biblical Theology of the Church's Mission* (Grand Rapids: Zondervan, 2010), 222–43.

Could it be that Jeremiah gave the instruction of verse 7 because he had a rose-tinted view of Babylon? Did he imagine that Babylon itself had somehow become God's favorite spot on earth, so that the Israelites could enjoy living there forever? Not at all. We know exactly what Jeremiah thought of Babylon. In another diplomatic postbag Jeremiah sent the massive oracle against Babylon that we now have in chapters 50 and 51. Jeremiah was under no illusions. Babylon itself stood under God's judgment, and its time would come. But this truth applied to all nations and all the earth, *and it still does*. The role of God's people in the midst of such reality is still to pray for and seek the welfare of the people they live among, even when we are aware that people in every nation and culture stand under God's judgment.

A SURPRISING FUTURE: FROM VICTIMS TO VISIONARIES (VV. 8–14)

The immediate future must be faced, and it was not what the prophets and diviners among the exiles were telling them (vv. 8–9). The exiles' dreams of a swift return were nothing but lies, and they were no more sent by God than Hananiah had been (Jer. 28). Their ending (29:20–23) would be even worse than his. No, the exiles were in Babylon for the long haul, commensurate with the long-term sins for which they were now suffering judgment. Such words from Jeremiah about the present reality bore no surprise at all. They are what he had been saying for decades.

So his next words about the future are truly and gloriously unexpected and surprising beyond belief. It would not be quick, but it would be certain. Babylon their oppressor, Babylon seemingly supreme and unrivaled, the greatest power in the world, Babylon about which Nebuchadnezzar boasted, "Is not this the great Babylon I have built as the royal residence, by my mighty power and for the glory of my majesty?" (Dan. 4:30)—Babylon's time would come, and within seventy years Babylon would be past history. A similar fate was, and is, in store for all human empires, ancient and modern.

And then what? Then God would "come to you and fulfill my good promise" (v. 10; literally, "establish upon you my *good word*"). The future was "good," for God said so. And verse 11 goes on to spell out just how good it would be. It was not merely that God would eventually bring the people back to their land, but that his overall plans for them were now plans of *shalom* and not *ra'ah* ("evil"), to give them "hope and a future" (29:11; this verse stands as a direct reversal of 18:11). And all of these plans are underlined by the emphatic "*I know*" of verse 11. This promise is not some remote possibility, but something securely determined in and by the mind of God. Jeremiah 29:11 probably ranks as one of the most quoted and most claimed promises of the Bible. It is found on countless text calendars, pretty pictures, and sacred ornaments. It is rightly trusted as a very precious word of assurance from God.

But do we take note of its context? This verse is a *surprising* word of hope to a people who stood under God's judgment. It is not a glib happy feeling: "God's going to be nice to us all, me especially." We should note that the "you" of verse 11 is plural, not individual; the statement is primarily a promise to the people as a whole. This declaration is the robust affirmation that, even in and through the fires of judgment, there can be hope in the grace and goodness of God. That is God's ultimate plan and purpose. The promise stands firm, but it does not preclude or neutralize judgment. Rather, it presupposes but transcends judgment.

What, then, should be the response to such a surprising word of amazing grace? Not gleeful celebration. Not mere relief: "Well, that's all right then; everything will turn out fine. Let's have a party!" Rather, the people are called to respond to the restoring grace of God with renewed prayer and seeking him (vv. 12–14). The language here is taken straight from Deuteronomy 4:29–31, which had anticipated just such a return to Yahweh in the wake of the judgment of exile and had promised that, when Israel would thus return with all their heart and soul, they would run into the arms of the God of forgiving grace. "For the LORD your God is a merciful God; he will not abandon or destroy you or forget the covenant with your ancestors, which he confirmed to them by oath" (Deut. 4:31).

We should notice the Gospel of these verses, contained in the repeated indicative verbs: "then you will . . . and I will." The movement of the people's heart to seek God is itself a gift of God's grace, even while it is at the same time the necessary condition in which they can receive his grace.[5] God's grace gives what God demands.

---

5. This understanding is the same as God's interpretation of the "good figs" (24:5–7), to which this passage is closely linked.

Similarly here, the statements "you will seek me and find me" (v. 13) and "I will be found by you" (v. 14) are both promissory statements. They tell us that it is God's supreme will to be found and known, which is the only source of his people's life and blessing. Their hope lies in God's willingness to be found, not in Israel's ability to search.

This time we know that Daniel was aware of Jeremiah's words, for Daniel tells us that, at some point in his study of Jeremiah's prophecies, he understood that the "seventy years" for Babylon must be coming to an end soon.[6] And what was his reaction? Not to call in his friends for celebration, but to respond exactly as Jeremiah 29:12–14 portrayed—by seeking God in prayer and confession, appealing to God to act in forgiving and restoring grace, as God had said he would (Dan. 9:1–19).

Here, then, was a surprising hope for the future that turned victims into visionaries. It enabled the exiles to look up and look forward and believe. They were not going to get the quick fix the false prophets were dreaming of. But they could trust that God would be true to his promise and that there was a future for the coming generations of God's people which (as we now know) would eventually be a future and hope for the nations.

The message of the whole letter could turn refugees, mourners, and victims into resident missionary visionaries. The challenge is: Which are we going to be?

6. Daniel's statement indicates that some edited text of Jeremiah's words was present among the exiles in Babylon, even though Jeremiah himself ended up in Egypt.

10

Somali Refugees Received by Mennonite Congregations in Pennsylvania, US: Two Case Studies

Peter M. Sensenig

In early 1953 the first Protestant missionaries to begin Christian work in Somalia disembarked in Mogadishu, the capital city.[1] At the time there was no dock, so the missionaries were precariously lowered from the ship in a basket, much like Paul escaping from Damascus (Acts 9:25). These missionaries hailed from a tight-knit community of Mennonites in Pennsylvania, a community awakened by a fresh calling to carry the Good News of Jesus to the ends of the earth.[2]

When they arrived, however, the Mennonites discovered that the ends of the earth were like home in surprising ways. Traditional Somali and European Mennonite cultures both emphasize genealogies, dependence on cows or camels, and oral tradition.[3] At the same time, the cultural differences were immense, not least the fact that the Mennonite Christians found themselves in a context with a strong Islamic identity from time immemorial.

---

1. For the sake of confidentiality, the names of the congregations and individuals involved in these case studies, both Somali and North American, have been changed or initialized.

2. Peter M. Sensenig, *Peace Clan: Mennonite Peacemaking in Somalia* (Eugene, OR: Pickwick Publications, 2016), 3.

3. Bertha Beachy, "My Pilgrimage in Mission," *International Bulletin of Missionary Research* 35 (2011): 208–12.

The Mennonites were welcomed as guests in their Somali home, where they set up schools and clinics that shaped generations of Somalis. The road was not smooth, however; the Mennonite Mission was dismissed from the country on several occasions, only to be welcomed back when the political winds had shifted once again. This precarious presence continued through national independence, war, dictatorship, famine, martyrdom, and nationalization of the Mennonite schools. But over time a remarkable rapport was built that lasts to the present day. In Toronto, Atlanta, or Hargeisa one meets Somalis who studied in the Mennonite schools and speak affectionately of their Mennonite teachers; some even refer to themselves as Mennonite Muslims.[4]

Within forty years of the Mennonite arrival in Somalia, however, the roles of guests and hosts were suddenly reversed. Civil war deposed the dictator Mohamed Siad Barre, and competing warlords threw the country into chaos. This crisis, combined with devastating famine and foreign military intervention, displaced many thousands of Somalis in the early 1990s. When Somali families began to arrive in Pennsylvania and were received there by Mennonite individuals and congregations, it was thus the continuation of a longer story.

This chapter addresses the experience of two Mennonite congregations in Pennsylvania in receiving Somali Bantu refugee families. After considering the immigration dynamics of Somalis resettling in eastern United States, I address the two cases in turn. Finally, I reflect on what wisdom can be gleaned from the experiences of these two congregations. What lessons might other congregations who are receiving immigrant families take from their example?

STAGES OF SHOCK:
SOMALI REFUGEES IN THE UNITED STATES

Refugees generally cycle through four stages as they learn to acclimate to their new homes. In stage 1, they begin with anticipation and excitement, dreaming of a good life without worry and pain. Then the reality of adjustment sets in (stage 2), followed by culture shock and the trauma of resettlement, which can produce depres-

4. Sensenig, *Peace Clan*, xxi.

sion and anxiety (stage 3). Many refugees finally find ways to cope and accept their new life (stage 4), but at any point in their journey, they can be thrown back into earlier stages.[5]

It is difficult for Westerners to grasp the reality of relocating as a displaced person from the Horn of Africa to a North American context. But recognition of these stages of adjustment can provide a first glimpse into the challenges, and welcoming teams from both Mennonite congregations could observe the refugee families dealing with each of these stages. For example, reality obtrudes the moment a person picks up a phone. One member of a welcoming team commented, "We defeat non-English speakers quite quickly when public institutions are involved. When you place a call you never get a person, but a message directing you what to do."[6] The result very often is neglected medical appointments, prescriptions, and school activities.

Both Somali families in these case studies are Bantu in ethnicity, meaning that they are descendants of ethnic tribes from the southeast coast of Africa who were captured in the nineteenth-century Arab slave trade and sold in Somalia. Bantu Somalis are ethnically and culturally distinct from the majority Somali clans and are marginalized in significant ways as a result of their slave status, including denial of access to education and other basic needs. As Danielle Mayfield puts it, "The Somali Bantu are a people who have been kicked in the teeth by the world. . . . When the violence broke out between the warring tribes and clans in Somalia, the Bantu were the first to feel shocks—much of their farming and agriculture was taken, or burned, unspeakable acts were done to the women and children, and so many men were killed."[7]

When the background of trauma and oppression, including a significant amount of time spent in refugee camps, is added to the stress of navigating a new culture, language, and climate, it is no surprise that refugee families seek out communities of people like themselves. Relocation to a large Somali community is espe-

5. Danielle L. Mayfield, "Preface: Stateless Wanderers," in *Assimilate or Go Home: Notes from a Failed Missionary on Rediscovering Faith,* Kindle edition (New York: HarperCollins, 2016), location 79.

6. R.H. (Oak Creek Welcoming Team), email to author, November 15, 2016.

7. Mayfield, "Anticipation and Excitement," in *Assimilate or Go Home,* location 442.

cially likely for those lacking education or other advantages.[8] Certain cities such as Minneapolis, Columbus (Ohio), and Seattle have become hubs for Somali immigrants, but other locations where Somalis are received by resettlement organizations and churches often serve only as stops along the way, as the nomadic spirit and desire for a critical mass of fellow Somalis lead refugees to keep moving. For that reason, the number of Somalis in the Pennsylvania community where these case studies occurred fluctuates between several dozen and over a hundred.[9]

Although the area lacks the critical mass found elsewhere, Somali families continue to come to eastern Pennsylvania in large part because of the work of Church World Service (CWS), a cooperative ministry engaged in refugee resettlement. The preferred modus operandi of CWS is to connect refugee families with congregations that can facilitate their adjustment to the new context. CWS faces an overwhelming number of refugees and thus can provide support to new families for only three months. Furthermore, the services CWS provides are distributed among all the clients, limiting the attention any given family unit receives. Families are given an orientation of three to five days upon arrival, which is acutely insufficient for navigating a new social system, and in some cases language translation is unavailable.[10]

In short, churches play a vital role for refugee families in need of help. CWS notes a huge difference in the rate of successful acclimation between families that have church sponsorship and those that do not. Without a church sponsor, families often miss appointments, find it harder to get employment, and are more likely to move away from the area.

SPRINGFIELD MENNONITE CHURCH

In 1967 a Mennonite doctor working in Somalia delivered a baby boy named Suleiman. Born into a Christian Bantu family connected to Mennonite missionaries, Suleiman walked the risky path of living as a person of a minority faith in his home context. He worked

---

8. B.W. (CWS volunteer), Skype interview by author, September 30, 2016.

9. I.L. and M.E.L. (Springfield Welcoming Team), Skype interview by author, October 9, 2016.

10. Suleiman Juba, Skype interview by author, September 25, 2016.

with Mennonite organizations to resettle Somali Bantu families in Tanzania during the civil war in the 1990s. After receiving death threats because of his faith, by 2010 Suleiman could not continue to live in either Somalia or Kenya.

The doctor who delivered Suleiman, now retired and living in Pennsylvania and having had no connection to Suleiman since his birth, caught word from a Mennonite mission agency that Suleiman and his family were in danger and needed to relocate. The doctor's congregation, Springfield Mennonite Church, sprang into action to form a welcoming team. According to a CWS worker, the team essentially took over the task of resettling the family.[11]

Springfield has a history of sponsoring refugee resettlement, and the welcoming team was well prepared when the Juba family of four arrived in December 2012. The team found a house for the Jubas, furnished it with help from the congregation, drove the family to appointments, and made school arrangements for the children. The church included resettlement expenses in their budget and paid the family's rent for a year. Whenever household items were needed, church members quickly responded, and one person even donated a small car. As one welcoming team member put it, "With Suleiman's family, we were on 24/7 call if there was a problem."[12]

One major factor in the successful acclimation of the Juba family was, as Christians, their being able to plug directly into congregational life from the outset. Although Suleiman's wife knew no English upon arrival, the family began attending Sunday services, participating in a Sunday school class and other church events. They also participated in monthly gatherings to pray for Somalia. They found the church and the pastoral leadership to be warmly intentional about fostering diversity, and as a result CWS and another resettlement agency often refer interested refugee families to Springfield.[13]

The relationship has developed into a dynamic of mutuality. While the congregation has provided a wide range of logistical help, from driving lessons to a teen mentoring program, the Juba family has been an important part of congregational revitaliza-

11. B.W., interview.
12. I.L. and M.E.L., interview.
13. Ibid.

tion. Suleiman agrees: "Many people did not know about Somalis or had negative views, but now they have learned from us who Somalis are. And they are now awaiting any Somali family; they keep asking me if I know anyone who is coming."[14]

WIDENING THE MINISTRY CIRCLE: SULEIMAN JUBA

Finding work is a major challenge for refugees, and for Suleiman the difficulty was compounded by the fact that he is without one of his legs. His ability in Somali, Swahili, English, and Bantu Somali languages did provide him with some part-time translation work, but from the moment he arrived in the United States he experienced the pull of other work to be done. Suleiman says, "I felt the Holy Spirit guiding me to be helpful, because the way that I experienced being a refugee, I knew others would have the same experience. I saw how Somali families are struggling. It's informal, but CWS calls me to help with particular families."[15]

Springfield donated a van, and before long Suleiman had a driver's license and was transporting Somali refugees to medical and school appointments, Somali stores, and wherever they needed to go. Suddenly Suleiman, as a refugee sponsored by Springfield Mennonite Church, was the liaison between the Somali refugee community and their new host culture. Even after Suleiman found a job at Goodwill, he continued to serve his Somali compatriots with his van.

Suleiman's role in the community goes far beyond logistics; he observes Somali refugees in all stages of adjustment. Dreams of an easy life in the United States are quickly shattered and—without someone like Suleiman to answer questions and provide encouragement—confusion, depression, and anxiety become powerful traps. Furthermore, as an ambassador between the communities, Suleiman is often privy to the ways that deeply held assumptions are challenged. He observes, "Muslim families have told me, 'What we believed before was that Christians are our enemies. But when we came to the United States that idea was washed out; now we know that they are not enemies but are helpful to us.'" For some Somali Muslims, interacting with Christians is a stretch, let alone setting foot in a church. Yet in spite of

14. Juba, interview.
15. Ibid.

this barrier, Suleiman has Muslim friends who join him on occasion in attending Springfield's services.[16]

Just as Suleiman's ministry extends to the Somali Muslim community in Pennsylvania, it also extends to Somali Christians around the world. He has regular contact with Somali believers in different corners of the globe, some of whom he has never met in person. A member of Springfield's welcoming team observes, "Suleiman's contact with believers around the world by phone and Internet constitutes a worldwide fellowship."[17] In turn, he keeps Springfield abreast of what is happening in Somalia. Through Suleiman, Springfield's simple but intentional ministry to one family has impacted both the local community and individuals around the world. Suleiman has received a powerful calling and ministry to Somali immigrants, to whom he commits much time and energy. He attributes this calling directly to Jesus, advising Christian congregations, "Let churches follow the way Jesus said himself: to receive those who are new, to not discriminate. I learned from Springfield how to do that."[18]

OAK CREEK MENNONITE CHURCH

When the escalating Syrian crisis hit the news in 2015, it sparked an interest in being involved with refugees in another Mennonite church in the area, Oak Creek.[19] Although several members of the congregation had served in Somalia, Oak Creek expected to sponsor a Syrian family. But when CWS connected them with a Somali Bantu family, the response was, "This is who God brought us!" [20] The church formed a welcoming committee consisting of eight to ten members with experience in different areas: medical, financial, and educational. One member of the welcoming team observes, "For those of us not called to go overseas, this is a way to be the hands and feet of Jesus here at home."[21]

16. Ibid.

17. I.L. and M.E.L., interview.

18. Juba, interview.

19. S.S. (pastor, Oak Creek Mennonite Church), email to author, November 15, 2016.

20. Oak Creek Mennonite Church Welcoming Team, Skype interview by author, November 13, 2016.

21. K.H. (Oak Creek Welcoming Team), email to author, November 16, 2016.

Suleiman was delighted to discover that he knew the family, who came from a neighboring village in Somalia. He says, "I almost cried, and I got in touch with them in the refugee camp. I met them at the airport, and they were overjoyed."[22] From the moment of their arrival in March 2016, the Gosha family had both a cultural interpreter in Suleiman and a sponsoring congregation in Oak Creek.

Like Springfield, Oak Creek pulled together as a congregation to set up a house for the Gosha family before they arrived. On the very first Sunday that the welcoming team posted a sign-up sheet with all kinds of household needs, everything was provided. The family continues to practice their Islamic faith, but several months after their arrival they attended one Sunday service at Oak Creek in order to introduce themselves and to express their gratitude from the pulpit. Only at that point did the Gosha family fully realize that the people helping them had been a church and not just a group of random people.[23] The family later participated in the church's community-day event.

For two weeks after the Gosha family's arrival, the welcoming team came to their home every day. While CWS made all the initial connections for medical appointments and for meeting all the government requirements, the team did virtually everything else for them.[24] After the initial move, the team's involvement with the family settled into three categories. First, a team member stopped in regularly to spend time with the three preteen daughters—playing games, cooking, visiting local sites, helping with schoolwork or English skills.[25] Second, the team helped with medical and school-related appointments. Third, one member worked with the father of the family on banking, budgeting, and paying bills. The goal was to foster more self-sufficiency; as the family became more independent, the number of team members required to keep up with appointments decreased.[26]

22. Juba, interview.

23. K.H., email.

24. Ibid.

25. A.G. (Oak Creek Welcoming Team), email to author, November 14, 2016.

26. L.N. (Oak Creek Welcoming Team), email to author, November 14, 2016.

In spite of the caring sponsorship of a church, the path to acclimation is a rocky one. The Oak Creek welcoming team has observed the Gosha family in all stages of adjustment.

Anticipation and excitement. Eagerness to jump in and get started with everything (school, work, buying and driving a car) makes it difficult to takes things in the required order. The oldest son expressed frustration that they had been in the United States for three weeks and none of them had a job yet.[27] The family purchased a car and promptly got into an accident, though no one had a driver's license or insurance. Furthermore, some other Somali refugees have given skewed information about life in the United States.[28]

Culture shock. The sheer force of difference hits one almost immediately: the weather, grocery stores full of unknown foods, the medical and educational systems, ideas about time management, differences in health and medicine, and perhaps most important, the language.[29]

Depression and anxiety. Anxiety and depression can arise at any time, from any direction. The trauma of the experiences in the refugee camp follows them (such as violent reports and images and animal attacks), yet they are reluctant, or have no venue, to work through the trauma. A team member relates, "It took months before we started hearing bits of their story. [The oldest son] talked about how nice it was to have law and order in the United States, and that there were not bribes for the police to protect people."[30] Also contributing to anxiety is the undercurrent of anti-Muslim sentiment, tensions within the Somali immigrant community, and the plethora of factors conspiring against the urban poor: overpriced and unhealthy food, housing issues, and the appeal of unaffordable products.[31]

27. Ibid.

28. A.G., email.

29. A.K.-G. (Oak Creek Welcoming Team), email to author, November 21, 2016.

30. L.N., email.

31. R.H., email.

Coping and acceptance. Resettlement to the US has been difficult for the Gosha family, and it remains to be seen how they will find ways to cope with their new life. Certainly one of the hardest points was when one of the daughters disappeared, only to emerge in another part of the country with a man. When this happened, according to Suleiman, the family surely would have left the area had it not been for the church's support; "Oak Creek has been with them 100 percent. They said to me, 'We cannot believe that Christians did this for us.' I really thank God for churches' doing this."[32]

DISCOVERIES

In assessing the experience of these two Mennonite congregations, we can identify four practices that foster greater effectiveness and accountability, which may be of aid to other congregations engaged in receiving refugees.

Do your homework. Members of a sponsoring congregation will have much greater success in relating to refugees if they take time to learn as much as possible about their cultural, historical, and religious mores. In this case, to have some familiarity with Somali culture would clue one in to the nomadic history ("Don't take it personally if they decide to move to another state," a CWS worker says),[33] to issues of trauma and mental health related to conflict and resettlement, and to religious practices such as avoiding pork, eating halal, and celebrations.[34]

Distribute the tasks. According to the pastor at Oak Creek, the strength of this endeavor is that it emerged organically from within the congregation, neither relying solely on pastoral leadership nor resting on one person's shoulders. Rather, the team consists of people who have taken leadership on behalf of the church.[35] Another strength is that the welcoming team has a diverse set of skills and interests, including a medically trained person, a social worker, and someone who spent years in East Africa. Likewise, the team

32. Juba, interview.
33. B.W., email to author, October 2, 2016.
34. I.L. and M.E.L., interview.
35. S.S., email.

includes men and women of various ages, who are better able to relate to different members of the family.[36] Although often impossible, ideally a team would include someone with some ability in one of the languages of Somalia, especially if a family has little or no English upon arrival.[37]

Be patient. When one bears in mind what a huge transition it is to resettle as refugees—and even more when it is not just an individual but a family system—then the necessity of patience becomes clear. It is crucial to check expectations, both on the part of refugees and on the part of those welcoming them, and to celebrate even the smallest of accomplishments. For example, to try to shift an entire way of thinking to the US American concept of time is unreasonable. But to take one appointment at a time and to celebrate each success reduces frustration on all sides.[38]

One team member at Oak Creek notes, "There are so many things for families to learn, and we still don't know all of the things they misunderstand. There was confusion about turning lights on (they often sat in very dark rooms) or how to open the windows when it was very hot outside. We have just tried to teach and explain as different issues arise, yet try to be respectful of their culture and ability to make decisions about things."[39]

Define mission broadly. Both churches responded to an impulse of hospitality to strangers emerging from their congregational DNA and from their Christian faith. Convinced of the intrinsic value of welcoming refugees, they were not driven by ulterior motives of proselytization. Indeed, CWS makes it very clear when orienting church sponsors that proselytizing is not acceptable, and recognizing the vulnerable status of refugees makes it easy to see the logic of this policy. In the case of the Juba family, the family integrated into the life of the congregation. But Muslim families will likely not be interested in attending church, and many Somalis are quite suspicious about any church activity. Muslim Somali families have reported attempts to prosely-

36. A.G., email.
37. K.H., email.
38. R.H., email.
39. L.N., email.

tize them, including receiving evangelistic videos and invitations to Sunday school. A former CWS worker comments, "It's not recommended to give them Christian material until you have known them for a while and have discussed whether they would be interested."[40]

CONCLUSION

The challenge of determining what it looks like to witness faithfully to Jesus is one that every congregation does and should wrestle with. The fact that relating to a refugee family complicates those questions is actually a blessing, because simple acts of friendship take on much greater significance. The small moments of sharing life can turn out to be the most profound ministry of all. After years of relating to Somali Bantu refugees, Mayfield observes, "The older I get, the more I realize that the ministries I once thought so trivial I now think are the most radical."[41]

What emerges is conversion—of hearts, of vision, of congregational life—as a genuine sense of mutuality develops. A team member at Springfield comments, "We are *not* to demonstrate a patronizing spirit toward the refugees coming to us needing help . . . but to develop a relationship which is a *mutual blessing* in which we value and respect their lives and culture and what they can teach us."[42] This mutuality is not a fantastic ideal, but a reality that can actually be observed in the lives of individuals and churches. An Oak Creek welcoming team member who spent years in East Africa states, "It's one of the ways we can be the face of Christ and pay forward God's generosity and Christ's love to us. One of the persons on the team commented that he wanted to be stretched and he has been. For me, it's been fun watching persons who have had few of the enriching experiences of living among others of another culture begin to see things a bit differently, through this family's eyes."[43] Transformed vision is a gift beyond measure.

40. B.W., interview.

41. Mayfield, "Stabilization," in *Assimilate or Go Home*, location 2515.

42. M.E.L. (Springfield Welcoming Team), email to author, October 9, 2016.

43. A.K.-G., email.

QUESTIONS FOR REFLECTION

1. How did the Mennonite history in Somalia prepare Mennonite congregations to receive Somali refugees in Pennsylvania?

2. What kinds of help could Suleiman offer to his fellow Somali refugees that the Mennonite churches could not?

3. Is it necessary for refugees to pass through the four stages of acclimation to their new context (anticipation and excitement, reality check, depression and anxiety, coping and accepting)? What role might churches have in helping refugees adjust well?

4. Why is *patience* important in receiving refugees as a congregation?

5. What does it mean that refugees and receiving congregations are a *mutual blessing* to one another?

Response
to
"Somali Refugees Received by Mennonite Congregations in Pennsylvania, US"

Calvin W. Choi

The torrent of Syrian refugees in recent years has made it clear that refugees no longer represent a local or regional issue, but a global crisis. In 2015 the world witnessed the heart-gripping image of a three-year-old Syrian boy whose dead body had washed ashore on a Turkish beach. Six years of ongoing war and internal conflicts not only have brought chaos and made visible unspeakable atrocities committed by an irresponsible regime but have also left the nation depleted and hopeless.

One nation that understands the Syrian people's frustration and that has experienced similar disastrous consequences is Somalia. A predominantly Islamic nation, Somalia has been torn by perpetual war, internal tribal conflicts, and increasing terrorist activity. In 2015 the Somali diaspora was estimated to number two million, 55 percent of whom were refugees.[1] Many other Somalis are displaced within the country. Having children fall behind in school and lose family members to violence and suffering has, unfortunately, become a norm.

The majority of Somali refugees now live in neighboring countries on the African continent. But the spread of the refugee

1. Phillip Conner and Jens Manuel Krogstad, "Five Facts about the Global Somali Diaspora," Pew Research Center, June 1, 2016, www.pewresearch.org/fact-tank/2016/06/01/5-facts-about-the-global-somali-diaspora.

crisis to the Western world has left people there bitterly divided. While some resist the presence of refugees and others simply tolerate them, many are looking for ways to cooperate with and accommodate refugees. Given the geopolitical climate, the question we want to ponder is what the biblical response is to this crisis. What role can local congregations play in aiding refugees and helping to alleviate their plight? In doing so, can they not simply be a resource for humanitarian aid but ultimately promote the mission and the Gospel of Christ? Two Mennonite churches in Pennsylvania believe congregations can accomplish the latter.

Peter Sensenig has helpfully looked into the joys experienced and challenges faced by these two Mennonite churches as they have served Somali refugee families. Given the growing anti-immigration and anti-Muslim sentiment within the Western world, Sensenig's chapter offers a timely word on intentional steps congregations can take to embrace the globalizing communities all around them—and thus to carry out Christ's mission.

PARTNERSHIP

Undertaking refugee resettlement is a daunting task. For this reason, many churches avoid involving themselves in such missions, thinking such a project to be beyond their ability to manage. It is worth noting, however, the example provided by the two churches on which Sensenig reports. Even with a history of over six decades of missions in Somalia, they choose to synergize with Church World Service (CWS), a mission agency engaged in refugee resettlement. Sometimes churches want to "do it alone" with their own resources and network of missionaries and are reluctant to be confined by policy restrictions imposed by mission agencies. Conversely, mission agencies often view local churches as a source of finance and prayer and are less enthusiastic about receiving input regarding the implementation of programs and initiatives. The two churches and CWS offer a model for mutual cooperation, drawing on the strengths and resources of each. It is encouraging to know, as Sensenig observes, that church sponsorship tends to lead to a higher success rate in refugees' overall adjustment to their new culture and environment.

Refugee families are given orientation by CWS, though Sensenig notes that the orientation seems to be inadequate. It would have been interesting to have an overview of the content of this orientation. Were the welcoming teams also provided orientation, or were they involved in the refugees' orientation process, and if so, to what extent? What orientation is given to sponsoring churches' welcoming teams when refugee families are not Christian but of another faith?

INTEGRATION IS A TWO-WAY STREET

It may be easy to look at the case of Springfield Mennonite Church (SMC) and attribute its success simply to the fact that Suleiman's family was Christian. While true, something significant was at play that must not be overlooked—and it had to do with the word *intentional*. SMC did well in understanding that integration is a two-way street. Aid givers can easily feel superior and advantaged, thereby causing aid recipients to feel inferior and disadvantaged. In such situations, relationships can only go in one direction.

Sensenig notes that the pastoral team intentionally took steps to foster diversity by creating an atmosphere of mutuality. They intentionally undertook to increase their cultural awareness and to understand better those who were culturally different from themselves. Such an attitude of intentionality builds a community of mutual care, respect, and support. Instead of an attitude of "we are here to help you," it fosters an outlook of "we are here to get to know each other and learn from each other." Such intentionality seeks the posture of humility by seeking the interest of others (see Phil. 2:4). SMC did not view Suleiman's family merely as aid recipients; it also recognized and utilized their assets and strengths and empowered him to serve other Somali refugee families in the community. The relationship was not a one-way street, but a two-way passage, built on mutual respect and love.

For Oak Creek Mennonite Church (OCMC), acclimation of the Gosha family did not go as smoothly. OCMC was aware that the goal was not conversion to Christianity, and they carried out their responsibilities for the family promptly. Their conscientiousness was admirable, but I cautiously wonder whether OCMC had been well informed and was fully ready for the Somali Muslim family. Sensenig asserts that OCMC's goal was to "foster more self-sufficiency; as the family became more independent, the number of team members required to keep up with appointments decreased" (158). Having grown up in the Middle East, I understand that non-Westerners can sometimes view Westerners as outsiders who have no genuine interest in neighboring people's affairs. Westerners can be perceived as persons who wish to do no more than fulfill their duty and move on. Many Muslims, in contrast, are community oriented. They place a higher emphasis on, and derive more meaning from, relationships. Often much sharing and listening is required before getting to the first point you wish to talk about. A ride to the grocery store, school, or hospital may leave a good impression, but that impression wanes quickly if a genuine relationship has not been established.

Just as refugee families pass through the four stages of acclimation that Sensenig mentions—moving from anticipation/excitement to culture shock, to depression and anxiety, and finally to achieving coping and acceptance—sponsoring churches are susceptible to a similar cycle. A sponsoring church may receive a refugee family with great enthusiasm. When expectations between a refugee family and a sponsoring church are not met, the result can be discontent, disappointment, and misunderstanding on both sides. A sponsoring church, however, may still feel obliged to cope with the situation by at least fulfilling its duty. Formally, the mission may be accomplished, but without genuine interest and engagement between the two parties. Understanding that integration is a two-way street is critical for the refugee family, as well as for the sponsoring church.

GOING BEYOND "ASSIMILATE OR GO HOME"

How can we encourage churches and inspire them to engage in receiving refugees? In view of what Sensenig writes, two thoughts come to mind: We are all refugees, and Be intentional. The former is attitudinal; the latter, practical.

We are all refugees. People often think that the church would be the last place in which to find racial tension. Unfortunately, the reality is different. In their well-researched study of congregations, Michael Emerson and Christian Smith point out that racial division has been a perennial problem within evangelical churches.[2] We all have inclinations toward ethnic pride and ethnocentrism.

---

2. Michael O. Emerson and Christian Smith, *Divided by Faith: Evangelical Religion and the Problem of Race in America* (Oxford: Oxford Univ. Press, 2000), 170–72.

In the Bible, the term "refugee" is synonymous with the word "alien." Abraham is regarded as both a refugee and an alien. The Israelites were aliens/refugees in the wilderness, as well as during the exilic period. Peter calls Christians aliens/refugees (1 Pet. 1:1; 2:11). According to Scripture, refugees consist of two types—those who take refuge in God and those who take refuge in the world. God's refugees are called to good works to give glory to the Father in heaven (Matt. 5:16). When we are in a position of giving aid, however, it is tempting to view ourselves as above others and to have the attitude of "assimilate or go home." As aid givers, we may find it too easy to assume that we are able to impose our way of thinking and expect conformity. The acknowledgment that we are all refugees is an important step in supplanting such an attitude of pride and prejudice with one of humility, marked by counting others more significant than ourselves (Phil. 2:3–4).

Be intentional. Making an intentional effort to get to know refugees and to build relationships with them is key. Running errands for them is great, but it may not necessarily translate into building relationships. Getting to know people's culture and family history, learning their past heartaches and hardships, taking time to listen to the story of their journey, holding special events to inform the community of the needs of the refugees, setting aside opportunities to recognize and celebrate their strengths and attributes, and involving them so they can contribute their talents are all part of the process of building relationships. Jesus did not sit down and immediately tell the woman at Sychar that she needed to be saved. Only after he had gotten to know her past did he begin to reveal himself to her.

As eager as someone might be to proselytize those of another faith, the priority is to imprint in them the love of Christ as visibly as possible by building relationships in deeds and words; the Gospel is always shared best when it is made visible first. Our deeds of love may not yield an immediate harvest, but they will never be forgotten. Intentional love shared in hardship leaves a lasting impact.

CONCLUSION

Failure to meet the needs of refugees has become a global crisis. For their part, churches have two options: to look the other way or to seize the opportunity to fulfill God's mission. While the church is not called to resolve the refugee crisis, the two Mennonite churches of which Sensenig writes challenge the global church by demonstrating how congregations can be involved in global missions locally. Through their experience these churches provide helpful insights for churches undertaking such a missional task. By their example, they summon congregations to look beyond themselves and to offer an openhearted response to an urgent crisis of our time.

11

Overseas Filipino Workers: Unknown Heroes of the Kingdom of God

Samuel Lee

Whether in Amsterdam or Barcelona, Kuwait or Riyadh, Singapore or Seoul, New York or Quebec, meeting Filipinos is unavoidable. Over the past twenty-three years, I have had the privilege of working with Filipinos, who are among the most devoted and passionate people I have encountered throughout my ministry.

The number of overseas Filipino workers (OFWs) equals about 10 percent of the total Philippine population of 103 million people. According to the Philippine Overseas Employment Administration, in 2013 there were 10,238,614 OFWs employed in 191 nations.[1] It is possible that the current numbers might be even higher. These OFWs have been contributing to the economic well-being of the Philippines; in 2016 they sent US$29.7 billion back to the Philippines, making it the world's third largest recipient of remittances, according to the World Bank.[2] That is, the Philippines exports labor, and its overall economy benefits from the resulting remittances.

1. Philippine Overseas Employment Administration, "Stock Estimate of Overseas Filipinos as of December 2013," www.cfo.gov.ph/images /stories/pdf/StockEstimate2013.pdf.

2. World Bank Group, *Migration and Remittances Factbook 2016*, 3rd ed. (Washington, DC: World Bank, 2016), http://siteresources.wor ldbank.org/INTPROSPECTS/Resources/334934-1199807908806/454902 5-1450455807487/Factbookpart1.pdf, 29.

These overseas Filipinos work in various labor sectors: administration and management, clerical, sales, service, agriculture, production, and, finally, professional, technical, and related areas.[3] The motivation for OFWs going abroad varies, though the search for economic gain is paramount. Many hope to earn more income in order to better support their families and loved ones; others are hoping to cover education expenses for their children, settle debts, or pay for medical treatment for an ill family member. This complex journey toward economic happiness, however, also has its drawbacks. First, skilled workers are going abroad instead of contributing directly to the development of the Philippines. On the societal level, the situation becomes much more complex; children raised without parents tend to exhibit more mental illness than children born in secure family settings with parents in the home. Furthermore, families that depend on remittances tend to work less, which is a significant factor hindering the government's efforts to develop the country.[4]

On a personal level, some OFWs end up in debt because of the huge sums of money they have to pay for placement agents to arrange for their journeys. Workplace difficulties, contract abuses by employers, and sexual harassment are some of the horrible new realities that OFWs may face abroad, especially in Middle Eastern countries. Finally, some of these OFWs end up working illegally, which makes them vulnerable to all kinds of abuse.

It is exactly amid such challenges that faith and church begin to play an important role. Despite the hardships that OFWs face, some of them become passionate for God, leading them to become active in evangelism, social action, and care for both their fellow countrymen and the people in their host nation.

---

3. Jodesz Gavilan, "What You Need to Know about Overseas Filipino Workers," *Rappler*, December 19, 2015, www.rappler.com/newsbreak/iq/114549-overseas-filipino-workers-facts-figures.

4. Kriengsak Chareonwongsak, "Advantages and Disadvantages of the Philippines Labour Export Policy," www.kriengsak.com/Advantages%20and%20Disadvantages%20of%20the%20Philippines%20Labour%20Export%20Policy.

FILIPINOS AND THE JESUS CHRIST
FOUNDATION CHURCH

I sketch here the story of Jesus Christ Foundation (JCF) Church, which is relevant for understanding more completely the story of OFW believers worldwide.[5] I planted JCF Church in 1994 in a suburb of Amsterdam. Since then, the work has grown to Cyprus, Lebanon, Philippines, Ghana, and South Africa.

When Filipinos attended JCF church for the first time, I had no way of knowing that they would come to play an important role in the church. I will never forget an experience I had as a young pastor preaching to an audience that included some migrant Filipinos. After I had preached a sermon on John 14:2, a Filipina approached me with a startling question: "Pastor, how about right now—do you have a room for me?" She was referring to my text ("My Father's house has many rooms; if that were not so, would I have told you that I am going there to prepare a place for you?" NIV). As an undocumented (illegal) Christian who had lost her contract, this woman was desperately in need of a house and a job. She needed to hide, and there was nowhere for her to do so. Eventually, our church members helped her to find a suitable place to stay.

Another needy Filipino woman was Lorie, who left her country because of the illness of her son. She first worked in Singapore, then left to work in the Netherlands to provide medical care for her son, who was dying from cancer. In Amsterdam she found her way to JCF. Her son eventually died, but even after twenty years had passed, Lorie was still an undocumented migrant trying to make ends meet by doing domestic work while she continued to send money home for her other son. I will never forget the time our church family was having a fellowship meal in a brother's house. Lorie's phone rang, but as soon as she answered it, she fell to the floor with a scream. Many of us panicked, not knowing what was happening, but we quickly learned that it was her husband giving her the sad news that their second son, nineteen years old, had been murdered at a basketball court by a gang that happened to pick on him. There in that tragic moment, she was faced with a new dilemma: if she went back to the Philippines, she might never be able to

5. See Jesus Christ Foundation, www.jcfchurch.com.

return, because she was undocumented, and then she would lose her job and her ability to feed the rest of the family. But if she remained, she would not be able to bury her son. Eventually, she decided to stay in the Netherlands for a couple of years, after which she did return to the Philippines. Despite her grief, Lorie never stopped worshiping the Lord and maintaining a testimony that touched many people's lives. Indeed, her story was covered on national television, where she glorified the Lord before an audience of thousands.

THE WITNESS OF OVERSEAS FILIPINO WORKERS

The former national director of the Philippine Missions Association, Rey Taniajura, makes a distinction between missions and incidental missions as these terms relate to the OFWs: *missions* are "activities engaged in by Christians [with the intent] to fulfil the Great Commission mandate expressed in Matthew 28:19–20," and *incidental missions* refer to "activities done by Christians in the furtherance of the Great Commission mandate which are occurring merely by chance or without intention or plan."[6] Though outsiders may tend to assume that Christian OFWs fall under the category of incidental missions, in many cases OFWs have in fact organized themselves in the form of independent churches and fellowships that may very well fit the definition of missions as described below. They may not look like missionaries, however, for they have no tie with established mission agencies.

In advancing this thesis for consideration, I am not claiming to be presenting here a comprehensive social-scientific analysis of the mission practices of OFWs. Rather, my comments are a reflection and a personal report of what I have observed as a pastor and sociologist over the past nearly quarter century. I am convinced that the Philippines is a strategic nation within global Christianity because of the expression of Christ's love and the spread of Christ's message through the OFWs to the nations in which they live and work. I offer this report as a testimony to the work of God through these Filipinos as they are scattered throughout the world.

6. Rey Taniajura, "Incidental Mission: Philippine Case Study; 'Moving the OFW Missions Phenomenon from Incidental to Intentional,'" www.scribd.com/document/348663520/incidental-missions.

As the number of OFWs increased in our JCF church, I observed the following three major realities concerning the scope of their Christian witness:

- *mission:* Filipinos became marketplace evangelists.
- *community:* Filipinos became active in social networking.
- *social justice:* Filipinos became active in justice movements.

Filipinos as marketplace missionaries. The OFWs who practice their faith are the modern-day Daniels, Mordecais, Esthers, and servants of Naaman. Many of these Filipino migrants are God's chosen instruments to witness to the nations that host them. These marketplace missionaries are typically not salaried or supported by a mission agency; rather, they share the Gospel in the course of practicing their profession.

The OFWs, especially those working in the household sector, remind me of Naaman's maidservant in 2 Kings 5:1–10. In the eyes of Naaman, an important military leader, his maidservant was merely a domestic worker, but it turned out that she had the only answer to his problem; he was suffering from leprosy. She directed him to meet Elisha, the prophet in Israel, whose God was able to heal him from his dreaded disease.

Today, thousands of OFWs are active in household service in the Middle East, Asia, and Europe. Many of these Filipinos—as well as other migrants—are telling their employers, neighbors, and colleagues that only Jesus Christ can heal them and that he will do so when they surrender their lives to him. They play a role similar to the one that Naaman's maidservant played in his life. In the Netherlands, there is a sister from the Philippines who cleans houses, but because of her faith and her devotion to the Lord, many of her employers seek her advice and prayers. At one point she herself was ill and needed an operation, and several of her employers got together to raise funds to cover her costs, so great was her impact on their lives.

The influence of OFWs includes the Muslim world—even, to a certain extent, in Saudi Arabia, which ordinary missionaries or evangelists may not enter. Many OFWs who practice their faith there, however, have been arrested—and some have even been executed—because it is forbidden to evangelize in Saudi Arabia.

Cases of enforced Islamization of OFWs in Saudi Arabia have been reported. The OFWs often have no choice if they want to keep their jobs, though some have refused conversion even under pressure.[7] In September 2010 a Filipino nurse died in the hospital in Riyadh after being raped and left to die. Local Christians believe that she was attacked because she refused to convert to Islam.[8] Although OFWs cannot openly share the Gospel in Saudi Arabia, the situation is different in Kuwait. There, OFWs sometimes find openings for conversation and discussion with their employers about matters of faith.

There are five JCF churches in Cyprus, which consist all together of about 150 women and only one man: Carlos, the pastor of the church. Together with his copastor-wife, Imelda, and their daughter, Natasha, they have been serving the Lord there for twenty years. I met Carlos and Imelda two decades ago when I visited Cyprus for the first time, not knowing that one day they would become the pastors of the JCF churches on the island. Both Carlos and Imelda have secular jobs, while at the same time pastoring a vibrant Filipino community. Many in JCF churches are domestic workers and au pairs who come to Cyprus for work with contracts that generally last only four years. After four years, some renew their contracts, but most either return to the Philippines or find contracts in other nations. During these four years in Cyprus, though, they are trained in biblical studies offered through our Bible school, and if they have a pastoral calling upon their lives after graduating, they are ordained as pastors and go through an internship within the JCF church branches. Most of them become active in the local churches or establish a new chapter of JCF when they return home or go to another country. So far, JCF Cyprus has trained more than fifty women in this school, of whom at least fifteen have been ordained. Pastors from Cyprus have gone to Lebanon, where with OFWs there they have planted JCF Lebanon, a church that collaborates with other evangelical churches in Lebanon.

7. Santosh Digal, "Christian Filipino Migrants Forced to Convert to Islam," *AsiaNews.it*, January 28, 2010, www.asianews.it/news-en/Christian-Filipino-migrants-forced-to-convert-to-Islam-17478.html.

8. John L. Allen Jr., *The Global War on Christians: Dispatches from the Front Lines of Anti-Christian Persecution* (New York: Image, 2016).

Another aspect of OFWs is their prayer for the influential people in society. Since most OFWs work for prominent and wealthy segments of the population, they have access to ministers, businessmen, ambassadors, artists, and athletes. On one notable day, OFWs in Cyprus, including Pastor Carlos, gathered to pray for the president of Cyprus, encouraging him in his election campaign. I believe the story of JCF Church in Cyprus is not unusual; most Filipino churches, whether evangelical, Pentecostal, Charismatic, or Catholic, have a similar interest in interacting spiritually with the people in their circles.

Filipinos and community. Whether they worship at a non-Filipino church, such as a JCF Church, or in a congregation composed of Filipino expatriates, OFWs create their own networks to support their fellow countrymen, especially newcomers who have just arrived from the Philippines. For instance, the JCF Church in Amsterdam includes a group called the JCF Filipino Community. This group makes sure that help is available, for example, when a new au pair arrives in the Netherlands and asks for assistance. Whether the newcomer needs a house, a room, or a job, the network already in place is prepared to help with the need. This help is not limited to Filipinos; it is occasionally extended as well to brothers and sisters from Ghana or other places. A good example of this assistance is the Filipino church practice of supporting a fund for paying off the debts of fellow Filipinos. Often, the amounts involved have been in the thousands of euros. By means of such a community fund, which is supervised by the pastors, massive debts can be paid off at once and the persons in debt will pay back the money to the community fund without any interest. At the same time, the persons in debt must sign an ethical and spiritual agreement to manage their finances properly, under the mentorship of the pastor and the team.

Filipinos and social justice. For the past fifteen years, I have been involved in the Commission for Filipino Migrant Workers (CFMW), a nonreligious NGO supporting the rights of OFWs and those from other nations. JCF Church in Amsterdam offered a platform for CFMW, Trusted Migrants, and other such organizations to educate and empower domestic workers in the Netherlands. Being an undocumented immigrant is a very difficult experience. But even the thousands of OFWs who do have the proper documents and labor contract often undergo violation of their rights. I have conducted various interviews with Filipino sisters concerning their labor rights, and what they have shared is often most disheartening. For example, a Christian sister who lives in a European country told me that her employer's dog has its own air-conditioned room, yet she sleeps in a basement without air conditioning. When she complained, her employer threatened to send her back to the Philippines. In another case, a Filipino worker was raped by her employer and left lying in the street, wondering where to go. Filipino brothers and sisters took her in and gave her shelter; after a yearlong process of inner healing and counseling, she is now back in the Philippines and active in local ministry.

JCF Church and CFMW work together with trade unions and participate in lobbying activities and demonstrations for the rights of domestic workers at the International Labor Organization (ILO). Through arts and theater performed in the church, CFMW has trained many Filipinos to stand up for their rights. As of 2016, Filipinos in the Netherlands are active in campaigning and lobbying with the Dutch Parliament to ratify ILO Convention 189, the Domestic Workers Convention, which recognizes domestic work performed by both documented and undocumented workers.

In 2012 the collaboration between JCF Church and CFMW gave birth to what is known as the School of Integrated Human Rights.[9] Most of the teachers in the school are Filipino migrants themselves: scholars, professors, and human rights activists, sharing their experiences not only with their fellow Filipinos but also with others from Ghana, Nigeria, Sierra Leone, Kenya, Ethiopia, and other nations. Cofounder of the school Jille Belisario, for example, spoke at the United Nations on September 19, 2016, as it adopted the New York Declaration for Refugees and Migrants, a document that expresses the political will of world leaders to save lives, protect rights, and share responsibility on a global scale. For this event, a video was created in which Jille Belisario was interviewed together with other migrants.[10] Thanks

9. See www.i-humanrights.com.

10. The video can be viewed at www.youtube.com/watch?v=VeL_30ss7ps.

to the CFMW, JCF Church, and the School of Integrated Human Rights, Filipinos and other migrants have been trained in lobbying, critical thinking, and studying the Universal Declaration of Human Rights.[11]

CONCLUSION

The stories of Filipinos shared here are only a few of thousands yet unheard and unvoiced by many Christians around the world. These mothers, sisters, brothers, and fathers who have left home to pursue happiness for their families and loved ones are now considered to be national heroes of the Philippines, the *bagong bayani* (new heroes).[12] Besides the role of these Filipinos as heroes for their country, many of them also are unknown heroes of the kingdom of God. They are not officially called missionaries, and perhaps what they do qualifies them only as incidental missionaries, but they work hard, using their free time and weekends to evangelize in apartments, old buildings, parks, and anywhere else that people will listen. These missionaries are not sent by agencies and receive no support from a mission organization or church, but they minister to their fellow Filipinos and to the people of their host nations. They are also active in their communities for social justice. By this fact OFWs are holistic missionaries, not only preaching salvation, but also providing means for their fellow men and women to live—indeed, to survive—in some of the most hostile and difficult situations in life. We have no way of knowing what percentage of the more than 10 million OFWs scattered around the globe are Christians who actively practice and witness to their faith. But if even 1 percent are thoughtful missionaries in this sense, it would mean that over 100,000 OFWs are scattered abroad serving in the *missio Dei*, giving themselves for Christ in the cause of world evangelization.

Despite the trials and tribulations of their journey, as well as the risks and pain most of them have experienced, many OFWs are choosing to serve the Lord. Though OFWs in general have gained much scholarly attention from academia, the mar-

11. The United Nations' Universal Declaration of Human Rights is available at www.un.org/en/universal-declaration-human-rights.

12. Gavilan, "What You Need to Know about Overseas Filipino Workers."

ketplace Filipino missionaries have not received the recognition they deserve, certainly not the publicity that missionaries who are linked to an official mission agency receive. The mission of the OFWs, by the grassroots and for the grassroots, deserves far more attention and prayer. May the works of these "unknown heroes of the kingdom of God" become better known to many in the coming days and years!

QUESTIONS FOR REFLECTION

1. Since many Overseas Filipino Workers (OFWs) have organized themselves in the form of independent churches, communities, and fellowships, do you see their activities as "incidental mission" or simply as "mission"?

2. The OFWs reported on in this chapter are organized around three major realities: mission, community, and social justice. Do you consider the participation of Christians in community work and in the social justice movement as mission, or is mission proper limited only to evangelizing?

3. Why does the author refer to the Christian OFWs as "unknown heroes of the kingdom of God"?

Response
to
"Overseas Filipino Workers"

Daniel Ahn

I wish to express appreciation for the focus supplied by Samuel Lee's chapter "Overseas Filipino Workers: Unknown Heroes of the Kingdom of God." It is a privilege for me to offer several comments in response. The Filipino diaspora provides us with a good vantage point for illumining significant issues in contemporary mission theory. I look first at several beneficial points made by Lee before respectfully offering my own reservations and then suggesting two areas for further exploration.

STRENGTHS

By presenting a case study of current trends within the diaspora ministry of Filipino domestic workers in the special context of the Netherlands, Lee makes a valuable contribution. In the face of today's global diaspora movements from the Global South to the Global North, the missiological priorities of the Christian church will have to be reoriented. Missiology needs to take into account the new demographic realities as diasporas move across the globe, including into Europe.[1] Thus, Lee's case study helps to reinforce the need for us to make a missiological paradigm shift away from an outlook of "from the West to the rest" and toward viewing mis-

---

1. Amador Remigio Jr., "Globalization, Diasporas, Urbanization, and Pluralism in the Twenty-First Century: A Compelling Narrative for the Missio Dei?," in *Scattered and Gathered: A Global Compendium of Diaspora Missiology*, ed. Sadiri Joy Tira and Tetsunao Yamamori (Oxford: Regnum Books International, 2016), 36.

sion as carried out "from everywhere to everywhere." More specifically, Lee shows us that, by acting as "marketplace missionaries" and "incidental missionaries," overseas Filipino domestic workers are "unknown heroes of the kingdom of God," ambassadors of Christ from the Global South who are bringing the Gospel to the Global North, including to the Netherlands.

The chapter gives a clear description of ways that the Jesus Christ Foundation (JCF) Church provides tangible, holistic ministry to Filipino workers through spiritual, logistic, financial, and legal help. First, JCF Church provides spiritual help by offering Bible school courses in which Filipino workers are trained as pastors or lay leaders. Second, JCF Church forms a community of Filipinos in which they are provided essential logistic and financial assistance. Third, JCF Church is deeply involved in protecting the human rights of Filipino workers, including "undocumented immigrants," in cooperation with the Commission for Filipino Migrant Workers (CFMW). It is impressive that JCF Church and CFMW actively participate in lobbying for the human rights of domestic workers at the International Labor Organization, and that their involvement has led to the formation of the School of Integrated Human Rights. The ministry of JCF Church supplies a good model of holistic ministry for the diaspora in Europe.

RESERVATIONS

Despite the strengths of "Overseas Filipino Workers," I wish to suggest several ways that its missiological and theological perspective might be reshaped and thereby enhanced.

Marketplace missionaries. The chapter argues that Filipino workers can be identified theologically with the maidservant of Naaman (2 Kings 5:1–10), Daniel, and Esther. Such identification, however, might not be biblically the best, for those characters in the Old Testament are not directly relevant to the case of the Filipino diaspora workers. Though both groups are used by God's hand as missionaries, the Filipino workers voluntarily go abroad to work, while the maidservant, Daniel, and Esther did not go voluntarily to the Aramaic kingdom or to Babylon to work. That is to say, the Filipino workers are drawn by a clear motivation to work abroad (pull factor), while the biblical characters were compelled to dislocate because they were captives and were exiled as slaves (push factor).

I would offer a caution that we carefully interpret what the Bible says about Naaman's servant, Daniel, and Esther before identifying the Filipino workers with them.

Missiological theories. Several missiological theories come to mind that are relevant to this case but that are not mentioned. First, we can observe two missional dimensions of the Filipino community. On the one hand, a centripetal dimension is present: we see the Filipino Christian community embracing other Filipino domestic workers by welcoming and helping them. This is Christian ministry directed within the community. On the other hand, we observe a centrifugal dimension: they preach the Gospel in their workplaces. This is Gospel ministry directed beyond the community.

Second, though the chapter underscores the JCF Church's remarkable growth in many countries, no clear analysis is made of any missiological reason for the growth. Is the church's fast growth derived from the Homogeneous Unit Principle, for which Donald McGavran argued—he contended that a congregation consisting of a homogeneous ethnic group could grow faster than a hetero- or multiethnic church. Or does JCF Church's rapid growth arise from its passion for the Gospel? Though the JCF Church is composed of Filipino workers as well as members of other ethnic groups from various countries including African nations, the chapter does not help us to understand how much the Filipinos relate culturally to other ethnic groups within the JCF Church and to what extent other ethnic groups contribute to the fast growth of this church.

Third, the chapter does not mention what types of cross-cultural training the JCF Church offers for Filipino workers who are exposed every day to the quite different cultural contexts found in the Netherlands, Cyprus, Lebanon, Ghana, and South Africa, nor does it indicate how well the Filipino workers contextualize the Gospel in those different contexts. Although Filipino workers in Islamic countries boldly share their faith with their Muslim masters, readers may wonder whether the JCF Church provides any cross-cultural training for those Christians' interfaith dialogue with adherents of different religions, including Islam. Unless the JCF church provides them with cross-cultural training, it can be expected that Filipino Christians would tend to stay within their own cultural safety zones, with the loss of God's calling to be incidental missionaries, or that their outreach would meet with rejection because of a lack of cross-cultural sensitivity. From a missiological perspective, lack of discussion of such issues can be a serious blind spot.

"Mission" vs. "missions." It can become a nicety of missiological terminology, but one might ask whether the chapter makes clear use of the distinction between "mission" and "missions." In general, "mission" stands for God's mission, or the *missio Dei*, whereas "missions" refers to the specific work of local churches and mission agencies as they participate in the *missio Dei*.[2] Specific missional tasks carried out by Filipino domestic workers—or others—would therefore be labeled "missions," rather than "mission."

I hope that these few comments will be found helpful. Shaping the discussion in the light of missiological concerns will strengthen it as an example of current global diaspora missions in Europe.

LOOKING MORE BROADLY

Throughout the Bible, we can observe that God revealed himself among the nations and fulfilled his redemptive plan for the nations by working together with persons in diaspora such as Abraham, Joseph, Moses, Daniel, and Esther in the Old Testament, and refugees and diaspora persons from the Jerusalem, Samaritan, and Antioch churches in the New Testament. I draw attention here to two groups of unknown heroes from the history of missions (diaspora missionaries) who might provide partial parallels to the Filipino workers. The first group consists of the unknown missionaries sent out from the church in Antioch during the early years of the church. This church not only sent the famous missionaries Paul and Barnabas to the Roman Empire in the west; it also sent unknown tentmaking missionaries to the east beyond the Roman Empire. Moving toward the Middle East, Central Asia, South Asia, and Far East, these missionaries, whose names are unknown to us, shared their faith in Jesus Christ with the Eastern nations by using

2. See A. Scott Moreau, Gary Corwin, and Gary B. McGee, *Introducing World Missions: A Biblical, Historical, and Practical Survey* (Grand Rapids: Baker Academic, 2015), 9.

their professional skills. As a result, the Christian community was planted throughout these regions from the church's very beginning in the first century.[3]

The Moravian missional refugee/diaspora community in Europe in the eighteenth century constitutes the second group. The Moravians were followers of Jan Hus, who in the fifteenth century initiated the Reformation in Prague, now the capital of the Czech Republic. In the face of Roman Catholic oppression of Protestants, the Moravians fled as refugees to Herrnhut in Saxony, Germany. They became a missional refugee/diaspora community under the leadership of Count Zinzendorf, a key figure of the Pietist movement in Germany. The Moravians first sent their missionaries to the Netherlands, where the missionaries prepared themselves to go overseas aboard the Netherlands' well-developed maritime force. As they were doing so, the missionaries planted several Moravian churches among the Dutch. As a result, from 1732 to 1768, a total of 226 Moravian tentmaking missionaries were sent to Greenland, England, North America, Central America, South Africa, India, and Russia. Those Moravians assigned as missionaries had their passage to the field paid by the Herrnhut community, but once on the field they were expected to provide their own support through their labor as crafts persons and their commercial engagements, something that parallels the way the Filipino Christians abroad witness to Christ while supporting themselves. Back at the community of Herrnhut, the so-called Moravian prayer chain provided intensive twenty-four-hour intercessory prayer support for the missionaries.

Samuel Lee highlights for us that, just as God has been fulfilling his missional redemptive plan for the nations by unknown heroes since the Old Testament period, he is now doing the same with another group of unknown heroes, Filipino domestic workers, in Europe in the twenty-first century. Whether in the past, present, or future, God remains always the same.

3. Samuel H. Moffett, *A History of Christianity in Asia*, vol. 1, *Beginnings to 1500* (Maryknoll, NY: Orbis Books, 2005).

12

Reverse Migration Ministries from Korea: A Case Study of Onnuri Community Church's M Mission

J. Nelson Jennings

A central feature of God's dealings with humanity is his providential guidance of people's movements and settlements —so that we all might come to know him (see Acts 17:26–27). God's orchestration of the movements and settlements of so-called Asian peoples is evident in the example of immigrants intersecting with Christian witnesses in the Republic of Korea, including witnesses in Onnuri Community Church (OCC).[1] Indeed, the tapestry of God's numerous introductions over many generations of Asian peoples to the Good News of Jesus includes his drawing, during the most recent generation, of many Chinese, Mongolians, Sri Lankans, Iraqis, and others to enter what has become the robust Korean economy and urbanizing society. During these same growth years of Korea's economy and cities, OCC (and many other churches) came into being and then explosively expanded. How God has used OCC in the lives of certain immigrants in Korea, and particularly how God has then guided those believers into ministry back in their countries of origin in what I am calling reverse migration ministries, is the subject of this study.

1. Onnuri's ministry among immigrants in Korea is one of several case studies presented in Enoch Wan and Chandler H. Im, "New Opportunities and Strategic Practices of Diaspora Missions in South Korea," in *Global Diasporas and Mission*, ed. Chandler H. Im and Amos Yong (Oxford: Regnum Books International, 2014), 193–223; for Onnuri M-Center, see 204–5.

Before examining the wider context and then programmatic development of OCC's mission to immigrants in Korea, a ministry they call *M Mission*, I share an example of God's orchestration of the Gospel's fruit in and through two brothers from Mongolia. Their story well illustrates the focus of this study.

MONGOLIAN TESTIMONY

In December 2002 a thirty-one-year-old Mongolian man named Galt was found lying on a street in Seoul and was rushed to a hospital. Despite chronic renal failure, Galt survived, but he remained hospitalized.[2]

OCC pastor Kyung Hee Lee and Mongolian Christians in the M Mission visited Galt in the hospital and shared the Gospel with him. That night Jesus appeared to him in a dream, whereupon Galt confessed his faith in Christ and began studying the Bible. He returned to Mongolia, where he died a few years later.

Through Galt's conversion and testimony, his parents and family also came to faith in Christ. Galt's younger brother Achit earned an MDiv at Seoul Bible Theological Seminary and served a Mongolian church near Seoul. Achit and his wife, Tumae, went through Onnuri's short-term missionary training program Turning Point, and in April 2016 they were appointed as missionaries to Mongolia with OCC's Tyrannus International Mission (TIM).

Achit and Tumae first served on a short-term mission assignment with a Korean missionary in Russia. As of July 2016, Achit was preparing to plant a church in Mongolia, ready to serve anywhere God might lead him.

THE WIDER CONTEXT OF OCC'S M MISSION

Since 1993, when the church launched its migrant workers' bazaar, this vibrant and growing ministry of OCC among foreigners in Korea has, as of May 2016, seen 456 baptisms among twenty-five national or linguistic groups. OCC's M Mission, or Migrant Mission, has grown in proportion to the increased numbers of foreigners coming to South Korea and its growing economy.[3] It is no sur-

2. OCC pastor Kyung Hee Lee, who formerly served in Vietnam, related the story of Galt to me.

3. The numbers of immigrants to Korea has sometimes fluctuated. At least one set of data indicates a net loss of immigrants entering South Korea during the 1990s, perhaps because of increased emigration from

prise, then, that in Korean missiological circles, diaspora missiology writings, conferences, and related efforts have seen a dramatic increase over the past decade.[4]

Two types of migration movements have drawn the attention of Korean churches and mission organizations. First are the approximately seven million Koreans living in diaspora outside the Korean Peninsula.[5] Second are immigrants who have come to South Korea. Some of these immigrants are themselves part of the Korean Diaspora but have lived outside Korea long enough to have become foreigners by culture, language, and citizenship. Most immigrants are not of Korean descent but have immigrated because of work, education, marriage to a Korean, or some other factor that draws them.[6]

As of August 2016, the more than 2 million foreign residents in South Korea belonged to the following national groups:

1	China	1,045,533
2	United States	150,778
3	Vietnam	144,362
4	Thailand	92,417
5	Philippines	54,182
6	Uzbekistan	53,816
7	Cambodia	45,610

South Korea to destinations such as the United States, plus the economic slowdown associated with the 1997 IMF crisis. See "Net Number of Migrants by Country, 1950–2015 (by Five-Year Intervals)," Migration Policy Institute (MPI) Data Hub, www.migrationpolicy.org/programs /data-hub/maps-immigrants-and-emigrants-around-world.

4. In addition to Korean-language publications, see, for example, S. Hun Kim and Wonsuk Ma, eds., *Korean Diaspora and Christian Mission*, Regnum Studies in Mission (Oxford: Regnum Books International, 2011), and *Torch Trinity Journal* 13, no. 2 (2010).

5. Young Woon Lee, "Brief History of Korean Diaspora and Educational Issues of Korean Diaspora Churches," *Torch Trinity Journal* 13, no. 2 (2010): 173. Available figures for the size of the Korean Diaspora range from 6.4 million ("Korean Diaspora," in *New World Encyclopedia*, June 25, 2014, www.newworldencyclopedia.org/entry/Korean_diaspora) to 7.25 million ("World's Widest Diaspora Born over 100 Years Ago," *Korea Joongang Daily*, October 2, 2013, http://koreajoongangdaily.joins.com/news /article/Article.aspx?aid=2978298).

6. Akli Hadid, "South Korea Redefines Multiculturalism," *Diplomat*, July 18, 2014, http://thediplomat.com/2014/07/korea-redefines -multiculturalism.

8	Indonesia	42,110
9	Japan	41,236
10	Mongolia	35,091
11	Nepal	33,221
12	Taiwan	30,985
13	Russia	30,098
14	Canada	27,363
15	Sri Lanka	27,360
16	Myanmar	21,534
17	Bangladesh	15,151
18	Pakistan	12,511
19	Hong Kong	11,460
20	India	10,637
21	Australia	9,764
22	United Kingdom	7,896
23	New Zealand	3,917
24	Other	87,846
	Total	**2,034,878**

Source: Adapted from "Nationalities of Legal Foreign Immigrants in South Korea as of August 2016," https://en.wikipedia.org/wiki/Foreigners_in_Korea.

Note: The total number of foreign residents in Korea represents roughly 4 percent of Korea's population of just over 50 million persons.

ANSAN CITY

Located in the southwest of the greater Seoul metropolitan area, Ansan City in particular is a place where thousands of immigrants have come to work in factories and small businesses such as restaurants and supermarkets. Ansan's foreign residents number almost 54,000, which is approximately 7 percent of the city's total population of 765,000.[7] Within Ansan's "Borderless Village," or "special multicultural district" in Wongok-dong, about 70 percent of residents are foreigners, their ranks having been "swollen by newcomers from emerging Asian economies ranging from India and Pakistan to Indonesia and Vietnam."[8] OCC's M Mission has thus heretofore focused its efforts within Ansan.

7. According to the City of Ansan's website, at www.iansan.net/english/aboutAnsan/statisticsMeterial/PopulationUnit.jsp?menuId=01012005.

8. "Foreigners Transform Neighborhoods," *Korea Joongang Daily*, November 4, 2013, http://koreajoongangdaily.joins.com/news/article/article.aspx?aid=2979860. See also Mee-yoo Kwon, "Ansan City to Build Town for Foreigners," *Korea Times*, May 4, 2009, www.koreatimes.co.kr/www/news/nation/2009/05/117_44319.html.

DEVELOPMENT OF OCC'S M MISSION

Eight years after the founding of OCC in 1985, the church first served migrant workers programmatically through a bazaar. In late 1994 a prayer meeting for the ministry was launched, followed by a shelter and other ministries of compassion. Next, one-to-one discipleship (one of OCC's foundational ministry programs) was begun among Burmese migrants. The initial phase of the M Mission's development focused on ministries of compassion, then matured further in mid-1996 with the beginning of a worship service for Chin migrants from Myanmar.[9]

Multiple worship services. With a new Korean-language class in January 1997, and soon thereafter with the inauguration of multiple worship services (Nepalese, Pakistani, and Mongolian), what had been named "Onnuri Mission" grew broader and deeper. A seeker-friendly service was started in 1997, welcoming all types of migrant workers, including Muslims, Buddhists, and various minorities.

After the initial two-year phase focused on compassion and then the second phase of multiple worship services, a third phase (approximately 1998–2005) began as migrants involved in the Onnuri Mission grew as disciples and became "reverse mission" missionaries.[10] The Mongolian example described earlier, as well as a pair of Iraqi testimonies given below, demonstrates God's continuing maturing of OCC's Gospel ministry among and through

9. Information for this section on the historical development of OCC's M Mission comes from three main sources: (1) the current M Mission leadership, most particularly M Mission pastor Kyu Suk (Joshua) Rho, OCC pastor Kyung Hee Lee, and former OCC missionary to Sri Lanka Yong Kook Yoon; (2) the "Onnuri M Mission 2016 Manual" (version 3.0; unpublished); and (3) OCC's thirty-year anniversary volume, *Onnuri Community Church: The First Thirty Years*, Jae Hoon Lee, publisher; Changgeuk Moon, editor in chief; Chi-hyung Roh and Cheol Suh, editors (Seoul: Onnuri Community Church, 2015; English trans. by Onnuri Mission R&D in preparation). One difference in how sources (2) and (3) characterize the M Mission's various phases will be noted later.

10. This more detailed distinction between phases is from the thirty-year volume. The 2016 Manual (p. 4) uses three overall phases for 1993–2015: "Ver 1.0, Mercy Ministry (1993–2005, Seobinggo)," "Ver 2.0, Worship Ministry (2005–2015, M-Center)," and "Ver 3.0, Multi-Community Ministry (2016–25, New M-Center)."

immigrants he had guided to Korea and then sent back to their home contexts. Discipleship materials for one-to-one mentoring were translated into Nepalese, Urdu, and Mongolian. More worship services were begun: Iranian, Russian (in Seobinggo, at OCC's main campus), Arabic, Indian, Russian (in Ansan), Mongolian (in Ansan, in addition to the previously established one at Seobinggo), Sri Lankan, Filipino, and Bangladeshi. With the expansion of ministries among migrants in Ansan, OCC opened a new Onnuri M-Center in rented facilities there. While conducting specifically religious ministries, the M-Center welcomed all migrants simply to come, rest, and be holistically served in any number of ways.

Training programs. In 2005 new training programs began, both for migrants and for Korean Christians to minister among migrants. A second M-Center, also in rented facilities, was opened near the first one in Ansan. Several Christian immigrants have received scholarships for formal theological training at Torch Trinity Graduate University, in Seoul. New worship services have continued to sprout up as well, including in Cambodian, Thai, and Vietnamese. New outreach events have flourished, including Harvest Festival, a multiday, international festivity held at Onnuri's Acts 29 Vision Village in Yangji, one hour south of Seoul.

OCC's ministries to university students support the M Mission's equipping of university students as reverse missionaries. One example is the "Vitamin C" program, which hosts Christian leaders from China for exposure to OCC and ministry training. Some of those Chinese Christians have sent their children to study in Korea, and OCC has served and equipped those students before their return to live and serve in China. The M Mission similarly sees its multifaceted ministries as including international students, Chinese and otherwise, as among those it equips for Christian service back in their home countries.

Holistic ministries. According to its vision statement, the M Mission's vision is "to be the Acts 29 church by winning, training, and resending the migrants in Korea to establish healthy reproducing churches in 10/40 Window countries." The mission statement spells out that vision in greater detail.

1. *Win*: Until we REACH all Migrant Peoples in Korea with the Gospel.
2. *Train*: Until we see CHRISTLIKENESS in the lives of disciples, we will devote ourselves to Quiet Time, One-to-One Bible study, and Cell ministry.
3. *Send*: Until the ends of the earth hear the Gospel of Jesus Christ, we will send Migrant Christians as Missionaries to their respective countries.[11]

The vision statement's mention of Acts 29—to manifest the Spirit's work in continuation of the Book of Acts—is distinctive of OCC's vision articulated by founding pastor Ha Yong-jo. The second of the three parts of the mission statement, emphasizing OCC bedrock programs of a quiet time (QT), one-to-one discipleship, and small groups, is also characteristic of OCC.

At the same time, social ministry explicitly goes hand in hand with cross-cultural mission in OCC's M Mission, both in what is stated and in what is practiced.[12] Free medical and dental care is offered to immigrants who need it. Korean-language instruction, legal and employment advocacy, and "lifelong education" are ongoing ministries.[13] Special attention is given to children, including through the M-Center's day school, Star Tree Academy.[14] As with OCC as a whole, the M Mission seeks to be missional in a holistic sense while focusing on evangelism and church-planting in a traditional evangelical way.

Present phase and future plans. Currently there are 500 migrant churches in Korea. Of this number, 20 (in fourteen different languages) are part of OCC's M Mission: 12 in Ansan, 4 in OCC's main Seobinggo campus, and 4 in various other OCC locations.[15] The M Mission vision is to have 100 worshiping communities by 2020, and thereafter eventually grow to 200 churches.

Pastor Kyu Suk (Joshua) Rho, having served as an OCC missionary in the Middle East, was inaugurated in December 2014 as

11. "Onnuri M Mission 2016 Manual" (ver. 3.0), 3.
12. Ibid.
13. Ibid., 4, 17, 20, 22.
14. Ibid., 15–16.
15. Ibid., 8–9. There are 25, including children's worshiping groups.

the fourth OCC M Mission pastor. With the opening in May 2016 of the newly constructed Onnuri M-Center in Ansan, OCC prayerfully hopes to see God increasingly bring migrants to faith and maturity in Jesus Christ and then to see them serve as "reverse mission" servants like the twenty-seven others who have already done so.16 The goal is to have thirty by 2020 and eventually two hundred missionaries sent back to their home countries.

A recent development is the involvement of OCC's TIM missionaries (Korean and others) in M Mission ministries. Such involvement takes place during missionary training as well as during home assignments in Korea. An expanding role is foreseen for TIM missionaries in the M Mission, including in both long-term service and short-term training or furlough assignments.

TWO IRAQI TESTIMONIES

In this section, we see the examples of Iraqis Malath and Bashar, who in different ways received training and encouragement in Korea and then ended up together in a church-planting ministry back in Iraq.[17]

Malath. For several years OCC's mission teams have cooperated with the Baghdad Alliance Church (BAC, belonging to the Christian and Missionary Alliance). The church's pastor, Ghassa Thomas, recommended that Brother Malath study theology in Korea for the sake of BAC's future partnership with OCC. Malath thus was enrolled in the MDiv program at Torch Trinity Seminary in Seoul. He also served with the Arabic Service at OCC's Seobinggo Campus as a part-time M Mission pastor.

During his service, Malath learned about OCC's vision for mission and experienced the character of OCC's cultural evangelism and mission through the church's Love Sonata ministry in Japan. He was also trained in street evangelism through sharing with Arab Muslims in Itaewon, Seoul, with Korean volunteers from OCC's Arabic Service.

Malath graduated from Torch Trinity Seminary in early 2009

---

16. Ibid., 27 (as of March 2016).

17. The following two accounts were provided by former OCC missionary to the Middle East and current M Mission pastor Kyu Suk (Joshua) Rho.

and took OCC's Turning Point training for short-term missionaries, offered at OCC's Acts 29 Vision Village in Yangji. He was then sent back to Iraq as a short-term missionary in February 2009, serving with BAC. In 2011 Malath moved to the Kurdish town of Erbil, in northern Iraq, where he planted a house church. That group grew to the point of meeting at a hotel, then in 2013 in a rented facility. Missionary Malath was invited to OCC's thirtieth anniversary celebration in October 2015, where he gave a ministry report.

Bashar. Bashar met OCC missionary Joshua Rho (now the M Mission pastor) at an Iraqi pastors' seminar in Amman in 2006. Bashar was a medical doctor at that time and attended the seminar as a young adult leader of the Baghdad Full Gospel Church. A friend of Malath, who was then studying at Torch Trinity Seminary, Bashar told Joshua Rho about his interest in studying theology in Seoul and committing himself to church ministry.

As a result, in 2007 Bashar entered the MDiv program at Torch Trinity Seminary and followed Pastor Malath in 2008–9 in serving with OCC's Iraqi ministry. While Bashar was serving with OCC, his wife, Saba, came to visit him in spring 2008. A pediatrician at Baghdad National Hospital, Saba was pregnant at the time. During her visit she gave birth to a son, Salam, who was born three months prematurely, weighing only 890 grams (just under two pounds).

When Bashar graduated from Torch Trinity, he also took OCC's short-term missionary training program Turning Point, and then in February 2010 was sent back to Iraq as a TIM missionary. He first served with the Baghdad Full Gospel Church, then teamed up with Malath to plant Erbil International Alliance Church. Missionary Bashar is currently serving there as a discipleship pastor. He visited Korea and Onnuri Community Church in August 2016.

EVALUATION, ANALYSES, AND RECOMMENDATIONS

Along with other Christian ministries to recently arrived immigrants in Korea, Onnuri's M Mission is a sign of God's tenacious, faithful connecting of Asian peoples, whose movements and settlements he oversees, with messengers of the Good News of Jesus Christ. God's raising up of OCC over the past three decades has borne fruit within the Republic of Korea, as well as internationally through OCC's many ministries that focus on peoples outside of Korea. These ministries include television station CGNTV, overseas missionaries sent through OCC's TIM and other agencies, BEE (Bible Education by Extension), and Better World (OCC's NGO). It has become increasingly evident that OCC's international ministries in Korea—coordinated by and focused on migrant workers through the M Mission—are bearing Gospel fruit through migrant Christians back in their homelands.

One organizational matter not yet mentioned involves the separate ministry structures of M Mission and of OCC's International Ministries involving English, Japanese, Chinese, and other language ministries. Because of timing, different levels of earlier presence in Seoul, and possibly the types of work and standards of living involved, the later-developing M Mission has come to focus on migrant workers in Ansan. The English, Japanese, and Chinese services and ministries developed earlier and structurally have their own separate status within the church's overall ministries; they are grouped together under the umbrella of International Ministries. Whether or not these structural differences should be done away with is a question at least worth reconsidering. Structural clarity must not be sought at the expense of needed recognition of historical and other distinctions, but the reasons behind the present structures, as well as possible improvements that could be made, need attention.

Many migrants (e.g., Indonesians) are involved with OCC's M Mission while simultaneously being involved with other churches and ministries. This sort of collaboration in ministry is a valuable testimony to Christian unity and should continue to be cultivated.

The M Mission happily shares its experience and resources—especially now that it is housed in a new facility—with other churches and ministries that desire to learn. This spirit of sharing also should continue. At the same time, Onnuri Church always needs to keep in mind that its large size and abundant resources (of people, materials, finances, and programs) can overwhelm other ministries and unwittingly stifle smaller groups' Spirit-led creativity and initiatives. Onnuri's M Mission should therefore be deliberate in seeking to learn from other ministries, especially those that are smaller or younger and possess fewer resources. God's commitment to peoples whose movements and settlements he is orchestrating is shown through all kinds of avenues, including through ministries that are self-consciously weak and inexperienced. The M Mission's stated mission to train disciples through Onnuri's distinctive QT, one-to-one Bible study, and cell ministry must not restrict its vision for how God grows Christians through various and diverse methods, patterns, and ministries.

In related fashion, the M Mission must keep from inflating its own importance as though it saw itself as solely responsible for reaching all immigrants in Korea—apart from what other ministries are doing. The wording in its mission statement, that "*we* REACH *all* Migrant Peoples in Korea with the Gospel" (emphases mine), might seem to indicate such an attitude. Thankfully, ministry among recently arrived migrants inherently reminds everyone involved of the fact of our weakness and limitations and of the need for humility.

An important area in which the M Mission may bear more fruit in the future is in the self-identity of OCC as a whole, namely, that OCC is also fundamentally made up of "aliens and strangers" in this world. Those of us well settled in our various contexts can all too easily allow our Christian identities to become too tightly entangled with those contexts, including those of ethnicity and nationality. OCC needs regular reminders of its identity as a kingdom outpost that is part of God's worldwide and macrohistorical mission. How OCC's Korean identity is affected by the identities of fellow Christians of other ethnic and national backgrounds involved in the M Mission is an important matter. Practical issues related to structures, communication, and financial systems need to be considered here.

Finally, how non-Korean TIM missionaries—particularly those previously involved with the M Mission—receive OCC financial support for projects may need further clarification and reconsideration.

May God continue to honor his name and the Gospel of Jesus Christ through his commitment to all people, including through ministries like OCC's M Mission.

QUESTIONS FOR REFLECTION

1. What are the best ways for Onnuri Community Church to stay involved with M Mission "reverse missionaries"?

2. What are potentially harmful ways for Onnuri Community Church to stay involved with M Mission "reverse missionaries"?

3. What should the relative emphases be for Onnuri Community Church between sending out Korean missionaries and sending M Mission "reverse missionaries"?

4. How might M Mission "reverse missionaries" serve Onnuri Community Church?

5. What are the most constructive roles for the M Mission to play in the overall life of Onnuri Community Church?

Response
to
"Reverse Migration
Ministries from Korea"

Craig A. Noll

In his presentation "Reverse Migration Ministries from Korea,"
Nelson Jennings opens a window on the intriguing mission life
of Onnuri Community Church (OCC)—in particular, its M Mission,
or Migrant Mission.[1] This mission to migrants arose out of a prayer
meeting in 1994. By 2016, this ministry was sponsoring twenty-five
non-Korean worshiping centers in Korea, from which there had
been 456 baptisms. Already twenty-seven migrant believers had
been trained and commissioned as missionaries and sent back to
serve in their countries of origin—Mongolia, Iraq, and elsewhere
in Asia. Thus, in barely a single generation, a Gospel movement of
"reverse migration" had begun. In the vision of OCC, this number
is but a trickle compared with the river of migrant-missionaries that
the church confidently envisions sending back to their native lands.

A LARGER VIEW OF OCC AND MISSION

After Jennings prepared his chapter on OCC's reverse migration
ministries, he published a longer account of Onnuri's extensive

---

1. Another fascinating window on OCC's missions was opened at
KGMLF 2015; see Jae Hoon Lee, Daniel S. H. Ahn, and Tae Kyoung Ham,
"The Accountability of Megachurches in Missions: Onnuri Church, Seoul,"
in *Megachurch Accountability in Missions: Critical Assessment through Global
Case Studies*, ed. Jinbong Kim et al. (Pasadena, CA: William Carey Library,
2016), 32–46. See also the response to that chapter by Wesley Granberg-
Michaelson, 47–52.

mission efforts, all of which flow from the missiological grounding present in the very founding of the church in 1985. Specifically, he notes the "wind" that is the Spirit blowing freely in and around the mission efforts that OCC engages in.

> First, I affirm the Holy Spirit's presence and work among and through OCC and its mission initiatives. The fruit of the Spirit is evident, the gifts of the Spirit (e.g., in Ephesians 4) are undeniable, the presence of the Spirit among OCC individuals and gatherings is real, and the ministry fruit in peoples' lives that have been changed . . . [is] abundantly confirmed by testimony and renewed lifestyles. The work of God's Spirit throughout the earth and across the generations has included forming and enlisting OCC in His mission.
>
> Second, OCC leaders and members consciously depend on the Holy Spirit for guidance and empowerment; and, they testify that the Spirit leads and empowers OCC's mission vision, programs, and efforts. I have been privy to many aspects of this dependence and testimony, for example in leaders' consistent refrain that OCC's foundation consists of "The Word and Spirit," as well as in the plethora of regular prayer groups devoted to OCC mission causes. Moreover, published records of OCC history and [founding] Pastor Ha's own accounts point to the Spirit as having shaped and empowered OCC and its mission.[2]

What an encouraging assessment! Would that similar words celebrating the Spirit's presence could be said of each of our churches!

BIBLICAL PERSPECTIVES

In the final section of his presentation, "Evaluation, Analyses, and Recommendations," Jennings mentions six aspects of OCC's M Mission that are worth watching carefully. I consider four of these areas here, offering considerations that perhaps shed further biblical light on the issues.

M Mission vs. traditional international missions? The M Mission focuses on ministry to migrants now resident in Korea. This minis-

2. J. Nelson Jennings, *Missional Missions: A Missiological Case Study of Onnuri Community Church / Sungyojeok gyohweieui sungyosayeok: Sungyo-hakjeok sarye yoenku—Onnuri Gyohwei* (Incheon, Republic of Korea: Onnuri Church, 2017), 104–5.

try includes a wide variety of social services and helps, as well as efforts that are more along the lines of traditional evangelism and church planting. Tyrannus International Mission embraces OCC's church planting efforts outside of Korea. Can these two very large programs be joined structurally within OCC? Or should they be kept separate? If they were blended into a single program, would something be lost—perhaps a sense that the priority of evangelism was being diluted with an overemphasis on holistic ministries, which have blossomed as OCC tries to meet the practical needs of migrants? Echoes of this concern indeed reverberate here among us in this gathering—and within the congregations and mission communities of which we are a part.

On this point we could appeal to the idea of "integral mission," so clearly affirmed in the 2011 Cape Town Commitment.[3] Perhaps more deeply, we could reaffirm trust in the guidance of the Holy Spirit, who is as ready now as ever to give a definite No or Yes as needed to any issue requiring an answer. For example, "Don't speak the word in Asia!" (Acts 16:6); "Do go to Macedonia!" (Acts 16:10). In one sense, the Spirit is very predictable (e.g., always bringing glory to Jesus [John 16:14], always promoting unity in the body [Eph. 4:3]). In another sense, we do *not* know what he will do next (John 3:8)—so we must ask and wait for an answer. Candid, spirited debate over this question or any issue and prayerful, humble listening are two sides of the same coin if we are to "keep in step with the Spirit" (Gal. 5:25 NIV; see also 1 Thess. 5:21). Debate, concerns, and disagreements *can*, under the Spirit's leading, come to resolution, perhaps in ways we have never before imagined—if only we ask, personally and corporately!

Too strong for the weak? Jennings explicitly warns that OCC's "large size and abundant resources (of people, materials, finances, and programs) can overwhelm other ministries and unwittingly stifle smaller groups' Spirit-led creativity and initiatives" (194). How hard this exhortation might be for a thriving megachurch to fully embrace, we in smaller churches can only imagine!

Scripture is clear that, in terms of numbers, God's choices of the wise, the powerful, or the strong are "not many" (1 Cor. 1:26).

---

3. *The Cape Town Commitment* (Lausanne Movement, 2011), I.7.a, I.10.b, www.lausanne.org/content/ctc/ctcommitment.

In a related point using a body metaphor, the apostle Paul implies that the feet and ears in the body of Christ may need help in confidently using their gifting alongside the more attractive hands and eyes, who may subconsciously be telling themselves, "I really have no need of you less dexterous, less attractive feet and ears!" (see 1 Cor. 12:15–16). Weaker parts of the body—and, could we add, weaker churches?—can take great encouragement from Scripture's teaching that they are actually "indispensable" (1 Cor. 12:22). As Jennings rightly notes, M Mission and such stronger ministries must be "deliberate in seeking to learn from other ministries . . . that are smaller or younger and possess fewer resources" (194–95).[4]

Goals too ambitious? In its vision statement, the M Mission lists a goal of "winning," which will go on until "we REACH all Migrant Peoples in Korea with the Gospel" (195). Jennings notes that such wording, especially the "all," could reflect an attitude of inflated self-importance.

In the thirty-plus-year history of OCC, vision statements have played a hugely important role, none more so than the "2000/10000" vision announced by founding pastor Ha in 1994. It called for the church (then around 7,000 members) to "send out 2,000 missionaries by the year 2010, as well as raise up 10,000 lay mission leaders."[5] Immediately, the church surged in growth,

4. Words written in a somewhat different context by Jae Hoon Lee point to how, practically, disparate parts of the body can practice mutual accountability in ministry: "The concept is rather simple: the greater the number of opportunities to visit each other, to have input into each other's major decisions, and to teach and counsel each other, the greater the chance of genuine care and prayer occurring, which promote unity in the body of Christ" ("Response to 'An American Church's Policy on Greater Mutual Accountability,'" in *Family Accountability in Missions*, ed. Jonathan J. Bonk [New Haven, CT: OMSC Publications, 2013], 134).

Along the same lines, I note an interesting recent suggestion by OCC's Pastor Lee that the church "might better consider itself as Onnuri *Communitas* Church. Doing so would stress the common experience and intimacy among OCC, even as members humbly intermingle with others, rather than demarcating OCC off from others by emphasizing its own name, programs, and structures" (Jennings, *Missional Missions*, 160). With or without the name change, interacting with potential mission partners with such an attitude would go far toward eliminating the unfruitful separationist tendencies of the greater body's feet, ears, hands, and eyes.

5. Jennings, *Missional Missions*, 155.

with the number of missionaries sent out by OCC eventually reaching the 900s.

The value to any organization of a clear, compelling vision is evident. For churches, however, there is the additional factor that members of the body are called to "grow up in every way into him who is the head, into Christ" (Eph. 4:15; see also Col. 1:28–29). To the extent the vision of a pastor reflects the will of Christ, there need be no conflict between the two. Yet, keeping a lively, personal sense of following the leading of Jesus our Chief Shepherd can easily be diluted, if not supplanted in practice, in the course of devoting oneself to an often more visible and urgent churchwide vision or a charismatic senior pastor. This caution applies both to smaller bodies that may come into partnership with a larger church and to the rank-and-file members of an OCC. "*Follow me* as I follow Christ" (1 Cor. 11:1 MEV), says the church leader—yes! "My sheep hear my voice. I know them, and *they follow me*" (John 10:27), says the church Leader—also yes![6] How to be intentional, thoughtful, and zealous in both followings requires the Spirit's ongoing counsel. Without such guidance, how can a strong leader realistically hope to avoid obscuring the preeminence of Christ, which our Lord rightfully claims, given his position as "head of the body, the church" (Col. 1:18)?

Korean church or kingdom outpost? Jennings aptly comments, "OCC needs regular reminders of its identity as a kingdom outpost that is part of God's worldwide and macrohistorical mission" (195). Growth of the M Mission has meant closer rubbing of shoulders with the migrant population in Korea today, now over two million strong. Migrants receive holistic care from OCC through its M Mission, generous help and services in countless areas of life which for them as foreigners in Korea are often so unsatisfying and frustrating (see David Chul Han Jun's presentation at this forum).[7] Migrants from North Korea face especially difficult challenges, as

6. From a brief online review of some of OCC's quiet time materials, it seems the church is very aware of the need for *each member* to cultivate a personal sense of hearing and obeying the Lord's voice. (See, for example, www.duranno.com/livinglife/images/sena_about1.jpg.)

7. For an overview of some of the significant difficulties facing migrant workers in Korean factories, see the chapter in this book by David Chul Han Jun, "The Importance of Migrant Missions in South Korea" (86–96).

Ben Torrey has documented.[8] Furthermore, Korea's acknowledged cultural homogeneity is a factor that silently but powerfully pushes against meaningful kingdom loving of cultural outsiders.

A reminder needed for answering this question rightly must include renewed attention to Philippians 2:4–5: "Let each of you look not to your own interests, but to the interests of others. Let the same mind be in you that was in Christ Jesus." We could start with noticing the interest of Jesus himself, who is the "one shepherd" of the "one flock" (John 10:16)—not just numerically one, but "completely one," as fully so as Jesus and his Father are (John 17:22–23). Do migrants (and others equally unlike ourselves) feel complete oneness with us in our churches?

These four questions may not have quick, easy answers. As always, however, our best, first choice is to come running—boldly, with confidence in the full access our great High Priest has provided— to our merciful Father, whose grace is both findable and timely (Heb. 4:16). And to Jesus, whose promise of rest is crystal clear to all who come to him (1) ready to "take my yoke upon you" and (2) humble enough to learn from him (Matt. 11:28–30). Amen!

8. See, in this book, Ben Torrey, "North Korean Migrants in South Korea: How Can the Korean Church Best Serve Them?," 1–13.

13

Educating Syrian Children in Lebanon's Refugee Camps

Mary Mikhael

Throughout history, human beings have witnessed countless occasions of human movement, displacement, and migration. The reasons for dislocation are many, ranging from natural disasters to poverty, oppression, and war. Even in the Bible we find stories of migration and displacement. Abraham was told, "Leave your own country, your kin, and your father's house, and go . . ." (Gen. 12:1 REB). Later we see the whole house of Jacob fleeing from one place to another. As a young man Jacob ran away from his own brother; then as an old man he and his entire family fled from hunger by going to Egypt (Gen. 46). Later, the Israelites spent forty years under the leadership of Moses, wandering from one location to another in the Sinai wilderness. Perhaps the most famous emigration in the Bible is that of Joseph, Mary, and baby Jesus, who fled from Herod's violence in fear for their lives. Such experiences of being uprooted from one's home and country are truly part of the human story.

In the modern Middle East, the main recorded stories of migration involve poverty, oppression, and war. To look at the miserable camps of Palestinian refugees in Lebanon and other places ever since the establishment in 1948 of the State of Israel in Palestine is to feel the depth of the human tragedy caused by displacement and being uprooted from one's own home.

Since 2011, however, the tragedy of displacement within and emigration from the Middle East is beyond parallel, with most of the displacement stemming in particular from the so-called Arab Spring. What violence this movement has brought to the Middle East![1] The idea of spring normally conveys the hope of renewal, but this spring has instead become the cause for the displacement and emigration of millions of people. In what follows I look at one part of the tragic story of Syria, that involving Syrian children in refugee camps in Lebanon.

A SHORT OVERVIEW OF THE SITUATION IN SYRIA

The Arab Spring in Syria was different than it was in other countries. Formerly, Syria was one of the most stable countries in the entire Middle East. Despite much need for reform and change, people in general enjoyed relative freedom and almost complete security. The Syrian people enjoyed freedom of worship, free education, and free hospitalization. They were generally unhindered in moving about the country and in conducting their business.

The country has been under the sway of one political party, the Baath Party, for well over a half century and under the rule of one political dynasty for some four and a half decades. (The Baath Party took over in 1963. A coup brought Hafez al-Assad to power in 1970; upon his death in 2000, his son Bashar al-Assad succeeded him.) There have been tensions with Israel, which has been occupying part of Syria's land since the late 1960s. Because of these tensions and the threat of war with Israel, the government enforced emergency rules and imposed limitations on political freedom. Though all were convinced that reforms were needed, changes were somehow continually delayed and slow to take place. The Syrian government has maintained its power through emergency rule throughout the decades since.

The initial flickering flames of the Arab Spring in Syria appeared in 2011 in a high school located in southern Syria near the Jordanian border. Students wrote on the school walls, "The people demand change of the regime." Unfortunately, the students were treated harshly, which led to protests by the parents. The protests grew into demonstrations calling for reform of the regime.

The regime did in fact begin to respond. Slowly but surely,

1. See Mary Mikhael, "The Syrian War and the Christians of the Middle East," *International Bulletin of Missionary Research* 39, no. 2 (April 2015): 69–70.

it reformed some laws, appointed a committee to consider a new constitution, lifted emergency rule, prepared for parliamentary elections, and took other measures.

However, violence soon broke out; the situation seemed like dry tinder waiting only for a spark, an opportunity for conflagration to erupt. Demonstrations spread quickly from town to town, and soon the demand arose for change of the regime, not merely for reform. Violence appeared unexpectedly as institutions were attacked, military personnel were killed, electrical and water stations were bombed, and archaeological and historical sites were targeted. Almost every week new fighting groups sprang up, each under a name that had religious connotations.

Eventually, fighters from eighty-three countries rushed in to take part in what they called a jihad, fighting for God or on behalf of God. Calls were issued for the establishment of an Islamic state, and Sharia law was enforced in areas declared to be Islamic emirates. Crime and acts of violence spread everywhere. All non-Syrian fighters seemed to be financed by the Persian Gulf States, trained and armed by other countries, and given free access to Syria across open Turkish borders, all of which complicated the situation as never before, anywhere, in any troubled area. Escalation of violence day by day became the rule of life.

Christians and all minorities were threatened, and many were killed. Others were kidnapped and held for ransom. Still others had to pay a special tax just to be allowed to stay in their own homes. And even a call was issued for Islamic conversion of non-Muslims. The situation has caused millions to run away to seek safety in other areas, leaving their homes, property, and jobs behind.[2]

As of April 2017, according to World Vision, 6.3 million Syrians had been internally displaced, and 5 million had become refugees in other countries. That is, more than 11 million persons—some estimates are higher—have been affected out of a population of 23 million.[3] Furthermore, hundreds have drowned in the Mediterranean Sea while attempting to reach Europe. In areas touched by the fighting, emigration has become everyone's desire.

2. See "Syrian Refugees: A Snapshot of the Crisis—in the Middle East and Europe," September 2016, http://syrianrefugees.eu.

3. World Vision, "Syria Refugee Crisis: Facts You Need to Know," April 13, 2017, www.worldvision.org/refugees-news-stories/syria-refugee-crisis -war-facts.

"How can these people be helped?" became the pressing question for everybody, especially for the church. But can the church really offer help when its own existence is threatened? Does the church have a mission to displaced people and refugees when its resources are insufficient for even its own members? What help can it provide?

Indeed the church does have a mission for all the needy, and in fact it did become involved in relief work as early as 2012, despite its limited resources. Up to the present day, it continues in a struggle for which it was never prepared. In what follows I concentrate on one facet of what the church has done: that is, its effort to provide schooling for children in Lebanon's refugee camps.

SYRIAN CHILDREN IN LEBANESE REFUGEE CAMPS

After a period of planning and preparation, schools were opened, and church ministry with children from the refugee camps began on February 1, 2016. That session ended in August 2016. The second session began in September 2016 and ran up to February 2017, thus marking a full school year. The initial plans, set up by the National Evangelical Synod of Syria and Lebanon, called for two years (2016–17 and 2017–18), four sessions in all, always in the hope for peace. We are now convinced, however, that the need will continue beyond this two-year period. On the one hand, we are earnestly praying that peace will be realized soon in Syria and that all the refugee children will be able to go back to normal life and schooling. On the other hand, we live in the present and act accordingly.[4]

When war broke out, Syrian families fled to nearby Lebanon in large numbers, but Lebanon was not prepared to handle more refugees. Since 1948 it has been struggling to cope with the presence of Palestinian refugees, many of whom still lack much in the way of basic needs. Now with this latest wave of refugees, the country was in danger of being overwhelmed.

We can appreciate the difficulties facing Lebanon—a small country with limited space and resources—with a great number of refugees now within their borders who do not know when, if ever, they will be able to return to their home country. Some of the large

4. See "Refugee Schools in Lebanon," in Syria Lebanon Partnership Network, *Ministry Updates*, www.syrialebanonpn.org.

number of Syrian refugees entered through legal entry points; others came over the mountains. The majority of Syrian refugees were and still are living in squalid camps; they are forced to live in the mud, lacking most of the basics of life.

Accurate reports on the number of Syrian refugees in Lebanon are hard to obtain. The total number of refugees is much larger than the figures that are supplied for "registered" refugees.[5] Some estimates put the number of Syrian refugees in Lebanon at around 1.5 million (as of March 2017), with nearly one-third of them being between the ages of three and fourteen.[6] Other estimates put the total figure higher, with about half of the total being children. These children are being denied a normal childhood and normal schooling.

The children are scattered on the streets of towns and cities, with nothing to look forward to except begging for food and pennies. We must also face the reality that these children are being exploited in a variety of ways. Many are being recruited by criminals, are being trained as thieves, or are intended eventually to become fighters.

With its limited resources, Lebanon has been unable to include Syrian children in existing Lebanese schools. The reasons are various but substantial: the large numbers of refugee children, limited space in the schools, differences in curriculum, differing languages (that is, Syrian schools teach all subjects in Arabic and only introduce a foreign language in the fifth grade; Lebanese schools teach in Arabic and English or French simultaneously as well as adding a third language in elementary classes), and of course the cost. Only a few Syrian children anywhere in the Middle East can afford to pay the cost of a private school, but none of those from the camps could do so.

THE CHURCH'S RESPONSE

The church could not overlook or ignore this great need to rescue as many children as possible from life on the streets. But how

5. See the figures supplied by the UN High Commissioner for Refugees, "Syria Regional Refugee Response," http://data.unhcr.org/syria nrefugees/regional.php.

6. See European Commission, European Civil Protection and Humanitarian Aid Operations, "Lebanon: Syria Crisis," https://ec.europa.eu /echo/files/aid/countries/factsheets/lebanon_syrian_crisis_en.pdf.

could it carry such a burden? Here I speak about the effort of only the Presbyterian Church—specifically, the National Evangelical Synod of Syria and Lebanon. This church indeed wanted to help by opening schools to educate children and save them from a life of destitution. The first step was to set up a special committee to plan what could be done. We called the project "A Church Educational Ministry for Syrian Refugee Children."

We immediately recognized that such a ministry must be near the camps. An accompanying conviction was that, wherever possible, the schools should be located in church facilities. Next, the church had to address the question of definition: What kind of education could it as a church provide in such a situation?

Formal education requires a full curriculum, permission from the Ministry of Education, certified teachers in every subject matter, proper facilities for sports, and the ability to provide appropriate legal papers to the children for whenever they might have the opportunity to move on to a fully accredited school. In the present circumstances, the church was not in a position to open an institution that could provide all of these features, which is precisely why it identified this project as a "church educational ministry." Nevertheless, the church sought to educate and prepare the children attending its schools, allowing them to grow in a normal school atmosphere. It wanted to enhance their lives so that they could be ready to enroll in accredited schools without loss of years when the time came.

An opening step was to visit families in the camps and inform them about the church's school. They were invited to allow their children to benefit from this ministry. In most cases, families welcomed this opportunity. The committee assured the parents of the church's intention to rescue the children and lovingly serve them, showing them that God loves and cares for them.

Getting the project launched, however, required that obstacles in local churches be overcome. The immediate need was to convince local churches to agree to host such ministries. A common fear was that, if refugee children attended church schools in the villages, they would bring their parents as well, something that would not be welcomed by the villagers, who mistrust the refugees. It took the church over a year to get beyond this and other obstacles.

Eventually the church was able to open schools in five locations near camps—in the south, the north, and the Bekaa Valley. Each area had its own challenges. In total, about 400 children enrolled in the five locations. In each one, buses picked up the children in the morning and returned them later in the day. All children were provided with school materials, books, stationery, uniforms, and one meal a day. The schools provided education in the first three levels, enrolling children from five to nine years old.

In the hope that the children would be able to return to Syria and become enrolled in Syrian schools, the church followed the Syrian school curriculum for its four main subjects: language (Arabic and English), arithmetic, science, and ethics.

Since we are serving the first three grade levels, we have started to think that we must add another level for children who succeed in level three, which, I am pleased to report, most will. Requests have already been received from two school locations, asking that another grade level be added. These requests are being evaluated and I believe we will make a decision soon. Still our prayers are that by 2018 peace will come back to Syria and that the children will go back to Syrian schools.

CHALLENGES

This ministry of the church providing elementary schooling for refugee children has encountered various challenges. In one location a school opened with seventy-five children. A few months later some UN and other organizations also began offering schooling for Syrian refugee children, but they offered money to parents who would allow their children to come to their schools. Not surprisingly, the church received requests for similar payments. The church refused, considering this a form of bribery. As a result, the number of pupils enrolled in this location for the second term dropped to only fifty children.

In a second location fifty children were enrolled for the first term, which grew to seventy-two in the second term. Soon, however, six pupils dropped out to go to a school that taught the Qur'an.

The school in a third location began with fifty-four children. We were unable to restrict enrollment to youngsters between five to nine years old, however, for many parents wanted to enroll their three- and four-year-old children also, having no other place for them. The committee consented, sympathizing with the need.

The enrollment went up to fifty-seven, with more requests being received every day. The committee agreed that enrollment could be allowed to increase to one hundred.

Sixty-one children showed up for school in the fourth location. Some of them were up to eleven years old. When it became possible for the older children to enroll in a government school in the city, they left, which brought the number enrolled down to fifty-four.

The fifth school, located in the northern Bekaa Valley, began with fifty children. A number of refugees were concentrated there, and soon parents were requesting that the school accept more children. The committee then opened an afternoon session with room for sixty more children, giving a total of 110 in attendance. One challenge faced by the school was that parents had trained their children to fast during the month of Ramadan. Despite concern for the children's well-being, the school accommodated their fasting. Other than that issue, school life at this location went on smoothly.

As might be expected, the schools faced problems relating to discipline and good manners. Children who had experienced only life in the camps needed help in developing their communication skills and in relating with other children, as well as with adults. The committee scheduled seminars to assist teachers and to train them so that they could help children with discipline or learning difficulties. At the same time, the committee invited professionals in arts and play to visit with the children and to spend time with them. The church also invited a child psychologist to visit the schools and arranged for physicians to examine the children from time to time.

CONCLUSION

Despite numerous challenges of various kinds, the church is committed and determined to educate and rescue as many children as it can. A study carried out by a group of Syrian professionals found that, because of the tragic events in Syria, 5.5 million Syrian children have been affected in a variety of ways, ranging from mental trauma to living without parents to lack of schooling to being recruited by militias to be trained as fighters.

What does the world have to offer these children? The church seeks to provide the children—who became refugees neither by their own choice nor by that of their parents—with the experience of a normal, loving, and nurturing human environment. The church has set its heart on sustaining this educational ministry for refugee children through the 2017–18 school terms. At the time of this writing, the decision of whether to continue beyond the February 2018 had not yet been made. Our hope remains that peace will be realized in Syria and that all the children will ultimately be able to go back to a normal life and childhood.

To God be the glory!

QUESTIONS FOR REFLECTION

1. Are children included in the mission of the church? How can children observe the commands of Jesus? In what ways can children benefit from this mission?

2. In times of conflict and war, how can or how must the church carry on its mission? When the church is only a minority and its own life is threatened, should the church get involved? in what ways?

3. When violence and war become the rule of life, causing multitudes to become displaced and refugees, must the church confine itself to offering material relief work, even with its limited resources?

4. In most cases of human displacement, care for children suffers, even to the point that they may be treated as of secondary importance. What can be done to rescue children who are living and dying in extreme situations?

5. When the church reaches out to rescue refugee children, must the church work to make those children become Christians?

6. What mission does the church have for children?

Response
to
"Educating Syrian Children in Lebanon's Refugee Camps"

Keung-Chul (Matthew) Jeong

I sincerely appreciate the contributions made by the Presbyterian Church in caring for Syrian refugee children, and it is an honor for me to respond to Mary Mikhael, who identifies critical issues at five schools sponsored by this church.

My response to her is informed by my background of serving Muslims and churches in Korea and various Muslim countries, especially Pakistan, since 1985. In addition, I studied at Arab Baptist Theological Seminary (ABTS), Beirut, Lebanon (2014–17), and had the privilege of attending the Middle East Consultation (MEC) 2016, whose theme was "The Refugee and the Body of Christ: Exploring the Impact of the Present Crisis on Our Understanding of Church." Held June 20–24, 2016, at ABTS, MEC 2016 brought together over 230 participants from all corners of the globe. It increased the depth of my understanding of this topic.[1] My Korean colleagues Moses and Maranatha Kim, who have been serving Syrian refugee children in Lebanon since 2015, have also taught me much.

My comments fall under three headings: history and politics, issues involved in relief work, and an urgent appeal for help.

HISTORY AND POLITICS

How do we address the political issues that have led to this crisis of so many refugees fleeing Syria? Mikhael's comment, "What

1. See https://imeslebanon.wordpress.com/2016/07/14/christ-trans forming-his-global-church-by-meeting-us-in-our-syrian-sisters-and-brot hers-highlights-from-middle-east-consultation-2016.

violence this movement has brought to the Middle East!" (204), is, some would say, a one-sided interpretation of the so-called Arab Spring. Some have argued that we need to be critical of both the Assad regime and the opposition.[2] The cry for justice and human rights in Tunisia, Egypt, and Syria that led to the Arab Spring was very genuine and thoroughly justified.[3] Millions of young people were protesting against one-party states, dictatorship, corruption, lack of freedom, police brutality, and lack of jobs.

If the Old Testament prophets had so much to say about the politics of their own nation and the surrounding nations, should Christians today not have something to say about the situations that have led to the refugee crisis? If Christians are concerned about justice, should they not be calling for social justice in Syria and in other countries of the region? Should Christians not have something to say about the root causes of all these problems?

ISSUES INVOLVED IN RELIEF WORK

I wish to focus on three specific issues in the education of Syrian refugee children.

Care for Syrian refugee children in trauma and without parents. Education in the classroom is good, but is it enough when so many personal, psychological, and social needs are present in the community? In addition to the mental trauma they have experienced in the conflict in Syria, many of the 5.5 million Syrian refugee children live without their parents and are not able to attend school.[4]

2. See Nikolas van Dam, *Destroying a Nation: The Civil War in Syria* (London: I. B. Tauris, 2017). Van Dam, a Dutch diplomat in Syria, "attempts to set out coldly what the opposition as well as the Assad government did wrong," according to Robert Fisk ("When Did Protest against Assad Govt Turn to War in Syria?," *Independent*, September 2, 2017, www.independent.co.uk/voices/syria-civil-war-rebellion-isis-assad-western-intervention-arms-a7921526.html). In his view, Syria lies in ruin, and the West is largely to blame.

3. See James Barr, *A Line in the Sand: The Anglo-French Struggle for the Middle East, 1914–1948* (New York: Norton, 2013), who writes of the importance and value of the Arab Spring.

4. For a valuable resource on trauma, see Harriet Hill, Margaret V. Hill, Richard Baggé, Pat Miersma, and Ian Dale, *Healing the Wounds of Trauma: How the Church Can Help* (New York: American Bible Society, 2016).

Moses Kim has commented to me that abnormal family life and the treatment of families by the Lebanese have made Syrian refugees downtrodden; as he has said to me, "They are hurt psychologically almost every day." As a result, in the words of Patricia Miersma, "Some have developed post-traumatic stress disorder (PTSD) or other conditions that exacerbate and prolong the pain."[5] What types of wider support—at the schools and in their communities—does the Presbyterian Church provide for Syrian refugee children facing these problems?

Sharing the Gospel with refugees. How is our Christian witness conveyed through our relief work among refugees? Is providing schools a sufficient witness in itself? What place is there for explicit, verbal Christian witness? During MEC 2016, Ghassan Khalaf (former president of ABTS) urged, "We must not be ashamed to preach the Gospel, because that is the mission of the church." Nadia Accad, director the Tahaddi Health Center in Beirut (www.tahaddilebanon.org), also observed at MEC 2016, "The church is not [a collection of] professionals like an NGO. Healing and transformation flow out of relationship, not just the delivery of service."

It has been my great joy personally to know many churches and NGOs engaged in relief work in Lebanon that, beside their practical service to the people, are engaging in open Christian witness. Many of the Muslims who benefit from their work have no objection to Christians sharing their faith in an open way. I have heard many stories of Muslims attending church services and midweek meetings. As reported by a participant at MEC 2016, a Muslim sheikh who had trained in Egypt's Al-Azhar University said in 2011, "In 1,430 years of Islam we did not experience the love we have experienced from Christians for the last three months." Many Syrian Muslims have asked Lebanese Christians, "Why are you helping us Syrians, although we have created many problems for you? Please tell us the truth about why."

Helping Syrian Christian families as a priority. Is there a case to be made in the Presbyterian Church for channeling some Christian

5. Patricia Miersma, "Counselling Victims of Human-Induced Trauma," in *Sorrow and Blood: Christian Mission in Contexts of Suffering, Persecution, and Martyrdom*, ed. William D. Taylor, Antonia van der Meer, and Reg Reimer (Pasadena, CA: William Carey Library, 2012), 453–54.

aid to Syrian Christian communities? Because of murders, kidnappings, and persecution, the number of Christians in Syria has decreased by 40 percent since 2001. How are these Christian families being cared for by the Presbyterian Church? What priority is given to the biblical injunction to "do good to all people, especially to those who belong to the family of believers" (Gal. 6:10 NIV). I trust that the church is giving good attention to its fellow Christians in both Lebanon and Syria.

AN URGENT APPEAL FOR HELP

The global church must listen to the united cry of all churches in Lebanon and Syria. On August 29, 2015, the churches of Syria and Lebanon circulated the document, "Urgent Appeal from the Supreme Council of the Evangelical Community in Syria and Lebanon to All the Evangelical and Protestant Churches and Organizations across the World." It reads, in part:

> Accordingly, and in view of our awareness of the danger of the present crisis, and in compassion with the sufferings and tragedies our people are facing, we urge our partners in ministry, being the entire community of Evangelical and Protestant Churches across the world, as well as all their social and humanitarian organizations, to act as soon as possible in order to: quickly urge governments and decision makers in your countries to (*a*) raise the awareness of all to the imminent dangers of the situation, (*b*) act immediately to stop the depletion, as well as the forced and ordered displacement of individuals and communities from their homelands, under the threat of arms, (*c*) work for a long term strategy aimed at putting an end to the phenomena of cruel violence and indiscriminate murder. . . . (sec. 8)

> We must work together to heal the wounds and to preserve what is left of the Christian community in those lands. We also must work towards strengthening our sustainable joint communal living with our Muslim brothers and sisters in spite of the widening confessional conflicts and the ever-growing cycle of senseless violence. (sec. 12)[6]

6. The full document is available at www.abtslebanon.org/Default.asp
?PN=%27News2%27&SubP=%27DNewsStory%27&gn=&DivisionID
=&DepartmentID=&SubDepartmentID=&NewsID=67555&ShowNav
=&StoryGroup=Current.

How has the global church responded to this appeal? Christians in other countries need to rally in response to this cry for help from Lebanese and Syrian Christian leaders. They need to provide the kind of resources required by the immensity of the work among Syrian refugees. Christians from elsewhere, however, also need to be aware that Christians in Lebanon and Syria have various opinions regarding the political issues facing their countries, which makes it difficult for them to speak with a clear prophetic voice.

But are there other ways in which the worldwide Christian community can help? Many commentators have pointed out that other countries in the region, as well as Western countries, have contributed to the conflicts in Syria through their interference over many decades.[7] As one Syrian Christian leader has said, "Syria is suffering from the game of nations." Christians worldwide may therefore need to be much more concerned than they currently are about international politics and questions of social justice and about the foreign policies of their own governments.

As followers of Christ, we need always to be reminded of the teaching of Paul, who met Jesus on the road to Damascus 2,000 years ago. He offers a Christ-centered approach to the kind of challenges we face: "If it is possible, as far as it depends on you, live at peace with everyone. Do not take revenge, my dear friends, but leave room for God's wrath. . . . Do not be overcome by evil, but overcome evil with good" (Rom. 12:18–21 NIV).

We hope and pray that before long Syrians will be able to write a new history for their own country.

7. In an interview, Nikolas van Dam, author of *Destroying a Nation: The Civil War in Syria*, stated, "If there had not been any Western influence . . . the country would not be in rubble, so many would not have died, [and] you would not have had so many refugees." Robert Fisk comments, "It's not that Van Dam blames the . . . West for the war, but he holds it to account for the influence and interference it exercised so promiscuously." See Fisk, "When Did Protest against Assad Govt Turn to War in Syria?"

14

Your God Reigns (Isaiah 52:7–10)

Christopher J. H. Wright

We are "Gospel people," we like to say, and sharing the Gospel in all possible ways is of the essence of the mission of God's people. Most of us are aware that the Old English word "gospel" means "good news," which is also at the core of all the "evangel-" words in Greek in the New Testament.[1]

The mission of God's people is to bring *good* news to a world where *bad* news is depressingly endemic. The New Testament vocabulary of gospel and evangelism actually has its roots in the Old Testament, specifically in the Book of Isaiah (and some psalms, as we shall see). The gospel words go back, in fact, to the good news that came to the exiles in Babylon.

GOOD NEWS FOR THE EXILES

In 587 BC the unthinkable had happened—Nebuchadnezzar had destroyed the city of Jerusalem. The people were in exile, having lost their land, city, temple, and hope. Fifty years had passed, and two generations had gone by. Jerusalem still lay in ruins, and so did the hopes of the people. If ever Israel needed to hear some good news, they did at this time. And good news is what they did hear in the soaring words recorded in Isaiah 40–55.

---

1. Some of the content of this Bible exposition has been adapted and edited from my book *The Mission of God's People* (Grand Rapids: Zondervan, 2010), chap. 11. Unless noted otherwise, Scripture quotations are from the New International Version.

God had promised through several prophets that the exile would not be the end for Israel. God would again deliver his people and bring them back to their land and city. The question was, When? For several chapters in the Book of Isaiah, the prophet has been anticipating the good news that the return would happen soon, that God would be victorious over his enemies, and that his people would be delivered.

Then the prophet announces (Isa. 52:7–10):

> How beautiful on the mountains
>   are the feet of the one who brings good news,
> who proclaims peace,
>   who brings good tidings,
>   who proclaims salvation,
> who says to Zion,
>   "Your God reigns!"
>
> Listen! Your watchmen lift up their voices;
>   together they shout for joy.
> When the LORD returns to Zion,
>   they will see it with their own eyes.
>
> Burst into songs of joy together,
>   you ruins of Jerusalem,
> for the LORD has comforted his people,
>   he has redeemed Jerusalem.
>
> The LORD will lay bare his holy arm
>   in the sight of all the nations,
> and all the ends of the earth will see
>   the salvation of our God.[2]

This chapter, Isaiah 52, had begun by summoning Zion to wake up and believe that the bad days of its desolation and captivity were coming to an end. In verse 7 the prophet calls on the exiles and us (his later readers) to exercise our imagination. We see ourselves back in the ruins of Jerusalem, anxiously gazing out toward the east, where the exiles were languishing in captivity, waiting every day for news that God has won the victory he promised, that the exiles are coming home.

---

2. Verse 7 is my translation; the messenger is singular in Hebrew.

At last, in verse 7, we see the running feet of a messenger speeding across the mountain ranges to the east of Jerusalem. A *single* running messenger—rather than the straggling remnants of a defeated army limping home—will mean good news of a victory. And so it proves.

As he runs nearer, the messenger gasps out the good news: "It's peace! It's good! We're saved!" At last, in verse 7, he reaches the city itself and calls out to those within, "Your God reigns!"

God Reigns (v. 7)

Yahweh reigns, the key message, is the truth that explains the other three items in the messenger's good news. For what does it mean to say that Yahweh, the Lord God of Israel, reigns? What does the good news of the kingdom of God bring with it? It brings everything the messenger has said, but along with it, rich meanings from the larger biblical framework.

The reign of God means "shalom." It will be a reign of peace. It will mean the end of the violence and conflict and of all the brokenness and shattering that war brings. God's reign will bring wholeness and fullness of life, when all things are as God intended them to be, when we are at peace with God, with ourselves, and with the world.

This yearning was an Old Testament longing and vision that expressed, certainly, a literal desire for the end of actual physical warfare (e.g., Ps. 46:9–10; Isa. 9:5–7). But the desire went deeper to the levels of restored peace and harmony in all relationships, and in that sense the image of the messenger who proclaims peace took deep root in Jewish hopes and informed New Testament understanding of the work of Christ, as we shall see (Acts 10:36; Eph. 2:17).

The reign of God means "good." When God acts in the way the prophet has been saying, it will be good news for the whole creation, for creation will be restored to what God said when he first created it, that "it was very good" (Gen. 1:31). When God reigns over all creation and over all humanity, it will be good, for God is good.

The reign of God means "salvation." The victory of God means the end of all that holds people in slavery. It will be the great rescue, deliverance from the literal captivity of the Israelite exiles and from captivity to all forms of oppression, addiction, and bondage. The reign of God breaks the chains of evil, sin, and Satan and removes the ultimate dangers of judgment and death. "Salvation" is an incredibly rich and complex word throughout the Bible. It was the distinctive, defining characteristic of Yahweh in the Old Testament and the personal name of Jesus (which means "God saves") in the New Testament.[3]

So when God reigns, there will be peace, life will be good, and we shall be saved. This announcement sums up the content of the evangel borne by the beautiful feet of the Lord's messenger. This is Gospel truth. John Oswalt puts it well:

> What does God's rule entail? It entails a condition where all things are in their proper relation to each other, with nothing left hanging, incomplete, or unfulfilled (*peace, šālôm*); it entails a condition where creation purposes are realized (*good, ṭôb* . . .); it entails a condition of freedom from every bondage, but particularly the bondage resultant from sin (*salvation, yᵉšû ʿâ*). Where God reigns, these follow. Of course, this is exactly congruent with what the Christian faith considers its good news (*euangelion*) to be. This is the content that Christ instructed his disciples to preach from village to village (Matt. 10:1–7): that which Isa. 52:7–10 had spoken of was now present and at hand. . . . Christianity understood itself to be about what Isaiah was about, declaring the good news of the universal rule of God in the world, with concomitant peace, good, and salvation.[4]

God Returns (v. 8)

In verse 8 the single voice of the running messenger is joined by an ensemble of watchmen, the imaginary sentries on the broken-down walls of Jerusalem. They now join together in a great chorus of joy. Why? Because they can now see beyond and behind the messenger, and what they see is Yahweh himself.

The Lord is on his way home! And so the God who reigns is the God who returns. God is coming back to his city, coming back *to* and coming back *with* his own people.

3. For a survey of the breadth of the biblical understanding of salvation, see Christopher J. H. Wright, *Salvation Belongs to Our God: Celebrating the Bible's Central Story* (Downers Grove, IL: IVP Academic, 2007).

4. John N. Oswalt, *The Book of Isaiah, Chapters 40–66* (Grand Rapids: Eerdmans, 1998), 368.

When Nebuchadnezzar destroyed Jerusalem in 587 BC and took its people into captivity, the exiles were not the only ones to leave the city. In a sense, God himself departed, too. In the terrible vision that was probably the lowest point of his whole ministry (second only to the death of his wife), Ezekiel had witnessed the glory of Yahweh leaving the temple and moving away, deserting the city (Ezek. 8–11). God had left the building. Would he ever come back?

Already Isaiah has given the answer in chapter 40, verse 3. God is on the move, so get the roads ready. It had already been heralded as "good news to Zion" (Isa. 40:9). Now the watchmen in Jerusalem are singing because they see him on his way! God is returning to Zion!

- As indeed he did, when the exiles returned in 538 BC, with the permission and sponsorship of the new king on the block, Cyrus of Persia. The city was inhabited again. The temple was rebuilt. Worship was restored.
- As he would do again, in a more significant way, when the Lord returned to his temple on the first Palm Sunday.
- And as he will do yet again, when the Lord returns to claim the whole creation as his temple and to dwell with his redeemed humanity forever.

God Redeems (vs. 9–10)

This song is infectious. From the gasped gospel of the single running messenger (v. 7), it has spread to the small choir of sentries (v. 8). But now the ruins of Jerusalem are personified, given voice to sing of their own redemption (v. 9). And the impact will go further still. In verse 10 the ends of the earth will see the salvation that these singers are celebrating. The theme of the song remains the same—the Lord God himself, who not only reigns and returns, but also redeems.

What does it mean? Comfort and redemption. Redemption means being comforted and liberated. The two words that describe what God has done for his people are repetitions of phrases that the prophet has used most emphatically already and filled with rich meaning. The opening words of Isaiah 40 double up "comfort,

comfort my people" and expand the theme with "speak tenderly," which is, literally, "speak to the heart." Comfort brings relief to pain and grief, bereavement and sorrow. The exiles have suffered their great loss and trauma long enough. God is pouring in his comfort (49:13; 51:3).

But comfort by itself can be impotent—mere words, as we say. So the second word is crucial. God has *redeemed* his people. By the time we reach chapter 52, the word "redeemed" (*ga'al*) is one Isaiah has already used several times (41:14; 43:1, 14; 44:22, 24; 48:17, 20). It comes from the world of Israel's economic life. Within Israel the term "redeem" spoke of the commitment of a family member to stand up and champion other members of the family who were in some situation of loss, danger, or threat. It implied decisive, powerful action, payment of whatever cost was needed (literally or in the sense of effort) and the achievement of liberty, release, or restoration. Yahweh applies this term and this role to himself repeatedly on behalf of Israel—especially in these chapters of Isaiah. It is an exodus-flavored word, since the earliest uses of it in a theological sense with Yahweh as the subject come in God's declaration of intent to "redeem" Israel out of Egypt (Exod. 6:6–8) and in Moses' celebration of that event in song (Exod. 15:13). The return from exile will be exodus reloaded—God redeeming his people out of captivity.

How will it be accomplished? The arm of the Lord. Verse 10 hints at how God will accomplish this great redemptive work: "The Lord will lay bare his holy arm." We recognize this terminology immediately as an anthropomorphic metaphor. You roll up your sleeves for vigorous work. Or the imagery may come from the battlefield, as a soldier throws off his cloak, baring his right arm for combat with the enemy.

Isaiah has used the expression "the arm of the Lord" before, and there are other flavors to the metaphor.

- In 40:10–11 the arm of the Lord is a combination of sovereign power and tender compassion, the compassion of a shepherd who takes up struggling lambs in his arm and carries them close to his heart.

- In 51:9–10 the arm of the Lord is identified with Yahweh himself in his great demonstration of saving power in bringing the Israelites out of Egypt and through the sea.

- In 51:5, however, the arm of the Lord is described in exactly the same terms as had been used for the servant of the Lord in 42:1–4, which suggests that God will accomplish his redeeming work through that servant—the personified Arm of the Lord.

- In 53:1, the so-called fourth Servant Song, which follows immediately after our text, this impression is strengthened as the arm of the Lord is identified with that servant who would live a life of rejection and die a death of horrendous injustice but would ultimately be vindicated and glorified by God. The Servant is the Arm of the Lord.

So it is a rich picture, then. The good news is that God will act and will accomplish redemption for his people. In one sense, he will do so unaided, acting solely by the power of his own arm, as at the exodus. And yet, we are led to expect that the arm of the Lord will be embodied in the servant whose calling, ministry, suffering, and victory so fill these chapters.

Who will benefit? All the nations. From a single runner to the ends of the earth, the good news spreads. Verse 10 does what this prophet does so characteristically: he opens up the promise of God from being a word directly for his own historical people (Old Testament Israel in exile) into a word that has universal scope and power. Verse 10 takes a word intended to bring hope to the exiles, centuries before Christ, and turns it into a promise of salvation to the world, quoting verbatim, as it does, from Psalm 98:3.

No wonder it is described as gospel. This good news is *for the world*, not just for Israel. *Israel's gospel is gospel for all nations*—as it was always intended to be (a point that Paul will build into the very essence of the Gospel he preached to the Gentiles).

The message of Yahweh's name, salvation, glory, and marvelous deeds constitutes good news, *a Gospel message* that, as Psalm 96:1–3 declares, the nations need to hear. The rest of Psalm 96 goes on to expose the futility of the idolatry of the nations and to invite them to abandon their nongods and to join in the worship of the only living God, in the beauty of his holiness.

And what is the content of the new song of Psalm 96, which is to be sung among the nations? Nothing less than the same truth we find in our Isaiah text—"Yahweh reigns" (Ps. 96:10). And if Yahweh reigns, then the old order of the world is turned upside down, transforming the whole creation into a place of reliability, righteousness, and rejoicing (Ps. 96:10–13).

The good news of the kingdom of God that is to go out to the ends of the earth, to bring comfort and joy to all nations, is the good news of the living God who reigns, who returns to his rightful inheritance, and who redeems the whole world. And all of these things God will accomplish through his mighty arm—that is, his Arm (his Servant) outstretched in gentle compassion, outstretched in suffering love, and outstretched in cosmic victory.

The Gospel is on its way.

GOOD NEWS IN JESUS

"Go, tell it on the mountain that Jesus Christ is born," proclaims a popular Christmas song, drawing its imagery from the messenger on the mountain in our text, as well as from Isaiah 40:9. And its instinct is right. For beyond the horizon of the exiles was the horizon of that greater arrival of God among his people in the person of Jesus of Nazareth. And all three parts of the gospel according to Isaiah's messenger in 52:7–10 are even more gloriously good news in Christ.

Jesus Was and Is God Reigning

The earliest gospel opens with the words "The beginning of the good news [euangelion] about Jesus the Messiah" and goes on to quote from Isaiah 40. Mark sees John the Baptist as the initial herald bringing good news, but both Mark and John quickly make it very clear that John was not the one who fulfilled the prophecies. They both point to Jesus in that role.

And so Jesus, when he begins his public ministry, functions as the messenger of good news, announcing that it has arrived. With his arrival, the reign of God is beginning (Mark 1:14–15). Luke records that one of the earliest acts of Jesus was to take upon himself precisely the role of the anointed preacher of good news whom we find in Isaiah just a few chapters after our text, using the same verb (Isa. 61:1–3).

> [Jesus] stood up to read, and the scroll of the prophet Isaiah was handed to him. Unrolling it, he found the place where it is written:
>
> > "The Spirit of the Lord is on me,
> >   because he has anointed me
> >   *to proclaim good news* to the poor.
> > He has sent me to proclaim freedom for the prisoners
> >   and recovery of sight for the blind,
> >   to set the oppressed free,
> >   to proclaim the year of the Lord's favor." (Luke 4:16–19,
> >   my italics)

For how many years had that Scripture been read in that synagogue? How many times would the local rabbi have encouraged the people to go on praying and trusting for the day when the one of whom it spoke would come and do those things? "May he come soon, O Lord! Bring us this good news in our lifetime. Perhaps tomorrow. . . ."

Then one Sabbath morning, the local carpenter's son shocked the whole town with the electric word, "Today!" No more waiting. What you have hoped for and longed for all these years is here in the one standing before you. The prophetic voice of the ancient text has become the living voice of the one now reading it to you. "Today this scripture is fulfilled *in your hearing*" (Luke 4:21, my italics).

And the things the text spoke of were exactly the things that Jesus pointed to as evidence that the kingdom of God had indeed come. God was reigning in and through Jesus, through his words and his works. To his challengers he said, "If I drive out demons by the finger of God, then the kingdom of God has come upon you" (Luke 11:20). When John the Baptist wondered if perhaps he had backed the wrong messiah, Jesus pointed to the same things, this time supported by yet another text of Isaiah (Isa. 35:5–6), but with the addition of the very significant words "and the good news is proclaimed to the poor"—literally, "and the poor are being *evangelized*" (Matt. 11:4–5).

And that reign of God, inaugurated by Jesus and indeed

embodied in him, continues to work within human history in the ways that Jesus said it would—like seed growing, like yeast leavening flour, like a net used in fishing (Matt. 13). The kingdom of God is at work in and through the lives of those who have "entered" it, that is, in whose lives God is reigning through repentance and faith in Christ, in those who are committed to the ways of Jesus Christ by submitting to him as Lord, in those who seek first the kingdom of God and his justice, who hunger and thirst for justice.

In short, the reign of God is found among those who understand their mission: to make *peace*, to do *good*, and to proclaim God's *salvation*. For those things, as Isaiah's gospel messenger called out, constitute the good news that "our God reigns." The Gospel is *good news about God*, as a foundation for all that makes it *good news for us*.

The Gospel, then, is fundamentally good news of the reign of God. It was the good news for which Israel had waited for centuries. They knew *what* the kingdom of God would mean; the question was *when* it would arrive. Jesus announced the good tidings—"It has come!"

It is also the good news for which the world is waiting still. "And this gospel of the kingdom will be preached in the whole world as a testimony to all nations, and then the end will come" (Matt. 24:14).

Jesus Was and Is God Returning

Our text from Isaiah is not the only place in the Old Testament where God promised to come, or to come back. The theme is found in several places, particularly in the postexilic period, when there was the feeling that, although the temple had been rebuilt, God himself had never really brought the exile to a true end by returning to his temple and keeping all the great prophetic promises. But he would do so and would send a messenger to prepare the way for his return (Zech. 9:9; Mal. 3:1; 4:5).

Jesus himself identified John the Baptist as the one who fulfilled the role of the Elijah "who was to come" (Matt. 11:14). But since Elijah was to come before Yahweh himself arrived, and if John was Elijah, who, then, was Jesus (whom everybody knew had come after John)? The day of the Lord had arrived, for the Lord himself was here in the person of Jesus.

And so, in a dramatic and totally deliberate piece of prophetic theater, Jesus came into Zion riding on a donkey (Matt. 21:1–11;

Mark 11:1–11; Luke 19:28–44; John 12:12–19). Having walked from Galilee, he had no need to ride the last few hundred yards. It was as clear as he could make it for all who had eyes to see and knew the Scriptures. The king was coming home, bringing God's righteousness and salvation.

We see that the horizon of our text stretches first to the return of the Lord to Jerusalem with the exiles, but then to the return of the Lord in the person of Jesus Christ in his first coming. The rest of the New Testament points to a further horizon when "this same Jesus, who has been taken from you into heaven, will come back in the same way you have seen him go into heaven" (Acts 1:11).

The Gospel is good news of the God who came, who came back as he first promised, and who will come again, bringing both judgment for those reject him and salvation for those who heed his call to repent and believe the good news.

Jesus Was and Is God Redeeming

The name "Jesus" means "salvation" or "Yahweh is salvation." The gospels festoon the story of Jesus' birth and ministry with scriptural quotations to show the full significance of his name. He was indeed "the one who was going to redeem Israel" (Luke 24:21); even though the two on the road to Emmaus thought such hopes had been dashed at Calvary, they had in fact been fulfilled there.

At Bethlehem the "Arm of the Lord" was rolling up his sleeves for Calvary. Finally he went to Calvary, and the "Arm of the Lord" was indeed stretched out there, stretched out on the cross for the redemption of the world. But God raised him from the dead, delivering his decisive No to death, and his decisive Yes to Jesus, Yes to creation, and Yes to all those for whom the risen Christ is the firstfruits from the dead. In Christ, "we have redemption, the forgiveness of sins" (Col. 1:14).

The gospel of Isaiah's messenger becomes the Gospel of Christ, which is also, as Paul would say just as easily, the Gospel of God.[5] In Christ the good news of Isaiah is realized. Jesus Christ is the reigning, returning, redeeming God. And God has kept his promise.

---

5. Paul speaks of "the gospel of God" seven times, and "the gospel of Christ" ten times.

GOOD NEWS FOR TODAY

That was then, but this is now. So what does this good news mean—for me, for you, for the world outside?

When I first prepared to preach on this text, I walked around the streets of London, where I live, asking myself: "What does it mean for me that Jesus is the reigning Lord, the returning King, and the redeeming Savior?" These are the ways I tried to answer those questions.

For me, to say that Christ is reigning means that I must look for the marks of the kingdom of God in the world.

When I reflect on the news of the world—for example,

- the unpredictable complexities of international life
- the flawed claims and counterclaims of moral rights and wrongs
- the posturing of military power
- the arrogance of cultural and economic dominance
- the scale of human suffering caused by wars
- the present refugee crisis around the world
- and much more—

I have to ask myself, "How and where do I see the signs of the reign of God in Christ in all of this?" In our topsy-turvy mad world, you might well wonder whether discerning such a sign is not altogether too complex and difficult.

It is probably no more difficult to discern the kingdom of God in the world today than it would have been in the sixth century BC, when Babylon ruled the world in which Israel lived. Probably it is not more difficult than in the first century AD, when Rome ruled the world of Jesus and the disciples. The Roman Empire was then the single superpower that dominated the world with a mixture of military superiority and economic self-interest—and yet gave the world much to be grateful for in the process. In all that ambiguity—then, as now—this text says to us: "Your God reigns!" "Jesus is Lord!"—not Caesar or any of Caesar's successors. And in that assurance I rest my confidence and hope!

For me, to believe that Jesus is returning means that I have hope in the midst of the waste. When I think of the "waste places" of the world (Isa. 52:9 KJV), the ruins of things God made beautiful—whether

- the appalling destruction of our planet's diversity and beauty
- the desolate waste places of human suffering (made so through the brutality and cruelty of the wicked or through our callous neglect)
- the sheer immensity of human and natural suffering, including, for example, HIV/AIDS, tsunamis—

then I remember that Jesus is also the returning King. He is the God who comes, who came, and who will come again.

When he comes again—when he returns—things will be put right and the whole of creation will rejoice:

> Let the heavens rejoice, let the earth be glad;
>   let the sea resound, and all that is in it.
> Let the fields be jubilant, and everything in them;
>   let all the trees of the forest sing for joy.
> Let all creation rejoice before the LORD, for he comes,
>   he comes to judge the earth.
> He will judge the world in righteousness
>   and the peoples in his faithfulness. (Ps. 96:11–13)

There is hope—not because, in some mythical world of monsters, good triumphs over evil—but because in the real world of men and women, God was in Christ reconciling the world to himself, and God will return to put things right forever.

For me, to believe that Jesus is the redeeming God means that I long for the day of deliverance. When I think of the vast numbers of the human race who live in all kinds of oppression and slavery imposed by

- poverty, hunger, and injustice
- forced migration as their homes are destroyed by war, persecution, or climate change
- violence, murder, rape, cluster bombs

- addictions
- AIDS
- sin and rebellion of their own choice
- ignorance of the Gospel

then I look forward to the day when "all the ends of the earth will see the salvation of our God" (Isa. 52:10). Then all who long for his appearing, all who turn to him in their need and despair, will see their Redeemer as he really is: Lord and King and Savior of the nations. That is the ending of the great story that the Bible tells.

But how? How and when can this be? All I can answer is in the words of William Fullerton's hymn:

> *I cannot tell* how he will win the nations,
> How he will claim his earthly heritage,
> How satisfy the needs and aspirations
> Of east and west, of sinner and of sage.
> *But this I know*, all flesh shall see his glory,
> And he shall reap the harvest he has sown,
> And some glad day his sun will shine in splendor,
> When he, the risen Savior of the world, is known.[6]

That is what the good news means to me.

But what about *them*? I thought as I walked along Tottenham Court Road in London. What about the people on the streets of London in their thousands? What does it mean to *them* that

- Jesus is the reigning Lord of history?
- Jesus is the returning King of creation?
- Jesus is the Redeemer and Savior of the world?

And the answer seemed to bounce back off the walls: "Nothing—nothing at all. How can it, if they don't know about it? And how can they know about it, if nobody has told them?"

Then my text seemed to bounce back also, but through the words of Paul, who quoted this text with similar questions in mind: "'Everyone who calls on the name of the Lord will be saved.' How,

---

6. William Y. Fullerton, "I Cannot Tell," *The Covenant Hymnal: A Worshipbook* (Chicago: Covenant Publications, 1996), 488–89, my italics.

then, can they call on the one they have not believed in? And how can they believe in the one of whom they have not heard? And how can they hear without someone preaching to them? And how can anyone preach unless they are sent? As it is written: 'How beautiful are the feet of those who bring good news!'" (Rom. 10:13–15).

CONCLUSION

Actually, there is nothing very beautiful about feet. The only thing that makes feet beautiful is when they are wearing running shoes for the Gospel of peace—as Paul also said in Ephesians 6:15.

Therefore, let's have our Gospel running shoes on so that we can . . .

- Go, tell it on the mountain—the mountain of human pride—that Jesus Christ is born and is reigning.
- Go, tell it on the mountain—the mountain of human despair—that Jesus Christ is born and is returning.
- Go, tell it on the mountain—the mountain of human bondage—that Jesus Christ is born and is Redeemer, Savior, and Lord.

15

Proclaiming Resurrection, Starting with the Refugee, Asylee, and Migrant

Seth Kaper-Dale

Blessed are the poor in spirit [those who have had the spirit beaten out of them], for theirs is the kingdom of heaven. Blessed are those who mourn, for they will be comforted. Blessed are the meek, for they will inherit the earth." Jesus' stump speech, the content of which we hear twice, once in Matthew as the Sermon on the Mount and once in Luke as the Sermon on the Plain, enunciates a preferential option for those who are suffering the most.

No population is more deserving of being first right now than the approximately 60 million forcibly displaced persons in the world—displaced by war and violence. In addition to the 60 million refugees and internally displaced persons, tens of millions more people are globe-hopping, accepting paltry wages and substandard living conditions because of the debilitating reality of poverty. Seeking to inherit just a small bit of earth and to eke out an existence, often for their children, workers leave family, friends, community, and culture. They do so without proper documents or a clear, safe plan. Jesus says to refugees and to all migrants, "In this new commonwealth that I am bringing about, you are blessed, you are first, you are loved."

There is a second part to Jesus' stump speech. A second group is blessed: "Blessed are the merciful, for they will receive mercy. Blessed are the pure in heart, for they will see God. Blessed are the peacemakers, for they will be called children of God. Blessed are those who are persecuted for righteousness' sake, for theirs is the kingdom of heaven." In this half of the speech, Jesus states the calling and purpose of those who are not among the poor and suffering of the world but who have the freedom to choose to stand with them. For many of our churches, currently located in places of safety and relative power, this second part of Jesus' speech is a message for us. It is the responsibility of the church, in the United States and other locations where it is currently not under high-level threat itself, to extend radical care to those who are beaten down, mourning, and powerless. In 2017 and beyond, the responsible church must hear Jesus Christ's clear call to be the gracious community for the sake of refugees.

Jesus' death, resurrection, and ascension, in the middle of history, showed the way in which this stump speech would become a living reality for the world. He was raised from the dead, not to heaven, but rather to earth, in a transformed body, showing that death and destruction are not the last word here on this earth, whether for himself or for others who, like him, have had the spirit beaten out of them. His resurrection was about the salvation of this world and about new life in this world. His resurrection and subsequent ascension kicked off an outpouring of the Holy Spirit that not only influenced changes in heaven, but also influenced the transformation of life on earth, especially for the poor and powerless. This was the salvation Christ was promising. Christ was resurrected in the middle of history and promised that we too would be resurrected for life upon the new earth that is what? —springing up? —spreading out? —descending from heaven? Scripture does state clearly that a final culmination of all things lies ahead, but it is equally clear in stating that starting now, through the outpouring of the Holy Spirit, resurrection of individuals, communities, and even the earth, is already under way.

At times Christian churches operate as if the goal of Christ was to get humanity "ascended," but no clear promise in Scripture announces that ascension away from the earth is Christ's ultimate goal for humanity. Resurrection, not ascension to heaven, is the message of Scripture—and resurrection is and has always been about resurrection to a fuller life on earth. The resurrected life is about helping the world to begin experiencing the resurrected life, as much as possible, in these last days. And Christ is clear, in his

Sermon on the Mount and elsewhere, that the starting place for creating resurrected life is among the poor and powerless, among the refugees, asylees, and immigrants.

THE CASE OF THE REFORMED CHURCH
OF HIGHLAND PARK

Church commitment to refugee resettlement in the United States has a long and exemplary history. The United States resettles, on average, around 75,000 refugees a year. Currently, because of the global refugee crisis, that number is 35,000 higher. The United States is usually the world's highest "third-country recipient" in the number of refugees received each year. That means that the country, though not bordering states in crisis, generously reduces the burden on those countries that are immediate neighbors to warring lands. The US resettlement system relies on nine non-profit organizations to receive families cleared by the US State Department and to disburse them responsibly in communities all across the country. Many of these nine organizations are directly affiliated with faith organizations—many of them Christian. Those faith-based nonprofits rely heavily on the goodwill of local churches to adopt families, mentor them, and help them ease into life in their new locale.

It is important, however, that our reflection on the US church's relationship to refugees, asylees, and undocumented persons not be confined solely to that particularly positive partnership with the government. The church frequently needs to be prophetic in its posture toward the US government, as opposed to playing the role of collaborative partner.

The Reformed Church of Highland Park (RCHP), in Highland Park, New Jersey, has become a leader in ministry to asylees, immigration reform, refugee resettlement, and advocacy. Sometimes we work collaboratively with government. Other times we are a thorn in its side. I have copastored that church, with my wife, Stephanie, since 2001. I would like to share briefly the story of our congregation as we have engaged the questions of migration and human dislocation and have tried to be accountable to Christ's Sermon on the Mount and confident of the good news of resurrection. This journey has been, for us, a central part of what it means to be in mission for the past fifteen years.

WHEN GOD FIRST MOVED OUR HEARTS CONCERNING MIGRATION AND HUMAN DISPLACEMENT

On September 9, 2001, my wife and I began our ministry in Highland Park as twenty-five-year-old graduates of Princeton Theological Seminary. On our first Sunday with the church we met the members of an Indonesian congregation that was sharing our building. Only a few of the nearly eighty members spoke English, so we knew that this immigrant community was newly arrived. We knew nothing else about them. Two days later 9/11 occurred, and suddenly the US public became fixated on the threat of Islamic terrorism. One year later Attorney General John Ashcroft announced the launch of the National Security Entry-Exit Registration System (NSEERS) that was set up to register males, ages fifteen through sixty-five, from the twenty-four largest Muslim countries in the world. Indonesia is the largest of those countries. I was called to a congregational meeting of the Indonesian Christian community, at which I learned that the entire congregation, and many in other newly started Indonesian congregations, were living in the United States on expired tourist visas. I also learned that the Indonesians in our church were ethnic Chinese Indonesian Christians. They had escaped to the United States after 1998 to be safe from the post–Suharto-regime bloodbath against anyone ethnically Chinese, and especially against Chinese Christians.

The question the community asked this young pastor was, "Should we comply with the government? Should we report ourselves as NSEERS requires?" The word from the government was "register or be considered a terrorist fugitive." With that threat looming, I encouraged them to register. I hoped that reporting would be seen as honesty, and I believed that this community could dodge the fury being levied against Muslims. I was, of course, concerned for Muslims through all of this, but I thought this particular Christian community would be safe if it reported itself.

I was wrong.

Honesty with the government was a bad idea for this community that had escaped a well-documented reign of terror in 1998 and whose relatives back home were still experiencing thousands of church burnings and ongoing threats. After registering with NSEERS, the entire community of Indonesian men (and Indonesian members of start-up churches sharing buildings with seven other US congregations) who were now out of the shadows began an arduous and expensive process of filing for asylum.

From late 2002 to the middle of 2003, members of my church and I accompanied Indonesian men as they reported to the Immigration and Naturalization Service. We also returned to Immigration Court with many members between 2003 and 2006 to bear witness to court proceedings as Indonesians filed for asylum and as they appealed cases. We saw only failed cases. A one-year time bar on filing for asylum was strictly applied, and they'd all been in the country for more than one year. It was our calling, during those years, to be in solidarity with those who were afraid and with those who were mourning. We hoped, even as cases failed, that Immigration and Customs Enforcement (ICE) would use its discretion to keep families together and would not exercise deportation.

In May 2006, after the Indonesian community in New Jersey had spent well over a million dollars on immigration lawyers in an attempt to stay safe, thirty-five of those husbands and dads were taken into custody by ICE in a very frightening predawn raid on an apartment complex where many of them were living. By this point many had children who were US citizens; those children were now alone with undocumented, single mothers. All the men were placed in our county jail, a jail making a tremendous amount of money by contracting with the federal government for such services. All thirty-five were deported. We learned, much later, that this was part of a nationwide round-up called Operation Return-to-Sender that the Bush administration carried out to show "muscle" as it pushed for an immigration bill that many saw as soft. Indonesians, along with others who self-reported, became low-hanging fruit for President Bush to send away as evidence of this "muscle."

From the time of that predawn raid until 2013, our congregation, with myself in the lead, was embroiled in a bitter battle with the US government. We claimed that the baptismal vows we made, to walk with families as they raised their children in the faith, called us to fight against family-breaking deportation. We were constantly in the news as we found creative ways to expose the abusive manner in which the government was carrying out its job. We were also in the news for creative solutions that we offered to the government for consideration.

From 2006 to 2012 the Reformed Church of Highland Park creatively lived into its identity as a blessed community. We were merciful to victims of an abusive system. We were peacemakers— fighting for real *shalom*. We were willing to be persecuted and reviled in order to defend the people with whom we had cove- nanted. Here are some of the actions we took.

We rallied for legislation introduced in Congress that would help keep US children from having their parents deported (The Child Citizen Protection Act). Through this effort our church mem- bers began to see how legislation could work to bring peace and justice to immigrants, asylees, and refugees.

We started visiting immigration detention centers to see our own members, and as we did so, we learned the value of visiting detainees who had no family. We got to know asylum seekers from all over the world. We formalized this effort in 2009 with a Monday night visitation program that continues to this day.

One dramatic morning in April 2009, when an Indonesian father of two US children, who was also an elder in the church, was about to be transferred from a New Jersey detention center to a detention center in Washington State and then deported to Indo- nesia, I used the "power of the collar" and talked my way onto the airplane in Newark. I just got on the plane to pray for him.

We learned how to utilize the media, especially taking my "plane incident" and turning it into a story that created the lever- age needed to get the ear of powerful people in President Obama's administration.

Late in 2009, after questions from his boss in Washington, the head of ICE in New Jersey called me and members of my congrega- tion to a meeting where he listened to our concerns for the Indone- sian community and offered a plan to protect them. This involved temporary benefits for all the men who had filed for NSEERS, now living in hiding. He invited all who were living with deportation orders to come forward to receive what were called Orders of Supervision. This was widely covered in the press, including on the front page of a Sunday morning edition of the *New York Times*. Nearly 100 Indonesian men stepped out of the shadows in New Jersey, and with the help of the *New York Times* article, similar pro- grams were set up in other places with Indonesian communities.

HOW THIS WORK CHANGED THE CHURCH

During these years our church grew in many ways. First, members grew in their belief that the church could influence systems in ways that would be better for immigrants and displaced persons. We would pray about real dilemmas, sharing testimonies and prayer requests during the Sunday service, and then we would follow up those prayers with definite actions.

Second, we grew in numbers. Part of that numeric growth was a multiethnic and multiracial growth, as our visitation ministry in the detention center led many asylees who were released to join our church. Often, when these detainees were released, the only phone number they had was that of the church.

Third, we grew in numbers among a population of young, enthusiastic, justice-and-peace-oriented Christians—people who want to see the world become a better place. Our numbers grew in this respect as we articulated, through action and words (in that order), a theology that was about liberation and transformation of systems on behalf of the poor.

Finally, we grew our interfaith community. The arrival of the kingdom of God, proclaimed by Jesus Christ and infused by the Spirit after Jesus' ascension, is an arrival that welcomes collaboration and partnership. The new earth that Christ is bringing about, the resurrected earth and community, is filled with people from a variety of religious, ethnic, and cultural traditions. As we worked to support the Indonesian community—and all the other migrant, asylee, and refugee communities that God led us to—we found many collaborative partners from other religions.

THE CHANGING WHIMS OF THE POWERFUL, AND THE FAITHFUL RESPONSE OF THE CHURCH

Leadership in federal agencies changes, and unfortunately for us, in 2012 the director of ICE in New Jersey was moved to Washington, DC. Despite our pleading, all commitment to the special deal made to protect the Indonesian community disappeared. ICE agents again began actively trying to deport our people, just two years after having given them special orders allowing them to stay. We responded, as a church, by writing a bill that we fought to get before the House of Representatives and the Senate, called the Indonesian Refugee Family Protection Act. All of the skills the church had learned over the previous ten years were put to use as we sought a sponsor for the bill and mobilized teams to visit Washington and as we sought endorsements from major religious groups and civil rights organizations. Finally, after two men were deported in early 2012, our church made the dramatic decision to offer physical sanctuary to any Indonesian who feared deportation. Nine men, most of whom had children who were US citizens, accepted our offer. For eleven months, the nine fathers lived in our facility while we drew attention to the outrage of family-breaking policies.

Each step in this process was important for our church community. The elders and deacons held lengthy and difficult conversations about the risk of challenging the government. We sought advice and direction from others who had taken such actions in the past. We learned to accept a level of risk as part of our calling. Once we extended sanctuary, the church community and the wider community stepped forward with great pride to participate. Each night a volunteer stayed in the church all night with our sanctuary guests, "standing sentry." Teams of church members visited Washington to share our sanctuary experience and to push legislation that we hoped would end the need for sanctuary. Other church members raised money to help pay the rent for families whose breadwinners were now stuck inside our church. In February 2013 the director of Enforcement and Removal Operations in Washington, who oversaw a $5 billion budget to remove individuals from our country, invited me to come and explain what was happening in New Jersey that led to such negative press for the agency. After hearing our story, the director issued special dispensations to allow those living in our church to be released. As we begin 2017, that arrangement is still in place. Not one Indonesian, with or without papers, has been deported since early 2012. It appears that the government does not want to mess with the church again!

REFUGEE RESETTLEMENT AT THE REFORMED CHURCH OF HIGHLAND PARK TODAY

The experience of working very intentionally with the Indonesian community that God clearly placed before us opened the hearts and minds of our church members to take seriously the struggles of refugees, asylees, and immigrants from all over the world. In 2014 we started incorporating into our Sunday morning prayers concern for people dying in boats and rafts who were trying to escape Syria, Libya, and other war-torn nations. Soon, a church family who heard those prayers invited us to consider supporting a new missionary couple heading to Italy to work with the Waldensian

Church and affiliated nonprofits supporting asylees and pushing for a "humane corridor," a safe passage across the Mediterranean. We started to contribute, and we started to pay closer attention.

In the spring of 2015 we started hearing about Rohingya Muslims escaping Myanmar, stranded off the coast of Indonesia. It was the Indonesian community in New Jersey, asylum-seekers themselves, who now, nearly twenty years after having fled, were praying that Indonesia would allow these boats to land. People were starving. We celebrated when God answered prayer and Indonesia opened its doors to the Rohingya. We did a fund-raiser that got great attention in Indonesia.

In the fall of 2015 our children's choir, made up of children from second through sixth grades, watched a documentary on Syrian children in refugee camps. Then they took quotes from the children and wove them through a rendition of the song "I Want Jesus to Walk with Me." This prayer, by the children of the church, led me, as pastor, to know we had to do something more to address the crisis.

In October 2015 a group of church members at RCHP met to discuss how we could start welcoming Syrian refugees and other refugees. We decided immediately to actively make this an interfaith effort. With all the examples of Islamophobia that were playing out in the United States, we wanted Muslim neighbors to be active with us from day one. We had an organizational meeting of interested congregations in October, and we agreed to have a kickoff event in early November, called the Take Ten Campaign. We were encouraging every municipality in central New Jersey to welcome ten families from Syria or from other suffering regions of the world.

Two days prior to our kickoff fund-raising event, in November 2015, the Paris terror attacks occurred. In a series of coordinated assaults, gunmen, one of whom the media said was a recent asylee, killed scores of people. We considered canceling our fund-raiser, in deference to the dead. We thought better of that idea, however, deciding that canceling it would somehow suggest that refugees are the threat to the world, as opposed to being the victims of the world. Three hundred people showed up for the walkathon, representing nearly thirty congregations and five major faith traditions. The event raised $10,000, and leaders from seven congregations spoke at various points along the walk. The day after our walk,

Governor Chris Christie declared that New Jersey would not receive refugees, "not even Syrian refugees under the age of five." Our well-publicized event, coupled with the governor's inflammatory remarks, led us into a public fight.[1]

Back in February 2015 our interfaith coalition, partnering with Church World Service, received our first family (a Congolese family of six), and in March, our second (an Afghani family of two). At the same time, we received, through our asylum-seeker connections, a Syrian family of three and two Nigerian men. We rented houses for all and provided wrap-around support, including accompaniment to social services, medical services, ESL, job training, and community integration.

With monthly meetings that pulled in participants from more than two dozen congregations, our efforts blossomed. By April we knew that we should continue formalizing our program and become our own refugee resettlement organization. Feeling emboldened by productive fund-raising and happy with the success of our first placements, we reached out to a Washington-based resettlement organization called US Committee on Refugees and Immigrants (USCRI) to see whether it desired a New Jersey affiliate. By May we had named ourselves Interfaith-RISE (Refugee and Immigrant Services and Empowerment). USCRI wrote us into their Request for Proposal for fiscal year 2017, and by October of 2016 we had been cleared by the State Department to be an official refugee resettlement site. We agreed to take fifty refugees in 2017.

In April, as a way to celebrate our new commitment to global refugees, we created Global Grace Cafe at RCHP. This cafe is run by the church, with daily volunteers who help to keep overhead costs down. Each day a different paid chef highlights the cuisine of a different place in the world. Most of the chefs are refugees or asylees (from Congo, India, Indonesia, Sierra Leone, and Syria). The menu changes as our refugee population changes. Global Grace is the way we say to the world, "What a blessing to have a global community!"[2]

1. For a number of news reports and videos posted online that are related to the steps taken by the Reformed Church of Highland Park, New Jersey, in response to the needs of refugees, including Syrian refugees, following Governor Christie's attempt to ban them from the state, see the appendix to this chapter.

2. See "Global Grace Cafe," www.rchighlandpark.org/global-grace-cafe.

COLLABORATION OR CONFRONTATION?
WHAT WILL THE FUTURE HOLD?

As I write this case study, the United States is on the verge of unprecedented change. A president-elect who has pushed Muslim registration and Islamophobia and who has used anti-immigrant, anti-refugee rhetoric will soon come into power. For the past few months our Interfaith-RISE efforts have been purely about collaboration with the government for the sake of caring for victims of the world's abuses. If the new administration, however, begins to make the situation of refugees, asylees, and migrants more dire, we will call upon our earlier experiences of pushing back for the sake of those who are last and least. It is our prayer that this time, with the strengthened interfaith reality in which we now operate, RCHP will be able to mobilize not only our Christian community, but also the entire interfaith community, to stand up for the last—those who God says are first in the kingdom of God.

APPENDIX

Following are a number of news reports and videos available online related to steps taken by the Reformed Church of Highland Park in response to the needs of refugees, including Syrian refugees after Governor Christie's attempt to ban them from the state. The entries appear by date of publication or their posting online.

Yuni Salim, "Simpati Diaspora Indonesia di New Jersey untuk Rohingya," *Voice of America Indonesia*, July 25, 2015, www .voaindonesia.com/a/2876478.html.

Brian Thompson, "Chris Christie Says He Wouldn't Even Take 'Orphans under Five' from Syria," *NBC 4 New York*, November 17, 2015, www.nbcnewyork.com/news/local/New-Jersey-Chris-Chri stie-Syrian-Refugees-Comment-Radio-351033021.html.

Brian Amaral, "Pastor Criticizes Christie, Pledges to Bring Refugees to N.J.," *NJ Advance Media*, November 17, 2015, www.nj.com /middlesex/index.ssf/2015/11/syrian_refugees_in_highland _park.html.

Michael George, "Syrian Refugee in New Jersey: 'I Found Peace, I Found a Chance,'" *NBC 4 New York*, November 19, 2015, www .nbcnewyork.com/news/local/Syrian-Refugee-Living-New -Jersey-Speaks-351552751.html.

"Syrians Welcome?," *Chasing News*, November 19, 2015, www .youtube.com/watch?v=5SWKi5nBDHs.

Karen Yi, "NJ Religious Leaders: We Must Accept Syrian Refugees," *Asbury Park Press*, November 23, 2015, www.app .com/story/news/world/2015/11/23/religious-leaders -we-must-accept-syrian-refugees/76109348.

Seth Kaper-Dale, "Sermon: 'Donald Trump, the Syro-Phoenician Woman, You and I,'" *Good Ole Woody's Blog and Website*, November 28, 2015, https://goodolewoody.me/2015/11/28/sermon-donald-tr ump-the-syro-phoenician-woman-you-i-by-rev-seth-kaper-dale.

Liz Robbins, "Syrian Family of Seven Is Settled in New Jersey against Christie's Opposition," *New York Times*, November 30, 2015, www .nytimes.com/2015/12/01/nyregion/syrian-family-of-7-is -quickly-settled-in-new-jersey.html?_r=1.

Kathleen O'Brien, "As Christie Seeks to Stop Syrian Refugees, Others Extend a Helping Hand," *NJ Advance Media*, December 2, 2015, www.nj.com/news/index.ssf/2015/12/as_christie_seeks_to _stop_syrian_refugees_others_e.html.

Seth Kaper-Dale, "Governor Chris Christie Committed a Most Dangerous Act a Couple of Weeks Ago . . . the Bridge Scandal Pales in Comparison," *Huffington Post*, December 7, 2015, www.huf fingtonpost.com/seth-kaperdale/governor-chris-christie -c_b_8725190.html?.

Mercedes Barba, "Jesus Was a Refugee," *NYUJournalism: Projects*, December 17, 2015, http://projects.nyujournalism.org/thene wamericans/jesus-was-a-refugee.

Larry Mendte, "Another Thing: Syrian Refugee Crisis," December 21, 2015, www.youtube.com/watch?v=ub4BxDItXAo.

Susan Loyer, "Global Grace Cafe Crosses International Borders," *myCentralJersey.com*, June 10, 2016, www.mycentraljersey.com /story/life/faith/2016/06/10/global-grace-cafe-crosses-interna tional-borders/85562708.

Deborah Amos, "As U.S. Politicians Shun Syrian Refugees, Religious Groups Embrace Them," *National Public Radio*, August 10, 2016, www.npr.org/sections/parallels/2016/08/10/487753289/as-u-s -politicians-shun-syrian-refugees-religious-groups-embrace-them.

Monsy Alvarado, "Café Offers a Taste of the World and a Chance to Help N.J.'s Newly Arrived Refugees," *The Record*, August 25, 2016, http://archive.northjersey.com/news/cafe-offers-a-taste -of-the-world-and-a-chance-to-help-n-j-s-newly-arrived-refug ees-1.1649711.

Raven Santana, "Highland Park Church Welcoming Refugees with Open Arms," *FiOS1 News*, August 26, 2016, www.fios1news .com/newjersey/highland-park-church-welcoming-refugees# .WMa3fY7aul5.

Jessica Formoso, "Helping Refugees," *Fox5 News*, n.d., www.fox5ny .com/news/210804192-video.

Response
to
"Proclaiming Resurrection"

D. David Lee

To protect the baby Jesus from being killed by Herod, Mary and Joseph fled with him to Egypt (Matt. 2:13–15). Jesus was thus a refugee in a foreign country. The UN High Commissioner for Refugees defines a refugee as "someone who has been forced to flee his or her country because of persecution, war, or violence."[1] As Seth Kaper-Dale points out, over 65 million people around the world have been forcibly displaced by conflict, persecution, violence, and war.[2]

The account Kaper-Dale gives concerning the steps taken by the Reformed Church of Highland Park (RCHP), in Highland Park, New Jersey, in behalf of the Indonesian asylees is a riveting example of what it means to love our neighbors here on earth. In this response I wish to voice questions and concerns I have in three areas: (1) issues of security and safety in an era of terrorism, (2) the priority of evangelism over social action and social services, and (3) political obligations in the context of today's global refugee crisis.

APPROPRIATE CONCERN FOR SAFETY
SHOULD NOT CUT OFF WILLINGNESS TO TAKE RISKS

As a church, RCHP and Pastor Kaper-Dale have acted like the Good Samaritan in Luke 10:25–37. They have shown love in action

1. See UNHCR, "What Is a Refugee?," www.unrefugees.org/what-is-a-ref ugee. See also UNHCR, "Refugees," www.unhcr.org/en-us/refugees.html.

2. UNHCR, "Global Trends: Forced Displacement in 2016," June 19, 2017, www.unhcr.org/en-us/statistics/unhcrstats/5943e8a34/global-trends-fo rced-displacement-2016.html?query=global%20trends.

as they have cared for the Indonesian congregation. They have visited detainees and have offered physical shelter to those in danger of being deported. RCHP has worked with the US Committee on Refugees and Immigrants to establish its own resettlement organization to enable it to accept and help resettle refugees coming to the United States. As Jesus taught in Matthew 25, RCHP truly feeds the hungry, gives something to drink to the thirsty, invites strangers, clothes them, visits them, provides a place to live, and even offers jobs. Members of the church have not looked after their own security or safety; they have been willing to take risks so as to help the least. Their love in action is highly commendable, and other churches must consider their example of following the way of Christ.

As a country, the United States is divided on the issue of immigration. Whereas the Obama administration was relatively pro-refugee, the tide has changed since the inauguration of Donald Trump. Trump is placing restrictions on accepting immigrants and has signed executive orders banning refugees from a subset of Muslim-majority countries. Evangelicals also stand divided on the issue of refugees. Robert Jeffress, pastor of First Baptist Church, Dallas, Texas, has claimed that border security is "God's idea."[3] Franklin Graham, president of Samaritan's Purse, commented to the *Huffington Post* that "it's not a biblical command for the country to let everyone in who wants to come, that's not a Bible issue. . . . There are laws that relate to immigration and I think we should follow those laws. Because of the dangers we see today in this world, we need to be very careful."[4]

Other evangelicals differ. Russell Moore, president of the Ethics and Religious Liberty Commission of the Southern Baptist Convention, criticized Trump's proposed ban on Muslims entering the country.[5] In addition, more than 100 evangelical leaders,

3. Samuel Smith, "Pastor Robert Jeffress: Securing US Border Is 'God's Idea,'" *Christian Post*, November 23, 2015, www.christianpost.com/news/pastor-robert-jeffress-securing-us-border-gods-idea-syrian-refgees-christians-bible-150735.

4. Carol Kuruvilla, "Here's How Franklin Graham Justifies Trump's Expected Refugee Ban," *Huffington Post*, January 25, 2017, www.huffingtonpost.com/entry/frankling-graham-refugees_us_5889049ce4b061cf898c6c42.

5. Russell Moore, "Is Donald Trump Right about Closing the Border

including Ed Stetzer, Rich Stearns, Stephan Bauman, Paul Ericksen, and Frank Page, affirmed the command to love our neighbors and the privilege of caring for refugees.[6]

Ensuring security is a crucial role of the government, and we must conclude that the US Department of Homeland Security has done an incredible job of screening refugees. Though over 3 million refugees have been resettled in the United States since the late 1970s, Bauman feels confident to assert that no terrorists have crept in among them.[7] Insofar as he is correct, we see that compassion and security can exist simultaneously.

EVANGELISM AND SOCIAL ACTION, WITH PRIORITY GIVEN TO EVANGELISM

Mission should always prioritize the proclamation of the Gospel for the saving of lost souls. Currently some missionaries tend to focus too much on social services and responsibilities, perhaps even to the exclusion of proclaiming the Gospel. Kaper-Dale and RCHP seem to misunderstand God's primary mission. Kaper-Dale believes that Jesus' resurrection is primarily about life in this world, not in heaven. His liberation theology shies away from balancing the Great Commandment with the Great Commission.

In 2005 David Hesselgrave identified three theological positions regarding the poor: radical liberationalism, holism (revisionist or restrained), and prioritism.[8] Kaper-Dale supports the first category insofar as he emphasizes social transformation to

to Muslims?," December 7, 2015, www.russellmoore.com/2015/12/07 /is-donald-trump-right-about-closing-the-border-to-muslims.

6. Ed Stetzer, "Christian Declaration on Caring for Refugees: An Evangelical Response," *Christianity Today*, January 8, 2016, www.christianityt oday.com/edstetzer/2016/january/church-leaders-speak-on-refugees .html. Also see Kate Shellnutt, "Evangelical Experts Oppose Trump's Refugee Ban," *Christianity Today*, January 25, 2017, www.christianitytod ay.com/news/2017/january/evangelical-experts-oppose-trump-plan-to -ban-refugees-syria.html; and World Relief, "World Relief Calls for a Swift End to Refugee Ban," January 27, 2017, www.worldrelief.org/pre ss-releases/world-relief-calls-for-a-swift-end-to-refugee-ban.

7. Stephan Bauman, "World Relief: We Must Help Refugees," *Christianity Today*, March 11, 2016, www.christianitytoday.com/edstetzer/2016 /march/world-relief-we-must-help-refugees.html.

8. David J. Hesselgrave, *Paradigms in Conflict: Ten Key Questions in Christian Missions Today* (Grand Rapids: Kregel, 2005), 118–25.

establish *shalom* on earth. I emphasize the third category, believing that priority should be given to spiritual transformation over social needs. As Hesselgrave states: "After all, people of good will of all religions and no religion can and do address the human need for food, clothing, shelter, health, education, justice and so on. But Christians—and Christians only—can be expected to preach the gospel, win men and women of all nations to Jesus Christ, and establish churches that will worship and witness until Christ returns."[9]

The apostle Paul reminds us that "the whole creation groans and suffers the pains of childbirth together until now" (Rom. 8:22).[10] I do sympathize with Kaper-Dale and RCHP's effort to bring *shalom* on earth, but we live in a world broken because of sin. Suffering and pain are thus inescapable aspects of human existence. We need to prioritize the most important aspect of God's mission. We must proclaim that through the cross Jesus gave "His life a ransom for many" (Matt. 20:28). Jesus said, "The Son of Man has come to seek and to save that which was lost" (Luke 19:10). The only begotten Son came so that those who believe in him could have eternal life (John 3:16), not merely the transformation of life here on earth.

While Christians should do their best in caring for the earthly needs of individuals, they should not forget, at the same time, to place priority on people's eternal salvation by proclaiming the good news of salvation in Jesus Christ. The apostle Paul had the eternal destiny of his own people (Rom. 9:1–3) as his overriding concern. His anguish resulted not from the social or political situation of his people under Roman rule; rather, Paul desired for them to be saved spiritually (Rom. 10:1–4). Our primary concern should be modeled on that of Paul.

POLITICAL OBLIGATION

Christ's followers should address moral and social concerns and advance ethical positions in the public arena, even while submitting to the governing authorities set in place by God. RCHP and

9. David J. Hesselgrave, "Will We Correct the Edinburgh Error? Future Mission in Historical Perspective," *Southwestern Journal of Theology* 49, no. 2 (Spring 2007): 144.

10. Unless otherwise noted, Scripture citations throughout this response are from the NASB.

Kaper-Dale are to be commended both for complying with government regulations and for working to reform government polices that cause hardship and distress through threats of deportation that would break up families.

The US government is not perfect in its policies toward refugees. Much good, however, has come from the work of the US government, particularly with its refugee resettlement program. The United States has, in fact, accepted more refugees for resettlement than any other country. See the accompanying table, which shows the number of refugees accepted for resettlement by the top five host countries over the decade 2007–16.[11] The number of refugees welcomed by the United States, double that of all other countries combined, is remarkable.

Number of refugees resettled, by country, 2007–16

	United States	Canada	Australia	Sweden	Norway	Others	Total
2007	48,300	11,200	9,600	1,800	1,100	3,300	75,300
2008	60,200	10,800	11,000	2,200	—	4,600	88,800
2009	79,900	12,500	11,100	1,900	1,400	5,600	112,400
2010	71,400	12,100	8,500	1,800	1,100	3,900	98,800
2011	51,500	12,900	9,200	1,900	1,300	3,000	79,800
2012	66,300	9,600	5,900	1,900	1,200	3,700	88,600
2013	66,200	12,200	13,200	1,900	—	4,900	98,400
2014	73,000	12,300	11,600	2,000	1,300	5,000	105,200
2015	66,500	20,000	9,400	—	2,400	8,800	107,100
2016	78,300	21,800	7,500	—	—	18,000	125,600
Total	661,600	135,400	97,000	15,400	9,800	60,800	980,000
Percent	67.51	13.82	9.90	1.57	1.00	6.20	100.00

As with any government policy, the US refugee resettlement program should be considered a favor, not a right. We should be grateful for what the US government has done and continues to do in terms of refugee resettlement, even while we keep our eyes open to areas of legitimate critique.

11. See UNHCR, "The Global Report," www.unhcr.org/en-us/the -global-report.html. The table was extracted by Global Fountains, "The United States, the World [sic] Largest Country for Refugee Resettlement, 2007–16," http://globalfountains.org/static/RefugeeResettlementStati stics.html.

CHALLENGE AND OPPORTUNITY

God moves people around the world, from east to west, from south to north. Migration and globalization have brought their share of challenges including cross-cultural issues, legal immigrant concerns, religious conflicts, and social problems. At the same time, we have in front of us the opportunity and privilege to love our neighbors and make disciples of all nations. On a closing note, as we do missions, we need to emphasize the importance of having a sound biblical theology and a high view of Scripture. Times may change, but God's Word remains the same. It is the very anchor for all we do.

16

A Place at the Table:
Migration and Mediation,
Mission out of Latin America

Ruth Padilla DeBorst

Long before they were called the Americas, these were lands of
people on the move. Our ancestors saw a bridge where others
saw only ice, and they made their way from Asia to what now is
called Alaska and ultimately down to Argentina. They crossed
mountains, deserts, and jungles; they founded cities and built
empires; they raised stone temples above the clouds. They were
later joined by those who braved their way across the ocean from
Europe, and those who willed their way to survive their sale out
of Africa. This is the story of my people, Latin Americans, young
and old, from the southernmost tip of the Americas to the border towns of Mexico and throughout North America—people
painfully clearing a way forward. Today war, violence, poverty,
and lack of opportunity all drive people to break a way forward
over walls, through rivers, across deserts. Often all they find is
death. They are guaranteed pain, loss, and discrimination. Many
are deported to places that were never theirs. At the same time,
another story needs to be told.

In 2015 the immigrant population in the United States
totaled over 43 million; as of that year, 1 in every 7.5 persons and
approximately 1 in 6 adults resident in the United States was not
born in the country.[1] Latin America accounts for almost 52 per-

---

1. Migration Policy Institute, "U.S. Immigrant Population and Share

250

cent of immigrants to the United States—and the majority of them are Christian.[2] Although in the social and political scene today immigration has become a contested, divisive, and polarizing issue, sociologists such as Stephen Warner are reporting that migrants in general play a mediating role between cultures and religions and that, far from de-Christianizing the United States, Christian migrants are reforming US Christianity by de-Europeanizing it.[3] Among these migrants, millions of Latin American Christians are participating in local churches, and they can serve as agents of renewal in the church and the broader community—*if* they are granted a place at the table.

This chapter does not offer an exhaustive study of Latin American immigration, nor does it seek to establish any overarching theory. It simply weaves together the stories of three Christian immigrants from Latin America, portraying the mediating role they play in the congregations of which they are members in the United States. It closes with a brief account of a local congregation that is striving to make a place at the table for immigrant agents of God's mission and poses a few questions for those who chose to embody a model of Christian mission that reverses the established expectation of mission from the haves to the have-nots.

THREE STORIES OF LATIN AMERICAN IMMIGRANTS IN US CHURCHES

I analyze here the stories of three Christian Latin Americans: Manuel (age 55), David (64), and Oscar (38). I gathered them through personal interviews with each of them and with the leaders of the churches with which they are involved in the United States.

---

over Time, 1850–Present," www.migrationpolicy.org/programs/data-hub/charts/immigrant-population-over-time.

2. Steven A. Camarota and Karen Zeigler, "Immigrants in the United States: A Profile of the Foreign-Born Using 2014 and 2015 Census Bureau Data," Center for Immigration Studies, October 3, 2016, https://cis.org/Immigrants-United-States; and Pew Research Center, "The Religious Affiliation of U.S. Immigrants: Majority Christian, Rising Share of Other Faiths," May 17, 2013, www.pewforum.org/2013/05/17/the-religious-affiliation-of-us-immigrants.

3. Stephen Warner, "Immigrants and the Faith They Bring," *Christian Century*, February 10, 2004, 20–23, available at www.religion-online.org/showarticle.asp?title=2946.

Pathways into "exile." Manuel loved his life in Mexico. He was happily married and enjoyed family life with his two sons. His twenty-five-year-long teaching career had been successful, particularly after completion of his PhD in Old Testament at Westminster Theological Seminary. He had always resisted the idea of taking a post in the United States, but an economic crisis hit Mexico in 1998, and no matter how hard he worked, Manuel could not make ends meet. Ten years later, he recalled the family decision to take a position in a church in the United States as "excruciatingly painful." His voice dimmed as he explained, "We simply *had* to go into exile."

David's PhD in psychology was granted by the Catholic University in Buenos Aires, Argentina. Further studies—and the family of his US wife—took him to the United States, where he earned a master's degree in peace studies and a PhD in practical theology at Princeton Theological Seminary. He and his wife wanted to return to Argentina, but there was no work for them there.

We enter Oscar's story at a different point: he is almost thirty years younger than David, and twenty younger than Manuel. Having graduated from the university in Monterrey, Mexico, with degrees in communication and anthropology—and although he had a tenured position in the Universidad Nacional Autónoma de México, and although his US-American wife had a good job in the city—he felt the itch to study theology. So he and his wife, with their two daughters, traveled to Philadelphia "for a spell." Back in Mexico he had volunteered in a poor neighborhood filled to the brim with Central American immigrants who had found jobs and stayed instead of continuing their travel to the United States. "Little had I imagined," he comments, "that the immigrant experience would be my story too!"

Not stereotypical working-class immigrants, the protagonists of these three stories are men with university degrees, whose wives also have higher education. Two of them were explicit about the main driving force in moving to or staying in the United States being the lack of paid work in their field in their home countries. All three talked with yearning about their land and their people, and each relished the times they were able to spend "back home."

The receiving churches. Although the immigrant experience was fraught with challenges, Manuel, David, Oscar, and their families actively sought out and created spaces of belonging in three local congregations in the United States. In all three cases, they chose to settle into churches of the same denomination as the ones they had attended in their home countries: a Christian Reformed Latino congregation, an English-speaking Baptist church, and a Mennonite fellowship, respectively. All three, along with their families, became actively involved in their new churches, providing leadership, preaching, teaching, and counseling, as well as serving on various committees. Essential to their integration was the attitude of the pastors and the congregations that received these immigrants.

Oscar's face expresses amazement when he recalls the words of Pastor Fritz upon his and his wife's arrival: "Oscar, you are the only Hispanic among us, so I want you to dream about what this church can be and do in relation to all the Hispanics in our area. Then you tell us what to do." The pathway had been opened for Oscar and Karen thanks to the readiness of the congregation. "A great number of the members were business people, who traveled and saw that the world was changing and who thought about how the church should change in light of those changes, as well as people in academia, in the university," Pastor Fritz explained. Oscar underlined the openness of the pastor: "He was one who saw that the church needed to change if it was going to stay alive." Today the number of Latinos continues to expand in this initially homogeneous Anglo congregation.

The work of David and his wife was one of pioneering, breaking new ground in a church that lacked awareness of people outside of the members' natural social grouping. Slowly but surely, however, their presence has made an impact on the attitude the other members display toward minorities. "He has opened up awareness of people from other cultures," affirms Pastor Will.

Manuel and Ramona, both Mexican and lacking previous cross-cultural experience, joined a small Latino church. Theirs was the groundbreaking role of challenging the settledness and vying for the acceptance of this community within a broader, dominantly Anglo-European denomination, which is slowly learning to integrate minorities.

THE GIFTS OFFERED BY THE IMMIGRANT CHRISTIANS

The testimony of the pastors interviewed points to the renewing potential inherent in the "reverse flow" of mission as the immigrants contribute to the established churches in their adoptive land. I mention here the three most significant contributions highlighted by the church leaders.

"Helping us see and opening the world to us." Pastor Fritz was categorical about the impact of Oscar's presence in a traditionally white, middle-class church. "Oscar became very helpful in sensitizing the congregation to the presence of Latino people in the community that this congregation probably never would have seen without his eyes—the neighbors, the workers in the community. We saw people show up at church we never knew were there before. Oscar would say, 'I met them down at the taco stand,' or 'I met them at a conference, and they live here in this community.' Those folk would start to come to church. And all of a sudden, we became aware of their presence in the community."

Oscar's "world-opening" role extended far beyond the local community. He joined a church team on a trip to Chile, during which he translated while also introducing church people to the larger Latin American culture and theological world. In addition, as a gifted and artistic photographer, Oscar continues today to open the world to the church members, who "become curious about the person behind the photos and the world behind that person."

Pastor Will's story about the impact of David's presence in the congregation also stressed his bridge-building role: "David has opened up our awareness to people of other cultures. He donates his time in a center for Latinos with counseling and other services. That helps us become more acquainted with younger families of Latino background. So we have made some significant changes in our congregation. Also, his being a part of the church is a gift by bringing Latin America to us—Peru, Puerto Rico, Argentina. When he travels to Argentina to see his mother, he is very faithful in sharing with us what he gleans from his trips."

David also insisted on building up the local congregation as a community of mutual concern, a welcoming space for foreigners, a supportive place for women to exercise their gifts without imposing "glass ceilings" on them, and a safe environment for children. "Relationships are a high priority for him," explained Pastor Will.

Gregorio talked enthusiastically about the impact Manuel has had on his Latino church, which offered classes and orientation to members as they negotiated relations to the dominant culture. In this context, Manuel—articulate, bilingual, and skilled cross-culturally—played a mediating role. "He is a true prophet in this society! He represents the Hispanic community to the Anglo church as a voice of those who have no voice. At the same time, he talks to the Latino community on behalf of the Anglo community. He is a mediator. He helps us look at one another differently, to understand one another."

The way in which these immigrants built bridges and strengthened relations between people within the congregations and far beyond illustrates Warner's conclusion that "across the board, new immigrants bring a more communal, less individualistic perspective to our society."[4]

Serving the less privileged. A natural consequence of this communal outlook is the concern expressed by Manuel, David, and Oscar for the less-privileged members of the community. David served in a clinic for immigrants in a nearby town. He saw this volunteer work both as an extension of the church and as a bond with Latin America. He has been influential in moving the congregation to consider its calling to serve the hundreds of immigrants in its broader community.

In one of his periodic visits to Mexico, Oscar took pictures of people in Chiapas and then assembled a presentation to bring awareness of poverty to his US congregation. Partly thanks to his creative insistence, the church began supporting a couple serving in an inner-city slum of Mexico City, as well as an economic development project among indigenous people in Chile. These social engagements are experienced by the pastors and these immigrant Christians as visible and inevitable expressions of their faith and theology.

Contextual theologizing. In the lives of Manuel, Oscar, and David, theological thought is not divorced from practice. Instead, they define Christian commitment as resulting from a dynamic dialogue between service, community, faith, and biblical teaching. Theirs is an ongoing theological reflection that is radically committed to the people in the midst of whom that reflection is being carried out and engages with the real-life issues they are facing. In that sense, it is contextual. It is "theologizing" in that it engages the mind, has cognitive content, and offers articulations

4. Warner, "Immigrants and the Faith They Bring."

about God, human beings, nature, and the interrelations among them, all in light of the biblical story.

The three pastors expressed appreciation for the manner in which the immigrants interviewed contribute to the theological praxis (reflection on action and action upon reflection) of the groups in which they are involved. Pastor Will commented about David, "When we are doing a Bible study, he's always very careful to provide the context for all he brings up. He helps us look at the culture, the history, the way people might have experienced a certain thing. You see it in the kinds of questions he raises, surprising ones. He brings in the experiential dimension of theology; he brings provocative points of view. It shows up in the way he interprets Scripture."

Manuel, in turn, explained his efforts to bring in a "contextually relevant *and* evangelical response" to the issues of the day. "I attempt to propose, at church and the seminary, a richer, deeper, more integral mission focus in theology. Many North Americans, like my colleagues in the seminary, are always looking to Europe—to Germany and England—for models. They find it hard to look South and to admit that anything good can come from there. I feel the resistance. But I insist, and slowly there is some openness to a way of doing theology that is not just about books but is connected to the real issues, including poverty, injustice, and broken families."

For these three immigrant brothers, theology—far from constraining Christians and isolating them from the broader context—is born in and intends to serve everyday life. None of these contributions would have come to fruition, however, if the receiving churches had not opened a place at the table to them.

DIGGING BELOW THE SURFACE

The capacity of these immigrants to function in the new communities and to contribute to them depended on a complex blend of personal, social, cultural, and economic factors. In the case of Oscar, David, and Manuel, they all shared a common affiliation with the Latin American Theological Fellowship (known as FTL, for its Spanish acronym) in their countries of origin. FTL's promotional brochure states:

> The FTL is a nonprofit organization integrated by followers of Jesus that are committed to the life and mission of God's people

in Latin America. We are an evangelical movement that, since the 1960s, has promoted spaces for theological reflection contextualized in our colorful and wounded Latin America. We yearn for a Latin American Church that, transformed by the Word and the Spirit into an agent of the Kingdom of God and God's justice, ministers in every area of society. The FTL, as part of the church, facilitates friendly spaces for dialogue and biblical-theological reflection from Latin America.

For several decades, the FTL has strengthened theological and interdisciplinary reflection that is contextually relevant, fostered much-needed ecumenical dialogue, encouraged Christians to act prophetically in the social arena, and provided a supportive ethos for lay initiative in integral mission. FTL members in Latin America have been the means for positive ferment within many churches and agencies, as well as diverse denominations. Although FTL is over forty years old and has chapters in many US cities, it is little known in North America, where liberation theologies have long been considered the only theological contribution representative of Latin America.[5] All three men—Manuel and Oscar in Mexico and beyond, and David in Argentina and beyond—experienced the FTL as an identity-building community that also propelled them into theologically reflexive engage-

5. The various liberation theologies generated within Latin America have been made known in North America through educational institutions, religious orders, and publications issued by Orbis Books. In contrast, the existence and production of the FTL are known far less well. Names associated with the beginnings of the FTL include Samuel Escobar, Orlando Costas, René Padilla, Peter Savage, Pedro Arana, Emilio Antonio Nuñez, and Rolando Gutierrez. For an overview of the FTL, see Daniel Salinas, "The Beginnings of the Fraternidad Teológica Latinoamericana: Courage to Grow," *Journal of Latin American Theology: Christian Reflections from the Latino South* 2, no. 1 (2007): 8–160. For a history of the FTL's continent-wide congresses, see Ruth Padilla DeBorst, "Latin American Congresses on Evangelization (CLADE), 1969–2012," *Journal of Latin American Theology* 5, no. 2 (2010): 107–24. The relationship between the FTL and liberation theologies is covered by Andrew Kirk, *Liberation Theology: An Evangelical View from the Third World* (London: Marshall, Morgan & Scott, 1979), and by Samuel Escobar, *La fe evangélica y las teologías de la liberación* (El Paso, TX: Casa Bautista de Publicaciones, 1987). Sharon Heaney provides an in-depth study of the FTL in *Contextual Theology for Latin America: Liberation Themes in Evangelical Perspective* (Milton Keynes, UK: Paternoster, 2008). Current information can be found at www.ftl-al.org.

ment in the broader society. As they entered the United States and joined new local congregations there, they drew on their experience gained in FTL and its outward-looking stance. Although none of them cited the formal statements issued by the FTL, their discourse, values, and actions express the core concerns, vision, and mission of the movement. The impact that these three immigrants have had in the United States has been a direct outgrowth of their experience in the FTL movement.

SUMMING UP THE STORIES

Manuel, David, and Oscar's stories are a rich treasure trove that can be looked at from different angles and that yields many valuable insights. Our focus has been particularly on the impact their presence has had on the US churches in which they have been involved. In these cases, regardless of the immigrants' length of stay, age, profession, or family conditions—and in spite of the struggles of assimilation, including language learning and cultural adjustments, they have faced in a new country—some plot elements have been constant in their stories, as highlighted by both the Christian immigrants and their pastors. The immigrants took agency in their new setting as:

- *eye-openers*—helping their congregations to see the surrounding community in all its diversity with new eyes, to open their doors, and to engage in service to the surrounding community;
- *community builders*—encouraging people in their churches to support one another in closer fellowship and mutual encouragement as a community; and
- *catalysts*—encouraging adoption of the contextual and communal theological praxis characteristic of their movement within Latin America.

MAKING A PLACE AT THE TABLE

A final story of a local congregation in the United States illustrates the journey toward recognizing the agency of Christian immigrants in God's mission. Three elderly Dutch-Americans constituted the missions committee of a certain urban church. They shared their concern with me over breakfast during my missionary home service: "Our entire neighborhood is changing! Those people are simply *too* different. We may have to move!"

"Interesting," I responded; "you know, those 'different' people are cousins, sisters, and brothers of the Central Americans I work with in El Salvador and for whom you pray every month. They are actually going through much the same experience as did your own European parents or grandparents. You might want to pray and talk through what God might be calling you to do as a church."

A year later they told me they had begun studying Spanish and were ready to open an after-school program for neighborhood Latino students. "But we need someone younger who knows Latino culture and can really engage with the students and their families," they explained.

"You may need to look beyond your church. Aren't there any Latino churches in your area?" I queried. "Might there not be some Christian leader among those immigrants who could lead your program with the support of your congregation?"

Since then, younger people have stepped onto the missions committee while the ever more elderly couples continue praying and advising. Mission, they insist, is not merely something special people do in far-off lands. Today, the after-school program held in the Anglo church is headed up by a Latino pastor from a neighborhood Latino church. Special events in the lives of the children and young people are celebrated in joint services of the two congregations. A new chapter began for that church the moment they recognized the newcomers as equal agents in God's kingdom. And its socially transforming presence in the broader community entered a new phase as the church sought ways to welcome the newcomers into their fellowship and to minister together.

NECESSARY QUESTIONS

The stories of Oscar, David, Manuel, their churches, and this local congregation pose questions to faith communities in a world of people on the move. Truly, newcomers can be eye-openers. However, is the church willing to look through new eyes at the surrounding community, even when looking may demand significant change in relationships, priorities, and budget allocation? Newcomers can serve as community builders. Yet, will church members listen to them, step out of the safety of their small circles, and allow the newcomers' culture to melt entrenched Western individualism? Will they open their ears to stories that may threaten the "official" ones regarding the virtue of the host nation and the impact of its power abroad? Newcomers can serve as catalysts for more holistic approaches to church life and mission. Are churches, however, ready to set aside presumptions of power and privilege in order to *learn* from people from outside their customary circles? In sum, will churches in privileged places recognize their need for renewal and welcome the fresh air brought by fellow Christians from the rest of the world?

Gone are the days when engagement with communities different from the one in which a person was born stood on a far distant horizon. Today, immigrants and refugees take the world to the world. In the face of such drastic changes, some individuals, families, and churches have perceived difference as a threat; allowing fear and mistrust to mark their decisions, they have closed their doors or fled to grounds they consider safe. Positive experiences like those told by Manuel, David, Oscar, and the pastors of their churches stand as bright reminders that other responses are not only desirable but also possible. Immigrants like these, who have already been forced to negotiate "multiple solidarities," have valuable skills, insights, perspectives, and relational patterns to offer—if only they are recognized and granted a place at the table of Christian fellowship.

QUESTIONS FOR REFLECTION

1. What challenges does the presence of foreign nationals present to South Korea as a "one-blood" nation?

2. What attitudes and actions do you believe the Gospel demands of Christian individuals and churches in relation to foreign workers in general?

3. Most of the 1.5 million registered foreign nationals in Korea work in 3-D jobs (difficult, dangerous, and demanding). What do you believe should be the role of Christians and the church in guaranteeing just policies regarding their treatment and well-being?

4. What gifts do you believe Christian foreign workers are bringing to Korea, and what could be done so that those gifts are better received by local congregations?

Response
to
"A Place at the Table"

Joon Juan Lee

Through her retelling of the stories of Manuel, David, and Oscar, Ruth Padilla DeBorst offers admirable insight into the potential spiritual contribution migrants can make in the new communities to which they relocate. To her account, I would like to add the perspective of a Korean–Latin American.

The US Census Bureau describes people of Hispanic or Latino ethnicity as "person[s] of Cuban, Mexican, Puerto Rican, South or Central American, or other Spanish culture or origin regardless of race." This definition places the Hispanic community as the largest minority in the United States. In 2015 the Census Bureau estimated that there were 54 million Hispanic people living in the United States, representing over 17 percent of the population.[1] The influence of Hispanics was felt in the 2016 US election, when they made up 11 percent of the electorate. By the bureau's projections, the year 2060 will see 119 million Hispanic people residing in the United States, and they will represent over 28 percent of the US population.

The definition used by the Census Bureau is expansive, counting people regardless of race. Today's ease of transportation and the rapid relocation possible in today's global society have allowed the creation of new types of Latinos—people who, like myself, have adopted Hispanic identity through new waves of immigration to Latin America. In the beginning of the peopling of the Americas, people made their way from Asia to what is now called Alaska and

1. "Hispanics in the US Fast Facts," *CNN Library*, March 31, 2017, www.cnn.com/2013/09/20/us/hispanics-in-the-u-s-/index.html.

ultimately down to Argentina. In similar fashion my parents flew from Korea to Buenos Aires as modern migrants, taking part in the birth of a new generation of Latin Americans such as myself. We were part of a host of migrants from Asia—some traveling to Europe and later Africa—seeking a new "American" dream. Today, I join with many Latin American people in crossing new borders into the United States. I have become part of the migrant story, just as have Manuel, David, and Oscar, whose personal stories Padilla DeBorst examines.

Evelyn Hu-DeHart, director of the Center for the Study of Race and Ethnicity in America at Brown University, Providence, Rhode Island, estimates that between 249,000 and 305,000 Chinese Latinos now live in the United States.[2] Also, the number of Chinese immigrants now living in Latin America—mainly, in the order in which Chinese immigrated to them, in Peru, Brazil, and Argentina—may exceed 2 million.[3] A great number of Asian immigrants in Latin America have come from Japan as well, followed by those from Korea. God is building new faces in this new global century.

Faith in God must understand immersion in social reality. I was a missionary in Mexico for twelve years; nine of those years were in Ciudad Juárez, a major Mexican city just south of El Paso, Texas. There I was able to join with faithful witnesses who saw the rise of life out of death and hope from despair when drug cartel wars were killing an average of twenty people per day in the city. People had to move away from such a desperate situation. Poor Christians in Latin America and their counterparts in the United States are now reshaping the established churches in terms of rereading and reflecting on Scripture. The stories of the three Latin American Christians Manuel, David, and Oscar show how the church is called to advance toward the margins of society, where Christ in the marginalized uses them. They serve as agents of renewal in the church and the broader community.

2. Erin Chen, "Identity Stew," *New York Times*, September 5, 2004, www .nytimes.com/2004/09/05/nyregion/thecity/identity-stew.html.

3. Jaqueline Mazza, "Chinese Migration to Latin America and the Caribbean," *The Dialogue: Leadership for the Americas*, October 2016, www .thedialogue.org/wp-content/uploads/2016/10/Chinese_Migration_to _LAC_Mazza-1.pdf.

NEW GLOBAL COMMUNITY IN JESUS

The new social changes found today in the surroundings of diverse communities in the United States call for the development of new forms of church. The churches on the receiving end of these changes need to understand the potential for renewal inherent in the "reverse flow" of mission. As mentioned by Padilla DeBorst, the immigrants contribute to the established churches present in their adoptive land. Change is a constant in history; change defines the church, which is continually being transformed by the human diversity around it. When Pastor Fritz speaks of Oscar "helping us see and opening the world to us" (254), when Pastor Will presents the story of the impact David made through his presence, and when Pastor Gregorio comments that Manuel was a "true prophet" and "mediator" (255), they provide trustworthy signs that these three men had become responsible agents in their new settings. These migrants served their new communities of faith as eye-openers, community builders, and catalysts.

Mission is no longer a one-way street. In God's mission, we learn that as we talk, we listen; as we give love, we receive love; and as we share, we get even more. David Shank writes, "We in the West are entering an era where we must learn to listen to what our brothers and sisters around the globe have to tell us. The nature of the world church requires it. Christ's new commandment to love one another calls for a reciprocity that goes beyond the motley band of twelve."[4] Sustained contact with other cultural communities provides an essential comparative perspective, from which each of us as individuals learns to raise deeper epistemological questions about faith, hermeneutics, and Christian praxis. Christianity and Christian mission have become truly international and global; in consequence, we need a paradigm change in our way of understanding how mission is taking place. The mission field is not far away any more. Cultural diversity as a conversation among the stories of different peoples within a society swirls at the church's doorstep. The Western church can profit from Latino spirituality, which has been formed through contextual theologizing.

Generally speaking, when we think of immigrants, we have

---

4. David A. Shank, *What Western Christians Can Learn from African-Initiated Churches* (Elkhart, IN: Mennonite Board of Missions, 2000), 4.

in mind the marginalized, the needy, the minority groups, and those who are underrepresented in powerful social, political, and economic arenas. Their "otherness" may be foremost in our minds. The Bible, however, places clear emphasis on compassion toward and care for immigrants; they are very important and are to be the recipients of compassionate treatment on the part of the people of God. The Bible takes an additional step, calling us to see immigrants as partners, colaborers, and coparticipants in the mission of God. They are to be, in the words of Padilla DeBorst's title, "granted a place at the table." When I was doing my studies at Fuller Theological Seminary, Paul Jeong wrote a dissertation that was later published under the title *Mission from a Position of Weakness*.[5] An element of mystery enters into mission when the dynamism of mission does not come from people in positions of power or privilege, or from the overwhelming dynamism of a superior civilization, but from below, from the little ones, from those who have few material, financial, or technical resources.[6]

The Bible develops this missiological perspective on migrants and immigrants, for in its pages we see how God uses them in a significant number of narratives. Among numerous others, we could mention the stories of Abraham, Joseph, Daniel, and David in the Old Testament, and the apostle Paul, Priscilla, and Aquila in the New Testament. Immigrants are not merely agents for carrying out preconceived methods of mission; they are also instruments for bringing into existence new attitudes toward and approaches to mission.[7] I believe that when we begin to understand the Bible's missiological and instrumental perspectives on immigrants, we may experience at least partially the vision expressed in 1 Peter 2 with regard to the immigrant and stranger. We are all immigrants and strangers in this world.

---

5. Paul Yonggap Jeong, *Mission from a Position of Weakness* (New York: Peter Lang, 2007).

6. Samuel Escobar, *A Time for Mission: The Challenge for Global Christianity* (Carlisle, UK: Langham, 2013), 7.

7. Here I follow the spirit of Charles Van Engen. See his *Mission on the Way: Issues in Mission Theology* (Grand Rapids: Baker, 1996), 17–43; and "Biblical Perspectives on the Role of Immigrants in God's Mission," *Journal of Latin American Theology: Christian Reflections from the Latino South* 2 (2008): 15–38.

CHANGES IN THE PRACTICE AND THEORY OF MISSION

At the opening of this twenty-first century, current means of travel, as well as today's colossal migration movements caused by economic changes and sometimes dire sociopolitical circumstances, allow Christians and churches everywhere to experience the world's rich and diverse expressions of Christian faith. In early 2017 my wife and I were invited to lead a family conference in London, not far from where Charles Spurgeon, one of the greatest pulpiteers in history, used to preach. As a Korean-Latino, I was teaching and preaching in Spanish to a large Spanish-speaking congregation, while simultaneously a Latina from Colombia who had grown up in England was translating into English for young 1.5- and second-generation Latinos growing up in England. Traditional Latino faces are changing as globalization brings people from anywhere to everywhere. Changing currents take Latin Americans out to the world, but they bring new challenges as well, as new immigrants come into Latin America. Stories like those of Manuel, David, and Oscar told by Padilla DeBorst are no longer stories just of Latin American immigrants in the United States; they represent also the new stories of new immigrants from Asia in the large cities of Latin America such as Mexico City, São Paulo, and Buenos Aires as they host new immigrants.

Can we imagine all that God might like to do through the new Hispanic/Latino people as agents of his mission in the reevangelization of North America and Europe?

17

Human Dislocation and the Local Church: A Diaspora Mission Strategy

Sadiri Joy Tira

Migration is a global reality that in the twenty-first century has greatly accelerated, becoming now a monumental movement of people. So pervasive is migration that the International Organization for Migration (IOM) dubbed 2015 "The Year of the Migrant." In the past decade, research on and response to migration has become a priority for countries, communities, and congregations.

This chapter presents a case study of Filipino-Canadian Christians engaged in mission and outlines a strategy for local church participation in diaspora missions. The case study draws on the experience of a Canadian migrant congregation, the First Filipino Alliance Church, in Edmonton, Alberta. The chapter is organized in three main parts: Filipinos in the global diaspora landscape, diaspora missiology, and mobilizing diaspora congregations for global missions.

FILIPINOS IN THE GLOBAL DIASPORA LANDSCAPE

Despite the misery that migrants and the countries that receive them may experience, it is important that we consider the bigger picture. In the words of IOM's director William Lacy Swing, "Migration is not a problem to be solved, it's a reality to be managed."[1] Hein

---

1. United Nations Regional Information Centre for Western Europe, "Migration Is Not a Problem to Be Solved; It's a Reality to Be Managed,"

de Haas, professor of sociology at the University of Amsterdam, describes migration as an "intrinsic part of a broader development process."[2] Writing in a seminal volume for diaspora missiology, the late Luis Pantoja Jr., a Filipino-American theologian, offers a helpful theological perspective: "Humankind is designed for mobility and conquest. . . . Mobility is endemic to human nature. People reside in or move from one place to another because God made them with such instincts."[3]

Currently, observes William Lacy Swing, mass migration is driven primarily by "demography; disasters; the digital revolution; distance-shrinking technology; north-south disparities; and environmental degradation."[4] In "Trends in International Migration, 2015," the Population Division of the UN's Department of Economic and Social Affairs reports that "the number of international migrants—persons living in a country other than where they were born—reached 244 million in 2015 for the world as a whole, an increase of 71 million, or 41 percent, compared to 2000."[5]

Continuing a long trajectory of economic and labor migration, the Filipino people are at the forefront of this movement of peoples beyond the borders of their countries of origin. The most recent statistics published by the Commission on Filipinos Overseas state that, as of December 2013, there were 10.2 million Fili-

---

May 12, 2015, www.unric.org/en/latest-un-buzz/29774-migration-is -not-a-problem-to-be-solved-its-a-reality-to-be-managed.

2. Hein de Haas, "About," *Hein de Haas*, February 25, 2016, https:// heindehaas.org/2016/02/25/551/.

3. Luis Pantoja Jr., "Formulating a Theology of the Filipino Diaspora," in *Scattered: The Filipino Global Presence*, ed. Luis Pantoja Jr., Sadiri Joy B. Tira, and Enoch Wan (Manila: LifeChange, 2004), 81. For a bibliohistorical study of "diaspora," key words, and theological foundations for diaspora missions, see Lausanne Committee for World Evangelization, *Scattered to Gather: Embracing the Global Trend of Diaspora* (Manila: LifeChange, 2010).

4. William Lacy Swing, "IOM Director General William Lacy Swing's Speech at the UN Summit on Refugees and Migrants and Signing of the IOM-UN Agreement, 19 September 2016," https://weblog.iom.int/iom -director-general-william-lacy-swings-speech-un-summit-refugees-and -migrants%C2%A0and-signing-iom-un.

5. UN Department of Economic and Social Affairs, Population Division, "Trends in International Migration, 2015," *Population Facts*, no. 2015/4 (December 2015), 1.

pino nationals living overseas.[6] The top ten countries of destination for diaspora Filipinos (all figures here in thousands) are the United States (3,536), Saudi Arabia (1,029), United Arab Emirates (822), Malaysia (794), Canada (722), Australia (398), Italy (272), United Kingdom (218), Qatar (205), and Singapore (203).[7] Furthermore, the IOM reports that in 2015 one out of every twenty citizens of the Philippines was living outside the country; according to the World Bank, the Philippines ranks third in the world's remittance-receiving countries with annual remittances of US$29.7 billion, following India and China.[8]

Just as global population movements are a reality of human experience, so for Filipinos international migration is a reality of their history.[9] Riding on the waves of colonial expansion—and literally aboard the vessels of their colonizers, Spain and then the United States—the people of the Philippines have exported their labor, even as they have struggled to forge their own national identity. Records and archaeological evidence reveal their lives as "Manila Men" aboard the Spanish galleons that crisscrossed the Pacific Ocean to the New World, then to universities of Europe and the United States as trophy children of their conquerors, as workers on American plantations and in factories, and as fighters in the American army and navy.[10]

Riddled with poverty and limited by uncertainty in their homeland, but equipped with the lingua franca of English (and to a limited degree, with Spanish) and American-style education, overseas Filipino workers have been prominent in the movement

6. Commission on Filipinos Overseas, "Stock Estimates of Overseas Filipinos," www.cfo.gov.ph/downloads/statistics/stock-estimates.html.

7. Commission on Filipinos Overseas, "Global Mapping of Overseas Filipinos," www.cfo.gov.ph/downloads/statistics/global-mapping-of-overseas-filipinos.html.

8. International Organization for Migration, "Philippines," March 29, 2017, www.iom.int/countries/philippines; World Bank Group, *Migration and Remittances Factbook 2016*, 3rd ed., https://siteresources.worldbank.org/INTPROSPECTS/Resources/334934-1199807908806/4549025-1450455807487/Factbookpart1.pdf.

9. See Center for Migrant Advocacy, "History of Philippine Migration," https://centerformigrantadvocacy.com/history-of-philippine-migration.

10. Floro L. Mercene, *Manila Men in the New World: Filipino Migration to Mexico and the Americas from the Sixteenth Century* (Quezon City, Philippines: Univ. of Philippines Press, 2007).

toward increased globalization. Deployed as engineers and field hands in foreign oil fields, as prized caregivers (from nurses to nannies in international homes and hospices), as celebrated entertainers on both land and sea, as trusted navigators delivering precious cargo across the seas, as valued managers and employees in international service industries, and, too often, enslaved as globally trafficked people, migrant Filipinos are ubiquitous. Their fortunes and plight are diverse and ongoing.

The colossal increase of migration, for Filipinos and other migrant peoples, presents a complex challenge and an urgent opportunity to the church. Government agencies, aid organizations, and community institutions contend with the demands of modern population movements, while denominations and local congregations, including diaspora congregations, mobilize to respond.

DIASPORA MISSIOLOGY

Integration of migration research into missiological study has resulted in practical diaspora missiology, a strategy for missions. Early attempts to define diaspora missiology showed a need for the concept to be refined. Initially described as "missiological study of the phenomena of diaspora groups being scattered geographically and the strategy of gathering for the Kingdom," the term "diaspora missiology" has evolved.[11] The Lausanne Diaspora Educators Consultation of November 2009 offered an enhanced definition of diaspora missiology as "a missiological framework for understanding and participating in God's redemptive mission among people living outside their place of origin."[12] It must be stated that diaspora missions are complementary to traditional missions, and diaspora missiology should not be perceived or touted as a replacement of traditional missiology. Nevertheless, it must be appreciated that diaspora missions are distinct from traditional missions. While

11. "Diaspora Missiology," in *Missions Practice in the Twenty-First Century*, ed. Enoch Wan and Sadiri Joy Tira (Pasadena, CA: William Carey International Univ. Press, 2009), 27.

12. Hosted by Torch Trinity Graduate School of Theology, Seoul, South Korea, November 11–14, 2009, the Lausanne Diaspora Educators Consultation convened missiologists and mission educators. For the Seoul Consultation's definition, see www.lausanne.org/content/statement/the-seoul-declaration-on-diaspora-missiology.

Protestant mission strategies have traditionally concentrated on a specific nation or geographic region, the focus of diaspora missions is *every person* outside the kingdom, *everywhere.*

In 1974 Ralph Winter popularized a missions strategy that emphasizes "unreached people groups" (UPG), coining what he called the E1, E2, E3 (or M1, M2, M3) strategies.[13] But by the time of the Lausanne Movement's 2007 Bi-Annual Leadership Conference, held in Hungary, Winter reflected (during personal interaction with me as the Lausanne Movement senior associate for diasporas) that "UPG M1, M2, M3 is no longer the only way of prioritizing missions because the world that we now live in has become borderless. . . . In 1974 the political climate was very different—it was the age of the Cold War, 'state dictatorship,' and many 'closed doors.'"[14]

Migration, particularly of those escaping regional conflicts, continues unabated, despite the recent rise of nationalistic and even nativist movements in traditional migrant-receiving countries (notably, the United States, United Kingdom, and Australia). The factor of migration highlights the challenges and opportunities presented to modern missions.[15] With the current state of migration, strategy and methodology must adapt as opportunities and challenges change.

In the 2014 edition of *Perspectives on the World Christian Movement: A Reader*, Ralph Winter and Bruce Koch's updated chapter, titled "Finishing the Task: The Unreached Peoples Challenge," acknowledges diaspora missiology: "As history unfolds and global migration increases, more and more people groups are being dispersed throughout the entire globe. Dealing with

13. For a presentation of various permutations of Winter's E-Scale, see Ralph D. Winter and Bruce A. Koch, "Finishing the Task: The Unreached Peoples Challenge," *International Journal of Frontier Missions* 19, no. 4 (Winter 2002): 15–25, www.ijfm.org/PDFs_IJFM/19_4_PDFs/winter_koch _task.pdf.

14. Ralph D. Winter, personal communication, June 22, 2007. The senior associate for diasporas, first installed by the Lausanne Committee for World Evangelization during the Hungary 2007 meeting, is now called the global catalyst for diasporas.

15. For one example, see the table "312 Diaspora Peoples without a Church. Populations over 25,000," prepared by Finishing the Task, Aliso Viejo, CA, 2010. To obtain online, enter "312 Diaspora Peoples without a Church" into Google. The table is in Chinese.

this phenomenon is now called 'diaspora missiology.' Not many agencies take note of the strategic value of reaching the more accessible fragments of these 'global peoples.'"[16] By 2017 an appreciable number of missiologists had begun concentrating on population movements and synthesizing current research to assist denominations and local churches in digesting the reality and opportunities of migration.

An essential first step for accountability in missions is to recognize that diaspora is an unavoidable reality. A good case in point is Canada. Early Canadian society was composed of people who had immigrated from Europe during the eighteenth and nineteenth centuries. During the past three decades, however, Canadian demographics have changed drastically. Consider the following information supplied by the Demography Division of Statistics Canada:

- The majority of immigrants to Canada now come from Asia. In 2012, nearly 6 in 10 (57.9%) immigrants to Canada came from Asia.

- In 2031, more than one in four Canadians could be foreign born. . . . According to the different scenarios of recent population projections, the proportion of foreign-born persons could reach just over one-quarter of the Canadian population (between 25% and 28%) by 2031. . . . Canada could have between 9.8 and 12.5 million foreign-born persons.

- Foreign-born population is increasingly ethnoculturally diverse. . . . This diversification could continue in the coming years. . . . According to the reference scenario for the most recent projections of the diversity of the Canadian population, more than half of the foreign-born population living in Canada could be Asian-born by 2031.[17]

16. Ralph D. Winter and Bruce A. Koch, "Finishing the Task: The Unreached Peoples Challenge," in *Perspectives on the World Christian Movement: A Reader*, 4th ed., ed. Ralph D. Winter and Steven C. Hawthorne (Pasadena, CA: William Carey Library, 2014), chap. 84.

17. Statistics Canada, Demography Division, *Canadian Demographics at a Glance*, 2nd ed., February 19, 2016, www.statcan.gc.ca/pub/91-003 -x/91-003-x2014001-eng.pdf?contentType=application%2Fpdf%20on%20 20; the quotations come from pp. 28, 34, and 14.

In 2015 the top five source countries of permanent immigrants received by Canada were the Philippines (50,846), India (39,530), China (19,533), Iran (11,669), and Pakistan (11,330).[18] Refugees represent a separate category; in 2016 the top ten countries of citizenship from which refugee claimants came were: China (1,498), Hungary (986), Pakistan (899), Nigeria (794), Colombia (696), Iraq (598), Syria (577), Libya (518), Somalia (505), and Afghanistan (495).[19]

Following Ralph Winter's UPG approach, the vital question for Canadian mission strategists becomes the following: Do immigrants and refugees in Canada include members of the least-reached people groups? If so, how can local churches engage them? According to the Joshua Project, as of April 2017 Canada was home to fifty(!) immigrant people groups categorized as unreached.[20] Diaspora peoples in Canada are indeed a mission field requiring new strategies.

In their planning, mission strategists must recognize three significant challenges and opportunities presented by migrants: urbanization, multiculturalism, and mobilization. Consider the following:

- Migration has fed *urbanization*. In 2014 Canadian cities were host to 82 percent of Canada's population, a proportion that is expected to rise to 88 percent by 2050.[21] The city

---

18. For data on immigration to Canada, see Government of Canada, *Statistics and Open Data*, www.cic.gc.ca/english/resources/statistics/index .asp. The figures given for 2015 are from "Canada—Permanent Residents by Source Country," www.cic.gc.ca/opendata-donneesouvertes/data/ IRCC_FFPR_15_E.xls. Also see Government of Canada, *Annual Report to Parliament on Immigration, 2016*, "Table 3: Permanent Residents Admitted in 2015, by Top 10 Countries of Citizenship," October 31, 2016, www.cic.gc.ca/english/resources/publications/annual-report-2016/ind ex.asp#s4.1.

19. See Government of Canada, Immigration, Regugees, and Citizenship Canada, "Statistics and Open Data, Facts and Figures," "10.2. Refugee Claimants by Top 50 Countries of Citizenship, 2006 to 2015," www .cic.gc.ca/opendata-donneesouvertes/data/IRCC_FF_39_E.xls.

20. Joshua Project, "People Groups, Resources; Country: Canada," https://joshuaproject.net/countries/CA.

21. UN Department of Economic and Social Affairs, Population Division (2014), *World Urbanization Prospects: 2014 Revision, Highlights*, 24, http://esa.un.org/unpd/wup/Highlights/WUP2014-Highlights.pdf.

is the focal point for diaspora missions and evangelization in Canada as migrants arrive and transform the urban face.[22] Accelerated and defined partnerships between like-minded denominations, local churches, and kingdom-building organizations must be encouraged (rather than indulging in "protecting our own castles").

- Migration has propagated *multiculturalism*. Gone are the days of Eurocentric Christianity. Local churches in Canada are called to engage migrant peoples with innovative strategies. Specifically, Christ's followers among the New Canadians must be nurtured in their faith and ultimately recruited and commissioned as church workers for missions. It is evident that an increasing number of Canadian missionaries are products of diaspora congregations. This pattern of growth in personnel deployment will continue within denominations that develop their mission agenda while keeping diaspora missions clearly in view.

- Migration has challenged traditional leadership *mobilization*. Crucial deficiencies in selection and training of leaders have hindered many denominations from undertaking successful cross-cultural evangelism and church planting. Migrants bring to Canada varying degrees of education and professional experience. Hence, local churches that adhere to strict requirements of college and seminary degrees for church staff often find themselves unable to keep abreast of developments in Canadian diaspora society. Church multiplication among diaspora groups requires a rapid output of workers. For this reason, denominations must bring the "academy" to the grassroots, as well as accelerate their nonformal education programs among the emerging leaders of diaspora congregations.[23]

22. Doug Saunders, *Arrival City: How the Largest Migration in History Is Reshaping Our World* (New York: Vintage, 2012).

23. SIM (Serving in Mission; https://www.sim.ca) is one agency actively seeking to train diaspora leadership. At the same time, formal pastoral training institutions cannot afford to see their graduates uninformed about migration. Seminaries and training institutions must design curricula for diaspora leaders by integrating diaspora missiology in their programs. Ambrose University in Calgary and Tyndale Seminary in Toronto are two institutions working toward such integration.

MOBILIZING DIASPORA CONGREGATIONS
FOR GLOBAL MISSIONS

In 2004 Winter observed that diaspora is an "undigested reality in mission thinking."[24] Since then, awareness of mass migration, or the diaspora phenomenon, has grown among many local churches in Canada's urban centers. Today it is not unusual to see local congregations intentionally reaching out to New Canadians (i.e., naturalized Canadian citizens), "temporary residents" (i.e., foreign workers and international students), noncitizen permanent residents, and tourists and refugees who are entering Canada. In Edmonton, which bills itself as Canada's Gateway to the North, local churches are strategically employing diaspora missiology.[25] The experience of Edmonton's First Filipino Alliance Church (FFAC) provides one example of what is taking place.

Despite Canada's bitter winters, the Philippines has been a top source of immigrants to the country for the past three decades, making the Filipino-Canadian community one of the fastest growing ethnic groups in Canada. According to the government of Canada, already in 2014 "over 700,000 Canadian residents [were able to] trace their ancestry back to the Philippines, and a growing number of Filipino citizens visit family and friends in Canada, study at Canadian colleges and universities, or immigrate to Canada as permanent residents."[26] In 2015 the Philippines was again the top source country for new immigrants (i.e., landed immigrants with permanent residence).[27] Consequently, the need to develop ministries in response to the influx of Filipino immigrants is readily apparent.

24. Ralph Winter's observation appears in a 2004 endorsement he wrote for Pantoja, Tira, and Wan, *Scattered: The Filipino Global Presence*.

25. For Edmonton's status as the "Gateway to the North," see www .thecanadianencyclopedia.ca/en/article/edmonton/.

26. Government of Canada, "Philippines—Top Source Country for Permanent Residents to Canada in 2014," May 8, 2015, www.canada.ca/en /news/archive/2015/05/philippines-top-source-country-permanent-res idents-canada-2014.html.

27. Government of Canada, 2016 *Annual Report to Parliament on Immigration*, "Table 3: Permanent Residents Admitted in 2015, by Top 10 Countries of Citizenship."

In 1983, early in this "immigration journey," the Filipino fellowship in Edmonton was born. With support from the Christian and Missionary Alliance (C&MA) in Canada and by its mother church—Edmonton's Millbourne Alliance Church— the Filipino fellowship, composed primarily of Filipino students studying at the University of Alberta, immigrant youth, and young professionals, quickly grew into a self-supporting, self-propagating, and self-governing congregation. In June 1989 the First Filipino Alliance Church of the C&MA in Canada was launched.

FFAC had a vision to be a catalyst in church planting and missions. That vision became the inspiration for many promising leaders to pursue further theological and ministerial training in Canadian seminaries, particularly at Canadian Theological Seminary, in Calgary, Alberta. Upon graduation, most FFAC-related students took church positions in various Canadian cities with the missional purpose of planting Filipino churches throughout Canada. They came to form the first generation of Filipino C&MA pastors and workers in Canada, launching the Council of Filipino Alliance Ministries in Canada (later changing the name to Conference of Filipino Alliance Ministries in Canada). Some of the students would go on to serve as international workers (i.e., career missionaries) with the denomination, often deployed overseas to limited-access nations with large expatriate Filipino populations.

FFAC also came to play a vital role in launching community outreach organizations to serve Edmonton's migrant populations, most notably Palm Ministries, which serves Muslim-background migrants in Edmonton. Influential non-Filipino leaders are also among the number who can trace their service to migrant communities back to early staff positions at FFAC.

FFAC's strong engagement in missions also led to the formation of the Filipino International Network (FIN). Launched in 1995, FIN exists "to motivate, equip and mobilize the Filipino diaspora to help fulfill the Great Commission" via evangelism, discipleship, and leadership training, as well as through prayer movement initiatives and family support ministries.[28] As one example, consider

28. Luis Pantoja Jr., Sadiri Joy Tira, and Enoch Wan, eds., *Scattered to Gather* (Manila: LifeChange Publishing, 2004), 160–61.

the Filipino congregation of the National Evangelical Church of Kuwait, which in March 2017 celebrated its twenty-fifth anniversary.[29] Its more than 800 members represent countries from around the globe. FIN was instrumental in discipling and training their leadership team.

Today, FFAC has a growing multicultural congregation composed of Filipino-Canadians, Indigenous Canadians (First Nations or Aboriginal Canadians), Canadians of European descent, Vietnamese-Canadians, Indo-Canadians (Canadians of South Asian heritage), Chinese-Canadians, Latin American Canadians, and second-generation Canadians of various other heritages. FFAC has been granted unique opportunities to make an impact both locally and globally. The impact of its mission initiative is disproportionate to its size, reaching across geographic and ethnic boundaries. I consider FFAC's birth as providential and, in God's sovereignty, strategic for global missions.

CONCLUSION

As the Philippines attempts to shed its colonial status and as its intellectuals focus on postcolonial discussion, it would be easy to view the country's economic poverty and political instability—and the consequent dislocation of millions of its people—through a myopically negative lens. The Spanish and US colonization of the Philippines was in many ways devastating, but viewed through a missiological lens, it has proved to be remarkably redemptive. However enduring the suffering of the Filipino people has been, it is overshadowed by the grace of God. The trajectory of colonization brought the Gospel, as well as Westernized education and skills, to the Philippines, preparing Filipinos for engagement in the global community. Filipinos, scattered across the globe, invite other nations to be gathered into the kingdom of God, transforming the immediately apparent cause of the Filipino diaspora for his glory. The sovereignty of God is evident in the dislocation and relocation of Filipinos globally for God's kingdom purpose.

In summary, local churches, regardless of size or budget, can implement the steps outlined by the Lausanne Movement's Cape

---

29. For information on the National Evangelical Church of Kuwait, see www.neckkuwait.com/populateHome.php?pid=4.

Town Commitment.[30] To actively participate in diaspora missions, local churches should:

- Recognize and respond to the missional opportunities presented by global migration and diaspora communities, including through strategic planning and offering of focused training and resources to those called to work among diaspora communities.
- Bear countercultural witness to the love of Christ in deed and word by obeying the extensive biblical commands to love the stranger, defend the cause of the foreigner, visit the prisoner, and practice hospitality through building friendships, inviting into our homes, and providing help and services.
- Discern the hand of God, even in circumstances that people might not have chosen, listen to and learn from immigrant congregations, and initiate cooperative efforts to reach all sections of Canada with the Gospel. (adapted from section IIC.5)

As with FFAC, more mission organizations, denominations, and local churches are coming to discern God's hand in human dislocation and relocation. As stated by Mary Wilder of Western Seminary, who addressed participants at the Conference of Filipino Alliance Ministries, hosted by FFAC and held at Taylor Seminary in Edmonton in August 2007, "A hundred years ago, the Filipinos were a mission field. Now, they are moving out to take their place in missions, reaching around the world in very creative ways!"[31] Just thirty years ago, freshly immigrated Filipino "New Canadians" were still, in Samuel Escobar's phrase, "mission fields on the move."[32] Today they are reaching out to their hosts and to other

30. The text of the Cape Town Commitment is available at www.laus anne.org/content/ctc/ctcommitment.

31. See Sadiri Joy Tira, "Every Person (from Everywhere)," *Evangelicial Missions Quarterly* 50, no. 4 (2014): 398–400.

32. J. Samuel Escobar, "Mission Fields on the Move: The Massive Global Migration We See Today Presents Unparalleled Opportunities for Ministry," *Christianity Today*, May 2010, www.christianitytoday.com/ct/2010/may/index.html.

scattered people in innovative ways. May many more congregations embrace migrants in Christ's name. Only God knows what roles diaspora engaged in God's mission will play in local churches and in mission globally in the days ahead.

QUESTIONS FOR REFLECTION

1. How can local congregations reach migrants or scattered peoples in their cities? How might congregations work to reflect multicultural diversity in ministry initiatives and in staff workers? How can larger and older congregations design appropriate budgets so as to balance overseas and local ministries?

2. In what way(s) could a traditionally diaspora/ethnic-minority congregation such as First Filipino Alliance Church reach out to the native/host/dominant population? How can ministries be intentional in reaching out to migrants and to the second and third generations? What kind of church government would it be willing to adopt?

3. Though First Filipino Alliance Church is a relatively young congregation, it has utilized diaspora missiology to minister both locally and globally. What could congregations of a similar size and age do to attain maximum impact with migrant communities both locally and abroad?

Response
to
"Human Dislocation and the Local Church"

Eun Ah Cho

The chapter by Sadiri Joy Tira has three main parts. First, it describes the presence of Filipinos within global population movements; second, it succinctly summarizes the historical development and implications of diaspora missiology; and, third—with the First Filipino Alliance Church (FFAC) of Edmonton, Alberta, as a case study—it shows how local diaspora churches can participate in God's mission. Tira is the Lausanne Movement's senior associate for diasporas and chairperson for the Global Diaspora Network. Throughout the chapter he helps us see migration as a grand opportunity for the church to participate in God's redemptive purpose for all nations.

Personally, as a woman whose life experience outside her land of birth began in Vancouver, British Columbia, and whose missionary engagements have been part of the outreach of a Korean diaspora church in Toronto, I find it to be truly a great joy to learn that a growing number of Canadian missionaries are products of diaspora congregations.

I agree with Tira that diaspora is "an unavoidable reality" (271) and that local churches around the world—which continue to grow in ethnic and cultural diversity and within which migration has now become commonplace—are blessed to reach out to the unreached, including those who have come from afar and have become literal next-door neighbors.

DIASPORIC CONGREGATIONS:
RESOURCES AND RESPONSIBILITIES

In a number of ways, diaspora congregations are uniquely equipped to participate in God's mission. The work of Howard Gardner on multiple intelligences, of David Livermore on cultural intelligence, and of Sherwood Lingenfelter on cross-cultural experience helps us to see the nature of this equipping. Gardner identifies seven kinds of intelligences: spatial, kinesthetic, musical, interpersonal, intrapersonal, linguistic, and logical. Persons in diaspora who live outside their land of origin are likely to acquire linguistic, interpersonal, and intrapersonal skills and intelligence, all of which enhance their capacity to serve the body of Christ in their new homelands.[1]

Livermore goes a step further in discussing *cultural* intelligence, an important quality especially for cross-cultural workers, but one that Gardner does not include among the seven intelligences that he identifies. According to Livermore, cultural intelligence is to be developed ultimately for the purpose of expressing love across the gap of cultural difference.[2]

Though the cross-cultural life experiences of diasporic congregations may uniquely position and equip them for participating in God's mission, these experiences do not mean that they can solely rely on what they have acquired naturally. As Lingenfelter reminds us, Christians in diaspora need to make intentional efforts to further develop their acquired skills and intelligences.[3] Here it seems important to remember that, when people face a crisis, they default to the values, expectations, and ways of doing things that they learned while growing up. Hence, when training and equipping diasporic congregations for cross-cultural missions, sufficient time and space should be made available for them to identify their own default culture and to refine and reinforce their acquired skills and intelligences.

Even more important, as Tetsunao Yamamori has noted,

1. Howard Gardner, *Multiple Intelligences: New Horizons* (New York: Basic Books, 2006).

2. David A. Livermore, *Cultural Intelligence: Improving your CQ to Engage Our Multicultural World* (Grand Rapids: Baker Academic, 2009).

3. Sherwood Lingenfelter, *Leading Cross-Culturally: Covenant Relationships for Effective Christian Leadership* (Grand Rapids: Baker Academic, 2008).

diasporic congregations can be "powerful agents for the extension of the gospel" because they have gone through the crucible.[4] They have experienced crises and have witnessed the power of the Gospel manifested in situations of vulnerability. The experience of vulnerability in the life of the landless may indeed be an invaluable ingredient for twenty-first-century missions to and beyond migrants.

Furthermore, diasporic congregations should be reminded of a God-given task assigned to them along with their new land. Before crossing the Jordan, when the Israelites' life of landlessness was about to end and their life as possessors of land was to begin, they were reminded, states Walter Brueggemann, that "being landed is *sola gratia*."[5] They were about to inherit a land that they themselves did not build, till, or plant. Land is thus a blessed gift. At the same time, as Brueggemann aptly illustrates, land can be a temptation because the abundance and security found in being "landed" can hinder one from remembering God, by whose divine plan and grace only can one ever be thus blessed.[6] For the landed to resist the temptation that having land presents, it is critical for them to realize that they have been given a task: to care for the poor, both the physically poor and the spiritually poor, who may be found within their host nations or beyond their boundaries. When landed migrants recall this God-given responsibility, they can be powerful agents for God's mission, just as FFAC has been. Thus, in their migration experience, it is imperative that diasporic congregations discern God's sovereign, loving, and redemptive purpose for all nations. In order to discern such a purpose, we need to nurture a sovereign mind-set that allows us to see God's hand at work in our circumstances. For example, Daniel had such a mind-set, which let him believe that the Most High God rules in the affairs of individuals, nations, and history. This outlook helped him to endure the hardship of being an exile.[7] Cultivating a sover-

4. Tetsunao Yamamori, Foreword, in *Scattered to Gather: Embracing the Global Trend of Diaspora*, Lausanne Committee for World Evangelization (Manila: LifeChange Publishing, 2010), 2.

5. Walter Brueggemann, *The Land: Place as Gift, Promise, and Challenge in Biblical Faith* (Minneapolis: Fortress Press, 2002), 46.

6. Brueggemann, *The Land*, 45–56.

7. See J. Robert Clinton, *The Bible and Leadership Values: A Book by Book Analysis* (Altadena, CA: Barnabas Publishing, 1993).

eign mind-set is crucial even when the experience of a nation thus far may best be categorized, in Andrew Walls's terms, as "Adamic" rather than "Abrahamic."[8]

FROM A LEADERSHIP PERSPECTIVE

I comment here on two observations from Tira's chapter, suggesting, primarily from a leadership perspective, further lines of reflection. First, at the beginning of his chapter Tira cites with approval a statement made by William Lacy Swing. According to Swing, migration is not "a problem to be solved" but "a reality to be managed."[9] I agree that migration is not a technical problem to be solved with technical solutions. I question, however, whether it is a reality to be "managed," that is, to be approached by controlling finances, time, and quality. Migration is not an impersonal object; rather, it involves the lives of actual people who, created in God's own image, are to be redeemed according to the riches of his grace, good pleasure, and purpose (see Eph. 1:7–11). Migrating people are to be viewed and valued in the wider trajectory of God's mission and his love for all nations.

Second, Tira indicates that leadership mobilization and nonformal education programs are one of three significant challenges and opportunities presented by migrants. I concur with Tira that college and seminary degrees are not mandatory prerequisites for successful cross-cultural evangelism or church planting. Nonetheless, I cannot fully embrace his statement that nonformal education programs should be accelerated for "a rapid output of workers" (273). What matters most, I would argue, is not the particular training mode that is chosen, but *what* is taught and *what end is in mind* as it is taught. Though diaspora missions may still be acknowledged to be a mission strategy whose significance has not yet been fully realized or digested, use of nonformal training modes should not

8. On Andrew F. Walls's development of the terms "Adamic" versus "Abrahamic," migration as bane or blessing, see his chapter "Mission and Migration: The Diaspora Factor in Christian History," in *Global Diasporas and Mission*, ed. Chandler H. Im and Amos Yong (Oxford: Regnum Books International, 2014), 21.

9. United Nations Regional Information Centre for Western Europe, "Migration Is Not a Problem to Be Solved; It's a Reality to Be Managed," May 12, 2015, www.unric.org/en/latest-un-buzz/29774-migration-is -not-a-problem-to-be-solved-its-a-reality-to-be-managed.

be preferred only for the sake of shortening the time for "a rapid output of workers." Given its urgency, leadership selection and development for God's kingdom work in, through, and beyond diaspora should be done carefully and prayerfully.

CONCLUSION

We should reflect on the scattering of peoples in multiple directions—something that often accompanies diverse and ongoing plight—in light of God's sovereign plan for the nations. As Sadiri Joy Tira articulates, we need to see "God's hand in human dislocation and relocation" (277). With this thought in mind, the First Filipino Alliance Church needs to remain faithful to its vision to be a catalyst, for it is of utmost importance that the *whole body of Christ*, whether diasporic or host, is encouraged and empowered so that each part can do God's kingdom work for his glory.

Diaspora mission summons the whole of God's people everywhere—both migrants and original residents, each of them called and equipped to work in faithful partnership with one another—to serve God and his kingdom. It is thus my earnest prayer that mission leaders around the globe will understand and fulfill their role as a "supporting ligament [that] promotes the growth of the body" (Eph. 4:16 HCSB) for God's kingdom and his glory.

18

The Refugee Situation in Europe: Reflections of a Theologian-Missiologist

Dorottya Nagy

"The earth is the LORD's, and everything in it, the world, and all who live in it" (Ps. 24:1 NIV) is an eschatological confession, one in which I wish to embed my theological-missiological reflections on the refugee situation in Europe in 2017. The eschatological stance of Psalm 24 applies to the refugee situation in Europe, for, as Jürgen Moltmann states, "From first to last, and not merely in the epilogue, Christianity is eschatology, is hope, forward looking and forward moving, and therefore also revolutionizing and transforming the present."[1]

SHARED TERMINOLOGY: LINKS TO THE WIDER WORLD

Discussing the refugee situation in Europe without linking it to discourses on refugees worldwide is meaningless. One constantly needs to ask the question, What kind of relationship exists between the internal dynamics of human mobility in Europe and the wider international scene? One obvious link is that the refugee situation usually goes together with the larger issue of other sorts of migration. Alongside flight connections between Europe and other parts of the world, connectivity

1. Jürgen Moltmann, *Theology of Hope: On the Ground and the Implications of a Christian Eschatology* (New York: Harper & Row, 1967; first published in Germany in 1964), 16. Moltmann was writing in light of the experience of World War II refugees, which continued into the 1960s.

becomes visible through long journeys by boat, on foot, and via other means of land transportation. As with airports, refugee camps and detention centers become signs of connectivity worldwide.

The idea of "fortress Europe" has been multiplied through the development of fortress countries all over the world.[2] The Darwinian voice of "us/me first" becomes a mantra for survival and security. The myth of the individualistic character of Western societies and the collectivistic character of Eastern societies falls apart when it comes to practicing the "us/me first" principle, whether in the form of neoliberal nationalism, Communist nationalism, or democratic nationalism (as long as modern democracies presuppose nationhood).

Similarly, the borders between so-called Christian discourses and non-Christian discourses become blurred. Hermeneutics of suspicion leads to contradictory readings of the Bible and to contradictory actions in refugee situations. Christians both build up walls and tear them down, and they do not always agree on the exact time for doing which. Divisiveness erupts when it comes to the issue of who may enter *our* gates, who may enter the lands that *we* possess.

Fear, anguish, threat, survival, risk, security, life, and future are keywords in the vocabulary that characterizes the refugee situation. Strikingly, those who fear easily become the ones feared, those who are threatened become those who threaten, and security and safety become concerns for those who never left home.

After all, talking about refugee situations means looking at two sides of the same coin: how societies—and Christians as members of societies—organize and negotiate political belonging, from documents, status, and rights on through the legal category of refugee and the ways that refugees change societies.[3] The coin consists of human interactions at large, intertwined with human sinfulness and righteousness.

2. See Ulrich Beck and Edgar Grande, *Cosmopolitan Europe* (Cambridge: Polity Press, 2007).

3. See J. Olaf Kleist, "The History of Refugee Protection: Conceptual and Methodological Challenges," *Journal of Refugee Studies* 30, no. 2 (2017): 161–69.

REFUGEE CRISIS IN EUROPE

The current refugee situation in Europe also cannot be isolated from its European past. Though people working with refugees had raised the alarm earlier, it was only the arrival in 2015 of more than one million people seeking refuge that caused a sense of crisis among large numbers of the European population.[4] Many people—Christian and non-Christian—numerous NGOs, and various faith communities responded with compassion to address immediate needs; yet only a small percentage of Europeans actually stepped forward to meet refugees.

The crisis needs to be placed in a historical framework that makes it clear that the refugees are not the cause of the crisis. Rather, the cause is the inability of leadership, mainly political leadership, "to adequately and jointly address the needs of people eligible for international protection," for in Europe fear creeps into all dimensions of life.[5] When I link accountability with leadership, I link it also with the people, as responsible citizens, and with ourselves as theologians and church leaders. In what ways could theologians, church leaders, ministers, and missionaries contribute to forming better expressions of faith and citizenship among people living in Europe?

Although Europe is larger than the European Union (EU), much of the refugee situation is being viewed through discourses and policies linked to the EU and its complex relationship to migration historically. After the political changes of 1989–90, the EU sought to achieve a harmonized Common European Asylum System based on solidarity, burden sharing, and transparency between member states. The Dublin Convention (1990) and

4. Tim Noble gives perspective: the "large numbers" of refugees arriving in Europe in 2015 amount to approximately 0.25 percent of Europe's total population. Proportionately, a town of 5,000 population would need to welcome and help only 12 new people. See Tim Noble, "Mission as Hospitality towards the Other," in *Reforming Theology, Migrating Church, Transforming Society: A Compendium for Ecumenical Education*, ed. Uta Andrée, Benjamin Simon, and Lars Röser-Israel (Hamburg: Missionshilfe, 2017), 192–97.

5. Jeroen Domernik and Birgit Glorius, "Refugee Migration and Local Demarcations: New Insight into European Localities," *Journal of Refugee Studies* 29, no. 4 (2017), 431. On fear, see Ulrich Beck, *World at Risk* (Cambridge: Polity, 2007); and Zygmunt Bauman, *Liquid Fear* (Cambridge: Polity, 2006).

the Amsterdam Treaty (1997) implied that asylum seekers are to be registered by the member state in which they first reach EU ground. The EU borders drastically changed in 2004, when Cyprus, Malta, and seven formerly Communist countries (Czech Republic, Hungary, Latvia, Lithuania, Poland, Slovakia, and Slovenia) joined the EU. As member states of the EU in Central and Eastern Europe took up their borderland function, they did so with strong undercurrents in their minds of the period in Europe's history when they acted as protectors of a Christian Europe. They are finding their new role to be a challenge. Both Eastern Europe and Western Europe seem to be more preoccupied with themselves than with the refugees.

Italy lies on the EU's southern border. In 2003–4 Italy (which was already hosting more than half a million Romanian citizens, a sign of the large intra-European human mobility) intensified its bilateral collaboration with Libya on refugee issues.[6] The EU also opened talks on the issue, for by that time "illegal immigrants" (a term often used for refugees) from sub-Saharan Africa present in Libya numbered between 750,000 and 1.2 million.[7] In 2004, a decade before the refugee crisis of 2015 and almost ten years before Pope Francis's visit to the Italian island of Lampedusa, Europe was seen as a place of refuge that, for many people, was approachable mainly via Lampedusa and the country of Malta in the Sicily Channel. For its part, in 2002 Greece signed a bilateral readmission agreement with Turkey. This agreement stands in the direct lineage of the readmission agreement signed between the EU and Turkey in December 2013 and the contested 2016 EU-Turkey deal on refugees.

Besides the refugees arriving from outside Europe, intra-European refugees further complicate the situation. The Ukrainian-Russian conflict, for example, has sent hundreds of thousands of refugees fleeing across Europe. In 2015 people from Albania and Kosovo formed the largest group of refugees—after those from Syria—to apply for asylum in Germany. The refugee

6. Silja Klepp, "Italy and Its Libya Cooperation Program: Pioneer of the European Union's Refugee Policy?," in *Unbalanced Reciprocities: Cooperation on Readmission in the Euro-Mediterranean Area*, ed. Jean-Pierre Cassarino (Washington, DC: Middle East Institute, 2010), 77–93.

7. European Commission, *Technical Mission to Libya on Illegal Immigration, 27 Nov–6 Dec 2004: Report; 7753/05* (Brussels: DG HI).

situation in Europe is part of a larger issue of migration management in which power relations function in tension with aspirations for well-being.

DIFFERENT READINGS

The above data offer at least two readings. First, political leadership in Europe tries, according to its best knowledge, to protect Europeans from an influx of millions of refugees and from possible dangers they might bring with them. Second, these efforts can also be read as practicing the "us/me first" policy, in which humanitarian catastrophes need to be managed by welfare states according to the desires of their citizens. These readings, however, also pose crucial questions concerning new ways of living together in Europe as a continent. In what ways can Christians be advocates for fullness of life for the migrating multitudes during this period of reconfiguring the inhabitation of the earth?

Where Christians develop apostolic and prophetic ecclesiological perspectives, good practices unfold. Yet, as stated above, one needs to be cautious when recommending Christian practices, for dissonances are observable between institutional engagements with refugees and the practices of people who identify themselves as Christian. For example, in Poland and Hungary many Roman Catholics feel uncomfortable with the pope's advice on matters related to refugees. Different ultimate concerns encounter and clash with each other, but too often the differences remain unacknowledged.

FEAR AND HOPE

Fears are also rooted in ultimate concerns. Although occupying different positions of power, refugees and nonrefugees in Europe may experience very similar fears.[8] Fear as a political emotion reflects values and character.[9] Properly speaking, fear is a mode of sin for it carries the sense of *homo incurvatus in se ipso* (in Martin Luther's

8. In the literature little attention is given to the fears of refugees. For a comprehensive account of the dynamics of fear within host societies, see Susanna Snyder, *Asylum-Seeking, Migration, and Church* (Farnham, Surrey, UK: Ashgate, 2012).

9. See Martha C. Nussbaum, *The New Religious Intolerance: Overcoming the Politics of Fear in an Anxious Age* (Cambridge, MA: Harvard Univ. Press, 2012).

famous phrase)—that is, a humanity whose primary concern is for itself. Fear as the central emotional response to the refugee situation in Europe cries out, seeking for hope.

Giving an account of one's hope (1 Pet. 3:15) is crucial in regard to the Christian presence in the complexity of the refugee situation. Political and legal frameworks always translate into concrete situations where people are agents. Christians born outside of Europe talk differently about hope in meetings with fellow refugees, just as Christians born in Europe do in talking with each other about hope versus fear. Concrete case studies can help us see what it means to proclaim hope in the refugee situation. The question of hope does not mean a burdenless life, but rather a borderless life in the love of God (Eph. 3:16–21).

19

Migration in Central Asia: Issues, Challenges, and Missional Tasks, with Focus on Kyrgyzstan

Joshua Aslanbek

Because of their geographic location, the countries of Central Asia have experienced a variety of cultural, economic, and religious interactions and exchanges throughout history, and the region exhibits a wide array of ethnic groups.[1] Wars in particular seem to have resulted in large-scale ethnic migration within Central Asia. In what follows, I briefly review migration issues present in Central Asia and share some of the missional challenges found there, focusing on Kyrgyzstan.

HISTORICAL AND SOCIAL CONTEXT RELATED TO MIGRATION

Large-scale migration in Central Asia during the twentieth century occurred primarily in two distinct periods: during the Soviet era and right after the Soviet Union's collapse. The main factors driving migration during these two periods were different. Mass migration during the former was mostly politically motivated and forced, whereas the movement of peoples following the dissolution of the Soviet Union was voluntary.[2] The collapse of the

1. The term "Central Asia" refers to five former republics of the Soviet Union: Kazakhstan, Kyrgyzstan, Tajikistan, Turkmenistan, and Uzbekistan. The author's name, Joshua Aslanbek, is a pseudonym.

2. Pavel M. Polian, *Against Their Will: The History and Geography of*

Communist regime led to independence for the countries of Central Asia, but as social and economic challenges increased, many citizens of those countries migrated to Germany, Korea, Russia, and Turkey, as well as other countries.

The emigrants following independence were neither political refugees nor war refugees. By the time emigration peaked in 2013, millions of migrants had gone to Russia—from Uzbekistan (2.7 million), Tajikistan (1.2 million), and Kyrgyzstan (0.6 million)—but they were mainly laborers who had left home seeking jobs.[3] Some people emigrated from Kyrgyzstan for other than economic reasons. For example, Jews and Germans went back to their original homelands in accordance with repatriation policies, and Russians and other Slavic peoples followed after them.

A recently released documentary film, *Moscow's Little Kyrgyzstan*, presents the situation of Kyrgyz people who have migrated to Russia seeking employment.[4] The film shows the hard lives and real problems of ten Kyrgyz who work as laborers in Moscow. Their main reason for leaving their home country, which they love, as well as their loved ones was that they could not find suitable jobs in Kyrgyzstan. They consider living as illegal immigrants—with ten to fifteen people crowded into a single apartment and an average monthly salary of about $300—better than living in Kyrgyzstan without a job.

After Kyrgyzstan declared its independence in 1991, Martin Schuler has noted three migration behaviors:

1. Migration followed a process of "opening" from a Soviet Union–wide horizon to a worldwide scale.
2. At the same time, a reduction occurred from this Union-wide horizon to a national orientation.

Forced Migrations in the USSR (Budapest: Central European Univ. Press, 2004), 99–100; Martin Schuler, "Migration Patterns of the Population in Kyrgyzstan," *Espace, Populations, Sociétés* 2007-1 (2007): 73–74, https://eps.revues.org/1967.

3. Józef Lang, "Central Asia: The Crisis of the Migration Model and Its Potential Impact on the EU," *Ośrodek Studiów Wschodnich* [Center for eastern studies], April 25, 2017, 1–2, www.osw.waw.pl/en/publikac je/osw-commentary/2017-04-25/central-asia-crisis-migration-model -and-its-potential-impact-eu.

4. Franco Galdini, *Moscow's Little Kyrgyzstan* (Surrey, UK: Journeyman Pictures, 2017).

3. Within the national context, the economic situation led to growth on the part of the rural population of the country, as well as to the strong expansion of the capital, Bishkek, and its surrounding areas.[5]

When considering Bishkek and Osh, the central city in the south of Kyrgyzstan, Schuler's assertions seem correct. Since independence from the Soviet Union, the Central Asian countries have emphasized their national identities, and each country has embarked on its own indigenous national preference policies, adopting the language of its people as its national language. Compared to the other Central Asian countries, however, Kyrgyzstan is more flexible in its national language policy, with Russian as an official language along with Kyrgyz. This policy can be seen as a gesture of consideration for other ethnic groups living in Kyrgyzstan. The Kyrgyz ethnic-centered policy of Kurmanbek Bakiev, the second president of Kyrgyzstan (2005–10), following a political revolution, however, provided the Kyrgyz people with more advantages than other ethnic groups, and the language policy was an important principle influencing migration in Kyrgyzstan.

Kyrgyzstan, moreover, was the first Central Asian country to legally establish a refugee policy.[6] Between 1992 and 1997, during the civil war in Tajikistan, more than 20,000 refugees crossed the border into Kyrgyzstan. Later, the majority of them went back home, but about 9,500 Tajikistan refugees remained. With the assistance of the Kyrgyzstan government, they were relocated to Ivanovka village, about an hour's drive from Bishkek. As of 2014, official refugee status had been granted to 466 of them from either the UNHCR or the Kyrgyz government, which afforded them the right to work.[7] The most recent wave of refugees in Kyrgyzstan has come from Afghanistan. Others hail from China, Iran, Paki-

5. Schuler, "Migration Patterns of the Population in Kyrgyzstan," 74.

6. In October 1996 the Kyrgyzstan government appeared willing to maintain a liberal refugee policy in accordance with the UN's 1951 Refugee Convention and its protocol of 1967. See John Anderson, *Kyrgyzstan: Central Asia's Island of Democracy* (Amsterdam: Harwood Academic, 1999), 97.

7. Timur Toktonaliev, "Kyrgyzstan: Refugees from Uzbekistan Fear Tashkent's Long Arm," *Eurasia Net*, December 11, 2014, www.eurasianet.org/node/71306.

stan, Syria, Tajikistan, and Uzbekistan. Over the period since independence in August 1991, Kyrgyzstan's most numerous block of immigrants, 100,000 strong, has been Chinese.[8]

A MISSIONAL APPROACH TOWARD MIGRATION AND THE RESPONSIBILITY OF THE CHURCH

What missional approaches to migrants are available? What responsibilities does the present massive migration place on churches and missionaries? Certainly, the situation and issues encountered by immigrants to Kyrgyzstan differ from those of emigrants *from* Kyrgyzstan. Both groups need active assistance on policy issues facing them at the national level and because of social tensions. Nevertheless, our focus should be on seeking ways to provide practical help to migrants, proclaiming the Good News of the kingdom to them, and serving them by living in this world as people of God who go beyond searching merely for political and social solutions.

Above all, we need to change our perspective toward immigrants. We need to take fully to heart that God created human beings according to his special purpose and will. We must strive to see migrants from the perspective of the kingdom of God, that is, as persons who are in need of knowing God's love and care for them.

It is right and proper to view immigrants as persons in need of God's loving care. Yes, all migrants need economic, medical, educational, cultural, social, and institutional help and care. At the same time, we need to change our outlook and see them as people who need to know God's love, people whom we can care for spiritually. In Russia and elsewhere, Kyrgyz migrants daily face unfair treatment and discrimination. God's people should be on hand to show empathy toward the sufferings of immigrants and to wipe away their tears.

RESPONSIBILITIES OF CHURCHES AND MINISTERS

Many Christian believers have migrated from Kyrgyzstan to either Russia or Germany, with the result that for a while churches in Kyrgyzstan experienced stagnation in growth or even a decrease in

8. Paul Goble, "Kyrgyzstan: Influx of Ethnic Chinese Causing Concern—Analysis," *Eurasia Review*, March 27, 2011, www.eurasiare view.com/27032011-kyrgyzstan-influx-of-ethnic-chinese-causing-conce rn-analysis.

numbers. From a kingdom perspective, however, "we cannot say that this is bad. Now there are three Kyrgyz churches in Moscow. Besides that, there are many other churches being planted among the Kyrgyz in other parts of Russia."[9]

A Kyrgyz church that I attend and serve is visited each year by emigrant church leaders who live in Germany. They migrated from Kyrgyzstan, and they share their spiritual situation and needs when returning to their home country. From this example, we can understand the significance of networking among migrants' churches. If Kyrgyz believers go to Moscow to work, a Kyrgyz church can be recommended for them to attend there. At the same time, the Kyrgyz church in Moscow should offer hospitality, practical care, and help.

Churches and leaders in Kyrgyzstan need to form a careful and strategic missional approach to refugees and migrants in the country. Even though the laws pertaining to religion have become stricter in Kyrgyzstan, diverse church activities have been carried out, mainly in registered churches where religious activities are permitted. For example, one sees students from Afghanistan, India, and Pakistan attending English worship services in Bishkek. Chinese believers also worship in the same church building at a separate time. We see God gathering them and building them into his church.

CONCLUSION

Churches, ministers, and missionaries should open up their minds and actively communicate the Gospel to migrants, who are socially "low on the totem pole." Ministries in Kyrgyzstan should be expanded and deepened so that the Good News of the kingdom of God can reach the migrants. God's people, who are invited to participate in his mission, should be grateful for the privilege. I hope to see the day when the people who have planted and watered faithfully will worship together with the fruit of their labor in the presence of God, who causes the growth.

9. Joshua Aslanbek, "Developing a Contextualized Church Planting Model: Fruitful Practices of Church Planting in Central Asia" (DIS diss., Fuller Theological Seminary, School of Intercultural Studies, 2016), 100.

20

Mission to and by the Japanese Diaspora: Hope for the Evangelization of Japan?

Eiko Takamizawa

In mid-September 2017 the population of Japan numbered 126 million.[1] In addition, approximately one out of every hundred Japanese lives in diaspora, residing in a number of countries around the world.[2] Japanese diasporas consist of four types. First, Nikkei are Japanese of the first generation and their descendants who have migrated abroad on a permanent basis, choosing to become citizens of their new country of residence. Their descendants often intermarry with the local people, and therefore tracing statistics for this group is difficult. Second, Permanent Residents (PR) are Japanese citizens who receive permits to reside permanently within their host countries while retaining their Japanese citizenship. Third, Long-Term Residents (LR) are Japanese citizens with Japanese passports who reside temporarily in host countries but who intend to return to Japan at a future date. LRs are usually company workers, business people, members of NGOs and NPOs, researchers, students, educators, working holiday visa holders,

1. See www.worldometers.info/world-population/japan-population.

2. Michael Hoffman, "Japan's Growing Diaspora Reflects Concern for the Country's Future," *Japan Times*, January 19, 2013, www.japantimes .co.jp/news/2013/01/19/national/media-national/japans-growing-dias pora-reflects-concern-for-the-countrys-future/#.WbgYt4qQyl4. For general information, consult the Japanese Diaspora Portal, Boston University Libraries, www.bu.edu/library/japanese-diaspora-portal.

religious workers, and so forth.[3] The fourth category of Japanese migrants consists of those who go abroad as spouses in international marriages.

The fourth category is statistically a part of either PR or LR but is distinct in terms of culture and mentality. While members of the first two diasporas incline to identify with their host countries, the LR identify more closely with Japan in terms of culture, self-consciousness, and legal status. The four types also differ in their response to Christianity.

The Japanese Ministry of Foreign Affairs reports that, as of October 1, 2016, the Japanese diasporas (categories 2, 3, 4) totaled 1,338,477. PRs numbered 468,428, and LRs 870,049.[4] LRs who have returned to Japan are called Returnees. Their presence exerts noticeable influence within Japanese society today. Schools arrange special classes for returning children, and most college admission programs set aside special seats for returnees. The growing needs of international trade lead some companies and organizations to employ returnees with special language skills.[5] Diaspora phenomena have spiritual implications; for example, except for Thailand, the top ten countries in which Japanese diasporas reside are majority Christian nations.[6]

CHRISTIAN AND MISSIONAL OPPORTUNITIES OF THE JAPANESE DIASPORA

How might Japanese diasporas relate to Christianity? First, Japanese in diaspora have an increased opportunity to encounter Christianity. Japan has 84,956 Shinto shrines and 77,304 Buddhist temples. Most of them are culturally part of Japanese life, which

---

3. These terms do not include short-term visitors abroad such as tourists and business travelers.

4. Annual Report of Statistics on Japanese Nationals Overseas, Ministry of Foreign Affairs of Japan, October 1, 2016, www.mofa.go.jp/mofaj /toko/page22_000043.html.

5. See "Nihon Kigyo niyoru Kaigai Kikokushijo no Saiyo to Jidaiteki Hensen [Recruitment and chronological transition of Japanese children returnees by Japanese companies], Tokio Nagamine, http://repo.lib.hosei .ac.jp/bitstream/10114/7161/1/12_nkr_12_2_nagamine.pdf.

6. Though some of these nations are regarded as post-Christian, they have certain cultural foundations based on Christianity that are not available in Japan.

includes child dedications, weddings in Shinto shrines, and funerals and ancestral rites in Buddhist temples. Christian churches, outnumbered 18 to 1, total approximately 9,070, of which 70 are Orthodox, 1,000 are Roman Catholic, and 8,000 are Protestant.[7] Together these three branches of Christianity constitute about 1.0 percent of the nation's population. Regular attendance in Protestant churches is a mere 320,000, or 0.25 percent of the country's population. Japanese people in Japan therefore have few opportunities to meet Christians. Moreover, destructive cultic activities in the recent past have led Japanese society to regulate religious organizations more strictly.[8] Members of Japanese diasporas living in countries with a Christian heritage clearly have greater opportunity to encounter Christianity than do their fellow Japanese living in the homeland.

Second, Japanese returnees have the potential to become missionaries. Japanese Christian Fellowship Network (JCFN) reports that Japanese living abroad are thirty times more likely to become Christians than are Japanese in Japan.[9] Statistically, each year about 1,700 LRs return to Japan as Christian converts. The average Protestant church in Japan has an attendance of 34. If the 1,700 converts returning every year to Japan were to start an average-sized Protestant church, it would represent the addition of 50 new churches annually. If these returnees were trained, they could hold great potential as evangelists in Japan.

CHRISTIAN MINISTRIES
FOR THE JAPANESE DIASPORAS

For the 1.3 million Japanese abroad, there are only 330 Japanese churches located around the world (see accompanying table). This number does not include Christian fellowship groups and house churches. Though Japanese churches outside of Japan are

7. Japan Mission Research reports these approximate numbers for 2014. See www.bunka.go.jp/tokei_hakusho_shuppan/tokeichosa/shumu/pdf/h26kekka.pdf.

8. The Act on Punishment of Organized Crimes and Control of Crime was enacted in 1999 as a result of the Aum Shinri cult's sarin nerve gas attack in 1995.

9. See http://jcfn.org/jcfnhome/index.php?option=com_content&view=article&id=767&Itemid=451&lang=ja. For information on JCFN in English, see http://jcfn.org/jcfnhome/index.php?lang=en.

also small in size, Japanese ministries on different continents hold large gatherings to encourage one another. The meetings include those of the Europe Japanese Christian Association, East Coast Japanese Retreat (United States), West Coast Japanese Retreat (United States), Mt. Hermon Christian Retreat (United States), and Asia Japanese Christian Family Camp. Although each church is small, the bigger gatherings may have 200 to 300 participants, which on the Japanese scale is quite a large number.

Japanese churches abroad

Area	Region	Churches
Asia	Korea	20
	Other countries	31
Europe		27
Middle East	Israel	1
North America	United States	192
	Canada	13
Oceania		12
South America	Brazil	30
	Other countries	4
Total churches		*330*

Source: Japanese Ministries Abroad, www
.jaspella.com/jp/jchurches

JCFN, which has been serving Japanese diaspora youth since 1991, focuses on young LRs in the United States and on returnees. It organizes programs and events to equip future returnees for reverse culture shock and to help them adjust to the culture of Japanese churches.[10] It sees the potential that returnees represent as witnesses to their family, friends, and other contacts. In the United States JCFN thus hosts the Equipper Conference, which provides leadership training for LRs. In Japan it organizes the Global Returnees Conference (GRC), which offers training programs and events for returnees there. Another organization, the Diaspora Network for Japanese (DNJ), has begun serving not only Japanese diaspora

10. JCFN hosts triennial Equipper Conferences to help LRs understand the Gospel and to train returnees. With over 400 participants, the Equipper Conference is the largest Japanese Christian gathering outside of Japan; see www.equipper.org/ec16/index .php?option=com_content&view=featured&lang=en.

youth, but more broadly LRs and returnees of any age.[11] JCFN and DNJ joined to host the All Nations Returnees Conference (ANRC) in 2009, 2010, and 2012. The first two conferences had 600 participants and more than 700 attended the one in 2012, making it one of the largest Christian gatherings in Japan. ANRC has now merged with GRC, and about 450 participants took part in the first GRC, held in 2015. GRC is now developing multiple regional gatherings in different cities in Japan.

JAPANESE MINISTRIES IN KOREA

Japanese ministries located in Korea are quite different from most Japanese-led churches in other parts of the world. In most countries, Japanese ministries focus mainly on the Japanese diaspora, but in Korea their congregations consist mostly of Korean Christians. This phenomenon arises from the fact that the Japanese Christian population abroad—and in Korea—is very small. There are approximately 38,000 long-term Japanese residents in Korea.[12] If we simply use the percentages given earlier, 0.25 percent of the Japanese living in South Korea (that is, about 95 persons) can be expected to participate in Christian worship. As there are approximately twenty Japanese churches in Korea, statistically each church would include four or five Japanese Christians. Convenient transportation is a crucial factor in attracting participants (see accompanying table).

Japanese churches in Greater Seoul

Church	Average attendance	Number of Japanese participants	Density of Japanese near the church	Convenient transportation
A	170	33	high density	very convenient
B	130	20	high density	very convenient
C	70	4	low	inconvenient
D	40	15	rather high	very convenient
E	40	5	rather high	very convenient
F	40	1	low	convenient
G	20	7	low	convenient
H	17	1	rather high	convenient
Totals	527	86		

11. See http://dnjonline.org/jp.

12. Short-term residents, including tourists and nonregistered visitors, increase the number of Japanese in South Korea by 19,000.

KOREAN ORGANIZATIONS
FOCUSED ON MISSION TO JAPAN

Japan Evangelical Mission (JEM), established in 1991, is one of the oldest mission organizations in Korea. It trains Korean Christians for mission to the Japanese, and today eighty JEM missionaries serve in Japan.[13] Japan Mission Fellowship (JMF) promotes mission among the Japanese by studying about and praying for Japan.[14] Korea Japanese Ministries Association (KoJaMA) is an association of ministries in Korea that focus on Japan. KoJaMA sponsors joint programs: Kizuna in the spring for prayer, and events at Christmastime for fellowship. At present, ministers from twenty churches in the Seoul area gather for networking and prayer.

OPPORTUNITIES FOR BOTH
JAPANESE AND KOREAN MISSIONS

Korea presents a number of opportunities for Japanese mission work. Likewise, Japan holds promise for Korean mission endeavor. For example:

Diaspora mission. Japanese ministries can reach 57,000 Japanese in Korea.[15] Korean language classes, children's educational programs, and house fellowships have proven to be attractive programs. Japanese women living in Korea as wives of Korean men are in great need of emotional support and fellowship.

Sending missionaries to Japan. Currently approximately 325 Korean missionaries serve in Japan. Facilitated by some similarities in language and culture, Korean missionaries can supply ministers for Japanese churches without pastors.

Receiving mission. Japanese who visit Korea are frequently amazed at the number of churches in the country. Korean churches can organize Christian tours for Japanese visitors, helping them to

13. See www.kjem.com.

14. JMF may be contacted via email: Inho Kim, chairperson, jmf-kih @hanmail.net.

15. About 37,000 PRs and LRs are registered in Korea. The number 57,000 includes tourists and those who do not register with the embassy.

enjoy Korean culture and church experience, as well as history. This ministry can be effective in reconciliation.

Media mission. In 1999 Onnuri Community Church founded Duranno Japan. In 2006 it launched CGNTV, which for the first time in Japanese history provides twenty-four-hour Christian programming.

Event evangelism. Over a span of ten years, Onnuri Church has organized twenty-six Love Sonata events in Japan. Record-breaking numbers of participants have taken part in these Christian events in each region. Love Sonata reports 4,100 decisions to follow Christ through these events.[16]

Short-term mission teams. A number of Korean churches and mission agencies send more than 100 short-term mission teams to Japan every year.

URGENT NEED FOR MISSIONARIES IN JAPAN

Japanese churches today face serious challenges: 1,000 churches lack pastors; the average age of pastors is sixty-eight; 80 percent of churches have fewer than fifty members, and 30 percent have fewer than fifteen. Few Christians are active witnesses to their faith.

Natural disasters present another urgent concern. The Japanese government has announced the possibility of a Nankai Trough Megaquake (M9) in the near future, which could be the cause of as many as 320,000 deaths in the western half of Japan.

The need for missionaries is desperate today. Diaspora converts can serve as missionaries to meet this urgent need.

---

16. See www.lovesonata.org and www.lovesonata.org/ja.

21

Accountability in Mission to Refugees in South Korea

Dae Hum Lee

The father's role in ancient Israel was that of economic provider, educator, and physical protector. In the same way, we understand God, our spiritual Father, to be the one who supplies these three things to us. When we consider refugees who come to Korea, we as God's children cannot ignore their need for economic help, doctrinal instruction, and physical protection. To address each of these needs, Peniel Presbyterian Church in Jinju, Korea, has set up a housing shelter, a counseling center, and a labor-management consultative body. Each of these is a nonprofit organization registered with the Korean government.[1]

Since October 2013 our shelter has been used by Nepalese migrants, Syrian refugees, and Islamic patients recuperating from treatment, as well as by international workers present in Korea under the Employment Permit System of the Korean Ministry of Employment and Labor.[2] Every day, persons living in the shelter

---

1. For similar efforts by a church in Ulsan, see Jang Suwon, "Chang-su-wŏn, kyo-hoe-ka i-chu-oe-kuk-in-tŭl-e-ke ŏ-ttŏn to-um-ŭl chul kŏs-in-ka" [How the church will help immigrant foreigners], in *21C sin-yu-mok-min si-tae-wa i-chu-cha sŏn-kyo* [Twenty-first century neo-nomadic era and migrant mission], ed. Chansik Park (Seoul: Christian Institute of Industrial Society, 2008), 350–57.

2. Ministry of Employment and Labor, "2014 Employment and Labor Policy in Korea," 42–45, www.moel.go.kr/english/pas/pasPubli_view .jsp?idx=1084.

can request to hold services of worship or prayer meetings; others may concentrate on evangelism or on supporting and nurturing one another.

ECONOMIC ACCOUNTABILITY

If you give a client some food, he or she can live for a day or a week, but if refugees find jobs, they can endure for months or years. Being relatively better off materially, Koreans are in a position to help refugees meet urgent needs. Individuals and small organizations are able to create links of cooperation with large churches and even international organizations. For example, the rice for our shelter is supplied by Changwon Migrant Labor Welfare Center and the world church (through Busan SegeRo Church).

The shelter operates at the lower end of the economic scale, and just as water flows to a lower spot, so poor people come to the shelter. Since our church is where the weak live, the migrants finding refuge in the shelter are constantly meeting the disabled, economically weak, homeless, exiles, and medically ill. Therefore, not only is their own need for shelter met, but migrant workers who have God's calling are also able to train for missions while staying in the shelter.

Migrants who come as refugees stay for six months before seeking employment. After six months they seek to move toward a job and economic self-reliance. As they become economically independent, they can begin transferring some of their earnings to their families outside of Korea. Our shelter has a foreign laborers support center and an industrial counseling center. Ongoing consultation is available to migrants to deal with any economic difficulties or regulatory problems.[3] These centers assist them in solving problems such as delay in receiving their pay, unfair treatment on the job, and difficulties in dealing with cultural differences.

RELIGIOUS RESPONSIBILITY

If we offer someone only shelter and food, we are treating them no better than we treat animals. As ambassadors of Jesus Christ, we must go further, advancing to training and missions. The nature of the program will vary according to the character of the church. In

---

3. Unlike the restrictions placed on workers within Korea's Employment Permit System (EPS), after six months refugees are free to change jobs.

Korea, churches meet for worship on Wednesday and for prayer on Friday. On Sunday, churches participate in church activities together. Syrians, Palestinians, and Muslims from various countries join in. In the course of this church life, study of the Bible and baptism of the Holy Spirit occur naturally.

Sometimes we have urged Coptic Christians to stand in our podiums to bear testimony and to be established as witnesses taking part in the work of world evangelization. Formerly, we had to go to the world to go on mission, just as Joseph was God's missionary sent to Egypt. Now the world has come to Korea; refugees and migrants from the ends of the earth have come to us.[4] South Korea has more than 2 million foreigners residing in it. We are doing overseas missions in our own country. As the number of refugees increases, Korea's share in the multicultural world grows with them. By coming to us, they are helping to draw Korea into the multicultural age.

Ministry to refugees should be regarded as a responsibility of missions, not merely as a means that may open the door for engaging in "real" mission.[5] Refugees frequently remain abroad for a long time; therefore, the one person out of every 113 in the world who is a refugee should be given missionary training as opportunities arise.[6] Such persons can then be sent as missionaries to their native countries or can serve as missional catalysts wherever they may go.

Mission beyond the borders of our own country of Korea is important, and we must spend much effort to evangelize the world. But the fact that the precious human resources of the countries to which we go have themselves come to Korea can be an important point of contact for missions.[7] Previously, "missions" meant only long decades of service abroad until one's bones were buried on

4. See Il Lee, "Status of Muslim Refugees in Korea, Understanding of the Refugee System and the Challenges of Korean Christian Churches" [in Korean], *Muslim-Christian Encounter* 9, no. 1 (March 2016): 88. *Muslim-Christian Encounter* is published by the Torch Trinity Center for Islamic Studies in Seoul.

5. Ibid., 101.

6. See Advocates for Public Interest Law, www.apil.or.kr/m/1993.

7. Sam-Hwan Kim, "Che-1-hoe kuk-che i-chu-cha sŏn-kyo p'o-lŏm hwan-yŏng-sa" [The First International Migrant Mission Forum Greetings], in *21C sin-yu-mok-min*, ed. Park, front matter.

the mission field. Mission to refugees is contributing to changing that picture. Also, mission teams from our churches go to China, Nepal, Uzbekistan, Vietnam, and elsewhere to carry out touring missions and enhance the work of "base" missions. Refugees can do similarly.

SOCIAL RESPONSIBILITY

Jesus embraced the socially underprivileged. He was touched by their problems. Many refugees are Muslim, but there are many Christian refugees also. As members of the church, we can introduce refugees to the social values of Christianity, such as monogamy and Christian perspectives on homosexuality. (I even include efforts against tattoos!) You can teach the Bible through such means.

Christian witness takes many forms. It includes citizens who understand the kingdom of God who can present to refugees, such as those from Syria, a cultural and economic vision for national recovery and restoration.

Early in 2017 we asked eight high school students in our church to conduct a survey. They asked refugees what they needed. The answers were a warm awareness of them, the need to feel welcomed by their host country, economic support, and a home.

Korean young people of marriageable age and refugees need to understand the many pitfalls before them if they decide to marry. The church has a role to play here in addressing false conceptions and insufficient understanding of and about refugees.

PHYSICAL RESPONSIBILITIES

Physical responsibilities include protective responsibilities. The church in mission must be an advocate for the powerless. Refugees in our shelter suffering from a fever, for example, have been unable to go to the hospital for months because they lacked sufficient insurance. Inadequate facilities make it difficult for the refugee shelter to support life. We must bear burdens together, which has meant suffering with the new members of the church and becoming a family, eating together, and sharing the same medical possibilities. The result? The church and the refugees live together as friends, just as friends do anywhere in the world. We now cooperate with the hospital as part of carrying out our ministry. And most of the refugees now have a relatively high income and economic stability.

Christians in the Muslim world who become refugees are still not free from the threat of violence. Ten years ago, for example, Indonesian Christians had gathered to pray in a certain place, but Indonesian Muslims who were passing by threw rocks at them. Now in 2017 we worked with the police to help Egyptian Coptic Christians deal with threats by unknown parties to murder their parents and to protect against attempts to hurt the refugees themselves. These kinds of violence between Islamic and Christian refugees take many insidious forms. We have an obligation to protect the refugees from physical harm.

The church and Korean society have many responsibilities toward refugees, but their fate is mixed with that of economic migrants coming to the country. Korean society is not yet ready to integrate refugees as full members of Korean society. In this report I have introduced a ministry that has been developed by one Korean church to assist refugees as they adapt to their new life in Korea. In distinction from both Europe's "salad bowl" refugee policy and the US melting pot immigration policy, we need to find an alternative that fits Korea. Our current constitutional discussion poses dangers of which the church needs to be aware. It is good to accept only what we can do. The world is watching our Korea.

Within a context of maintaining democratic peace, issues such as homosexuality, the Islamic influx, overcoming the isolationism of Korean politics, preparing evangelical policy with a view toward unification, advancing the Gospel, and improving living conditions for more refugees pose ongoing challenges before us.

22

Missional Multicultural Church Movement as Incubator and International Student Volunteer Movement as a Force for Mission in the Migration Mission Era

Young Sup Oh

Today we can discern the migrant mission era coming over the horizon. Key factors in its inauguration are the merging of the missional church movement and the multicultural church movement into today's missional multicultural church movement. Missional multicultural churches in turn are incubators for the International Student Volunteer Movement (ISVM) which holds promise to become a major force in the migration mission era.

GOD SENDS ALL NATIONS TO KOREA

In 2017 the world population surpassed 7.5 billion; of this number, 244 million (or 3.25 percent) were international migrants.[1] Slightly over 3 billion of the world's people belong to "unreached people groups."[2] If the same proportion are international migrants, then

---

1. See "Current World Population," Worldometers, www.worldome ters.info/world-population; and "244 Million International Migrants Living Abroad Worldwide, New UN Statistics Reveal," United Nations: Sustainable Development Goals, January 12, 2016, www.un.org/sustain abledevelopment/blog/2016/01/244-million-international-migrants-li ving-abroad-worldwide-new-un-statistics-reveal.

2. "Global Statistics," Joshua Project, https://joshuaproject.net/pe ople_groups/statistics.

over 100 million members of unreached people groups live abroad, that is, outside of their native country. South Korea, by economic and demographic necessity, is host to 2.2 million migrants.[3] With one of the world's lowest birthrates and an aging society, the country faces a "demographic cliff" in 2018. Discussions of Korea's future as a multicultural country proliferate online.[4]

The number of international students is also increasing rapidly across the globe. Worldwide, the total number of international students grew from 0.8 million in 1975 to 2.1 million in 2000, then 4.5 million in 2012, and it continues to grow.[5] Fifty-three percent of these students come from Asia: most from China, then India, and then Korea.[6] At the same time, the number of international students and other migrants coming *to* Korea continues to grow. Reasons for this growth include migrants' pursuit of the "Korean Dream," fueled by the country's economic development. Other reasons are the country's need for laborers, international marriages with (generally old) bachelors and birth of their children in the Korean countryside, Korea's encouragement of international students (as part of the Study Korea Project 2004), inflow of North Korean defectors and refugees, and the "Korean Wave," that is, the global increase in popularity of South Korean culture. The heart of God must be hidden in all of these factors.

3. Statistics Korea, "Current status of aliens by year (1998–2016)" [in Korean], July 26, 2017, www.index.go.kr/potal/main/EachDtlPa geDetail.do?idx_cd=2756#quick_02.

4. Choe Sang-Hun, "South Korea's Plan to Rank Towns by Fertility Rate Backfires," *New York Times*, December 30, 2016, www.nytimes.com /2016/12/30/world/asia/south-korea-fertility-birth-map.html?_r=0; Cho Kye-wan, "South Korea Could Be Heading for Its 'Demographic Cliff' after 2018," *Hankyoreh*, June 20, 2015, http://english.hani.co.kr/arti/eng lish_edition/e_business/696800.html; Faustino John Lim, "Korea's Multicultural Future?," AP Migration, http://apmigration.ilo.org/news/kore a2019s-multicultural-future.

5. South Korea Ministry of Education, "Expansion policy of attracting international students" [in Korean], July 7, 2015, p. 1, www.moe.go.kr /boardCnts/view.do?boardID=339&lev=0&statusYN=C&s=moe&m=02 &opType=N&boardSeq=59920.

6. Organisation for Economic Co-operation and Development, "How Is International Student Mobility Shaping Up?," *Education Indicators in Focus*, No. 14, July 5, 2013, www.oecd-ilibrary.org/education/how-is -international-student-mobility-shaping-up_5k43k8r4k821-en.

INTERNATIONAL STUDENTS IN KOREA:
WHERE THEY COME FROM AND WHAT THEY STUDY

The number of international students enrolled in Korean colleges and universities increased significantly from 2003 (12,314) through 2011 (89,537), dipped slightly for the years 2012 through 2014, and then showed strong growth in 2015 (91,332) and 2016 (104,262).

As shown in table 22.1, international students in Korea come from around the world, though the great preponderance come from other Asian countries. The largest block of students is enrolled in nondegree training courses, with nearly as many registered in undergraduate and technical college programs.[7]

Table 22.1. International students in Korea in 2016
by region of birth, showing program level of enrollment

Continent	Undergraduate and Technical College	Graduate School (MA)	Graduate School (PhD)	Subtotal	Training Course	Total	Percent
Africa	387	1,175	322	1,884	477	2,361	2.3
Asia	36,398	14,282	6,029	56,709	34,659	91,368	87.6
Europe	585	556	150	1,291	3,867	5,158	4.9
North America	1,181	898	312	2,391	1,659	4,050	3.9
Oceania	134	100	24	258	146	404	0.4
South America	259	271	41	571	350	921	0.9
Total	38,944	17,282	6,878	63,104	41,158	104,262	100.0

In 2016 the largest number of international students came from China (58%), followed in order by Vietnam, Mongolia, Japan, United States, and Taiwan (between 7 and 2 percent each). Also in 2016 the 104,262 international students in Korea were divided as follows:

- 38,944 at undergraduate institutions (including junior colleges), with the top three fields of study being humanities

7. The figures shown in table 22.1 and the paragraph that follows are based on statistics gathered, on April 1, 2016, by South Korea's Ministry of Education. See "Information on the status of foreign students in Korea in 2016" [in Korean], www.moe.go.kr/boardCnts/view.do?boardID=350&boardSeq=64729&lev=0&searchType=S&statusYN=W&page=1&s=moe&m=040103&opType=.

and social science (69%), engineering (14%), and physical education and art (10%);

- 17,282 at the master's level, with the top three fields studied being humanities and social science (70%), engineering (15%), and natural science (7%);

- 6,878 at the doctoral level, with the top three fields being engineering (38%), humanities and social science (32%), and natural science (20%); and

- 41,158 were enrolled in training courses, with 66 percent taking language training classes.

A MINISTRY FOR INTERNATIONAL STUDENTS OF ALL NATIONS

What might outreach to international students look like today? Launched in Seoul 2005, Landmarker Ministry (www.landmarkerministry.org) in 2014 began sponsoring significant new ventures in ministry to international students. Consider the following four examples:

Missional multicultural church. In 2014 Forest of Living Water Church (www.forestlivingwater.org) was created as an international church situated within Landmarker Ministry.[8] In the effort to create a missional church, Forest of Living Water Church is conducting adventurous experiments. It strives to be a cafe church that has a campus youth culture at its center. A multicultural church with ministry to international students at its core, Forest of Living Water Church can be viewed as the "base camp" for Landmarker Ministry. Four days each week it sends evangelism teams to three different university campuses to reach out to international students. The teams also lead Bible studies on ten different university campuses, inviting students to participate in powerful multicultural worship.

HUG Festival. Using HUG Festival (Happy food, Unique joy, Group dynamics), Landmarker Ministry is reaching out to international students through new cultural wineskins (board games, music and media, barbeque parties, and dinner festivals).[9] Launched in 2010

8. https://youtu.be/IqvH2xlGZKI.
9. See https://youtu.be/bwU-A26XYWE.

and updated in 2014, HUG Festival, ver. 2.0, is an evangelism program especially designed for youth. The church has been hosting trilingual HUG Festivals four times a year for international and Korean students enrolled on ten university campuses. At the same time, the church has also hosted an expanded version—HUG Conference, ver. 2.0—for the pastors and ministers of local churches and ministries in Siberia (Russia, 2016), Bulgaria (Europe, 2017), and Seattle and Alaska (United States, 2017).[10]

Multicultural Mission Network. In 2015 Landmarker Ministry began a network among pastors, missionaries, professors, and ministries that are involved in multicultural ministries. The desire is to encourage all to labor together in mission, culture, and scholarship, according to God's will—multiethnically, multiculturally, and multilingually—so that all persons can receive and enjoy the same grace and blessing. To support this vision, the Multicultural Mission Network has launched both a global forum and a global mission school. Plans for partnership in evangelistic outreach during the PyeongChang 2018 Winter Olympics, February 9–25, 2018, were a special focus of ongoing discussions.

RUSTA. In 2016 Landmarker Ministry joined with Onnuri Church's M-Center and the Commonwealth of Independent States (CIS) Pastors Association in founding RUSTA (RUssian Speaking nations To All nations).[11] RUSTA provides a network connecting migrants, churches, and ministries in eleven CIS countries and is a means for facilitating the evangelism of unreached people groups through use of adult camps, youth camps, and children's camps. It is especially significant that most of the unreached people groups in the 10/40 Window can be found on Russia's borders, so a reverse mission strategy is possible.

THE NEXT STAGE OF MISSION HISTORY: THREE PREDICTIONS

In 1980 David Howard advised mission leaders to recognize the role that students have played in every pioneering movement

10. For Siberia, see https://youtu.be/ZEyWk3WpOkE; for Bulgaria, go to https://youtu.be/laTUnHHTJyg.

11. See https://youtu.be/cb-piGygQRQ.

for world mission. He stressed the crucial impact of students' vision and effort in accelerating and strengthening the church in its work of evangelism. In much the same way, Taewoong Lee, a Korean mission leader, has written of the relationship apparent in church history between student movements and mission movements. Through their devotion and depth of community, Christian student groups have brought about turning points in mission history.[12] Viewed in this light, we can discern God's hidden intention in sending international students from all nations to Seoul. Looking ahead, we can foresee three characteristics of future missionary work.

First, a new stage in mission, the migration mission era, has already begun, and it will continue to accelerate. This new era will follow upon the three eras evident in modern mission history:

- the coastal mission era, associated with William Carey;
- the inland mission era, typified by Hudson Taylor; and
- the unreached people groups era, exemplified by William Cameron Townsend and Donald McGavran.

It might be proper for us to call this new era the "moving unreached people group era," but since we need totally new and different mission strategies for this new era, it is better to say that the unreached people group era has ended and that the migration mission era has begun.

Second, similar to the earlier Student Volunteer Movement and the Student Foreign Mission Fellowship, the new International Student Volunteer Movement (ISVM) will be a key force in launching the migration mission era. A central focus will be the new-style urban generation that is being formed in global cities around the world. This generation, heavily influenced by international students, will be multicultural, multiethnic, and multilingual.

Third, the ISVM will be incubated in and extended by the missional multicultural church movement. The outcome of a new paradigm, the missional multicultural church seeks to plant and

12. David Howard and Taewoong Lee as cited in Mission Korea, "Report on Future Mission Korea" [in Korean], workshop handout, October 28, 2015, 12.

grow multiethnic, multicultural, and multilingual congregations among the young urban generation in global cities.

The missional multicultural church movement is a new cultural force in which music and media dominate both online and offline. As I look forward to the return of Jesus Christ, I am pondering God's *heart* and *dream* for the missional multicultural church movement to incubate the ISVM, and for the ISVM in turn to become a force for inaugurating the migration mission era.

23

The Scattered People and Mission

Timothy K. Park

Those who had been scattered preached the word wherever they went. (Acts 8:4)[1]

Now those who had been scattered by the persecution that broke out when Stephen was killed traveled as far as Phoenicia, Cyprus and Antioch, spreading the word only among Jews. Some of them, however, men from Cyprus and Cyrene, went to Antioch and began to speak to Greeks also, telling them the good news about the Lord Jesus. (Acts 11:19–20)

Because of the rapid development of technology, humanity has experienced significant changes in every aspect of life. "Sociologists and futurologists have analyzed that the changes of the past 100 years are the same amount of changes as those of the previous 10,000 years, the changes of human history. In addition, the changes that will take place over the next 20 years are expected to match the changes of the last 100 years. In the end, it means that the changes over the next 20 years will be equal to the changes in human history as a whole."[2]

The Gospel is unchanging, but the environment in which

1. All Scripture quotations in this chapter are taken from the New International Version.

2. Yoon Sik Choi, *Han-kuk-kyo-hoe mi-lae-chi-to* [2020–2040 Future map of the Korean church] (Seoul: Word of Life, 2013), 104–5.

the Gospel is preached is changing constantly and rapidly. The church, which has been commissioned to implement Christ's Great Commission, ought to preach the unchanging message of the Gospel in acceptable ways in an ever-changing world. The apostle Paul, a model for missionaries of all times, was faithful to the truth (Gal. 1:6–9), yet he was flexible in how he communicated the Gospel to specific recipients or audiences (1 Cor. 9:19–23). Similarly, Christian messengers today who are commissioned to implement Christ's Great Commission must understand both the message to be preached and the changing world in which the message is to be preached.

One of the characteristics of today's changing world is globalization and the frequent migration of people. A variety of causes leads people to relocate, including business opportunities, better education, overseas job employment, and wars. We may refer to those who are relocated as diaspora, immigrants, migrants, refugees, relocated people, asylum seekers, or other terms. I like to call them "the scattered people."

Many people have mistakenly believed that the task of world evangelization is given only to missionaries who are officially commissioned by the church. God, however, uses all types of people, including officially commissioned missionaries, in restoring his rule on this earth. In attempting to implement the Lord's Great Commission, we need to use both traditional methods and new methods under the guidance of the Holy Spirit.

In "The Kingdom Strikes Back: Ten Epochs of Redemptive History," Ralph Winter pointed out four mechanisms of mission that God has used: *voluntary going* (such as Abraham to Canaan, Moses to Egypt, Paul and Barnabas to Asia and Europe, St. Patrick to Ireland, William Carey to India, Hudson Taylor to China, and today's commissioned missionaries), *involuntary going* (such as Joseph to Egypt, Jonah to Nineveh, Jewish war captives to Babylon, Christians captured by Vikings), *voluntary coming* (such as the Queen of Sheba to Solomon's court, Ruth from Moab, Greek men to Jesus, the Goths invasion of Christian Rome, and international visitors into the Christian West), and *involuntary coming* (Gentiles settled in Israel by Cyrus the Great, slaves brought from Africa to America, and refugees).[3] God has

3. Ralph D. Winter, "Ha-na-nim-ūi na-la-ka pan-kyōk-ūk ka-ha-ta:Ku-

used at least these four mechanisms in order that the whole world might acknowledge that Jesus is the King of kings and the Lord of lords (Matt. 28:18) and accept his rule.

PEOPLE WHO WENT VOLUNTARILY
WITH MISSIONARY INTENT

God has used people who have gone voluntarily with missionary intent. Abraham and Moses are the typical Old Testament examples of this kind of person. God said to Abraham, "Go from your country, your people and your father's household to the land I will show you" (Gen. 12:1). And Abraham went at the command of God to be a channel of blessings to all peoples on earth. Moses, though he was reluctant in the beginning, when God called him by saying, "So now, go. I am sending you to Pharaoh to bring my people the Israelites out of Egypt" (Exod. 3:10), went voluntarily at last with missionary intent to deliver the Israelites out of Egypt. New Testament examples of those who went voluntarily with missionary intent are Jesus (John 20:21), the twelve disciples (Matt. 28:18–20), the seventy-two disciples (Luke 10:1–20), and Paul and Barnabas (Acts 13:1–3). In church history, William Carey, Hudson Taylor, Donald McGavran, Yi Ki-Poong, Park Tai-Ro, Sa Pyeong-Soon, Kim Young-Hoon, and 27,205 Korean missionaries working in 172 countries today have gone out voluntarily with missionary intent, and God has used them.

PEOPLE WHO WENT INVOLUNTARILY
WITHOUT MISSIONARY INTENT

For the salvation of humankind God has used not only people who have gone voluntarily with missionary intent, but also those who have gone involuntarily without any missionary intent. Examples of the latter, many of whom went without missionary intent, but were greatly used by God for the proclamation of the rule of God include Joseph, Daniel and his three friends, the Israelite servant girl at Naaman's home, and Naomi.

Joseph certainly did not go to Egypt with a missionary intent, nor did his father or brothers send him to Egypt with their sup-

---

sok-sa-e na-t'a-nan 10si-tae" [The kingdom strikes back: Ten epochs of redemptive history], *Peoseupegtibeu* [Perspective], ed. Ralph D. Winter, Steven C. Hawthorne, and Han Cheol-Ho (Seoul: YWAM, 2009), 466.

port. But we know that the missionary God sent Joseph to Egypt and used him for the salvation of Egypt and the nations. Notice Joseph's perspective: "And now, do not be distressed and do not be angry with yourselves for selling me here, because it was to save lives that God sent me ahead of you. . . . But God sent me ahead of you to preserve for you a remnant on earth and to save your lives by a great deliverance. So then, it was not you who sent me here, but God. He made me father to Pharaoh, lord of his entire household and ruler of Egypt" (Gen. 45:5–8).

Daniel and his three friends were taken to Babylon as war captives, but they were greatly used by God for the salvation of the people in Babylon, including the king of the empire. Daniel and his friends accomplished God's will for them by living lives that honored God (Dan. 3:28–30; 6:25–27). The Israelite servant girl who was taken to Naaman's home in Syria as a war captive did not go with missionary intent, but Naaman came to the Lord through her witness (2 Kings 5:1–19). Naomi went to the land of Moab because of the famine in Bethlehem. She went there without missionary intent, but eventually God used her for the salvation of Ruth (Ruth 1).

PEOPLE WHO CAME TO GOD VOLUNTARILY

God also has used those who have come to him voluntarily through having observed the presence of God among believers. The Queen of Sheba and Ruth are among those who came voluntarily by observing the beautiful life of God's people. The Queen of Sheba heard the news that God had blessed Solomon and came voluntarily to meet Solomon personally to confirm the news. She was greatly inspired by the wisdom God gave Solomon and realized the grace of God (2 Chron. 9:1–12). Ruth also came to God voluntarily and became a member of God's household through observing the faith and life of Naomi, her mother-in-law (Ruth 1:16–18).

PEOPLE WHO CAME TO GOD INVOLUNTARILY

God saved and used not only those who came voluntarily, but also those who came to the people of God involuntarily. Examples of those who came involuntarily, but eventually came to know God, are the Gentiles who came to the various towns of Samaria according to the resettlement policy of the king of Assyria (2 Kings 17:1–6, 24–33); Cornelius, a Roman army officer, who came to fear the Lord while he was stationed in Caesarea (Acts 10); and African slaves who came to faith after they were brought to Europe and America.

In the Old Testament most of the people who became light to the Gentiles were the scattered people. Although they went to other lands without an intention for mission, they honored God and became light and salt in the lands to which they were relocated and were greatly used by God for the evangelization of the world. The New Testament also shows us that scattered people such as Barnabas, Paul, and others who understood the language and culture of their host countries were better used cross-culturally than were the apostles in Jerusalem. The churches in Antioch and Rome were planted by scattered people, and these churches made great contributions to the evangelization of their host nations and the world.

We need to acknowledge that God uses for his mission purposes people in each of these four categories. In our world today, refugees, asylum seekers, overseas workers, foreign students, and immigrants are among the most common scattered people who live among us. But as we have seen in Scripture, scattered people are not only recipients of the church's mission; they are also great resources for mission. In the Old and New Testaments and in history, scattered people have made great contributions to the ministry of the kingdom of God, and they will continue to do so in the future. People who are scattered throughout the world in the providence of God will play an important role in twenty-first-century world mission. It is important to understand the missionary characteristics of scattered people and to help them make positive contributions to the coming of God's kingdom on earth, wherever God may place them.

SIGNIFICANT ISSUES RAISED BY THE PRESENTERS

Ben Torrey shares the experience of North Korean migrants in South Korea and the ministry that South Korean churches have to them. If there is open acceptance of and respect for differences, Torrey tells us, both North Korean migrants and South Korean hosts can learn from the other and can enrich each other's faith and life. He advises us to keep in mind the need for a strong, loving community—one that can provide healing and acceptance—and to remember the work of the Holy Spirit in bringing about true conversion and transformation in a person.

Andrew Walls reminds us that migration has been a recurrent feature of human life throughout history and that it is also a theme that runs through the Bible. He observes that the book of Genesis introduces us to two main categories of migration: the Adamic and the Abrahamic. The former is represented in the expulsion of Adam and Eve from paradise, where the migration is punitive, indicating deprivation and loss. Abrahamic migration is represented in the divine call to Abraham to leave his settled homeland and to assume the life of a nomadic herdsman, with the promise of receiving a better land for his children. Similarly, Jews settled all over the Hellenistic Greek-speaking world, bringing with them their Scriptures, their worship of God, and their complete rejection of all other divinities. Walls also well states that Koreans overseas are not only to be the focus of evangelization, but are also to be evangelists themselves.

Jesse Mugambi notes that "Africans were dispossessed and also dislocated from their ancestral homelands; even more significantly, they were dispossessed of their cultural and religious identity in the name of Christian mission" (53). The African Christian diaspora, however, is contributing toward vibrant expressions of Christianity in various European countries. Not only are there churches in the West whose membership is entirely African, but also others that are fully integrated, enfolding members from the host nations, yet with African leadership. He emphasizes that "mission and evangelization, as biblical mandates, are no longer the monopoly of missionaries from Europe and North America to the rest of the world. In the twenty-first century, participation of the African diaspora in Christian mission and evangelization is vibrant, influential, and innovative, attracting attenders and converts from the host countries," including Western countries that previously sent missionaries to Africa (58).

John Chung writes of the sufferings of Iraqis after the Gulf War, the Iraq War, and the emergence of ISIL and of the care he and Jordanian churches extended to the Iraqi refugees. I myself had the opportunity to preach the Word of God to Iraqi refugees during their worship in an evangelical church in Amman where John Chung has served. I encouraged them to trust in the Lord as Joseph did in Egypt and as Daniel and his three friends did in Babylon. These Iraqi refugees, like other scattered people, have come to the Lord during their refugee life, and some of them have become missionaries to their own people, as well as to others.

David Chul Han Jun introduces us to his ministry among foreigners in South Korea. He reminds us that those who were scattered because of the great persecution in Jerusalem, though the dispersion itself was painful, preached the Gospel of Jesus Christ wherever they went (Acts 8). He states that God is now using the Korean diaspora as a missionary tool and that recognizing and using the Korean diaspora may be one of the most important strategies for the future of Korean overseas mission. On a different tack he writes that "since the 1990s, many churches and mission organizations have begun ministering to foreign workers in South Korea. At present, about 500 organizations are doing so" (91). Jun emphasizes the need for Korean churches and missions to do holistic mission among foreign workers and train foreign workers to become missionaries to their own people. Most churches, however, seem to lack knowledge of the needs of these foreign workers and the ways they could be involved in mission.

Timothy Hong shares the account of how he became a believer in Jesus Christ and how he has led persons from multiple ethnic backgrounds to Christ through his ministry. His testimony reminds us that it is God, not we, who works among people. It is God who calls us and uses us for the salvation of his people, and we can bear fruit when the Holy Spirit works through us. When God calls us, he gives us gifts to accomplish his purposes. God's challenge to Timothy Hong becomes a challenge to us all.

Ildoo Kwon presents the missionary work of Yoido Full Gospel Church (YFGC). He comments, "For many years, YFGC's main mission strategy has been focused on sending native Korean missionaries to foreign countries to share the Gospel and provide relief for medical and social needs of the people. . . . It is time now to empower and mobilize Korean-Chinese Christians residing in Korea for missionary service in China, instead of continuing to send only Korean nationals" (124). I believe that Koreans and Korean-Chinese in both Korea and China must work together. It should not be either/or, but both/and. Kwon emphasizes the importance of developing cross-cultural leadership for effective ministry.

Peter Sensenig relates the stories of two Mennonite congregations in Pennsylvania that have helped Somali refugee families. He observes that, in spite of the caring sponsorship of a church, the path to acclimation for refugees is a rocky one. Refugees pass through four stages while adjusting: anticipation and excitement, culture shock, depression and anxiety, and finally coping and acceptance. For the aid of other congregations engaged in receiving refugees, Sensenig identifies four practices to foster greater effectiveness and accountability: do your homework, distribute the tasks, be patient, and define mission broadly. Taking care of people in need is a blessing not just to the recipients, but also to the caregivers.

Samuel Lee reports that "the number of overseas Filipino workers (OFWs) equals about 10 percent of the total Philippine population of 103 million people" (170). He continues, "Many of these Filipino migrants are God's chosen instruments to witness to the nations that host them" (174). They enter countries that ordinary missionaries cannot. "They are not officially called missionaries, and perhaps what they do qualifies them only as incidental missionaries, but they work hard, using their free time and weekends to evangelize in apartments, old buildings, parks, and anywhere else that people will listen. These missionaries are not sent by agencies and receive no support from a mission organization or church, but they minister to their fellow Filipinos and to the people of their host nations" (178).

Nelson Jennings observes that more than 2 million foreign residents dwell and work in Korea, approximately equal to 4 percent of Korea's population, and he introduces the ministry of Onnuri Community Church for foreign residents in Korea. He reports that Onnuri Community Church, a local church in Seoul, leads foreigners in Korea to Christ and trains them to become missionaries to their homelands upon their return to their own countries. What a wonderful ministry this is to scattered people—both for them and through them!

Mary Mikhael tells about the situation of 1.5 million Syrian refugees in Lebanon. She shares how Christians in Lebanon have taken care of the refugees, particularly in the area of education of Syrian children. She reports that "because of the tragic events in Syria, 5.5 million Syrian children have been affected in variety of ways, ranging from mental trauma to living without parents to lack of schooling to being recruited by militias to be trained as fighters" (210). "Despite numerous challenges of various kinds," she concludes, the churches in Lebanon are "committed and determined to educate and rescue as many children as [they] can" (210).

Seth Kaper-Dale narrates the story of the ministry of the Reformed Church of Highland Park, New Jersey, USA. This church, according to Kaper-Dale, has become a leader in ministry to asylees and in the areas of immigration reform, refugee resettlement, and advocacy. He reports on the way he and his church became involved in this ministry and how God worked through them. He states that the church has grown in many ways during the years it has ministered to the immigrants. For example, members of the church have grown in their Christian convictions, the church community has grown in number, and the number of young, enthusiastic, justice-and-peace-oriented Christians within the church constituency—people who want to see the world become a better place—has grown. "Finally," Kaper-Dale reports, "we grew our interfaith community" (238).

Ruth Padilla DeBorst informs us that "Latin America accounts for almost 52 percent of immigrants to the United States—and the majority of them are Christian" (250–51). She introduces the life and work of three particular Latin American immigrants and the contributions they have made to American Christians. Three most significant contributions, as highlighted by American church leaders, were helping American churches to see and opening the world to them, serving the less privileged, and modeling contextual theologizing. Padilla DeBorst also articulates that mission is not from the haves to the have-nots and that mission is not merely something special people do far-off lands. She emphasizes that "immigrants like these, who have already been forced to negotiate 'multiple solidarities,' have valuable

skills, insights, perspectives, and relational patterns to offer—
if only they are recognized and granted a place at the table of
Christian fellowship" (260).

Sadiri Joy Tira presents a case study of Filipino-Canadian Christians
engaged in mission and outlines a strategy for local church participation in diaspora missions. He suggests that local churches that
participate in diaspora missions should do three things:

- Recognize and respond to the missional opportunities
  presented by global migration and diaspora communities, including through strategic planning and offering
  of focused training and resources to those called to work
  among diaspora communities.
- Bear countercultural witness to the love of Christ in deed
  and word by obeying the extensive biblical commands to
  love the stranger, defend the cause of the foreigner, visit the
  prisoner, and practice hospitality through building friendships, inviting into our homes, and providing help and
  services.
- Discern the hand of God, even in circumstances that people
  might not have chosen, listen to and learn from immigrant
  congregations, and initiate cooperative efforts to reach all
  sections of Canada with the Gospel.

CONCLUSION

The presenters spoke on different topics, but all focused on ministry
among the scattered people or by the scattered people. This forum
helps us to understand better what God has been doing among
scattered people and through scattered people on all continents.
The forum has also challenged us to participate more actively and
effectively in ministry to the scattered people. Today's mission is
truly from everywhere to everywhere. It is no longer a one-dimen-
sional mission—speaking, teaching, giving, and loving—but rather
a multidimensional mission of speaking and learning, teaching
and learning, giving and receiving, and loving and being loved. As
we serve scattered people among us, if we are humble, we also can
become beneficiaries.

We must remember that God uses not only people who go

voluntarily with missionary intent, but also people who go involuntarily without missionary intent. God also uses people who come voluntarily by seeing God working among his people, as well as people who come to God's people involuntarily. Churches therefore need to proclaim the Gospel in word and deed and need to utilize different types of missionaries such as residential missionaries, nonresidential missionaries, short-term missionaries, and professional missionaries. Churches in the world should be concerned both with mission *for* scattered people and with mission *by* scattered people.

24

Migration, Human Dislocation, and Mission Accountability: A Concluding Summary

Jonathan J. Bonk

The case studies, responses, and discussion presented in this book illustrate and reinforce seven key Christian beliefs about the human beings God created to inhabit and care for the world and for one another.

KEY OBSERVATIONS

It is difficult for human societies to expand the category of "we"—but it is absolutely essential that Christians within those societies do so, so that "we" encompasses not only family, tribe, and nation, but also stranger, alien, and even enemy. This is a recurring emphasis in Jesus' teaching as recalled in the Gospels, and it culminates in his teaching about the great judgment at the end of time (Matt. 25:31–46), where distinguishing between true followers and bogus believers boils down to their treatment of society's most marginalized: hungry, thirsty, destitute, ill, imprisoned strangers ignored, abandoned, and harassed by conventional society.

Immigrants and refugees are not to be seen as mere fodder for statistics and impressive compilations of numbers. Each one has a name and a keen sense of personal identity; each one occupies a place in a family and network of relatives; each one has hopes that are both unique to the individual and common among humankind; each one is so valuable that Jesus gave his life to reconcile them to God and neighbor; each one is worthy of our personal interest and investment of time and resources.

Many living in nations commonly held to be Christian in pedigree and institutions and who self-identify as Christians do not welcome strangers, and many are active in political parties that actively promote xenophobia and dread of strangers. Their primary loyalty appears to be to the self-serving state rather than the self-giving Christ.

When churches passively ignore or actively resist the presence of so-called illegal immigrants and refugees, they effectively leave Christ outside, standing at the door, knocking. Christ enters our congregations and our lives through strangers and the marginalized in our world.

While all societies promote some level of xenophobia, some societies are so linguistically and culturally homogeneous that members, even Christian members, cannot imagine how outsiders could ever be at home legally, socially, or culturally. This factor is possibly why countries like Korea and Japan have such a sorry record of incorporating refugees. Incumbent groups have created outsider-proof systems of kinship and social organization.

The fact that xenophobia is almost always supported by laws and sustained by social custom can give Christians the false impression that their compliance is required as religious duty. But the long story told in our Scriptures—a story in which we now play our part—reminds us that the heart is deceitful above all things, and that we often mask, perpetuate, and protect gross injustice with our laws. These Scriptures also remind us that God can easily distinguish between legality and justice, and that his followers must learn to distinguish between them as well. Compliance with or support of evil in the guise of law will not exempt us from God's insistence that his followers practice justice.

It seems easier—as the chapters of this book make clear—for us to serve refugees outside of our countries than to make room for them inside our countries. Serving the marginalized far away is certainly good, but it is not the same as welcoming strangers, since those men and women and their families remain firmly excluded from our own homelands.

WHAT WE CAN LEARN FROM THE PRESENTATIONS

John Chung shows how difficult it was for a fellowship of Iraqi believers (ICRWC) to fully accept a convert from Islam, and yet this same convert was welcomed by a Jordanian church. The story reminds one of the understandable suspicion with which the conversion of Saul was regarded by believers in Damascus and Antioch (Acts 9), and how essential it was to have a man like Ananias who was able to bridge the fear gap and help Saul begin the process of assimilation into the church. Jewish believers found it difficult to trust and accept Paul. This story has its contemporary analogues in many countries where it is the accepted and even encouraged practice to persecute followers of Jesus. Chung also shows how churches can function as places of refuge and welcome in times of immense destruction, human suffering, and massive population relocation caused by war.

Timothy Hong, drawing on his experience in international student ministry at the University of Illinois, reminds us that human beings are most receptive to transformative religious change when they are far from home, with its secure but restricting social and religious obligations and practices. When socially and geographically dislocated, even if the dislocation is voluntary in pursuit of an education, people need a place to belong—a community that includes *"them"* in its *"we."* All humans thrive when they are associated with people who are genuinely interested in all dimensions of their well-being. This interest, expressed practically, is the essence of incarnational ministry.

Nelson Jennings shows how Onnuri Community Church's ministry to foreign residents in Korea has had a ripple effect far beyond those persons' lives as foreigners in Korea, extending the Gospel to the lands and communities from which they have come. Onnuri's hospitality is not only necessary in and of itself, because it is the right thing to do, but it has profound strategic implications, since every foreigner is defined by and connected to a large web of relatives, neighbors, colleagues, and acquaintances back in their homeland communities. As Hong reminded us in his case study, we humans are most receptive to change of any kind—including religious—when we are strangers in a strange land.

David Chul Han Jun, writing on migrant missions in South Korea, reminds us that immigrants are easily exploited within our own countries by unscrupulous employers, for whom foreigners are merely a means to personal ends. This attitude contrasts with that of followers of Jesus, for whom no human being, especially strangers and foreigners, who are most vulnerable, is a means to our ends. Each person is an end in and of himself or herself. Jun points to the acute social and linguistic isolation and exploitation experienced by vulnerable foreigners in Korea who can never, ever call Korea their home. The church must constantly guard against the all too common "telescopic philanthropy" of Mrs. Jellyby, satirized by Charles Dickens in chapter 4 of *Bleak House*, who focused time and energy on a remote tribe in Africa while turning a blind eye to the desperate but less glamorous plight of the needy right under her nose.

Seth Kaper-Dale shows us that being a faithful pastor in the United States in a time of politically incited fear and paranoia requires godly defiance of the state along with practical activism on behalf of the state's targeted victims—in this case Christian refugees fleeing for their lives from Indonesia, where their churches and homes were burned and their friends and families were harassed and murdered. His chapter shows that resistance requires more than mere defiance. As in the times of Daniel, energetic and constructive lobbying of the country's lawmakers is needed to help them make the country's laws truly compliant with God's standards of justice.

Ildoo Kwon's case study, building on sound theory and on-the-ground experience, highlights the exciting potential of Korean-Chinese in establishing an authentically Chinese church in China. He outlines practical approaches being taken or considered by the Yoido Full Gospel Church to assist men and women within this diasporic community to develop as effective ministers of the Gospel. Being both Korean and Chinese, they constitute a natural bridge between churches and ministry in the two countries. If the transformation of core cultural and ethical orientations that missionaries know as conversion is going to yield "fruit that remains," Korean diasporic believers will doubtless fulfill integral roles otherwise open only to cultural insiders.

Samuel Lee's presence among and advocacy for one of the great diasporic peoples of the twentieth and twenty-first centuries—Christian Filipinos scattered in large numbers all over the world and often exploited as migrant workers supporting families back in their homeland—gives us a glimpse both of the pathos of these brothers and sisters and of their positive witness to God's presence among them.

When reading *Mary Mikhael*'s report, one can only imagine the heartbreaking plight of refugees who have for many decades flooded into Lebanon from across the war-riven Middle East. Mikhael hints at the fatigue of encountering and caring for a relentless, never-ending stream of men, women, and children fleeing for their lives, their sheer numbers swamping the resources, infrastructure, and at times civility of the citizens of that venerable nation. The five loaves and the two fishes offered by the church in Lebanon seem to be so little for so many in need, and yet the Lord has blessed and multiplied these meager but generous offerings on behalf of the needy.

Jesse Mugambi reminds us that no country in continental Africa is unaffected by human dislocation on a scale that dwarfs that found in the rest of the world, and that this is an unsettling of peoples in which European colonial powers and the American slave economy played, and still play, a key role. Africa south of the Sahara is the most Christian region in the world, and the ancient Christianities of Egypt and Ethiopia continue to play vital and constructive roles in their societies, which shows us that God's work in God's world is not restricted to those who live comfortably, festooned with vast material possessions and the luxury of comfortable travel that enables them to view the rest of the world as tourist spectacle. Predominantly Christian countries such as DR Congo, Kenya, and Uganda, for all of the challenges they face, are far more welcoming to vast numbers of refugees than are any Western countries. We should not be surprised, since God has always worked through the weak and rejected the proud.

Ruth Padilla DeBorst addresses the myriad challenges faced by Latin American immigrants to the United States, the powerful neighbor to their north whose territories include millions of square miles

of territory once home to indigenous people, and whose expropri-
ation of those lands and forced exodus of their incumbent populations required brutality, enslavement, and genocide on a scale
that left the remnant demographically diminished and socially
broken. But through her stories of Manuel, David, and Oscar, she
demonstrates both the absurdity of alt-right promoted stereotypes
of "illegal" immigrants from Latin America and the contribution
of such immigrants to healthy worshiping and community-serving
congregations in the United States.

Peter Sensenig provides one of the most heartening case studies.
He chronicles the practical hospitality of two small congregations
in Pennsylvania in receiving, caring for, and sustaining Somali refugee families as they learn how to live in a strange land among
a people who are not uniformly welcoming. These congregations
serve as a witness within a US society that in these times has torn
away its pleasant mask to reveal the merciless face of anti-Christ in
the guise of Immigration and Customs Enforcement (ICE) opera-
tives, who obediently put their nation above God by contravening
our Lord's priorities as summarized in Matthew 25:31–46.

Sadiri Joy Tira's chapter complements Samuel Lee's case study,
reminding us to give thanks for the ways in which God is at work
in and through the Filipino diaspora. The point he makes is of special interest to me, since I live in Winnipeg, a cold North American
city with a large (40,000) population of Filipinos. Our city is blessed
indeed!

Ben Torrey is no stranger to South Korea or to the Korean Global
Mission Leadership Forum. He writes masterfully and movingly
about the complex challenges and opportunities of serving North
Korean migrants in South Korea and China.

In his address, *Andrew Walls* places current concerns about migration and human dislocation within a 4,000-year-plus frame of
human history. We do well to be reminded that there is nothing
unprecedented about the migration of humankind, even if the par-
ticularities of any dislocation are dreadfully tailored to the affected
individuals and communities, who can take small solace from the
knowledge of migrations of other times and other peoples. Never-

theless, for those who frame their lives in certitude of God's active engagement in the world of human affairs, there can be awareness that, at least in retrospect, our suffering might make some kind of sense. The Gospel travels with the dislocated and displaced people of God.

"WHOSE HEAD IS THIS, AND WHOSE TITLE?" (MATT. 22:20)

In line with Christopher Wright's three Bible studies, in this section I point to key elements of a theology of migration, human disloca-tion, and Christian accountability.

With the disintegration of civil society throughout the Mid-dle East—a disintegration to which the ignorant, self-serving, vio-lently exploitative policies and actions of Western nations have for the past hundred years contributed mightily—we have also seen a reversion to brutal racism and the exclusion of minorities at the highest levels in the United States, Great Britain, and some Euro-pean nations. In their militant, adamant objection to strangers, they are manifesting the spirit of the antichrist. In recent years we have witnessed and our nations have participated in the displacement of more than 65 million men and women, children and adults. That is considerably more than the entire population of South Korea. More than 40 million of these are refugees in their own lands. The other 25 million are on the move internationally, crossing borders, and undergoing perilous journeys. Wherever they go, they are often greeted by hostility or suspicion.[1]

What do such numbers mean, practically? For most people, not much. A life oriented to genuine hospitality (welcoming of strangers, *philoxenia*; see Rom. 12:9–21; Heb. 13:1–3) requires more than being overwhelmed by numbers. Each of "us" and each of "them" is more than simply a cipher buried in a statistic! The US citizen with a broken leg derives little consolation from the fact that in a given year some 6.8 million of his or her fellow citizens suffer from frac-tures or broken bones. Such information does not fix *my* or anyone else's bone, nor does such knowledge animate the physician who

---

1. Jennifer M. Welsh, *The Return of History: Conflict, Migration, and Geopolitics in the Twenty-First Century* (Toronto: House of Anansi Press, 2017), 113–69.

tends to my personal plight. Only in the person-to-person encounter between patient and physician can healing be facilitated.

Similarly, each refugee, each immigrant, each dislocated person is in and of himself or herself a special case, worthy of our close, practical, and sustained attention. It is telling that God incarnate chose to live life as an utterly parochial person, at the beck and call of insignificant people, in an occupied back eddy of the Roman Empire—as despotic and militaristic a regime as can be imagined. Jesus the Christ did not come as an influential wielder of political or economic influence, but as a dusty-footed itinerant carpenter-teacher—a "three-mile-an-hour God," as the late Kosuke Koyama put it.[2] Today, an itinerant healer trudging by foot from village to village in an occupied, violence-ridden country—say, Afghanistan—might serve as Jesus's contemporary analogue. Would you listen to such a person, let alone be persuaded to follow him?

No meaningful accountability in church or mission is possible without costly incarnation. This statement entails that, unless we become intimately and personally involved in the complex challenges faced by actual dislocated *persons*, all of our fine talk about migration and human dislocation in the tens of thousands or the millions remains nothing but pious platitudes. As followers of Jesus, we cannot be content to cite impressively marshaled and organized statistics, and then stride virtuously away as though we had actually done something for "the least of these"! When we get involved in the real world of dislocated persons, we quickly discover both *what* we *can* do and *how little* we can do. Incarnational engagement is ever that way.

Limitations of time and space do not permit me to tell stories about my family's personal engagement with refugees for most of our forty-nine years of marriage. Suffice it to say that living with refugees from China, Ethiopia, Iraq, Kyrgyzstan, Myanmar, Russia, Sierra Leone, and Syria has often been hard, inconvenient, intrusive, and expensive—but deeply rewarding. We are blessed with a large international family, and with grandchildren in abundance!

2. Kosuke Koyama, *Three Mile an Hour God: Biblical Reflections* (Maryknoll, NY: Orbis Books, 1982).

God's or Caesar's? When quizzed about what Caesar could legitimately claim as his due (Matt. 22:15–22), Jesus requested a coin and asked, "Whose head is this, and whose title?" (v. 20). We understand from our Scriptures that men and women are stamped with God's imprint. Each carries God's DNA and reveals God's face. No "Caesar" as Caesar—whether national or tribal—can legitimately make such a claim on fellow human beings, although many come perilously close when they declare outsiders to be *illegal*. To depict any human being as "outside the pale" pits Caesar against God. Surrendering to Caesar what can belong only to God is idolatry.

To be a Christ-one entails recognizing and resisting the terrible reductionisms of all self-serving nationalisms, tribalisms, and racisms—and their ever-attendant legalisms—that undervalue or even dismiss the stranger, the refugee, the immigrant, or indeed the enemy. When we cooperate in such systemic reductionism, we subvert our own identities as men and women created in the image of God, since we yield to Caesar something to which Caesar has no ultimate claim—human beings, including ourselves. *Legality*, for Christians, can never be an acceptable substitute for *justice*.

The challenge for Christians has always been *how* to follow their Lord faithfully while necessarily participating in human systems so evidently and unapologetically habituated to self-interest. Put another way, one might say that in applying a biblical plumb line to our theology—which is inseparable from *praxis*—we Christians must work back from the questions set for the final judgment as described by Jesus in Matthew 25. From these we deduce what the outcome of any God-honoring faith must be—whether explicitly "Christian" or *directionally salvific* (even if called by another name or by no name at all).

The end of the age will not see ideologues of various stripes between the poles of "socialism" and "capitalism" dividing up the new creation among themselves, but Jesus as sole Judge separating sheep from goats on the basis of *how the socially disenfranchised, politically marginalized, and economically destitute figured in their priorities.* There will be no questions about doctrines or about the legalities employed to rationalize complicity in injustice. Religious and nonreligious alike will be surprised to learn that ordinary human decency, kindness, and justice turn out to have been more important than tidy proprietary religious systems that insinuate or even claim a monopoly on goodness and that support the self-serving and self-preserving agendas of some political entity.

Both family resemblance and proof of affinity lie in one's concrete relationship to the socially marginalized neighbor: the destitute, the imprisoned, the orphaned, the homeless, the alien, and the enemy. If compassion is not the outcome of one's faith, that faith is ultimately useless both now and in the life to come. The margins are the center for all authentically *Christian* mission.

CONCLUSION

I conclude with selections from the Torah, echoing the Bible studies that have so admirably anchored this forum.[3]

> You shall not wrong or oppress a resident alien, for you were aliens in the land of Egypt. (Exod. 22:21)
>
> You shall not oppress a resident alien; you know the heart of an alien, for you were aliens in the land of Egypt. (Exod. 23:9)
>
> When an alien resides with you in your land, you shall not oppress the alien. The alien who resides with you shall be to you as the citizen among you; you shall love the alien as yourself, for you were aliens in the land of Egypt: I am the LORD your God. (Lev. 19:33–34)
>
> You shall have one law for the alien and for the citizen: for I am the LORD your God. (Lev. 24:22)
>
> For the LORD your God is God of gods and Lord of lords, the great God, mighty and awesome, who is not partial and takes no bribe, who executes justice for the orphan and the widow, and

---

3. For a select list of works giving background and orientation to this forum's topic, in addition to Welsh, *The Return of History*, cited above, see Kathleen R. Arnold, *American Immigration after 1996: The Shifting Ground of Political Inclusion* (University Park: Pennsylvania State Univ. Press, 2011); David L. Baker, *Tight Fists or Open Hands? Wealth and Poverty in Old Testament Law* (Grand Rapids: Eerdmans, 2009); Jonathan Glover, *Humanity: A Moral History of the Twentieth Century* (New Haven, CT: Yale Univ. Press, 2000); Ian Goldman, Geoffrey Cameron, and Meera Balarajan, *Exceptional People: How Migration Shaped Our World and Will Define Our Future* (Princeton: Princeton Univ. Press, 2012); Tony Judt, *Postwar: A History of Europe since 1945* (New York: Penguin, 2006); Russell King, *People on the Move: An Atlas of Migration* (Berkeley: Univ. of California Press, 2010); Howard Thurman, *Jesus and the Disinherited* (Boston: Beacon, 1996).

who loves the strangers, providing them food and clothing. You shall also love the stranger, for you were strangers in the land of Egypt. (Deut. 10:17–19)

You shall not deprive a resident alien or an orphan of justice; you shall not take a widow's garment in pledge. Remember that you were a slave in Egypt and the LORD your God redeemed you from there; therefore I command you to do this. (Deut. 24:17–18)

What possible role can be played by churches or by similarly minded individuals and mission societies when it comes to the plight of "the world's refugees"? More important, what is the responsibility of each believer to the refugee next door? How proactive *are* we, and how proactive *should* we be, in seeking their well-being? How many of our churches, seminaries, or missiological training centers explicitly identify kindness to refugees as *the* paramount sacred calling for those who call "Lord" one who was never satisfied with passive detachment from the plight of neighbors and strangers? What role should churches play in pressuring their governments at all levels—local, regional, and national—to welcome refugees? How can we learn to be decidedly and constructively disobedient to our beloved Caesars when they deny the legality of the strangers in our midst and demand of us what belongs to God alone?

Our answers to these and related questions, wherever we are in the world, must in some measure be influenced by our understanding the difference between Caesar's imprint on a coin and God's imprint on human beings. "Then he said to them, 'Whose head is this, and whose title?' They answered, 'The emperor's.' Then he said to them, 'Give therefore to the emperor the things that are the emperor's, and to God the things that are God's'" (Matt. 22:20–21).

Bibliography

Adamo, David T. *Africa and Africans in the New Testament*. Lanham, MD: Univ. Press of America, 2006.

———. *Africa and Africans in the Old Testament*. Eugene, OR: Wipf & Stock, 1998.

Allen, John L., Jr. *The Global War on Christians: Dispatches from the Front Lines of Anti-Christian Persecution*. New York: Image, 2016.

Alma, Carissa. *Thriving in Cross Cultural Ministry*. Lexington, KY: Pavilion, 2011.

Anderson, Allan H. *African Reformation: African Initiated Christianity in the Twentieth Century*. Trenton, NJ: Africa World Press, 2001.

Anderson, John. *Kyrgyzstan: Central Asia's Island of Democracy*. Amsterdam: Harwood Academic, 1999.

Andrée, Uta, Benjamin Simon, and Lars Röser-Israel, eds. *Reforming Theology, Migrating Church, Transforming Society: A Compendium for Ecumenical Education*. Hamburg: Missionshilfe, 2017.

Armstrong, Hayward. *M-Life Illustrated: Reflections on the Lives of Cross-Cultural Missionaries*. Lexington, KY: Rainer, 2016.

Arnold, Kathleen R. *American Immigration after 1996: The Shifting Ground of Political Inclusion*. University Park: Pennsylvania State Univ. Press, 2011.

Asamoah-Gyadu, Kwabena. "African-Led Christianity in Europe: Migration and Diaspora Evangelism." *Lausanne World Pulse Archives*, issue 7 (2008).

Aslanbek, Joshua. "Developing a Contextualized Church Planting Model: Fruitful Practices of Church Planting in Central Asia." DIS diss., Fuller Theological Seminary, School of Intercultural Studies, 2016.

Baker, David L. *Tight Fists or Open Hands? Wealth and Poverty in Old Testament Law*. Grand Rapids: Eerdmans, 2009.

Barr, James. *A Line in the Sand: The Anglo-French Struggle for the Middle East, 1914–1948*. New York: Norton, 2013.

Barrett, C. K. *A Commentary on the First Epistle to the Corinthians*. Peabody, MA: Hendrickson, 1987.

Barrett, David B. *Schism and Renewal in Africa*. Oxford: Oxford Univ. Press, 1968.

Bauman, Stephan. "World Relief: We Must Help Refugees." *Christianity Today*, March 11, 2016, www.christianitytoday.com/edstetzer/2016/march/world-relief-we-must-help-refugees.html.

Bauman, Zygmunt. *Liquid Fear*. Cambridge: Polity, 2006.

Beachy, Bertha. "My Pilgrimage in Mission." *International Bulletin of Missionary Research* 35 (2011): 208–12.

Beck, Ulrich. *World at Risk*. Cambridge: Polity, 2007.

Beck, Ulrich, and Edgar Grande. *Cosmopolitan Europe*. Cambridge: Polity Press, 2007.

Bediako, Kwame. *Theology and Identity: The Impact of Culture upon Christian Thought in the Second Century and in Modern Africa*. Oxford: Regnum Books International, 1992.

Bonk, Jonathan J., ed. *Family Accountability in Missions*. New Haven, CT: OMSC Publications, 2013.

Boyd, David. *You Don't Have to Cross the Ocean to Reach the World*. Grand Rapids: Chosen, 2008.

Brueggemann, Walter. *The Land: Place as Gift, Promise, and Challenge in Biblical Faith*. Minneapolis: Fortress Press, 2002.

Buswell, Robert E., and Timothy S. Lee. *Christianity in Korea*. Honolulu: Univ. of Hawai'i Press, 2006.

Camarota, Steven A., and Karen Zeigler. "Immigrants in the United States: A Profile of the Foreign-Born Using 2014 and 2015 Census Bureau Data." Center for Immigration Studies, October 3, 2016, https://cis.org/Immigrants-United-States.

Cassarino, Jean-Pierre, ed. *Unbalanced Reciprocities: Cooperation on Readmission in the Euro-Mediterranean Area*. Washington, DC: Middle East Institute, 2010.

Changwa, Mkwazu. "Causes of Conflicts in Africa." Rural Development, February 15, 2009, http://maendeleoyajamii.blogspot.co.ke/2009/02/social-change.html.

Choi, Hyung Keun. "Missional Conversion and Transformation in the Context of the Korean Protestant Church." *Mission Studies* 34, no. 1 (2017): 53–77.

Choi, Yoon Sik. *Han-kuk-kyo-hoe mi-lae-chi-to* [2020–2040 Future map of the Korean church]. Seoul: Word of Life, 2013.

Clinton, J. Robert. *The Bible and Leadership Values: A Book by Book Analysis*. Altadena, CA: Barnabas Publishing, 1993.

———. *The Making of a Leader*. Colorado Springs, CO: NavPress, 1988.

Clinton, J. Robert, and Richard Clinton. *The Mentor Handbook: Detailed Guidelines and Helps for Christian Mentors and Mentorees*. Altadena, CA: Barnabas Publishing, 1991.

Cone, James H. *The Spirituals and the Blues*. Maryknoll, NY: Orbis Books, 1992; orig. 1972.

The Covenant Hymnal: A Worshipbook. Chicago: Covenant Publications, 1996.

Domernik, Jeroen, and Birgit Glorius. "Refugee Migration and Local Demarcations: New Insight into European Localities." *Journal of Refugee Studies* 29, no. 4 (2017): 429–39.

Drobner, H. R., and S. S. Schatzmann. *The Fathers of the Church: A Comprehensive Introduction*. Peabody, MA: Hendrickson, 2007.

Elmer, Duane. *Cross-Cultural Connections: Stepping Out and Fitting In around the World*. Downers Grove, IL: InterVarsity Press, 2002.

Emerson, Michael O., and Christian Smith. *Divided by Faith: Evangelical Religion and the Problem of Race in America*. Oxford: Oxford Univ. Press, 2000.

Escobar, J. Samuel. *La fe evangélica y las teologías de la liberación*. El Paso, TX: Casa Bautista de Publicaciones, 1987.

———. "Mission Fields on the Move: The Massive Global Migration We See Today Presents Unparalleled Opportunities for Ministry." *Christianity Today*, May 2010, www.christianitytoday.com /ct/2010/may/index.html.

———. *A Time for Mission: The Challenge for Global Christianity*. Carlisle, UK: Langham, 2013.

European Commission. *Technical Mission to Libya on Illegal Immigration, 27 Nov–6 Dec 2004: Report*. 7753/05. Brussels: DG HI. www.statewatch .org/news/2005/may/eu-report-libya-ill-imm.pdf.

Finishing the Task. "312 Diaspora Peoples without a Church. Populations over 25,000" [in Chinese]. Aliso Viejo, CA, 2010.

Galdini, Franco. *Moscow's Little Kyrgyzstan*. Surrey, UK: Journeyman Pictures, 2017.

Gardner, Howard. *Multiple Intelligences: New Horizons*. New York: Basic Books, 2006.

Gatu, John G. *Joyfully Christian, Truly African*. Nairobi: Acton, 2005.

George, Sam. *Diaspora Christianities: Global Scattering and Gathering of South Asian Christians*. Minneapolis: Fortress Press, 2018.

Gilliland, Dean S., ed. *The Word among Us: Contextualizing Theology for Mission Today*. Dallas: Word, 1989.

Glanville, Elizabeth Loutrel. "Missiological Reflections on Difference: Foundations in the Gospel of Luke," *Mission Studies* 26, no. 1 (2009): 64–79.

Global Diaspora Network. *Scattered to Gather: Embracing the Global Trend of Diaspora*. Rev. ed. Manila: Lausanne Committee for World Evangelization, 2017.

Glover, Jonathan. *Humanity: A Moral History of the Twentieth Century*. New Haven, CT: Yale Univ. Press, 2000.

Go, Myong-Hyun. "Resettling in South Korea: Challenges for Young North Korean Refugees," Asan Institute for Policy Studies, Issue Briefs, August, 2014, http://en.asaninst.org/contents/resettling-in -south-korea-challenges-for-young-north-korean-refugees/.

Goldman, Ian, Geoffrey Cameron, and Meera Balarajan. *Exceptional People: How Migration Shaped Our World and Will Define Our Future*. Princeton: Princeton Univ. Press, 2012.

Grosheide, F. W. *Commentary on the First Epistle to the Corinthians*. Grand Rapids: Eerdmans, 1984.

Ha, Min Kee. *Shattering the Korean Dream: Korean Chinese Experiences in Seoul, Korea*. Ann Arbor, MI: UMI, 2001.

Habash, Jiries. "Evangelical Churches in Jordan." *MEATE* [Middle East Association for Theological Education] *Journal* 6, no. 1 (December 2011): 1–15.

Han, Gil-Soo. "Korean Christianity in Multicultural Australia: Is It Dialogical or Segregating Koreans?" *Studies in World Christianity* 10, no. 1 (2004): 114–35.

———. "An Overview of the Life of Koreans in Sydney and Their Religious Activities." *Korea Journal of Population and Development* 35, no. 2 (1994): 67–76, www.ekoreajournal.net/issue/view_pop .htm?Idx=2848.

Han, Joy J., and Gil-Soo Han. "The Koreans in Sydney." *Sydney Journal* 2, no. 2 (2010): 25–35.

Hanciles, Jehu J. *Beyond Christendom: Globalization, African Migration, and the Transformation of the West.* Maryknoll, NY: Orbis Books, 2008.

Heaney, Sharon. *Contextual Theology for Latin America: Liberation Themes in Evangelical Perspective.* Milton Keynes, UK: Paternoster, 2008.

Hesselgrave, David J. *Paradigms in Conflict: Ten Key Questions in Christian Missions Today.* Grand Rapids: Kregel, 2005.

———. "Will We Correct the Edinburgh Error? Future Mission in Historical Perspective." *Southwestern Journal of Theology* 49, no. 2 (Spring 2007): 121–49.

Hill, Harriet, Margaret V. Hill, Richard Baggé, Pat Miersma, and Ian Dale. *Healing the Wounds of Trauma: How the Church Can Help.* New York: American Bible Society, 2016.

Hofstede, Geert. *Culture's Consequences: Comparing Values, Behaviors, Institutions, and Organizations across Nations.* Thousand Oaks, CA: Sage, 2011.

Hofstede, Geert, and Michael Harris Bond. "The Confucius Connection: From Cultural Roots to Economic Growth." *Organizational Dynamics* 16, no. 4 (1988): 5–21.

Hood, Robert. *Must God Remain Greek?* Minneapolis: Fortress Press, 1991.

Hunt, Bruce. *For a Testimony.* London: Banner of Truth Trust, 1966.

Im, Chandler H., and Amos Yong, eds. *Global Diasporas and Mission.* Oxford: Regnum Books International, 2014.

Jennings, J. Nelson. *Missional Missions: A Missiological Case Study of Onnuri Community Church / Sungyojeok gyohweieui sungyosayeok: Sungyohakjeok sarye yoenku—Onnuri Gyohwei.* Incheon, Republic of Korea: Onnuri Church, 2017.

Jeong, Paul Yonggap. *Mission from a Position of Weakness.* New York: Peter Lang, 2007.

Judt, Tony. *Postwar: A History of Europe since 1945.* New York: Penguin, 2006.

Jun, David Chul Han. "Case Study of Church Planting through Diaspora Ministry in Korea" [in Korean]. *Korea Missions Quarterly* 16, no. 2 (December 2016): 56–57.

———. "World Christian Mission through Migrant Workers in South Korea and through the Korean Diaspora." Presentation at Tokyo 2010 Global Mission Consultation and Celebration, Tokyo, May 2010.

Jung, Jin-Heon. *Migration and Religion in East Asia: North Korean Migrants' Evangelical Encounters.* New York: Palgrave Macmillan, 2015.

Kalu, Ogbu, ed. *African Christianity: An African Story.* Trenton, NJ: Africa World Press, 2007.

Kang, S. Steve, and Megan A. Hackman. "Toward a Broader Role in Mission: How Korean Americans' Struggle for Identity Can Lead to a Renewed Vision for Mission." *International Bulletin of Missionary Research* 36, no. 2 (April 2012): 72–77.

Kang, Shin Ji. "Postcolonial Reflection on the Christian Mission: The Case of North Korean Refugees in China and South Korea." *Social Sciences* 5 (2016): art. 67, www.mdpi.com/2076-0760/5/4/67, doi: 10.3390/socsci5040067.

Keil, Carl Friedrich, and Franz Delitzsch. *Biblical Commentary on the Old Testament.* Vol. 1, *The Pentateuch.* Grand Rapids: Eerdmans, 1981.

Kim, Jinbong, et al., eds. *Megachurch Accountability in Missions: Critical Assessment through Global Case Studies*. Pasadena, CA: William Carey Library, 2016.

Kim, S. Hun, and Wonsuk Ma, eds. *Korean Diaspora and Christian Mission*. Oxford: Regnum Books International, 2011.

Kim, Youn-Young. "Dae-Ryang-tal-buk-nan-nin yu-yip dae-bi kyung-chal-eu dae-ung-ban-an" [A study on counter measures by Korean police against massive influx of North Korean defectors]. *Chee-an-jung-chak-yun-ku* [Journal of police policy] 29, no. 2 (September 2015).

King, Russell. *People on the Move: An Atlas of Migration*. Berkeley: Univ. of California Press, 2010.

Kirk, Andrew. *Liberation Theology: An Evangelical View from the Third World*. London: Marshall, Morgan & Scott, 1979.

Kleist, J. Olaf. "The History of Refugee Protection: Conceptual and Methodological Challenges." *Journal of Refugee Studies* 30, no. 2 (2017): 161–69.

Koyama, Kosuke. *Three Mile an Hour God: Biblical Reflections*. Maryknoll, NY: Orbis Books, 1982.

Kwon, Ho-Youn, Kwang Chung Kim, and R. Stephen Warner, eds. *Korean Americans and Their Religions: Pilgrims and Missionaries from a Different Shore*. University Park: Pennsylvania State Univ. Press, 2001.

Kwon, Ildoo. "The Development of Mentoring Practices Guidelines for Korean-Chinese in Yoido Full Gospel Church." DIS diss., Fuller Theological Seminary, School of Intercultural Studies, 2016.

Lane, Patty. *A Beginner's Guide to Crossing Cultures: Making Friends in a Multicultural World*. Downers Grove, IL: InterVarsity Press, 2002.

Lausanne Committee for World Evangelization. *Diasporas and International Students: The New People Next Door*. Lausanne Occasional Paper 55. 2005. www.lausanne.org/content/lop/lop-55.

———. *Scattered to Gather: Embracing the Global Trend of Diaspora*. Manila: LifeChange, 2010.

Lausanne Movement. *The Cape Town Commitment*. 2011. www.lausanne.org/content/ctc/ctcommitment.

Law, Samuel K. *Revitalizing Missions on the Cusp of Change: Complex Systems Science Mazeways for Mission Theory amid Twenty-First-Century Realities*. Wilmore, KY: Emeth Press, 2016.

Lee, Byoung Gil. "Missionary Roy M. Byram's accusation of Japan" [in Korean]. *Revival and Reform* [in Korean], August 30, 2015, www.kscoramdeo.com/news/articleView.html?idxno=8836.

Lee, Il. "Status of Muslim Refugees in Korea, Understanding of the Refugee System and the Challenges of Korean Christian Churches" [in Korean]. *Muslim-Christian Encounter* 9, no. 1 (March 2016): 79–104.

Lee, Jae Hoon, Chang-geuk Moon, Chi-hyung Ro, and Cheol Suh, eds. *Onnuri Community Church: The First Thirty Years*. Seoul: Onnuri Community Church, 2015.

Lee, Kyung-Nam. "The Issues of Mission to North Korea." *Han-Kook Gi-dok Kong-bo*, no. 3093 (June 2, 2017).

Lee, Soon-Ok. *Eyes of the Tailless Animals: Prison Memoirs of a North Korean Woman*. Bartlesville, OK: Living Sacrifice, 1998.

Lee, Young Woon. "Brief History of Korean Diaspora and Educational Issues of Korean Diaspora Churches." *Torch Trinity Journal* 13, no. 2 (2010): 173–90.

Lewellen, Ted C. *The Anthropology of Globalization: Cultural Anthropology Enters the Twenty-First Century*. Westport, CT: Bergin & Garvey, 2002.

Lingenfelter, Sherwood. *Leading Cross-Culturally: Covenant Relationships for Effective Christian Leadership*. Grand Rapids: Baker Academic, 2008.

Lingenfelter, Sherwood, and Marvin Mayer. *Ministering Cross-Culturally: An Incarnational Model for Personal Relationships*. Grand Rapids: Baker Academic, 2016.

Livermore, David A. *Cultural Intelligence: Improving your CQ to Engage Our Multicultural World*. Grand Rapids: Baker Academic, 2009.

Matsuoka, Fumitaka, and Eleazar S. Fernandez. *Realizing the America of Our Hearts: Theological Voices of Asian Americans*. St. Louis: Chalice Press, 2003.

Mayfield, Danielle L. *Assimilate or Go Home: Notes from a Failed Missionary on Rediscovering Faith*. Kindle ed. New York: HarperCollins, 2016.

Mazza, Jaqueline. "Chinese Migration to Latin America and the Caribbean." The Dialogue: Leadership for the Americas, October 2016, www.thedialogue.org/wp-content/uploads/2016/10/Chinese_Migration_to_LAC_Mazza-1.pdf.

Mbiti, John S. *Concepts of God in Africa*. 2nd ed. Nairobi: Acton, 2012.

———. *New Testament Eschatology in an African Background*. Oxford: Clarendon Press, 1971.

Mercene, Floro L. *Manila Men in the New World: Filipino Migration to Mexico and the Americas from the Sixteenth Century*. Quezon City, Philippines: Univ. of Philippines Press, 2007.

Migration Policy Institute. "U.S. Immigrant Population and Share over Time, 1850–Present," www.migrationpolicy.org/programs/data-hub/charts/immigrant-population-over-time.

Mikhael, Mary. "The Syrian War and the Christians of the Middle East." *International Bulletin of Missionary Research* 39, no. 2 (April 2015): 69–70.

Moffett, Samuel H. *A History of Christianity in Asia*. Vol. 1, *Beginnings to 1500*. Maryknoll, NY: Orbis Books, 2005.

Moltmann, Jürgen. *Theology of Hope: On the Ground and the Implications of a Christian Eschatology*. New York: Harper & Row, 1967.

Moreau, A. Scott, Gary Corwin, and Gary B. McGee. *Introducing World Missions: A Biblical, Historical, and Practical Survey*. Grand Rapids: Baker Academic, 2015.

Mugambi, J. N. Kanyua. *Christianity and African Culture*. Nairobi: Acton, 1992.

Nouwen, Henri J. M. *The Wounded Healer: Ministry in Contemporary Society*. New York: Doubleday, 1979.

Nussbaum, Martha C. *The New Religious Intolerance: Overcoming the Politics of Fear in an Anxious Age*. Cambridge, MA: Harvard Univ. Press, 2012.

Oden, Thomas. *How Africa Shaped the Christian Mind*. Downers Grove, IL: IVP Academic, 2006.

Organisation for Economic Co-operation and Development. "How Is International Student Mobility Shaping Up?" *Education Indicators in Focus*, No. 14, July 5, 2013, www.oecd-ilibrary.org/education/how-is-international-student-mobility-shaping-up_5k43k8r4k821-en.

Oswalt, John N. *The Book of Isaiah, Chapters 40–66*. Grand Rapids: Eerdmans, 1998.

Ott, Craig, and Harold A. Netland, eds. *Globalizing Theology: Belief and Practice in an Era of World Christianity*. Grand Rapids: Baker Academic, 2006.

Padilla DeBorst, Ruth. "Latin American Congresses on Evangelization (CLADE), 1969–2012." *Journal of Latin American Theology* 5, no. 2 (2010): 107–24.

Pantoja, Luis, Jr., Sadiri Joy Tira, and Enoch Wan, eds. *Scattered: The Filipino Global Presence*. Manila: LifeChange, 2004.

Paris, Peter. *The Spirituality of African Peoples*. Minneapolis: Fortress Press, 1994.

Park, Chansik, ed. *21C sin-yu-mok-min si-tae-wa i-chu-cha sŏn-kyo* [Twenty-first century neo-nomadic era and migrant mission]. Seoul: Christian Institute of Industrial Society, 2008.

Park, Chon Eung. "The Present Reality of Foreign Workers and Multicultural Policy Agenda" [in Korean]. Paper presented at the Shinchon Forum 22, Seoul, May 2008.

Plueddemann, James E. *Leading across Cultures: Effective Ministry and Mission in the Global Church*. Downers Grove, IL: IVP Academic, 2009.

Polian, Pavel M. *Against Their Will: The History and Geography of Forced Migrations in the USSR*. Budapest: Central European Univ. Press, 2004.

Rogers, Everett M. *Diffusion of Innovations*. 5th ed. New York: Simon & Schuster, 2003.

Rynkiewich, Michael A. "The World in My Parish: Rethinking the Standard Missiological Model." *Missiology* 30, no. 3 (2002): 301–22.

Salinas, Daniel. "The Beginnings of the Fraternidad Teológica Latinoamericana: Courage to Grow." *Journal of Latin American Theology: Christian Reflections from the Latino South* 2, no. 1 (2007): 8–160.

Sanneh, Lamin. *Translating the Message*. Maryknoll, NY: Orbis Books, 1986.

Saunders, Doug. *Arrival City: How the Largest Migration in History Is Reshaping Our World*. New York: Vintage, 2012.

Schuler, Martin. "Migration Patterns of the Population in Kyrgyzstan." *Espace, Populations, Sociétés* 2007-1 (2007): 73–89, https://eps.revues.org/1967.

Sensenig, Peter M. *Peace Clan: Mennonite Peacemaking in Somalia*. Eugene, OR: Pickwick Publications, 2016.

Shank, David A. *What Western Christians Can Learn from African-Initiated Churches*. Elkhart, IN: Mennonite Board of Missions, 2000.

Snyder, Susanna. *Asylum-Seeking, Migration, and Church*. Farnham, Surrey, UK.: Ashgate, 2012.

Stanley, Paul D., and J. Robert Clinton. *Connecting: The Mentoring Relationships You Need to Succeed in Life*. Colorado Springs, CO: NavPress, 1992.

Stieglitz, Joseph. *Globalization and Its Discontents*. New York: Norton, 2002.

Stott, John. *The Spirit, the Church, and the World*. Downers Grove, IL: InterVarsity Press, 1990.

Sydney Korean Women's Association. *Needs Assessment Report of the Korean Community in the City of Sydney, 2011*. Sydney: SKWA, 2011.

Taniajura, Rey. "Incidental Mission: Philippine Case Study; 'Moving the OFW Missions Phenomenon from Incidental to Intentional,'" www.scribd.com/document/348663520/incidental-missions.

Taylor, William D., Antonia van der Meer, and Reg Reimer, eds. *Sorrow and Blood: Christian Mission in Contexts of Suffering, Persecution, and Martyrdom*. Pasadena, CA: William Carey Library, 2012.

Thurman, Howard. *Jesus and the Disinherited*. Boston: Beacon, 1996.

Ti, Thiow Kong, and Edward S. K. Ti. *Singapore and Asia: Celebrating Globalisation and an Emerging Post-Modern Asian Civilisation*. Singapore: Partridge, 2014.

Tira, Sadiri Joy. "Every Person (from Everywhere)." *Evangelicial Missions Quarterly* 50, no. 4 (2014): 398–400.

Tira, Sadiri Joy, and Tetsunao Yamamori, eds. *Scattered and Gathered: A Global Compendium of Diaspora Missiology*. Oxford: Regnum Books International, 2016.

Toktonaliev, Timur. "Kyrgyzstan: Refugees from Uzbekistan Fear Tashkent's Long Arm." *Eurasia Net*, December 11, 2014, www.eurasianet.org/node/71306.

Trans-Atlantic Slave Trade Database, http://hutchinscenter.fas.harvard.edu/research-projects/projects/trans-atlantic-slave-trade-database.

Uka, Emele Mba. *Missionaries Go Home? A Sociological Interpretation of an African Response to Christian Missions*. Frankfurt: Lang, 1989.

United Nations, Department of Economic and Social Affairs. *International Migration Report 2015: Highlights*. 2016.

United Nations. Universal Declaration of Human Rights. www.un.org/en/universal-declaration-human-rights.

Utianiyo wa Mwiyai Yesu Kilisto. Translated by John S. Mbiti. Nairobi: Kenya Literature Bureau, 2014.

Van Dam, Nikolas. *Destroying a Nation: The Civil War in Syria*. London: I. B. Tauris, 2017.

Van Engen, Charles. "Biblical Perspectives on the Role of Immigrants in God's Mission." *Journal of Latin American Theology: Christian Reflections from the Latino South* 2 (2008): 15–38.

———. *Mission on the Way: Issues in Mission Theology*. Grand Rapids: Baker, 1996.

Wagner, C. Peter. "Colour the Moratorium Grey." *International Review of Mission* 64, no. 254 (April 1975): 165–76.

Walls, Andrew F. *The Cross-Cultural Process in Christian History: Studies in the Transmission and Appropriation of Faith*. Maryknoll, NY: Orbis Books, 2002.

———. *Crossing Cultural Frontiers: Studies in the History of World Christianity*. Maryknoll, NY: Orbis Books, 2017.

———. "Mission and Migration: The Diaspora Factor." *Journal of African Christian Thought* 5, no. 2 (2005): 3–11.

Wan, Enoch, and Sadiri Joy Tira, eds. *Missions Practice in the Twenty-First Century*. Pasadena, CA: William Carey International Univ. Press, 2009.

Warner, Stephen. "Immigrants and the Faith They Bring." *Christian Century*, February 10, 2004, 20–23, www.religion-online.org/showarticle.asp?title=2946.

Welsh, Jennifer M. *The Return of History: Conflict, Migration, and Geopolitics in the Twenty-First Century*. Toronto: House of Anansi Press, 2017.

Wenham, Gordon J. *Genesis 1–15*. Waco, TX: Word, 1987.

Wilmore, Gayraud. *Black Religion and Black Radicalism*. 2nd ed. Maryknoll, NY: Orbis Books, 1998.

Winter, Ralph D., and Steven C. Hawthorne, eds. *Perspectives on the World Christian Movement: A Reader*. 4th ed. Pasadena, CA: William Carey Library, 2014.

Winter, Ralph D., Steven C. Hawthorne, and Han Cheol-Ho, eds. *Peoseupegtibeu* [Perspective]. Seoul: YWAM, 2009.

Winter, Ralph D., and Bruce A. Koch. "Finishing the Task: The Unreached Peoples Challenge." *International Journal of Frontier Missions* 19, no. 4 (Winter 2002): 15–25.

World Bank Group. *Migration and Remittances Factbook 2016*. 3rd ed. Washington, DC: World Bank, 2016, http://www.worldbank.org/.

Wright, Christopher J. H. *The Message of Jeremiah: Grace in the End*. Nottingham: InterVarsity Press, 2014.

———. *The Mission of God's People: A Biblical Theology of the Church's Mission*. Grand Rapids: Zondervan, 2010.

———. *Salvation Belongs to Our God: Celebrating the Bible's Central Story*. Downers Grove, IL: IVP Academic, 2007.

Yang, Fenggang. *Chinese Christians in America: Conversion, Assimilation, and Adhesive Identities*. University Park: Pennsylvania State Univ. Press, 1999.

Yi, Soon-Hyung, Youn-Shil Choi, and Meejung Chin. *Buk-han-yi-tal-ju-min-eu jong-kyo-kyung-hum* [Religious experience of North Korean refugees]. Seoul: Seoul National Univ. Press, 2015.

Participants

Amos Aderonmu
Founder, Calvary Ministries
(CAPRO)
Lagos, Nigeria

Daniel S. H. Ahn
University of Amsterdam
Amsterdam, Netherlands

Jonathan J. Bonk
Director, *Dictionary of African
Christian Biography*
Research Professor of Mission
Center for Global Christianity
and Mission
Boston University School of
Theology
Boston, Massachusetts, USA

Stephen S. Cha
Lead Pastor, English Ministry
Onnuri Community Church
Editor, *Ministry and Theology
Journal*
Seoul, Korea

Steve Chang
Professor, Torch Trinity Graduate
University
English Pastor, Hallelujah
Community Church
Yongin, Korea

Han Lisa Chang
Youth Pastor, Hallelujah
Community Church
Yongin, Korea

Eun Ah Cho
Assistant Professor of
Intercultural Studies
Fuller Theological Seminary
Pasadena, California, USA

Yong Joong Cho
General Secretary
Korea World Mission Association
Seoul, Korea

Calvin Woosung Choi
Senior Pastor
Watertown Evangelical Church
Watertown, Massachusetts, USA

Inho Choi
Missionary
Korea Food for the Hungry
International
Korr, Kenya

Jae Ryun Chung
Associate Pastor
Onnuri Community Church
Seoul, Korea

Je Soon Chung
Executive Director
Arilac Graduate School of
Global Development and
Entrepreneurship
Handong Global University
Pohang, Korea

John Hyung Nam Chung
Missionary
Global Mission Society
Amman, Jordan

Keun Sam Chung
Medical Doctor, Yale/New
Haven Hospital
New Haven Korean Church
New Haven, Connecticut, USA

345

Yook Hwan Do
Director, Tyrannus International
    Mission
Onnuri Community Church
Seoul, Korea

Sam George
Global Catalyst
Lausanne Movement
Vernon Hills, Illinois, USA

Kyusam Han
Senior Pastor
Choonghyun Presbyterian
    Church
Seoul, Korea

Jisun Han
Missionary
Korea Food for the Hungry
    International
Korr, Kenya

Paul J. K. Han
Global Coordinator, KAMSA
Mission Pastor-Consultant
Onnuri Community Church
Seoul, Korea

Sungbin Hong
Branch Leader
WEC International
Bishkek, Kyrgyzstan

Timothy Hong
Senior Pastor
ESF International Church
Chicago, Illinois, USA

Jongboo Hwa
Senior Minister
NamSeoul Church
Seoul, Korea

John Hyunjo Hwang
Senior Pastor
Connecticut Vision Korean
    Church
Waterbury, Connecticut, USA

Jongyoun Hwang
Pastor, Acts29 Vision Village
Onnuri Community Church
Goyang, Korea

R. Darrell Jackson
Associate Professor of Missiology
Morling College
Sydney, Australia

J. Nelson Jennings
Mission Pastor, Consultant,
    International Liaison
Onnuri Community Church
Seoul, Korea

Matthew Keung-Chul Jeong
Dean of the Chapel and Associate
    Professor
Forman Christian College
    University
Lahore, Pakistan

Eimsook Joung
Rector
Holy Comforter Church
Rankin Inlet, Nunavut, Canada

David Chul Han Jun
President
Evangelical Holiness Church
    (Friends of All Nations)
Incheon, Korea

Dae Su Jung
Elder, Mission Department
Onnuri Community Church
Treasurer, Lausanne Committee
    Korea
Seoul, Korea

Jae-Han Jung
Director of World Mission
Yoido Full Gospel Church
Seoul, Korea

Soon Young Jung
Assistant, Global Mission
    Leadership Forum
Missionary, WEC Korea
Shelton, Connecticut, USA

Youngsoo Jun
Elder
Onnuri Community Church
Seoul, Korea

Wissam Paulus Kammou
Lay Minister
Christian Missionary Alliance
Erbil, Iraq

Seth Kaper-Dale
Senior Pastor
Reformed Church of Highland
    Park
Highland Park, New Jersey, USA

Chang Ok Kim
Secretary General, Better World
    INGO
Onnuri Community Church
Seoul, Korea

Hong-Joo Kim
Director, Mission Headquarters
Onnuri Community Church
Seoul, Korea

Jinbong Kim
Managing Director, GMLF
Coordinator, KGMLF
Shelton, Connecticut, USA

Jung Nyun Kim
Missionary
Biblical Education by Extension
    Korea
Sungnam, Korea

Nam Hyuk Kim
Pastoral Staff, International
    Ministries
Calvary Church
Grand Rapids, Michigan, USA

Sookhi Kim
Lay Leader
Seungdong Presbyterian Church
Seoul, Korea

Timothy Kyung Jong Kim
Senior Minister
St. Andrew's Presbyterian
    Church
Penang, Malaysia

Abe Kugyong Koh
Senior Pastor
Korean Grace Presbyterian
    Church
Fort Lee, New Jersey, USA

George Iype C. Kovoor
Chaplain to H.M. Queen
    Elizabeth II
Senior Pastor
St. Paul's Episcopal Church
Darien, Connecticut, USA

Ildoo Kwon
Director of International
    Ministries
Yoido Full Gospel Church
Seoul, Korea

Samuel Ka-Chieng Law
Associate Professor of
    Intercultural Studies
Singapore Bible College
Singapore

D. David Lee
Executive Director, Global
    Fountains
Associate Director, World
    Missions Center
Southwestern Seminary
Fort Worth, Texas, USA

Dae Hum Lee
Pastor, Peniel Presbyterian Church
Joy Industrial Counseling Center
Jinju Foreign Laborers Support
    Center
Jinju, Korea

Ho-Taeg Lee
Executive Director
Refuge pNan
Seoul, Korea

Jae-Hoon Lee
Senior Pastor
Onnuri Community Church
Seoul, Korea

Juan Joon S. Lee
Director
Latin American Leadership
    Center
Los Angeles, California, USA

Jung-Sook Lee
President
Professor in Church History
Torch Trinity Graduate
    University
Seoul, Korea

Peter Lee
Executive Director
Cornerstone Ministries
    International
Los Angeles, California, USA

C. Samuel Lee
President
Foundation University
Amsterdam, Netherlands

See-young Lee
President and Representative
Senior Mission Korea
Former Korean Ambassador to
    the United Nations
Seongnam, Korea

Mary Mikhael
Communicator with Partners
    and Interpreter of the Church
    Ministry with Syrian Refugees
Presbyterian Synod of Syria and
    Lebanon (NESSL)
Antelias, Lebanon

Jesse N. K. Mugambi
Professor of Philosophy and
    Religious Studies
University of Nairobi
Nairobi, Kenya

Dorottya Nagy
Professor of Missiology
Protestant Theological University
Amsterdam, Netherlands

Craig A. Noll
Freelance Academic Editor
Copyeditor, *International
    Bulletin of Mission Research*,
    1992–present
North Kingstown, Rhode Island,
    USA

Youngsup Oh
Founder and Representative
Landmarker Ministry
Seoul, Korea

Ruth Irene Padilla DeBorst
Provost
Center for Interdisciplinary
    Theological Studies
San Jose, Costa Rica

Bokyoung Park
Professor of Missiology
Presbyterian University and
    Theological Seminary
Seoul, Korea

Hyung Jin Park
Professor
Torch Trinity Graduate
    University
Seoul, Korea

Kyungnam Park
Director, Korea Branch
WEC International
Seoul, Korea

Timothy Kiho Park
Professor of Asian Mission
Director of Global Connections
Fuller Theological Seminary
    School of Intercultural Studies
Pasadena, California, USA

Yong Hae Park
Treasurer, Global Mission
    Leadership Forum
Elder, New Haven Korean Church
New Haven, Connecticut, USA

David Wayne Parsons
Bishop of the Diocese of Arctic
Evangelical Anglican Church
    Arctic Canada
Yellowknife, Canada

Kyu Suk (Joshua) Rho
Lead Pastor, M-Mission
Onnuri Community Church
Ansan, Korea

Timothy Hyunsung Ro
Associate Pastor
Ansan Dongsan Church
Ansan, Korea

Peter M. Sensenig
Regional Consultant
Mennonite Board in Eastern
    Africa
Zanzibar, Tanzania

Hunseung Shin
Elder
Head, Mission Committee
Onnuri Community Church
Seoul, Korea

Eiko Takamizawa
Professor of Mission/ICS
    Department
Torch Trinity Graduate
    University
Hallelujah Japanese Ministries
Seongnam, Korea

Sadiri Joy Tira
Catalyst for Diasporas
Lausanne Movement
Edmonton, Canada

Lourdes Tira
Advancing Indigenous Missions
Diaspora Associate
Edmonton, Canada

Ben Torrey
Chairman, Jesus Abbey
Executive Director, The Fourth
    River Project
Taebaek, Korea

Liz Torrey
Principal, The River of Life
    Middle and High School
Associate with Jesus Abbey
Taebaek, Korea

Andrew F. Walls
University of Edinburgh,
    Scotland
Liverpool Hope University,
    United Kingdom
Akrofi-Christaller Institute,
    Ghana
Aberdeen, United Kingdom

Ingrid Walls
Liverpool Hope University,
    United Kingdom
Akrofi-Christaller Institute,
    Ghana
Aberdeen, United Kingdom

Christopher J. H. Wright
International Ministries Director
Langham Partnership
London, United Kingdom

W. Stephen Yi
Director
Love for All Nations
Seoul, Korea

Jung Ja Yoo
Lay Leader
New Haven Korean Church,
New Haven, Connecticut, USA

Contributors

Daniel S. H. Ahn teaches World Christianity as a visiting scholar at the Free University of Amsterdam as well as lecturing on multiple continents. He draws on extensive cross-cultural ministry experience in training pastors and leaders of international, migrant, and refugee churches. He has special interests in global diaspora missiology, interfaith dialogue, and contextualization of Christianity into multicultural and multireligious contexts. He has contributed chapters to several books, including *Religious Encounters in Transcultural Society* (Lexington, 2017), *Megachurch Accountability in Missions* (William Carey Library, 2016), *Religious Transformation in Modern Asia* (Brill, 2015), and *Korean Church, God's Mission, Global Christianity* (Regnum, 2015).

Joshua Aslanbek (a pseudonym) is passionate about reaching out to Muslims in Central Asia and training local church leaders and expatriate workers. He worked on a multicultural church planting team, serving among Muslims in southern Kyrgyzstan for seven years, before moving to northern Kyrgyzstan, where his role was in organizational leadership. He mentors expatriate church planters and multicultural church planting teams. Aslanbek graduated from Chongshin Theological Seminary (Korea) with an MDiv, earned an MA in Intercultural Studies at Columbia International University (South Carolina), and obtained a DIS at Fuller Theological Seminary (California). Married with two children, he is associated with WEC International.

Dwight P. Baker served for thirteen years (2002–15) as associate editor of the *International Bulletin of Missionary Research*. In 2011 he retired as associate director of the Overseas Ministries Study Center, New Haven, Connecticut. Previously, he was director of the World Christian Foundations study program at the U.S. Center for World Mission (now Frontier Ventures) in Pasadena, California. He is coeditor of *Serving Jesus with Integrity: Ethics and Accountability in Mission* (with Douglas Hayward, 2010), and *The Missionary Family: Witness, Concerns, Care* (with Robert J. Priest, 2014).

Jonathan J. Bonk is president of the Global Mission Leadership Forum (GMLF). He is research professor of mission, Boston University, where he directs the *Dictionary of African Christian Biography* (www.dacb.org), an electronic, multilingual reference tool that he founded in 1995. He has served as professor of global Christian studies at Providence University College and Theological Seminary in Manitoba, Canada, and as adjunct professor of evangelism and mission at both Yale Divinity School in New Haven, Connecticut, and Presbyterian College and Seminary in Seoul. He now teaches World Christianity at Canadian Mennonite University in Winnipeg. He is executive director emeritus of the Overseas Ministries Study Center, New Haven, Connecticut (www.omsc.org), where he served 1997–2013. He was editor of the *International Bulletin of Missionary Research* (www.internationalbulletin.org) from July 1997 until June 2013. His best-known book is *Missions and Money: Affluence as a Western Missionary Problem* (Orbis Books: 2nd ed. 2007; orig. 1991).

David Dong-Jin Cho has been a pastor in Seoul, South Korea (1960–78), and a professor in the United States as well as in both South and North Korea. In 1963 he established the East-West Center for Missions Research and Development. He also was instrumental in founding the Asia Missions Association (1973), the Third World Missions Association (1989), and the Asian Society of Missiology (2003). He is the author of about thirty mission books, including *The Mission* and "Historical Anatomy of the Power Encounter of the Christian Mission with the Nation: A Paradigm for the Future" (PhD diss., 1993).

Eun Ah Cho is assistant professor of intercultural leadership at Fuller Theological Seminary, School of Intercultural Studies, Pasadena, California. She came to Fuller from AUTU-ACTS in Korea, where she served as a professor of intercultural studies. Cho's life, ministry, and teaching have been rich with multicultural experience. Originally from South Korea, she immigrated with her family to Canada as a teenager, and then attended university in St. Petersburg, Russia, earning her undergraduate degree in Russian philology. She went on to serve for five years as a missionary in Kazakhstan, planting a multiethnic church and training local leaders, before moving to Fuller for her master's and doctoral degrees.

Calvin Woosung Choi, by growing up in different parts of the world, has acquired a unique cultural background. Having lived in Korea, Iran, Turkey, India, and the United States, he is fluent in English, Korean, Persian, and Turkish. He now resides in Boston and currently serves as the senior pastor of Watertown Evangelical Church, Watertown, Massachusetts, and adjunct professor of preaching at Gordon-Conwell Theological Seminary, South Hamilton, Massachusetts. He is the author of *Preaching to Multiethnic Congregation* (Peter Lang, 2015) and has translated *Preaching with a Plan* (Zondervan, 2012) into Korean.

Inho Choi, a missionary with Food for the Hungry International (FHI), has served in Marsabit County, Northern Kenya, since 2003. He has also served as the East African coordinator for FHI Korea. He lives with a minor nomadic group, the Rendille people, who reside in Korr, Marsabit County. He and his wife are blessed with three children.

John H. N. Chung has served Iraqi Christian Refugee Worship Communities of Jordan Evangelical Churches since 1994. He has also been a professor at Jordan Evangelical Theological Seminary (JETS), and a research professor at Asian United Theological University / Asian Center for Theological Studies (ACTS) in Korea. He is the author of *Islam and the Issue of the Messianic Kingdom* (in Korean; CLC, 2009).

Sam George is an author, speaker, professor, and leadership coach. Of Asian Indian origin, he worked in industrial technology in Asia in the 1990s and pioneered family-based mission work in India and the United States. He has studied at Fuller Theological Seminary and Princeton Theological Seminary. His PhD from Liverpool Hope University, United Kingdom, focused on diaspora missiology and theology. He lives with his wife and two teenage boys in a northern suburb of Chicago, Illinois.

Jehu J. Hanciles, born in Sierra Leone, is the D.W. and Ruth Brooks Associate Professor of World Christianity at Emory University's Candler School of Theology, Atlanta, Georgia, USA, and has been a visiting professor at schools around the world. Before coming to Candler in 2012, Hanciles was associate professor of the history of Christianity and globalization, and director of the Center for Missiological Research at Fuller Theological Seminary, Pasadena, California. His current research surveys the history of global Christian expansion through the lens of migration. He has published extensively on issues related to the history of Christianity (notably the African experience) and globalization, including two books, *Euthanasia of a Mission: African Church Autonomy in a Colonial Context* (Praeger, 2002) and *Beyond Christendom: Globalization, African Migration and the Transformation of the West* (Orbis Books, 2009).

Timothy Hong is senior pastor of ESF International Church, Chicago, Illinois (1999–present). He worked in campus ministry at the University of Illinois at Chicago (UIC) from 1987 to 1998. His academic studies include a ThM in Christian Ethics (course work), Calvin Seminary, Grand Rapids, Michigan (1987), and a ThM in New Testament, Trinity Evangelical Divinity School, Deerfield, Illinois (1996).

Jongboo Hwa is the head pastor of NamSeoul Church in Seoul, Korea. Previously he served as lead pastor at an immigrant Korean church in Oxford, England, and at Jejadle Church in Seoul. He has published books on Galatians, Philippians, and the Sermon on the Mount, among other texts. His heart is to see the Korean church grow to be more healthy through solid expository preaching. He desires to play a part in recognizing the calling that the Korean Church has in North Korean and world missions. He studied political science at Yonsei University and theology at Chongsin Theological Seminary. He earned a master's degree in Scottish Reformation church history at Edinburgh University, Scotland.

R. Darrell Jackson is an ordained Baptist pastor with missionary experience in Europe. He serves as associate professor of missiology, Morling College and the University of Divinity, in Australia. He has taught as adjunct or visiting faculty at a variety of colleges, universities, and seminaries worldwide and is a regular conference speaker whose writing on migration and diaspora has been widely published, including *Mapping Migration: Mapping Churches' Responses in Europe* (2nd ed. with Alessia Passarelli; CCME, 2015). He is a member of the Australian Association for Mission Studies (secretary), World Evangelical Alliance's Mission Commission (associate), International Association for Mission Studies, National Leadership Team in Australia for Missions Interlink, Global Interaction (missiological consultant), and European Christian Mission International (board member).

J. Nelson Jennings, having been raised in a US-American Christian home, married Kathy in 1981. After Nelson earned his MDiv, in 1986, the Jennings family moved to Japan as church-planting missionaries. In 1995 Nelson completed his PhD dissertation, published in 2005 as *Theology in Japan: Takakura Tokutaro (1885–1934)* (Univ. Press of America). Jennings taught at Tokyo Christian University (1996–99) and at Covenant Theological Seminary (1999–2011), then served at the Overseas Ministries Study Center (2011–15) and with GMI (Global Mapping International, 2016–17). Since September 2015 Jennings has served as mission pastor, consultant, and international liaison for Onnuri Community Church, Seoul. Other publications include *God the Real Superpower: Rethinking Our Role in Missions* (P&R Publishing, 2007) and *Philosophical Theology and East-West Dialogue* (with Hisakazu Inagaki; Rodopi, 2000).

Keung-Chul (Matthew) Jeong has served in various capacities in Pakistan since 1993. He is currently associate professor and dean of the chapel at Forman Christian College University in Lahore, research fellow at International Islamic University in Islamabad, and commissary of the bishop of Peshawar Diocese of the Church of Pakistan for Far East Asia. He has served Interserve in various leadership roles. In addition to Pakistan, he has served in Canada, Cyprus, Malaysia, South Korea, Turkey, and the United Kingdom and is fluent in Korean, English, and Urdu. His focus as a missiologist has been on Muslim-Christian relations and on the poor in Muslim countries, with a special view to extending compassion to "one of the least" (Matt. 25:40) in Pakistan.

David Chul Han Jun serves, since 2001, as founding director of Friends of All Nations, in Korea. His previous ministries include Korea Harbor Evangelism, OM Ships, Mission in South Africa, and World Concern. At present for Every Community for Christ (ECC)/One Mission Society (OMS), he serves as church multiplication facilitator (CMF) for Vietnam and Philippines. He has taught at Seoul Theological Seminary.

Wissam Paulus Kammou became a born-again Christian in 1999. Since 2001 he has had the privilege of serving the Lord via teaching and discipleship in small groups. He has conducted this ministry in various cities in Iraq, such as Nineveh, Baghdad, and now in Erbil.

Seth Kaper-Dale and his co-pastor wife, Stephanie, have served the Reformed Church of Highland Park in New Jersey (RCHP) since 2001. In addition to traditional church ministry, Kaper-Dale has created a network of church-based non-profits that exist to provide affordable housing, disaster relief, re-entry support after prison, immigrant advocacy, and refugee resettlement. He serves on the board of the National Religious Campaign Against Torture and is a regular lecturer at universities, colleges and seminaries. Kaper-Dale is the author of *A Voice for Justice:*

Sermons that Prepared a Congregation to Respond to God in the Decade after 9/11 (Wipf & Stock, 2013). In 2017 he was the Green Party of New Jersey's candidate for governor.

Jinbong Kim, beginning in 1990, served for a number of years as a missionary in West Africa. He and his wife, Soon Young Jung, joined GMS (Global Mission Society) in 1994 and in 1998 joined WEC International as well. They spent two terms working among Fulani Muslims in Guinea, before moving to the Overseas Ministries Study Center in 2006. In 2008 Kim proposed that the Korean Global Mission Leadership Forum be organized. He is now managing director of the umbrella organization Global Mission Leadership Forum and has served as coordinator for each of the KGMLF consultations. Kim earned the DMin in intercultural studies at Grace College and Theological Seminary, Winona Lake, Indiana.

Ildoo Kwon serves as director of international ministries at Yoido Full Gospel Church, Seoul, Korea. He is also international coordinator for Asia Leaders' Summit (ALS) and Korea-China Christian Leaders Forum. He earned the MDiv at Fuller Theological Seminary as well as the DMiss in Intercultural Studies. He and his wife are blessed with two children.

Samuel Ka-Chieng Law is associate professor of intercultural studies, Singapore Bible College, and pastor-at-large, Evangelical Chinese Church of Seattle, where he has served as elder board chair and English ministry pastor. Previously, he has been senior pastor for the Lexington (KY) Chinese Christian Church and adjunct faculty in the Seattle Pacific University School of Theology's Global and Urban Missions program. Prior to entering the ministry, Law served on the staff of the National Institute for Alcohol Abuse and Alcoholism, part of the National Institutes of Health. He holds a PhD in biomedical engineering. He and his wife, Esther, have four children.

D. David Lee, an effective missions strategist and mobilizer, is the founding president of Global Ministries Inc. and the executive director of Global Fountains, a ministry dedicated to sharing the Gospel with refugees in the Dallas/Fort Worth metroplex area and to mobilizing local churches for Kingdom work. A graduate of Southwestern Baptist Theological Seminary (SWBTS), he served at SWBTS's World Missions Center (2008–17). He and his wife, Jee Su, are the parents of Shion, Siyoung, and Siyul. They live in Fort Worth, Texas.

Dae Hum Lee is pastor of Peniel Presbyterian Church in Jinju, Korea. Being burdened for South Korea's growing population of foreign laborers, his church pioneered the establishment of shelter housing and soccer teams in ministry to foreign workers. He organized the Jinju Foreign Laborers Support Center and the Joy Industrial Counseling Center. He holds first level certification from the Korea Industrial Counseling Academy for which his thesis was "Relationship between Job and Health in Foreign Laborers." Individuals from more than twenty nations attend his church, and people from ten nations use his shelter. He has published evangelical papers in Chinese and English and travels overseas to make disciples and engage in church planting.

Jae Hoon Lee has has served as senior pastor of Onnuri Community Church, Seoul, since 2011. In the United States, he pastored the Chodae Community Church, Norwood, New Jersey, for four years. As an evangelist, he leads what is regarded as one of the most creative megachurches in South Korea. He has been influential in both Christian and non-Christian circles throughout South Korea through innovative uses of social media, art, and publishing. He also serves as the chair of the Korea Lausanne Committee and the chair of the board trustees for Korea's Handong Global University. He earned a ThM at Trinity Evangelical Divinity School and is a candidate for the DMin at Gordon-Conwell Theological Seminary.

Joon John Lee (aka Juan, "John" in Spanish) served as a missionary in Mexico, providing leadership in theological education, pastoral formation, and lay leadership development. His missiological thinking has developed through reflection on praxis during his travel and ministry throughout Latin America. Lee currently leads the Latin American Leadership Center, in Los Angeles, while teaching at World Mission University, Los Angeles, and Fuller Theological Seminary, Pasadena, California.

Peter Lee is executive director of Cornerstone Ministries International, a ministry that has worked to bring the Bible and help to plant the church in North Korea. He earned the MDiv degree and a PhD in Intercultural Studies at Fuller Theological Seminary, Pasadena, California. He is author of *Bukhan Jiha GyoHwe Soonkyosa* (History of martyrdom of the underground church in North Korea), a Korean translation of his doctoral dissertation. A member of the Presbyterian Church of America, he and his wife are blessed with three children and four grandchildren.

Samuel Lee is president of Foundation University in Amsterdam, an institution that offers an affordable academic education for refugees and migrants. Since 1994 Lee has been senior pastor of Jesus Christ Foundation (JCF). Based in Amsterdam, JCF is also present in eleven other cities around the world. He is one of the coordinators for the Center for Theology of Migration at the Free University Amsterdam (VU Amsterdam), which offers a postgraduate program for migrant pastors and church leaders in the Netherlands. Lee's publications include *Understanding Japan through the Eyes of Christian Faith*, fifth ed. (2015), *The Japanese and Christianity: Why Is Christianity Not Widely Believed in Japan?* (2014), and *Blessed Migrants: A Biblical Perspective on Migration* (2009), all published by Foundation University Press.

Mary Mikhael was president of the Near East School of Theology, Beirut, Lebanon, and was the first woman to hold such a position in the Middle East. Following her retirement, she was assigned to the roles of communicator with partners on behalf of the National Evangelical Synod of Syria and Lebanon (Presbyterian), regarding the tragedy in Syria, and of interpreter of the Church's ministry among the internally displaced inside Syria. She was also assigned to start schooling for children from the camps in Lebanon. She has written on the topics of theological education and women in the church and has published *She Shall Be Called Woman*, a meditation on biblical women, *Joshua: A Journey of Faith*, and nine Bible studies, as well as a chapter, "The Issue of Women's Ordination," in *Toward a Modern Arabic Theology.*

Jesse N. K. Mugambi, born and educated in Kenya, is professor of philosophy and religious studies, University of Nairobi, Kenya, where he has taught since 1976. His research interests include phenomenology of religion, philosophy of religion, comparative study of religions, contemporary religious thought, religion and ecology, religion and culture, religion and education, religion and social reconstruction, interreligious relations, ecumenical relations, scriptural hermeneutics, and mission studies. He was Visiting Mellon Distinguished Professor, Rice University, Houston, Texas (1990–91) and has lectured as a guest professor in a number of other countries. His publications include *African Heritage and Contemporary Christianity* (1988), *From Liberation to Reconstruction* (1995), *Religion and Social Construction of Reality* (1996), and *Christian Theology and Social Reconstruction* (2003).

Dorottya Nagy is professor of missiology at the Protestant Theological University in Amsterdam, Netherlands, with research interest in migration, mission studies, ecclesiology, Christianity in post-Communist Europe, and innovative ways of theologizing. Her publications include *Migration and Theology: The Case of Chinese Christian Communities in the Globalisation-Context* (Uitgeverij Boekencentrum, 2009) and "Minding Methodology: Theology-Missiology and Migration Studies," in *Mission Studies* (2015). Nagy is president of the Central and Eastern European Association for Mission Studies (CEEAMS) and a member of the editorial board of its journal. She is an ordained Lutheran minister, is married, and is the mother of two children.

Craig Noll is a freelance academic editor, having worked twenty years as a staff editor with Eerdmans Publishing (Grand Rapids, MI) and over ten years as a freelance editor for various university presses and Christian publishers. Since 1992 he has been copyeditor and assistant editor of the *International Bulletin of Mission(ary) Research.* With an advanced degree in linguistics and an interest in New Testament Greek, he also has taught linguistics and Greek at the college and seminary levels.

Young Sup Oh is the leader of Landmarker Ministry (2005), which he founded for the sake of sharing the Gospel to all nations with a focus on city mission. He pioneered Forest of Living Water Church (2014) as a missional, multicultural church. He is presently building up the church as an experimental base camp of the International Students Volunteer Movement (ISVM) for the "Migration Mission Era." Oh co-founded and is general secretary of the Multi-Cultural Mission Network (2015) as a proving ground for united multiethnic, multicultural, and multilingual ministries. He also co-founded RUSTA (2016), uniting ministries among Russian communities in Korea who come from eleven CIS countries.

Ruth Irene Padilla DeBorst yearns to see peace and justice embrace in the beautiful and broken world we call home. A wife of one and mother of many, theologian, missiologist, educator, and storyteller, she has been involved in leadership development and theological education for integral mission in her native Latin America for several decades. She works with the Comunidad de Estudios Teológicos Interdisciplinarios (CETI, www.ceticontinental.org), a learning community with students across Latin America. She coordinates the Networking Team of INFEMIT (International Fellowship for Mission as Transformation, www.infemit.org), collaborates with Resonate Global Mission, and serves on the boards of A Rocha and the Oxford Centre for Mission Studies. She lives with her husband, James, in Costa Rica as a member of Casa Adobe, an intentional Christian community with deep concern for right living in relation to the whole of creation (www.casaadobe.org).

Timothy K. Park is the director of Global Connections and professor of Asian Mission at the School of Intercultural Studies of Fuller Theological Seminary, Pasadena, California. Before coming to Fuller, Park served as a cross-cultural missionary in the Philippines for fifteen years and was involved in church planting in Metro Manila and various locations on Luzon Island. He helped found the Presbyterian Theological Seminary in the Philippines (now PTS College and Advanced Studies), where he served as professor and president. Park also founded the Institute for Asian Mission (IAM) and Asian Society of Missiology (ASM). He works with other Asian missiologists to help Asian churches and missions through research, publication, consultation, and education. He has also served as head chairman of Asia Missions Association (AMA) and as president of the East-West Center for Missions Research and Development.

Peter Sensenig was born in Swaziland to missionary parents and lived as a TCK in Somalia. He is an ordained minister in the Mennonite Church USA. Sensenig has a PhD in Christian ethics from Fuller Theological Seminary, with a minor concentration in Islamic studies. He is a regional consultant for the Mennonite Board in Eastern Africa and lives in Zanzibar, Tanzania, where he teaches peace studies at Tumaini University. He has also taught in DR Congo, Djibouti, Ethiopia, Kenya, Somaliland, and United States. Sensenig is the author of *Peace Clan: Mennonite Peacemaking in Somalia* (Wipf & Stock, 2016).

Eiko Takamizawa is the first Japanese female missiologist in Asia. She teaches intercultural studies at Torch Trinity Graduate University, Seoul. She received the MDiv from ACTS, Seoul, and PhD from Trinity International University, Deerfield, Illinois. She serves widely as a conference speaker and seminar lecturer in Asia, North America, and other parts of the world. She is currently president of the Asian Society of Missiology, chair of the Korea Japanese Ministries Association, and pastor of Japanese ministries at Hallelujah Church in Korea.

Sadiri Joy Tira is the Lausanne Movement's catalyst for diasporas (formerly titled senior associate for diasporas) and vice president for diaspora missions for Advancing Indigenous Missions. He also serves as missiology specialist at the Jaffray Centre for Global Initiatives, Ambrose University and Seminary, Calgary, Canada. He ministered in Edmonton, Alberta,

Canada for over two decades, where he served (until 2006) as founding senior pastor of First Filipino Alliance Church. His publications include *The Human Tidal Wave* (LifeChange, 2013) and *Filipino Kingdom Workers: An Ethnographic Study in Diaspora Missiology* (William Carey International Univ. Press, 2012).

Ben Torrey and his wife, Liz, are members of Jesus Abbey, an intentional intercessory prayer community in Taebaek, Kangwon Do, Korea. He is director of The Fourth River Project as well as of The Three Seas Center. Born in the United States, he went to Korea at age 7, in 1957, with his parents. As a teenager, he joined them in pioneering Jesus Abbey, a community of prayer located in Taebaek. With his father and ten other young men, he lived in a tent for six months while clearing land and erecting the first Jesus Abbey building. Torrey and his wife returned to Korea in 2005 to prepare for the opening of North Korea. They operate the River of Life School dedicated to raising up the "unification generation."

Andrew F. Walls taught at colleges in Sierra Leone and Nigeria before accepting positions at the Universities of Aberdeen and Edinburgh, where he was director of the Centre for the Study of Christianity in the Non-Western World. He has been a visiting professor at Yale and Harvard Universities, National University of Lesotho, Princeton Theological Seminary, and Trinity College, Singapore. Among Walls's numerous publications are *The Missionary Movement in Christian History: Studies in the Transmission of Faith* (1996), *The Cross-Cultural Process in Christian History: Studies in the Transmission and Appropriation of Faith* (2001), *Crossing Cultural Frontiers: Studies in the History of World Christianity* (2017), all published by Orbis Books.

Christopher J. H. Wright is director of international ministries for Langham Partnership, which provides literature, scholarships, and preaching training for Majority World pastors and seminaries. He taught in India for five years. As well as commentaries on several Old Testament books, his books include *Old Testament Ethics for the People of God* (2004), *The Mission of God* (2006), *The God I Don't Understand* (2008), and *The Mission of God's People* (2010). He was the chief architect of *The Cape Town Commitment*, issued by the Third Lausanne Congress in October 2010.

Laura S. Meitzner Yoder is professor of environmental studies as well as director and John Stott Chair of Human Needs and Global Resources, Wheaton College, Wheaton, Illinois, USA. Her research focuses on human-environment interactions in remote villages and urban centers of Southeast Asia and Latin America. Most of her work has been in situations of conflict, disaster, chronic poverty, or political marginalization. Her ongoing work in Timor-Leste examines the interactions between customary and state authorities regarding land and forest management. Responding to the December 2004 Indian Ocean earthquake and tsunami in Aceh, Indonesia, she taught at the local state university and led a social research methods training program for hundreds of Acehnese professionals. This initiative contributed to social healing after the dual tragedies of the tsunami and the decades of civil strife in the province.

Index

9/11, 235
10/40 Window, 311

Abraham, 183, 315–16; as called by
    God, 22, 27, 44, 143; migration
    of, 31, 43, 168, 203, 282n8, 319;
    promise to, 144–45
Abrahamic migration, 31, 319
ABTS. *See* Arab Baptist Theological
    Seminary
Abugazala, Jiries, 76
Abu Karam, 82–83
Acacian Schism, 51n10
Accad, Nadia, 214
*Accountability in Missions: Korean
    and Western Case Studies*
    (KGMLF 2011), xxii
Achit (Mongolian believer), 186
Acts 29 Vision Village (Onnuri),
    190, 193
Adam and Eve, 31, 44, 319
Adamic migration, 31, 319
Adamo, David T., 59n26
Africa, significance of, 50–52
African diaspora, 57–58, 319
African Union, 55
Agenda 2063: The Africa We Want, 55
Agenda for Sustainable
    Development (2030), 49
Agutu, Nancy, 66n7
Ahad, Mahir Abdul, 71n5
Ahn, Daniel S. H., 180–84, 197n1,
    200n4, 350
Alexandria, 32–33, 51
Allen, John L, Jr., 175n9
All Nations Returnees Conference,
    299
Alma, Carissa, 112n8
Alsaka, Munthir, 83
Alvarado, Monsy, 243
Amaral, Brian, 242

Ambrose University (Calgary),
    273n23
Amman, Jordan, 69, 81, 193, 319
Amos, Deborah, 243
Amsterdam Treaty (1997), 287
Anaee, Faeza (Um Karam), 83
Anaee, Sabah. *See* Abu Karam
Anderson, Allen, 56
Anderson, John, 292n6
Ansan City, 90, 97, 188, 190–92, 194.
    See also M Mission
Ansan Immigration Center, 90
anti-Communism: as part of
    migrant education in South
    Korea, 7; as shaping South
    Korean culture, 12
Arab Baptist Theological Seminary,
    212, 214
Arab diaspora, 79
Arabic Service (Onnuri), 192
Arab migrations, 33–34
Arab Spring, 204, 213
Arana, Pedro, 257n5
Armstrong, Hayward, 107n2, 112n9
Arnold, Kathleen R., 334n3
Asamoah-Gyadu, Kwabena, 57–58
Ashcroft, John, 235
Ashe, Thomas, 66n9
Asia Japanese Christian Family
    Camp, 298
Asian Center for Theological
    Studies and Mission (ACTS),
    73n7, 351–52
Asian Society of Missiology, 357
Asian United Theological
    University, 73n7, 351–52
Aslanbek, Joshua, 290–94, 350
Assad, Bashar al-, 204
Assad, Hafez al-, 204
Atta, Fawzi, 76
Atta, Linda, 76